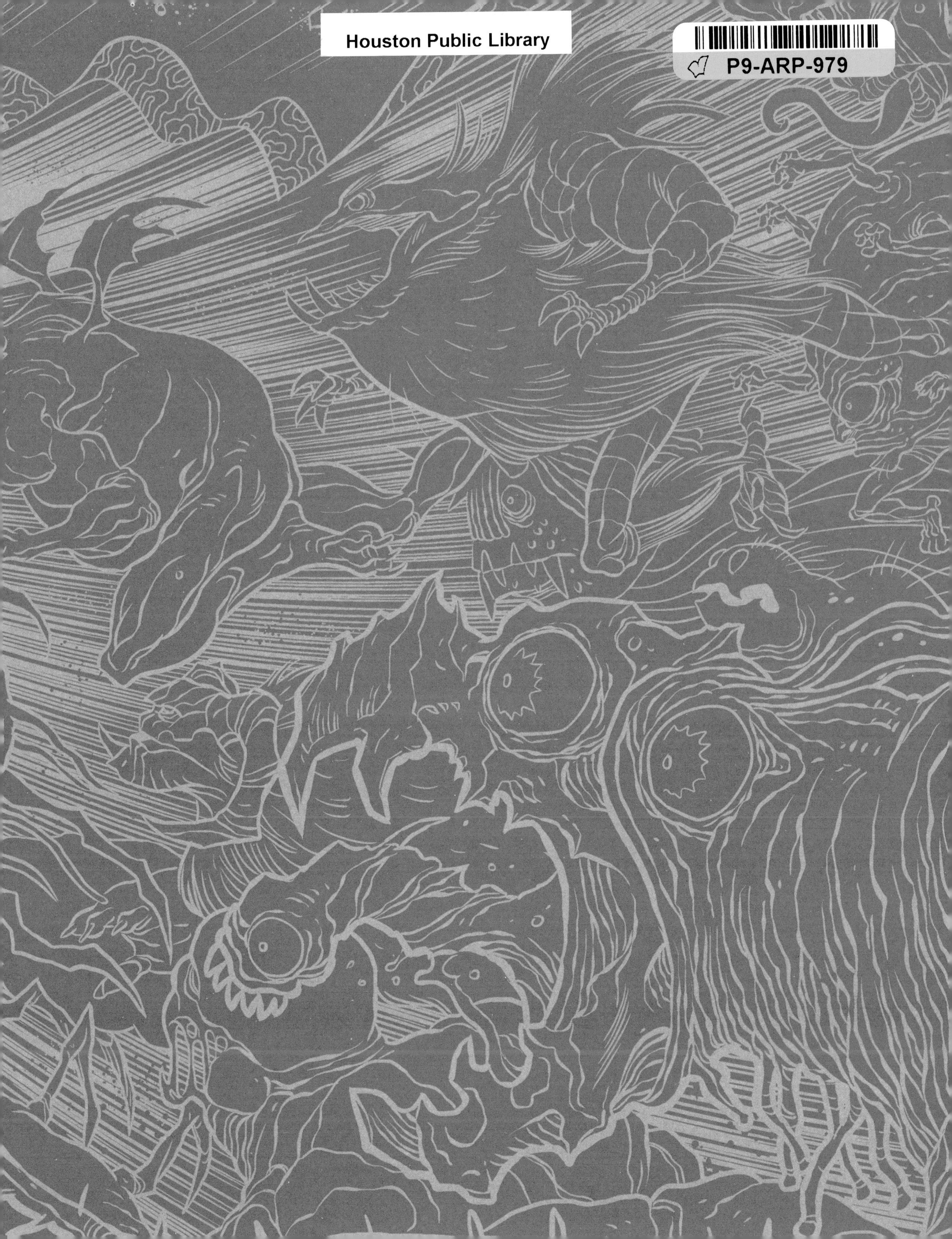

DOCTOR STRANGE

WRITTEN BY

BILLY WRECKS, NICK JONES & DANNY GRAYDON

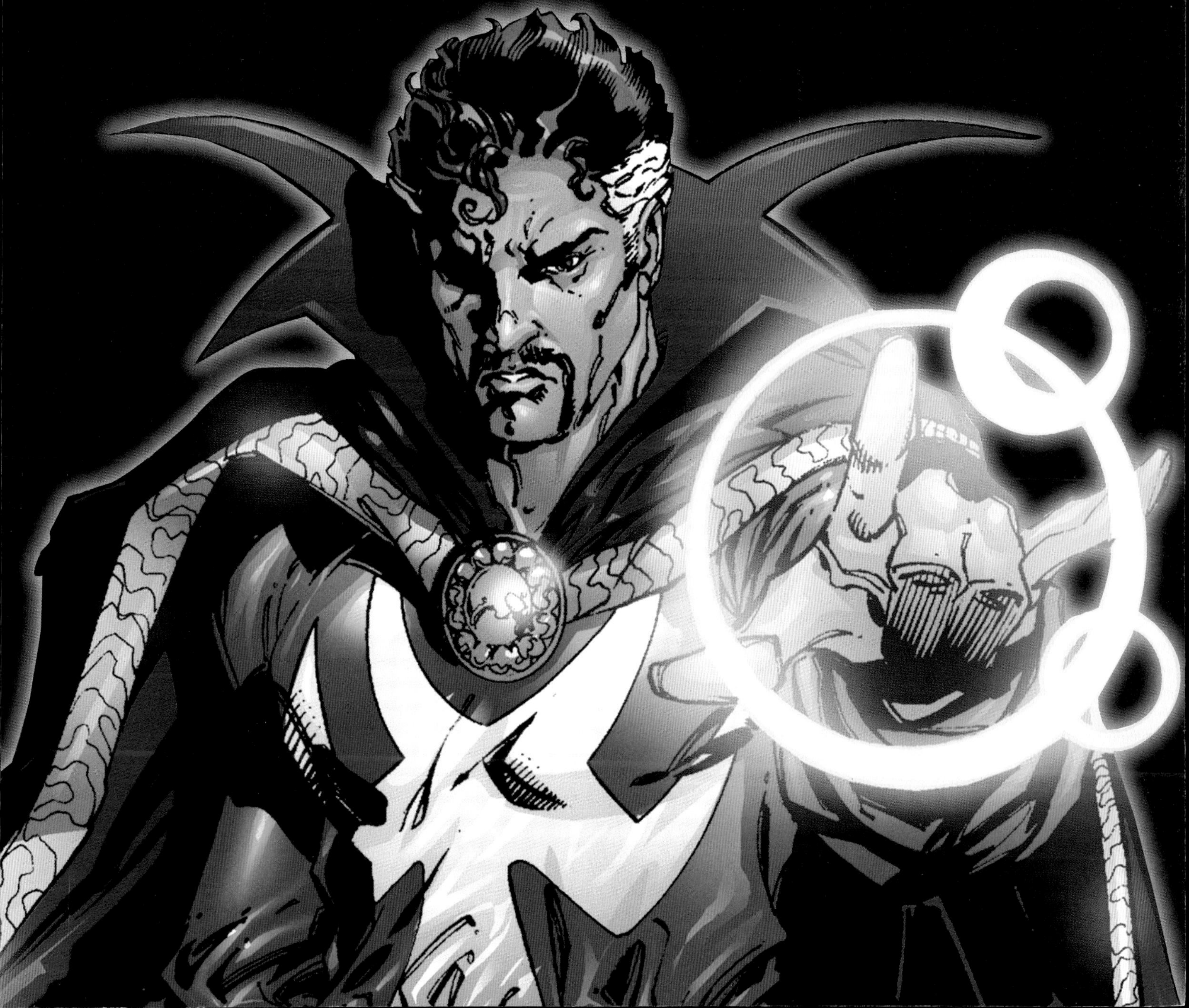

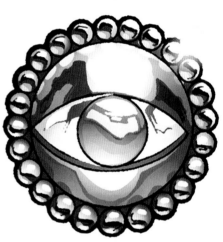

Senior Editor Cefn Ridout
Editor Lauren Nesworthy
Senior Designer Rob Perry
Designer Chris Gould
Pre-Production Producer Siu Yin Chan
Senior Producer Alex Bell
Managing Editor Sadie Smith
Managing Art Editor Ron Stobbart
Publisher Julie Ferris
Art Director Lisa Lanzarini
Publishing Director Simon Beecroft

Additional design by Amazing15

First American Edition, 2016
Published in the United States by DK Publishing
345 Hudson Street, New York, New York 10014

Page design copyright © 2016 Dorling Kindersley Limited
DK, a Division of Penguin Random House Company LLC
16 17 18 19 20 10 9 8 7 6 5 4 3 2 1
001–297716–Oct/2016

marvel.com
© 2016 MARVEL

A catalog record for this book is available from the Library of Congress.
ISBN: 978-1-4654-5557-4

DK books are available at special discounts when purchased in bulk for sales promotions,
premiums, fund-raising, or educational use. For details, contact:
DK Publishing Special Markets, 345 Hudson Street, New York, New York 10014 SpecialSales@dk.com

Printed and bound in China

ACKNOWLEDGMENTS
DK would like to thank Marcus Scudamore, Martin Stiff, and Nick Jones at Amazing15,
Sarah Brunstad, Jeff Reingold, Brian Overton, and Joseph Hochstein at Marvel,
and Joel Kempson and Julia March for editorial assistance.

A WORLD OF IDEAS:
SEE ALL THERE IS TO KNOW
www.dk.com

CONTENTS

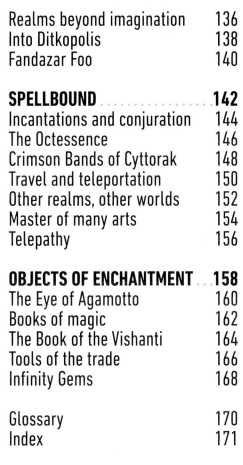

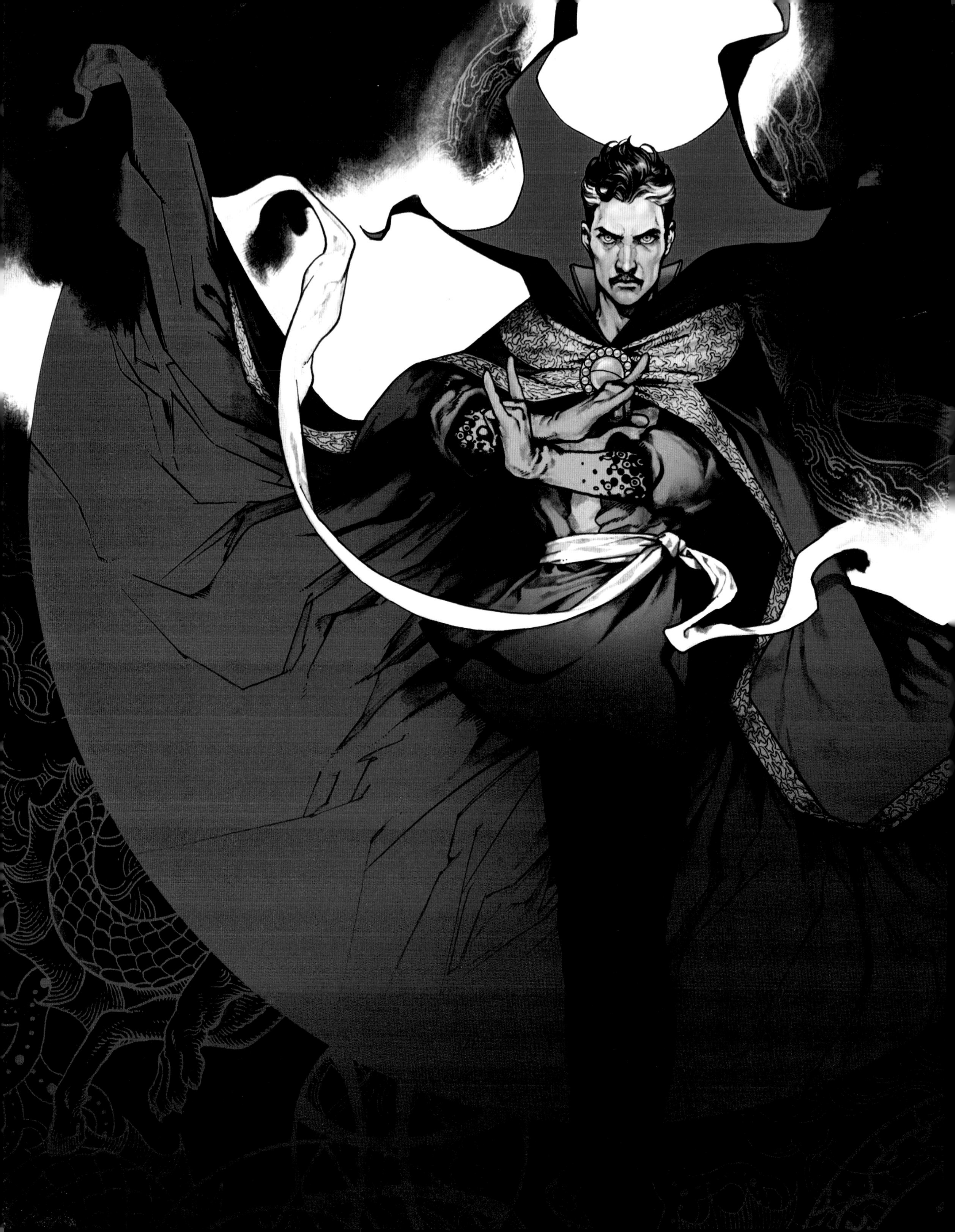

FOREWORD

"THE STORY OF DOCTOR STRANGE IS, AT ITS HEART, A STORY OF REDEMPTION."

Doctor Stephen Strange first appeared in an odd little story tucked into an issue of the comic book *Strange Tales*. In that introductory tale, the Doctor truly was a mystery. We knew only that his name was "spoken in whispers" around the world, that he was a man who dared to enter the realm of nightmares.

Within just a few issues, we learned the truth about this enigmatic man: How he had been a supremely talented—and supremely arrogant—surgeon, before surviving a career-ending accident. How he had searched the world in vain for a cure. How he had embraced the teachings of a mysterious mystic, and forged an entirely different life, employing his new-found knowledge to protect the world from forces beyond our darkest imaginings.

The story of Doctor Strange is, at its heart, a story of redemption. And over the years, that story has been told by some of the most talented individuals in the history of comics. From the earliest defining stories by Stan Lee and Steve Ditko, through the supernatural psychedelia of Roy Thomas and Gene Colan, to the cosmic tales told by Steve Englehart and Frank Brunner, and on to the latest adventures by Jason Aaron and Chris Bachalo... Doctor Strange has brought out the best in his creators.

I myself had the privilege of writing stories for this series. I was lucky enough to have my stories brought to life by a veritable Who's Who of comics artists... Tom Sutton, Michael Golden, Marshall Rogers, Paul Smith, and Mike Mignola, to name just a few.

And now, the talented people at DK have assembled this magnificent guide to the comics world of Doctor Strange. If this is your first exposure to the good Doctor, welcome. You are in for a treat. And if you have been following his adventures since that very first strange tale, welcome home!

CHAPTER 1
STRANGE MAGIC

Doctor Strange is one of the most powerful mystics in existence. He is Earth's primary protector against magical threats, whether from our world or the vast, eternal realms that exist beyond imagination. Noble and vigilant, he uses mysterious incantations and secret knowledge to battle practitioners of the dark arts, and to defend against ancient evils and demonic entities. Able to summon the power of the universe itself to guard against cosmic cataclysm, Doctor Strange is, in this reality and beyond, admired and feared as *the Sorcerer Supreme!*

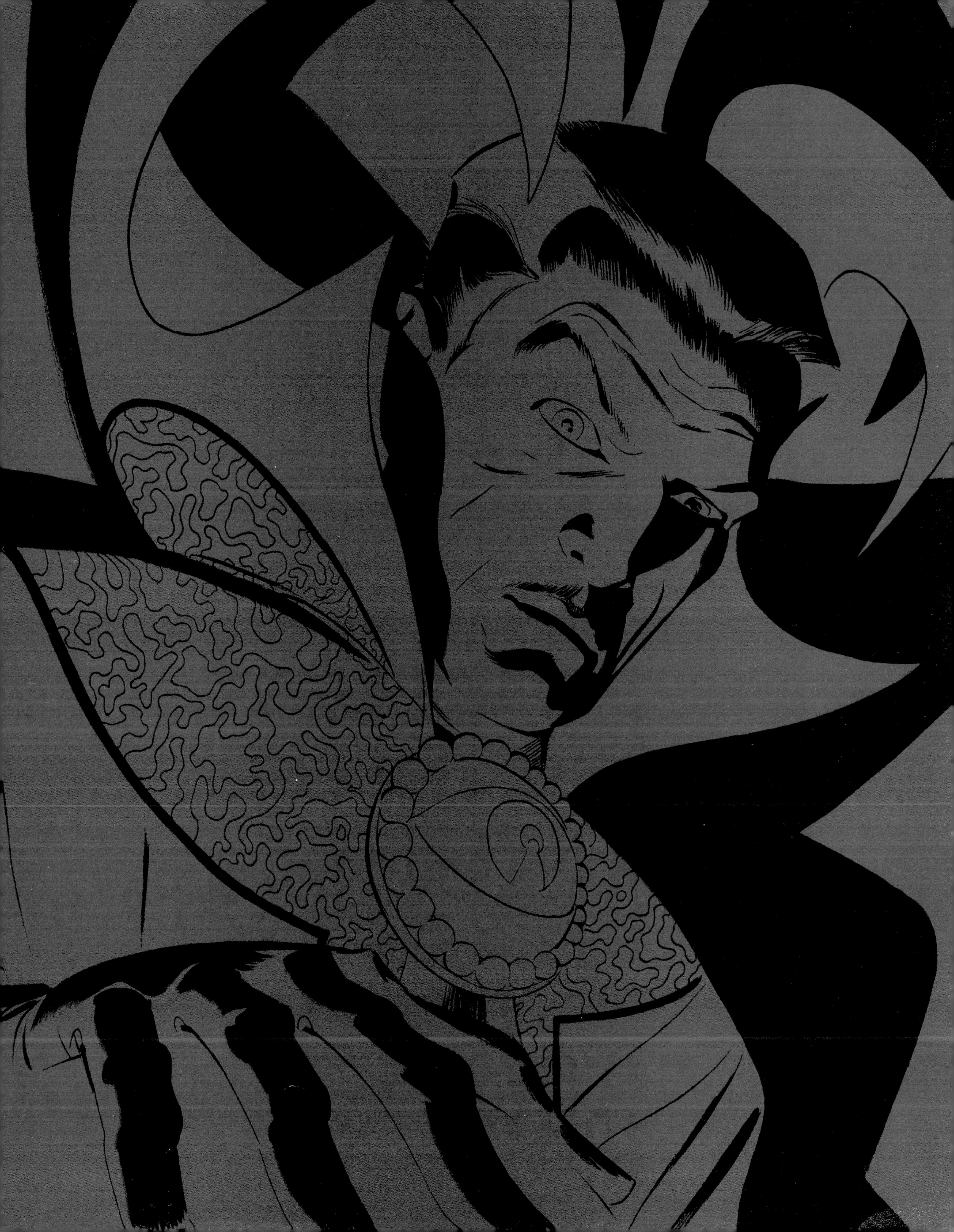

BIRTH OF A MASTER MYSTIC

Stephen Strange was a celebrated surgeon whose brilliance was matched only by his arrogance. His highly successful career came to an abrupt halt when a car accident left him with nerve damage to his hands. As a result, he was unable to perform surgeries. Consumed by self-pity and refusing to accept his dire circumstance, Strange used his fortune to search for a cure, a quest that reduced him to a homeless alcoholic.

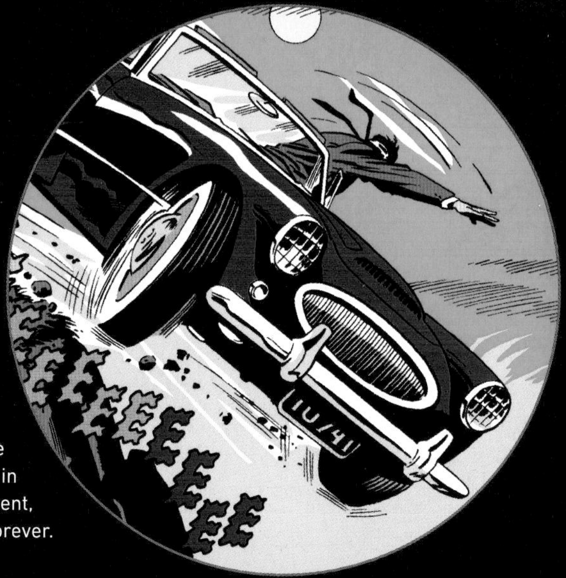

▶ ***Strange fate*** Distracted by thoughts of defrauding his wealthy patients, Doctor Strange missed a treacherous bend in the road. In that moment, his life changed forever.

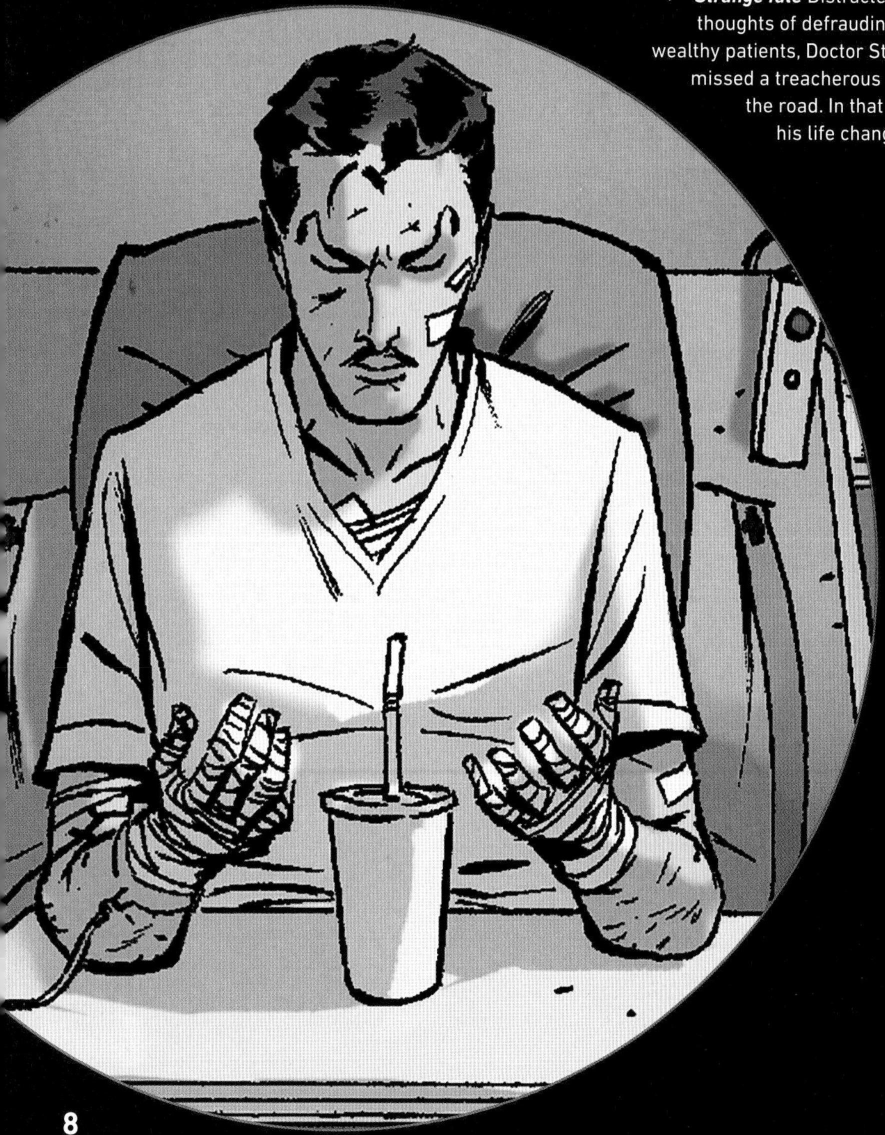

◀ ***Healing hands*** Contemplating his damaged hands, Doctor Strange was forced to realize his plight was beyond medical help.

PATH TO POWER

During these dark times, Doctor Strange heard rumors of a mystical healer named the Ancient One. Pawning his last possessions, Strange traveled to Tibet to seek the healer's aid—his desperation leading him to pursue remedies he wouldn't normally have considered.

Finding the Ancient One's palace, Strange was infuriated when the mystic initially refused to help him. However, he was astonished when he saw the aged man resist a savage attack from occult forces. Strange learned that the Ancient One was in fact Earth's magical defender, and that the attacker was his pupil, Baron Mordo.

When Strange attempted to warn the Ancient One, he was placed under a spell by Mordo, which prevented him from helping the venerable old man. Forced to accept that magic did exist, and that there were evil beings using such power, Strange overcame his own pride and selfishness and made a pledge to fight these malevolent forces.

◀ *Higher learning* At the Ancient One's temple in Tibet, Doctor Strange learned, to his surprise, that he was a natural student of magic.

I WANT TO BE ABLE TO MOVE WORLDS AND SHAKE THEM TO THEIR FOUNDATIONS."
Doctor Strange

Magical collection

Strange has an impressive collection of magical artifacts at his disposal. A key item is the powerful amulet named the Eye of Agamotto. It amplifies his mind's eye and gives him vast psychic abilities. Another item at the forefront of Strange's collection— and a vital part of his costume—is the Cloak of Levitation. It gives Strange the ability to fly.

The Ancient One was impressed, and being well aware of Mordo's treachery, removed his disciple's spell on Strange. He then offered Strange the opportunity to become his student. So began years of physical and spiritual healing, and training in the mystic arts. Strange learned how to tap into his own innate mystical powers as well as those of the world around him.

When the Ancient One died, Doctor Strange inherited his mentor's role as Sorcerer Supreme of Earth. Strange was selected for the position by the Eye of Agamotto, which would one day choose another worthy candidate for the role when Strange's time as Sorcerer Supreme was over.

Relocating to New York City, Doctor Strange set up the Sanctum Sanctorum, a sanctuary from where he defends Earth and the dimension in which it resides.

Immortality
Though human, Doctor Strange is technically immortal and does not age, having passed the Ancient One's test of "accepting" death.

STRANGE CHANGES

Doctor Strange is a striking and flamboyant figure, his distinctive costume usually framed by the mystical Cloak of Levitation. Yet over the course of his adventures, the Sorcerer Supreme has adopted a few different looks.

Doctor Strange's costume is a crucial component of his role as the Master of the Mystic Arts. Key elements of it—the Eye of Agamotto and the Cloak of Levitation—act as direct channels of mystical power. Over the years his costume has remained largely consistent, but in both his own dimension and alternate timelines, there have been minor and major alterations to his iconic attire. Some of these changes were by his choice, others were forced upon him by fiendish events.

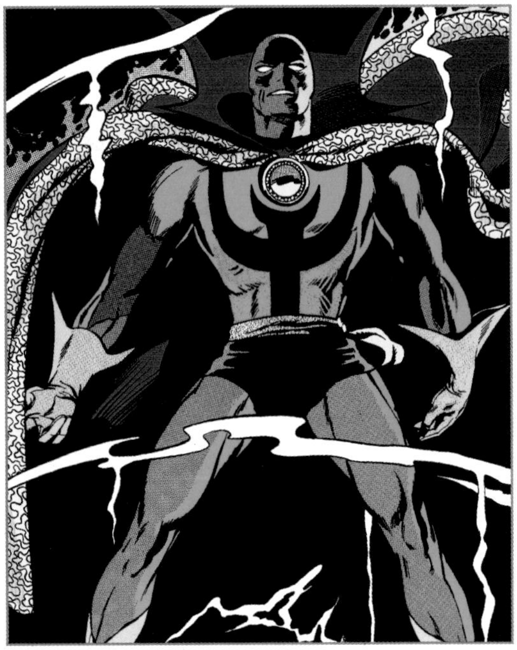

Masked mystic

When Asmodeus, the leader of the Sons of Satannish cult, stole Doctor Strange's face and body, Strange was forced to mask himself to re-enter Earth's dimension and battle the villain.

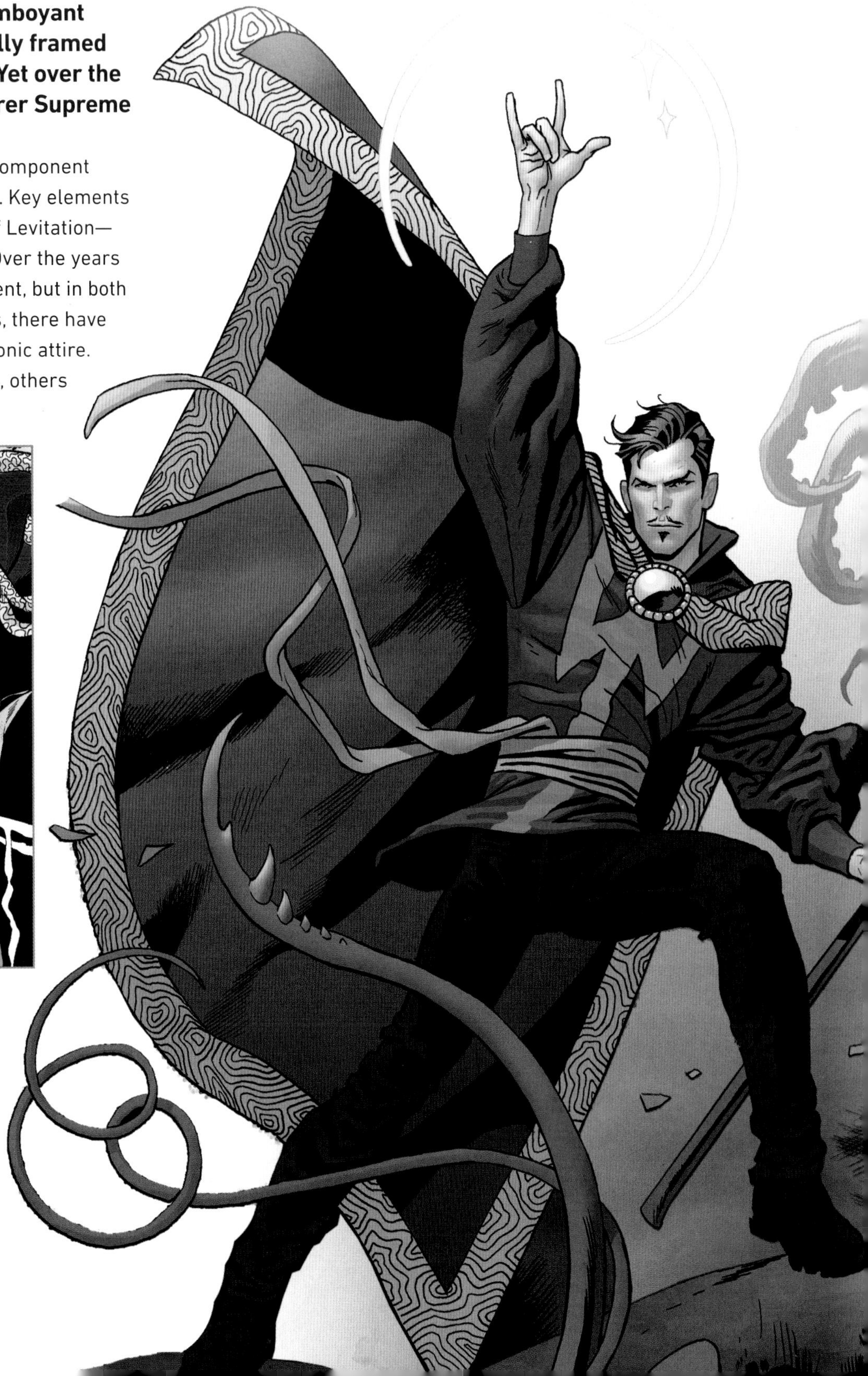

▶ ***A classic costume*** Doctor Strange's stylish outfit has seen a few changes over the years, but always returns to a variation on the unique original.

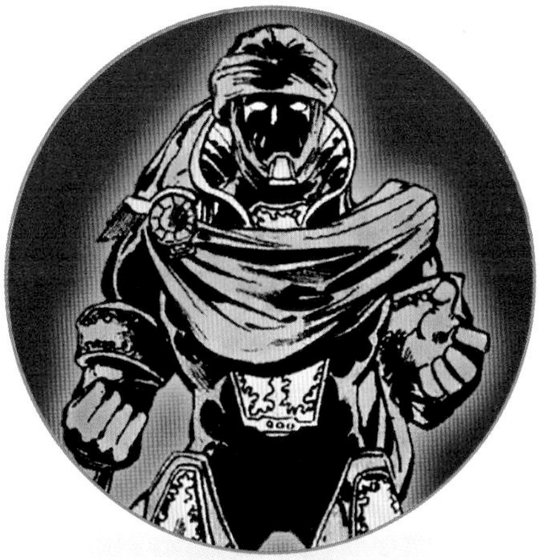

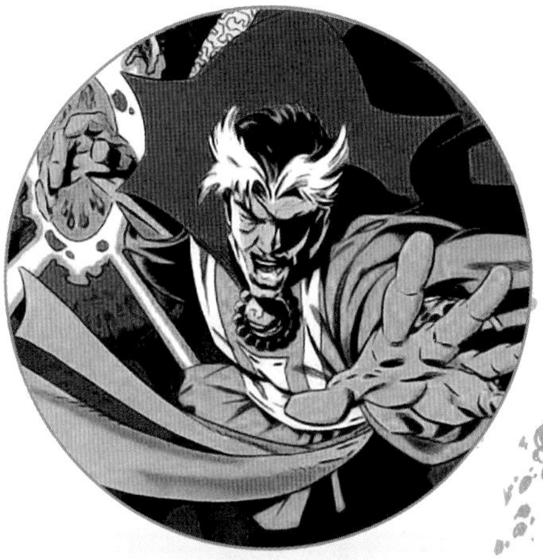

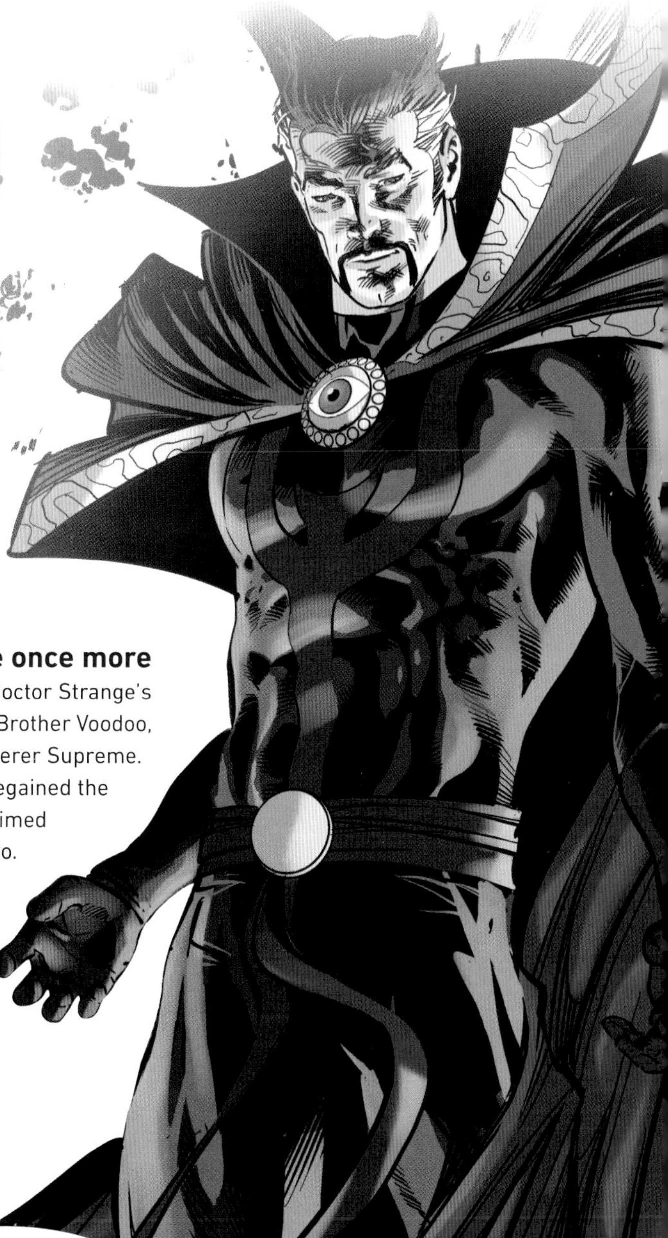

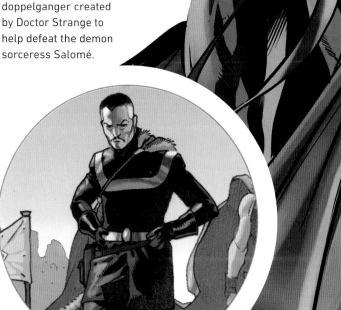

Seeing red

Mesmerized by the mystical Star of Capistan gem, Doctor Strange became the host body for the jewel's protector, the Red Rajah. This turbaned tyrant possessed all of Strange's powers!

A rough patch

Fighting alongside his enemy, Kaluu, against Shuma-Gorath, Strange became vulnerable when his eye was taken from him. The injury required the adoption of an eye patch.

Supreme once more

For a time, Doctor Strange's fellow mage, Brother Voodoo, became Sorcerer Supreme. When Strange regained the title, he also reclaimed the Eye of Agamotto.

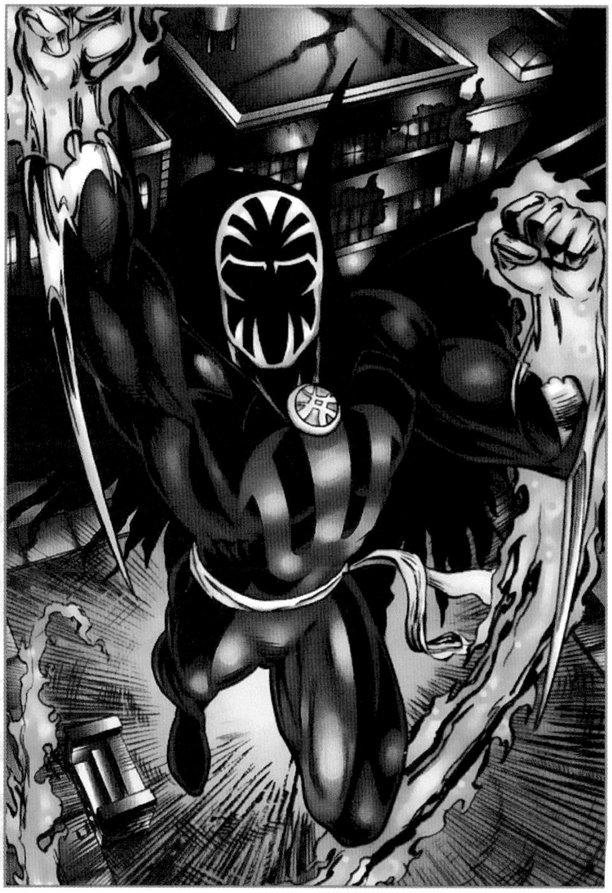

Second self

Paradox—also known as "Strange"—was a doppelganger created by Doctor Strange to help defeat the demon sorceress Salomé.

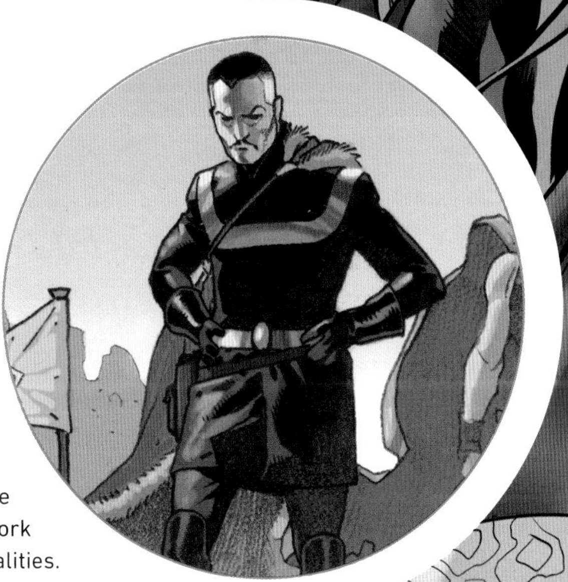

New sheriff in town

During a cataclysm involving the collision of multiple universes, Doctor Strange became the Sheriff of Agamotto on Battleworld, a patchwork planet made up of the remains of numerous realities.

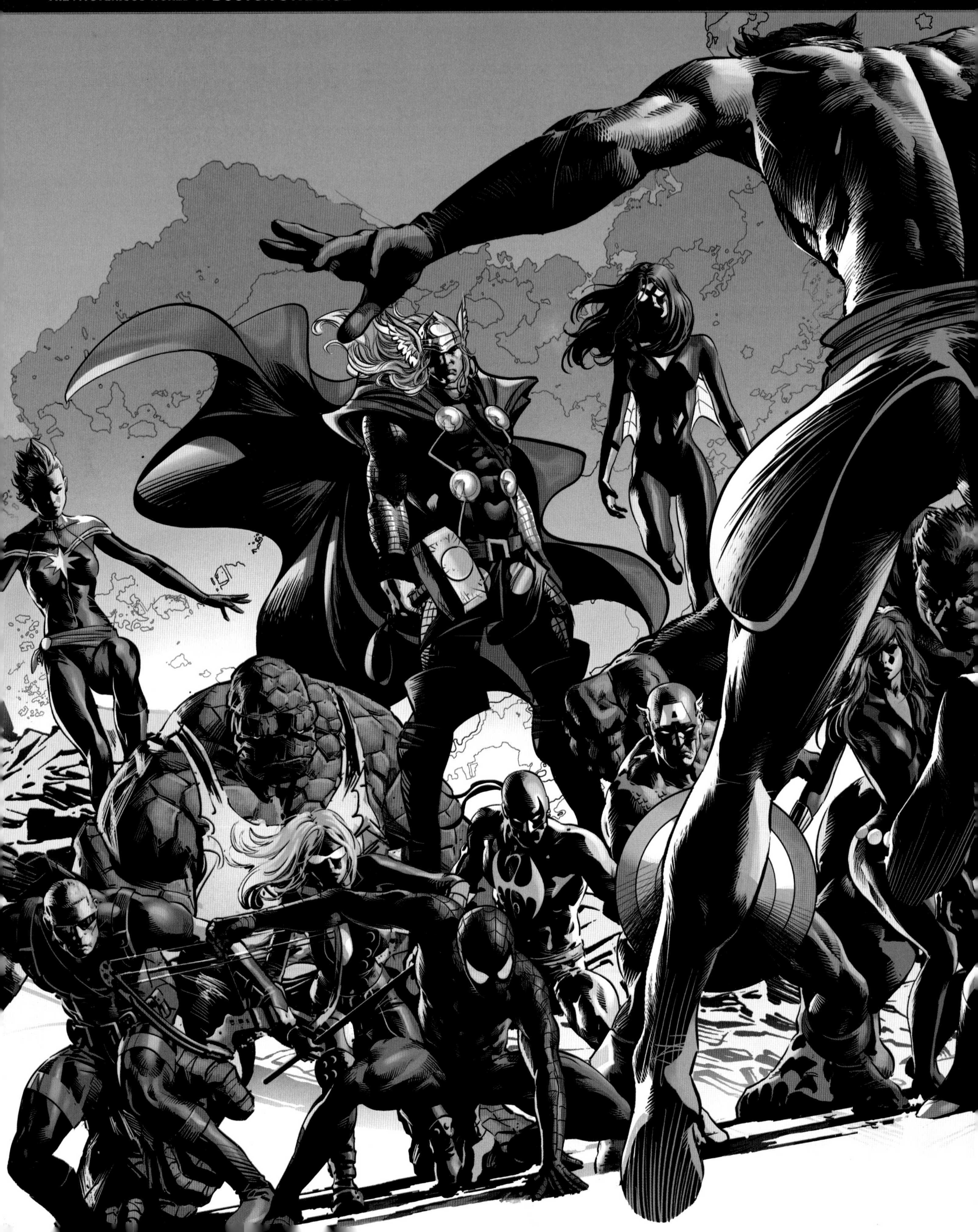

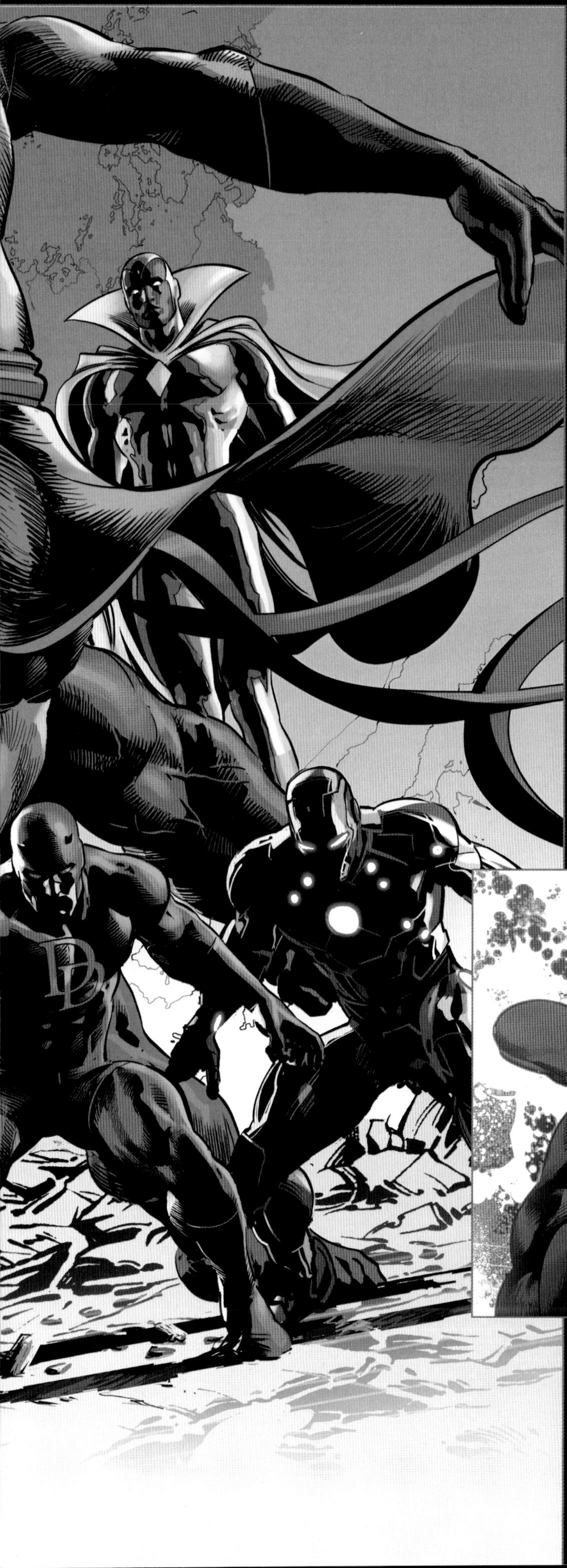

◀ ***Alone against the Avengers*** While Doctor Strange had faced all manner of mystical threats, the awesome physical power of 14 of the world's greatest Super Heroes proved a mighty challenge.

THE MYSTIC MIGHT OF DOCTOR STRANGE

For a time, the mantle of Sorcerer Supreme was passed to another mystic—Jericho Drumm, alias Brother Voodoo. But when Drumm was killed, Doctor Strange subsequently faced one of the greatest tests of his otherworldly powers, when he single-handedly fought all of the Avengers. The team had been possessed by the spirit of the sorcerer Daniel Drumm, who blamed Doctor Strange for the death of his brother. In the ensuing battle, Strange bested the Red Hulk, Spider-Man, the Thing, and Captain America, before resorting to the dark arts to vanquish Drumm's spirit. Bloodied, beaten, but unbowed, Strange became the Sorcerer Supreme once more.

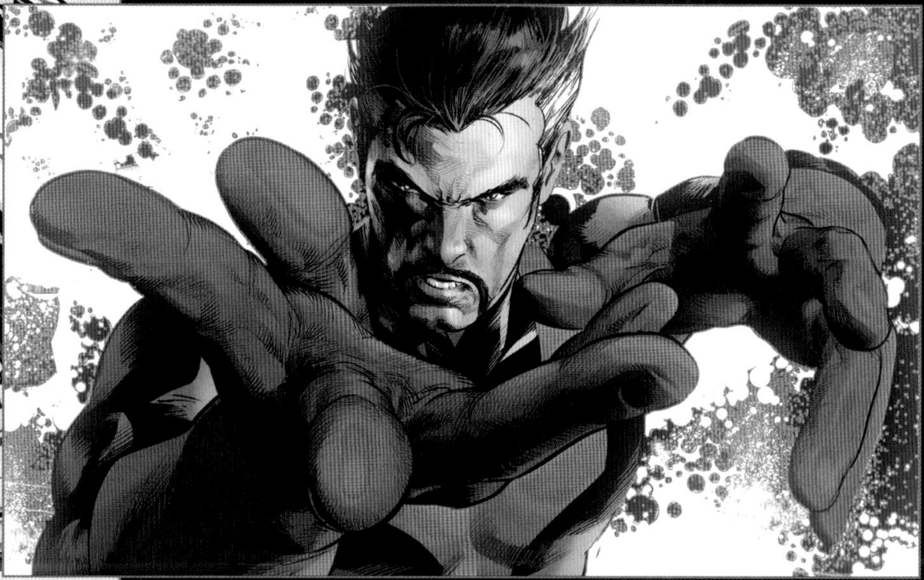

An inventive victory

Although Strange was not at full power when he fought the possessed Avengers, sheer bravery and ingenuity enabled him to overcome a mystical evil and aid his stricken comrades, the Avengers.

CHAPTER 2

SIDE BY SIDE

At first, Doctor Strange was aided on his mystical journey by those closest to him, such as the Ancient One, Wong, and Clea. Over the years, however, the Sorcerer Supreme has found allies amongst magical beings like the Scarlet Witch and Brother Voodoo, heroes such as Spider-Man and X-23, and even, when necessary, villains like Doctor Doom. Doctor Strange's skills have also ably served many Super Hero teams, such as the New Avengers and the Midnight Sons. He has formed his own team, the mighty Defenders, and helped to shape global and cosmic events as an indispensable member of the shadowy Illuminati.

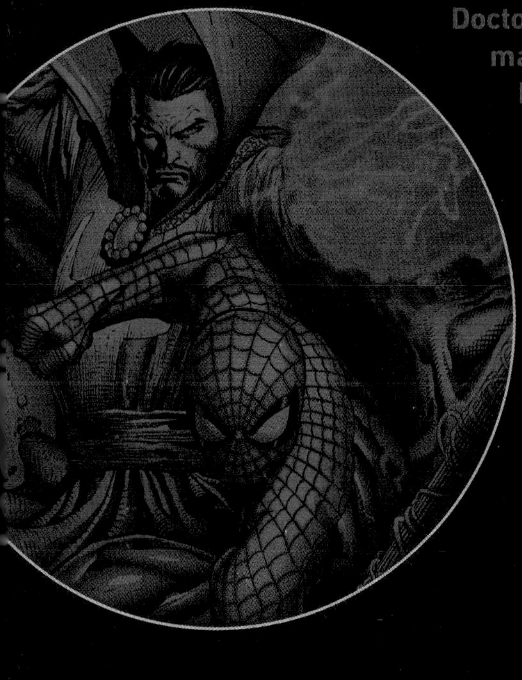

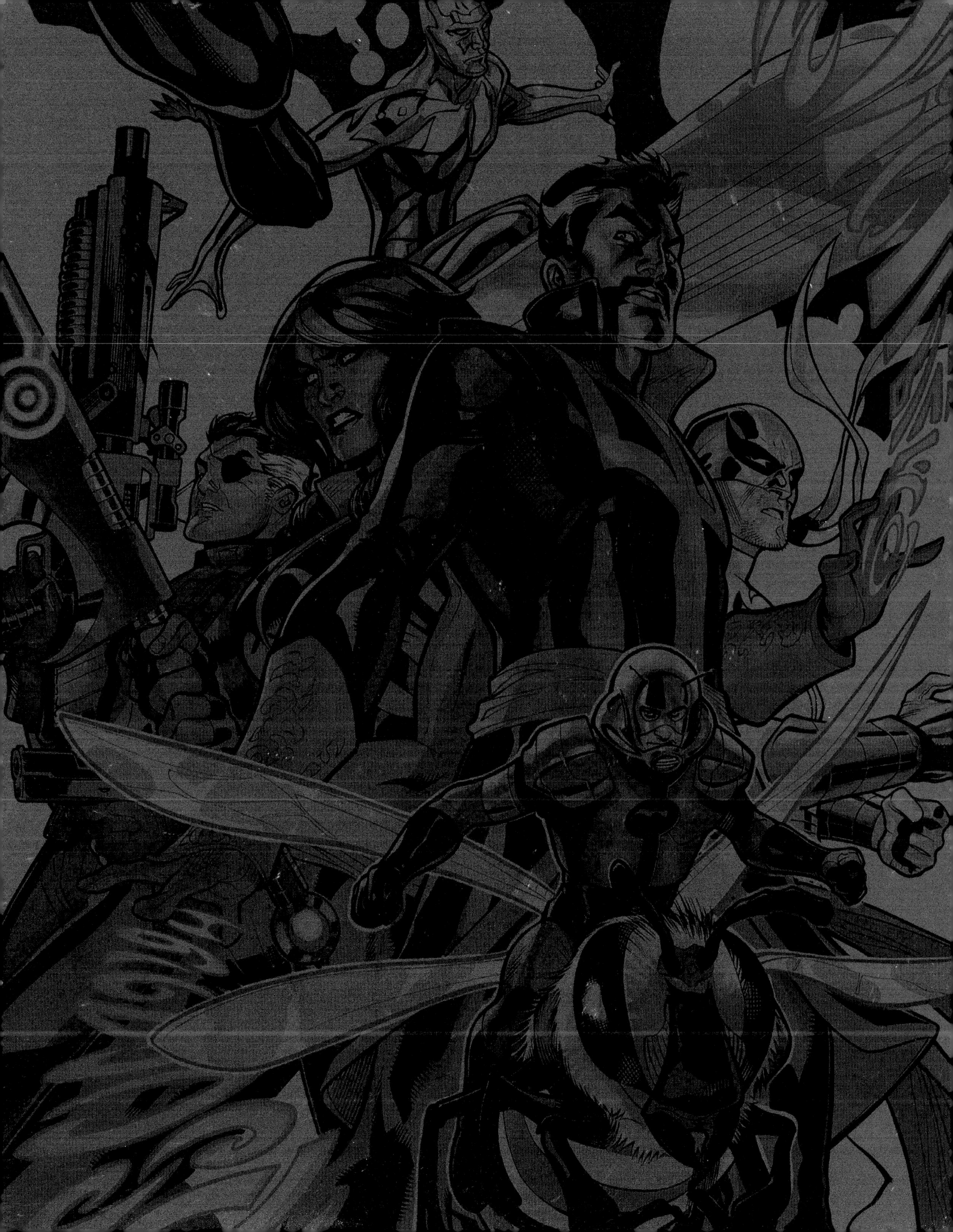

THE ANCIENT ONE

When all seemed lost for Doctor Stephen Strange, he made one last desperate gamble to find a mysterious Tibetan mystic who might heal his damaged hands. Reaching a snowbound citadel, Strange did indeed encounter a powerful mage. His life would be transformed and a universe of possibility revealed to him by this mysterious figure: the Ancient One, Earth's Sorcerer Supreme.

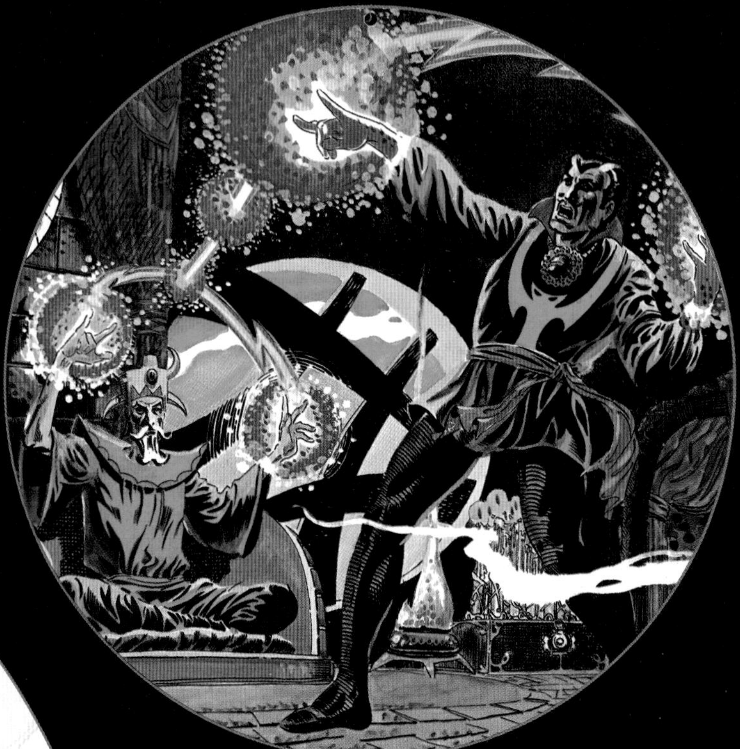

▲ ***Wise teacher*** The Ancient One gave Doctor Strange the training that he needed to become a great sorcerer.

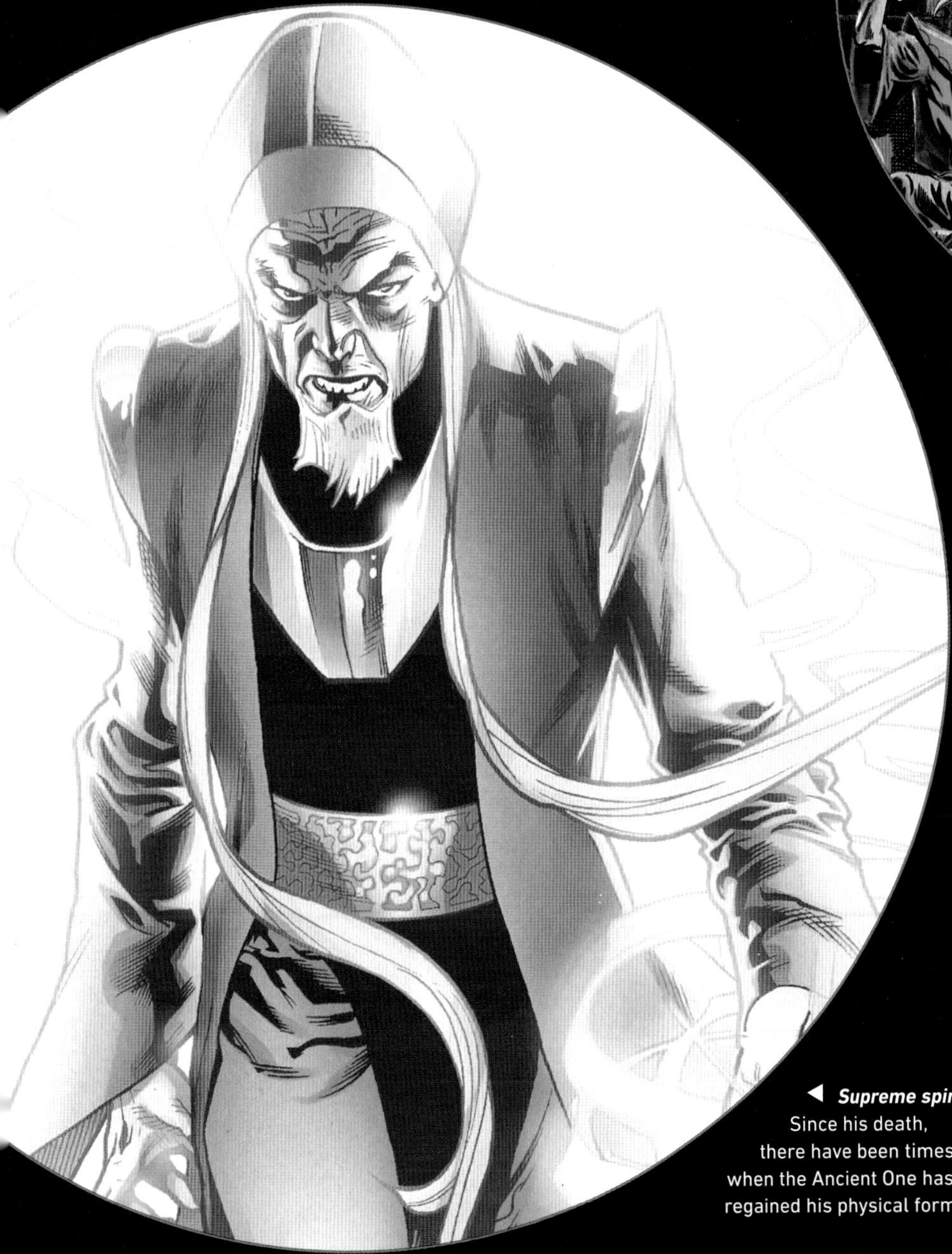

◀ ***Supreme spirit*** Since his death, there have been times when the Ancient One has regained his physical form.

STRANGE SALVATION

Over 500 years ago, in a small village hidden deep in the mountains of Tibet, the boy who would become the Ancient One was born. He was named Yao and was destined to be a common farmer. However, he met an older villager named Kaluu who shared with Yao his knowledge of sorcerey—including the secrets of immortality. Over time, Kaluu grew more interested in power and influence, while Yao sought more benevolent uses of magic.

While the pair initially used their new powers to eliminate poverty, disease, and ageing from their village, Kaluu was drawn farther into darkness. He used magic to manipulate and subjugate villagers to his will.

Dormammu
The Ancient One first fought the villainous Dormammu during the Great Fire of London in 1666, successfully banishing the evil mystic.

> "I MUST ALWAYS BE ON MY GUARD... THE FORCES OF EVIL ARE EVER PITTED AGAINST ME!"
> The Ancient One

Sorcerer Supreme

As Sorcerer Supreme, the Ancient One wielded extraordinary power. It was his duty to protect Earth from all manner of mystical threats.

The boy tried to stop Kaluu, but their conflict led to the destruction of the village. While Kaluu escaped to another dimension, Yao was stripped of his own immortality.

Devoted to using magic for good, Yao roamed the Earth for centuries before settling with a group of sorcerers named the Ancient Ones. Supremely skilled, Yao became the first human to meet Eternity and was entrusted with the all-seeing Eye of Agamotto, making him Earth's first Sorcerer Supreme.

Yao eventually made his home in the Himalayas, taking nobleman Baron Mordo as his apprentice. Sensing Mordo's corruption, Yao tried—and failed—to steer him towards good. However, it was only with the arrival of the stricken Stephen Strange that Yao ultimately found a worthy successor to inherit the mantle of Sorcerer Supreme.

▲ *Long life* The Ancient One may have lost his immortality, but the magic that he possesses allowed him to age extremely slowly, granting him an unnaturally long life.

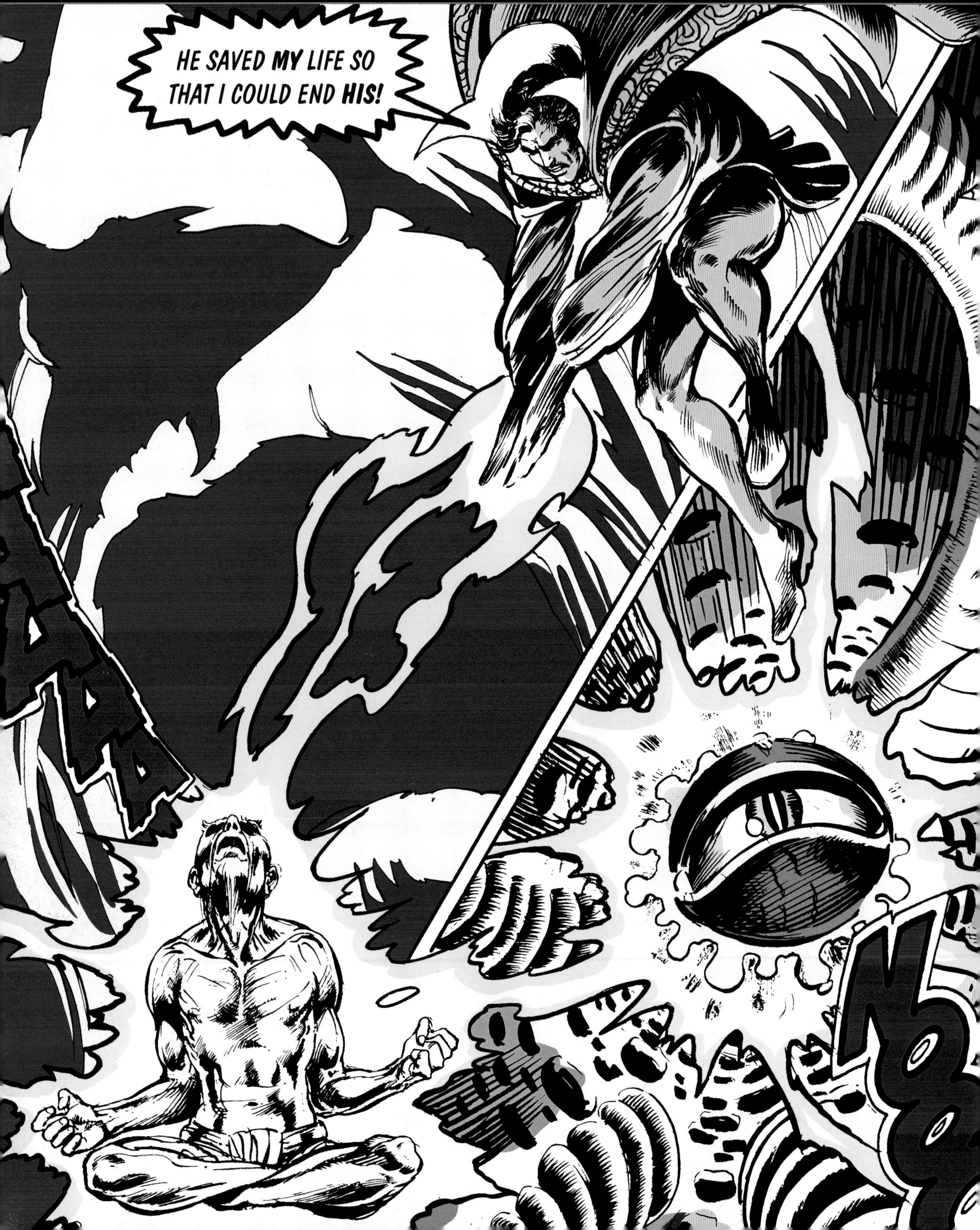
HE SAVED MY LIFE SO THAT I COULD END HIS!

◀ ***A terrible necessity*** Facing the dreaded possibility of Earth being invaded by Shuma-Gorath, Doctor Strange was forced to destroy his respected mentor.

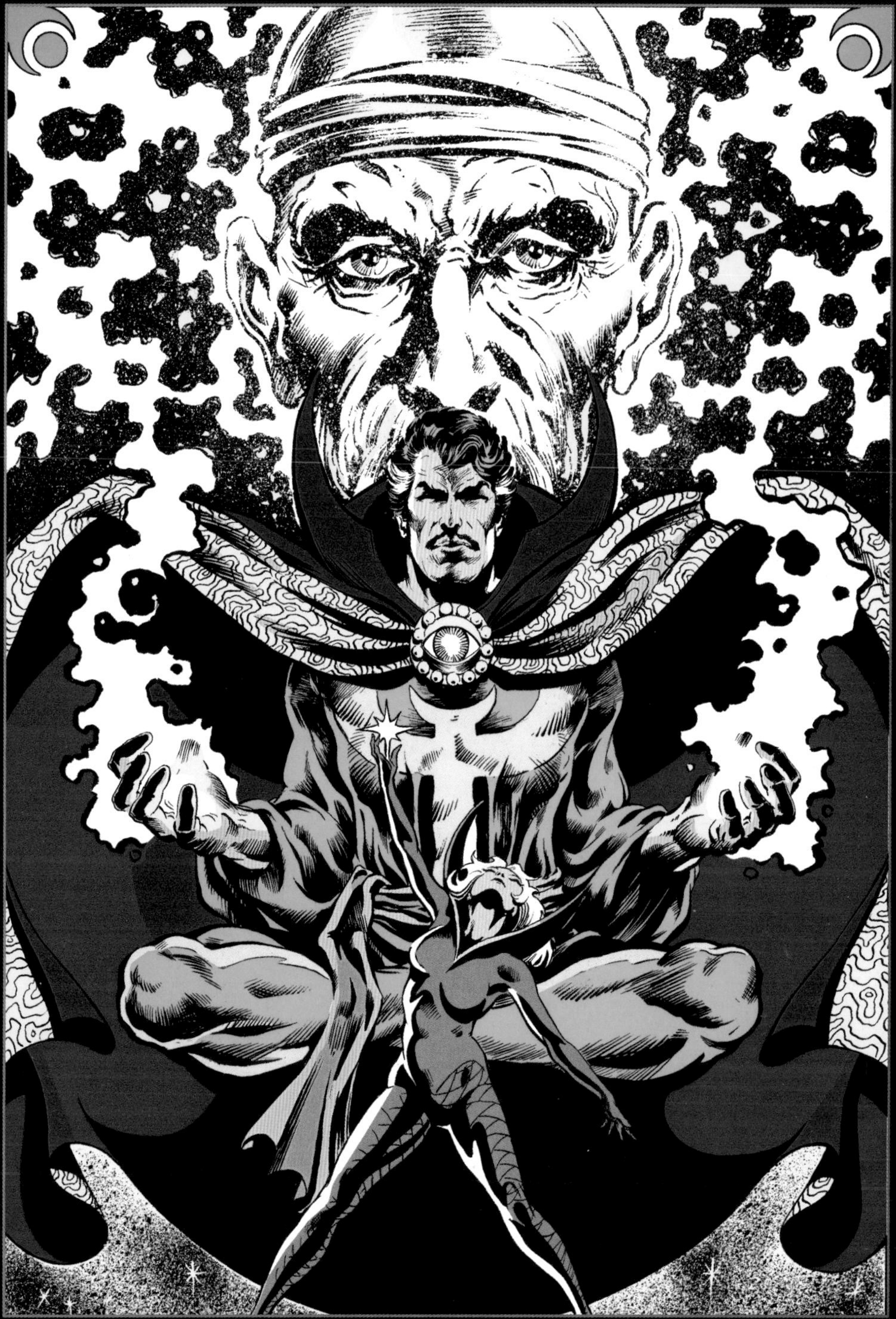

FROM DEATH TO ETERNITY

The Ancient One's centuries-long existence on Earth came to an end in a moment of supreme sacrifice. When the monstrous tentacled demon Shuma-Gorath tried to invade Earth through the Ancient One's mind, the aged mystic ordered Doctor Strange to destroy the part of his psyche that contained his ego. The desperate maneuver blocked Shuma-Gorath's entrance to Earth, but destroyed the Ancient One's physical form. However, his spirit achieved transcendence and became one with Eternity.

Mystic legacy The Ancient One's teachings would live on through Doctor Strange, who, in turn, passed them on to his own disciple, Clea, a sorceress from the Dark Dimension.

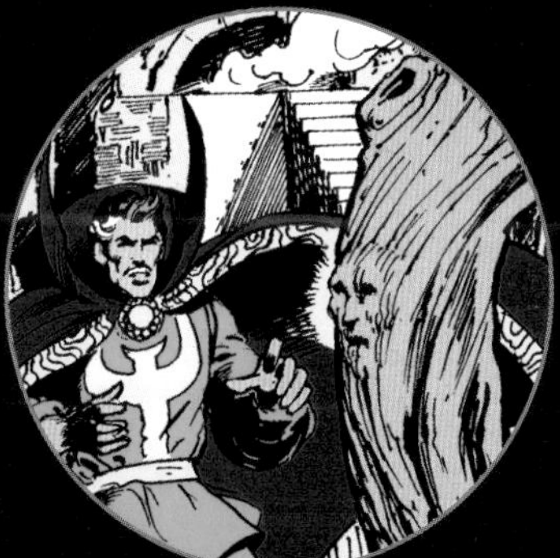

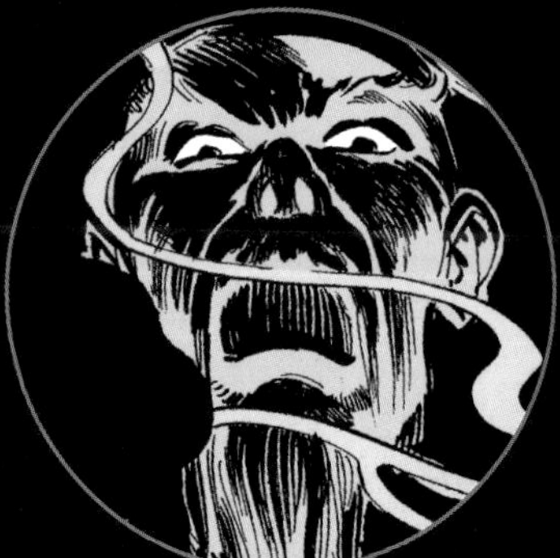

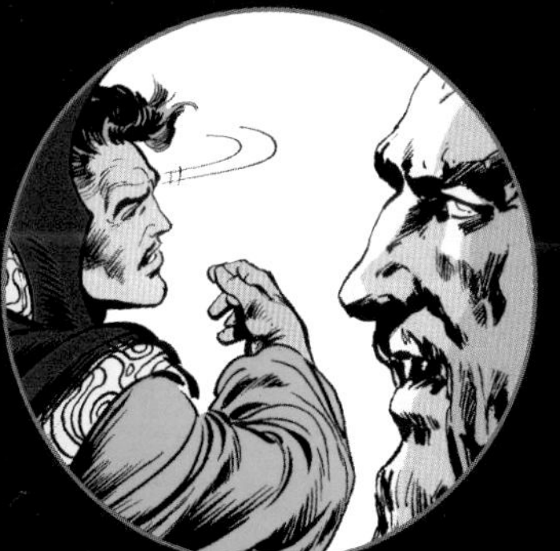

Wood, water, stone After his physical demise, the Ancient One continued to aid and counsel Doctor Strange, even manifesting his new presence in elemental forms that surprised and shocked the new Sorcerer Supreme.

CLEA

When Doctor Strange first ventured into the Dark Dimension to face Dormammu, he discovered a young woman who would have a huge influence on his life as he would upon hers: Clea. A powerful sorceress in her own right, she would come to rule the Dark Dimension, as well as join Doctor Strange in marriage.

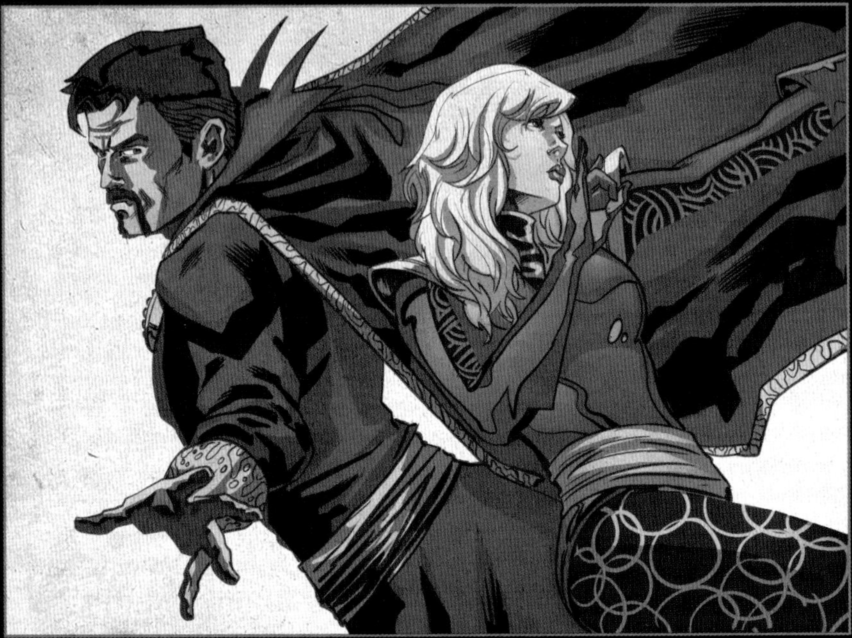

▲ ***Complicated history*** Clea's relationship with Doctor Strange is filled with love, but is also beset by constant challenges.

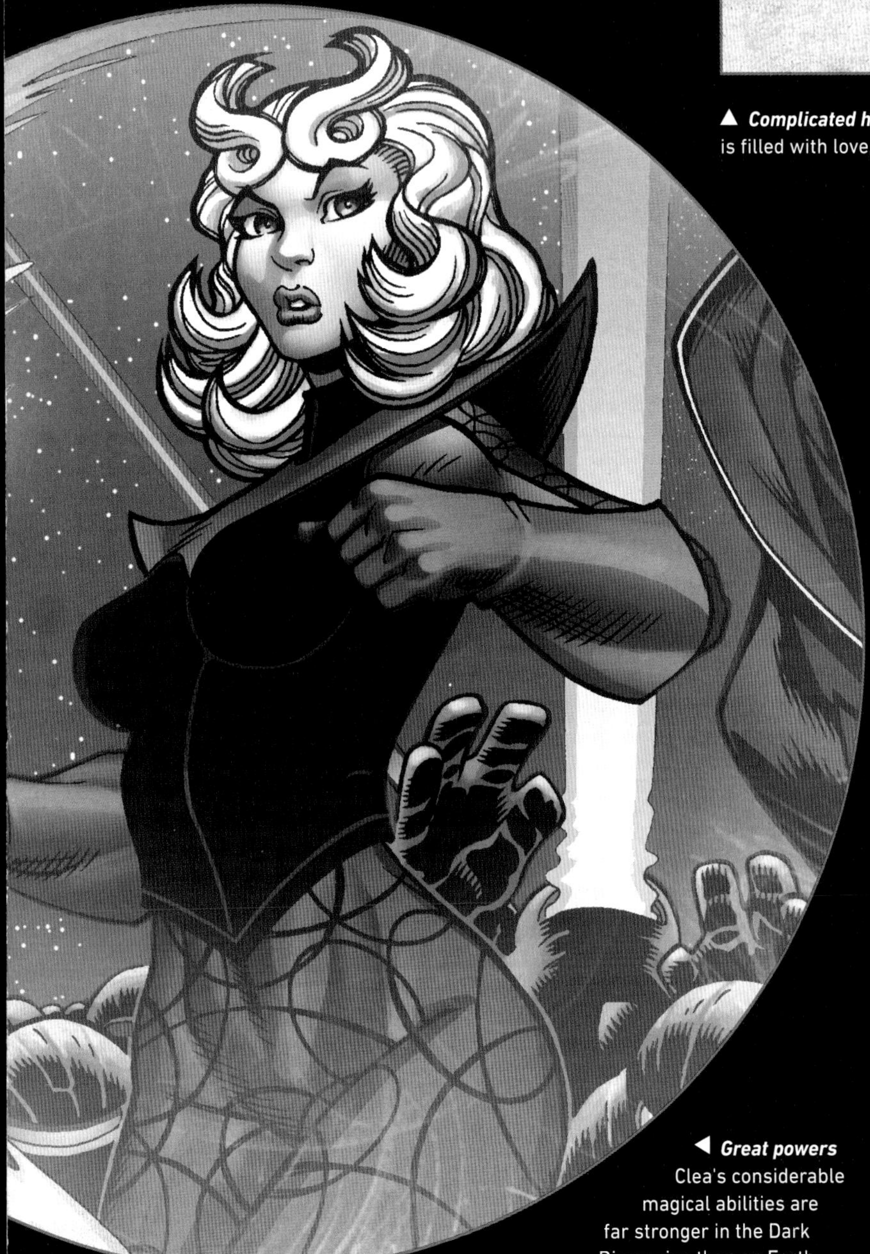

◀ ***Great powers*** Clea's considerable magical abilities are far stronger in the Dark Dimension than on Earth.

SORCERESS SUPREME

The silver-haired Faltinian princess Clea emerged from a turbulent heritage, born of a secret relationship between Prince Orini, rightful heir to the Dark Dimension, and Umar, sister of the despotic ruler, Dormammu. Umar abandoned Clea to be raised by Prince Orini, who hid the truth about her mother's identity from her.

Meeting Doctor Strange upon his first entry into the Dark Dimension, Clea aided him in his battle, risking the wrath of the ruler of the dimension (and her uncle), Dormammu, on multiple occasions.

Clea eventually journeyed to Earth with Doctor Strange, living in the Sanctum Sanctorum as his student. In the years that followed, Clea proved herself a supremely capable sorceress, with abilities rivaling Strange's own. She accompanied her mentor in many

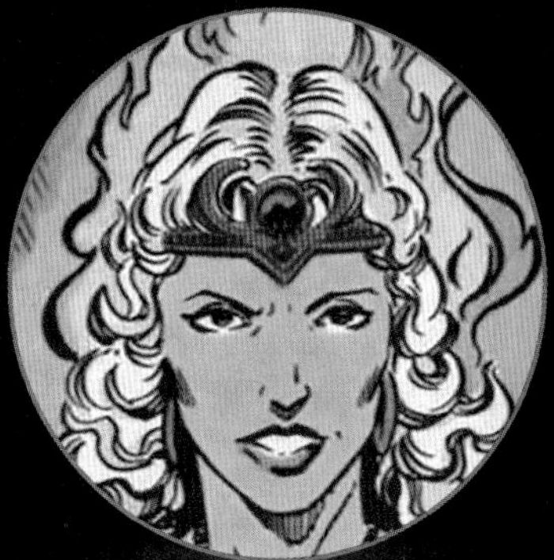

Fire power

The Flames of Regency are bestowed upon the ruler of the Dark Dimension. They made Clea strong enough to overthrow and banish her parents Umar and Orini from their kingdom, and take the throne... for a time.

Partners in magic With her mystical powers almost equal to those of Doctor Strange, Clea proves herself to be a vital ally in battle.

An exalted title
Clea is named as the Sorcerer Adept of the Dark Dimension. She possesses vast mystical abilities derived from extensive training with Doctor Strange and her Faltine heritage.

exploits, even becoming a regular member of the Defenders, an ad-hoc team of Super Heroes that Strange had formed to defend the Earth.

Clea returned to the Dark Dimension, learning that Umar had overthrown Dormammu. Joining the rebellion against Umar, Clea finally discovered from Prince Orini the true identity of her malevolent mother and ultimately fought her one-on-one. Victorious, Clea was named sovereign of the Dark Dimension and, shortly after, married Strange.

However, Dormammu returned and reclaimed his rule, forcing Clea's return to Earth. There, her relationship with Doctor Strange grew increasingly tempestuous, and she returned to the Dark Dimension, to lead the rebellion against Dormammu.

"I TARGET BIGGER MONSTERS THAN YOU EVERY NIGHT! AND THE NIGHTS ARE LONG IN THE DARK DIMENSION!"
Clea

Family betrayal
Dormammu imprisoned Clea when he discovered that she had aided Doctor Strange. When Strange helped Dormammu defeat the Mindless Ones, the dark lord was forced to free Clea in return.

Old soul It is thought that Clea is actually thousands of years old, despite her appearance as a young woman. Her father has aged very slowly over centuries, while her mother seems to be immortal.

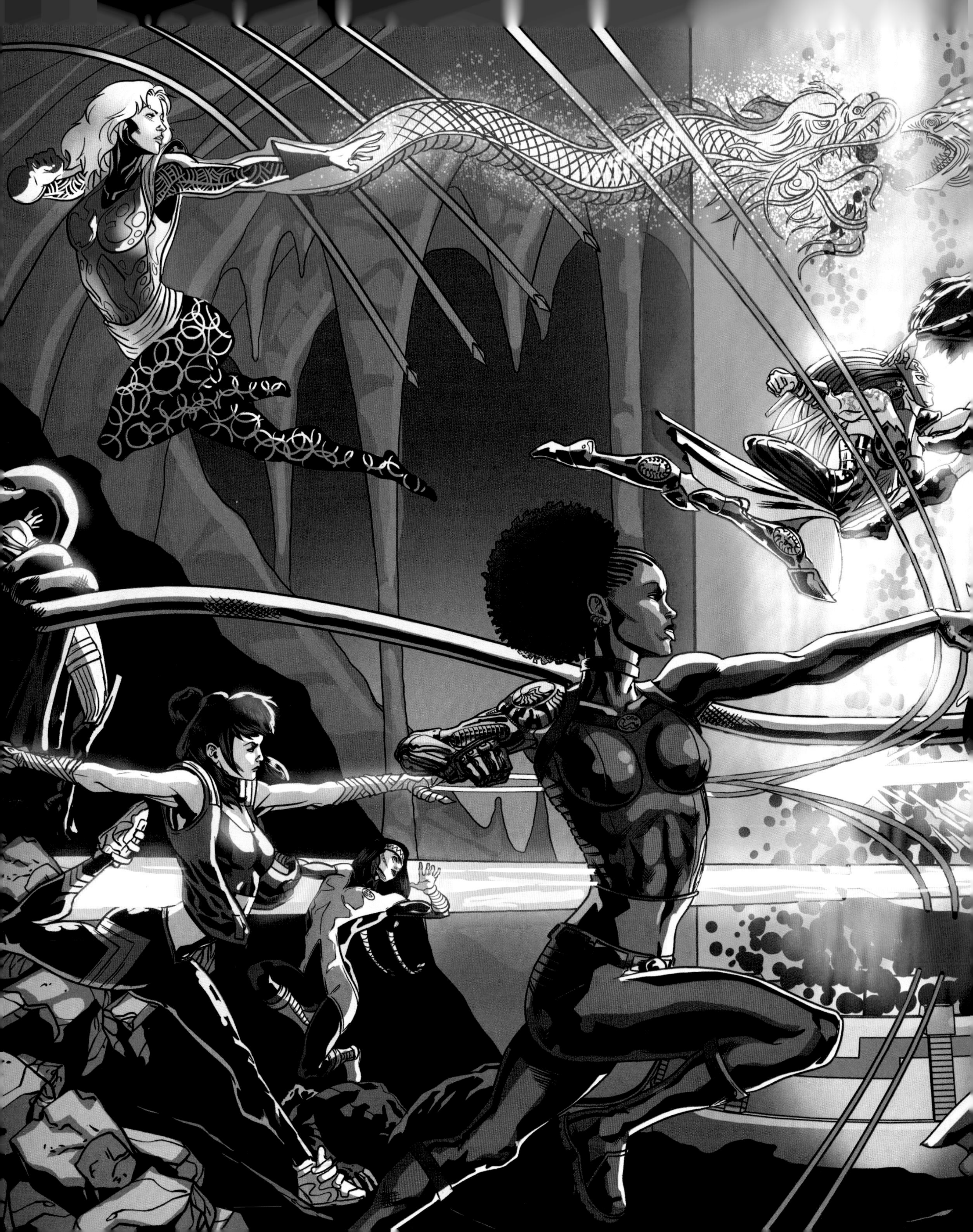

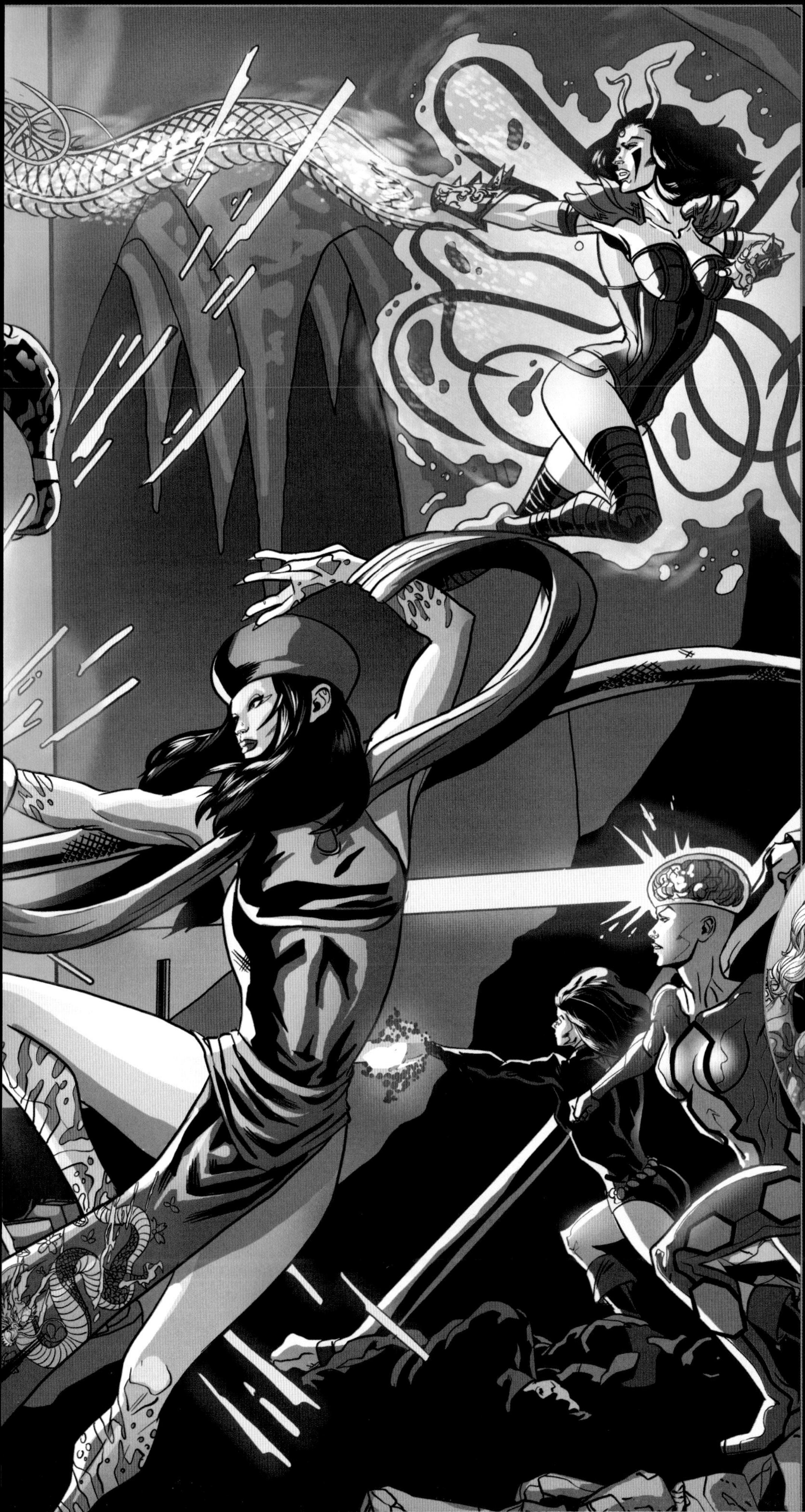

◀ ***Opposites repel*** During a pitched battle with the Doom Maidens, Clea took on the demonic sorceress Aradnea.

FEARLESS FEMALES

For a time, Clea joined an all-female team of Fearless Defenders, alongside the heroes Valkyrie, Warrior Woman, Ren Kimura, and others. The team met their ultimate nemesis in the shape of the Doom Maidens, a group led by Caroline Le Fay, daughter of Morgan Le Fay and Doctor Doom. The Defenders were able to vanquish the Maidens and prevent Caroline Le Fay from gaining the power she craved. However, they could not prevent her from achieving her real goal: to ally with her mother and bring her to the present day.

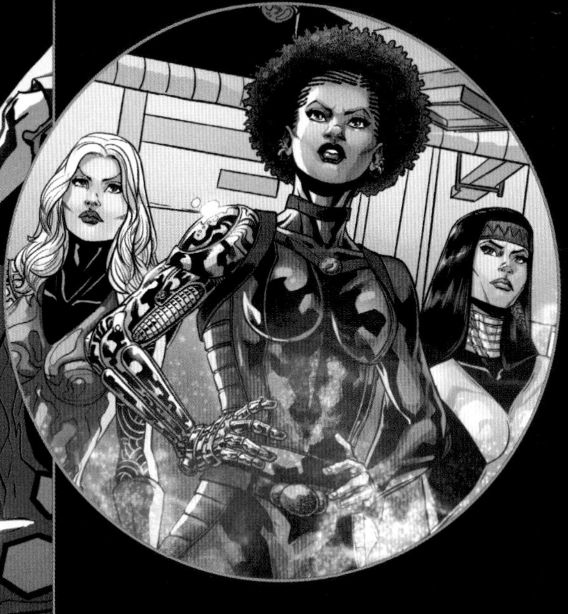

Soul sisters

Clea found much in common with her teammates, such as the private eye Misty Knight and the mutant telepath Dani Moonstar. Together they fought many foes, including the bizarre Headmen and the evil living sculptures known as the Pandemonium Axles.

WONG

As Doctor Strange's manservant, confidant, and housekeeper of the Sanctum Sanctorum, Wong is a vital source of support for Earth's Sorcerer Supreme. The Tibetan-born Wong is well-versed in the mystical arts, despite having no magical powers himself. A formidable martial artist in his own right, he has valiantly served as Strange's accomplice in many adventures.

An impossible choice

When Wong was diagnosed with a brain tumor, Strange traveled to another dimension to find an elixir to eradicate the disease. However, when the potion was spilled and only a drop remained, Strange faced a terrible dilemma: use the precious drop to save his dying friend or use it to replicate the elixir and save the world.

FRIEND AND ALLY

The descendent of a Chinese monk named Kan, Wong was born in the village Kamar-Tej—the birthplace of the Ancient One. Ten generations of Wong's family served the elderly mystic—including Wong's father, Hamir—and Wong followed in this proud tradition from an early age.

As a boy, Wong was sent to a remote monastery to study the martial and mystic arts of Kamar-Tej, in preparation for serving a master sorcerer. During his training, he became highly proficient at certain martial arts styles.

Once Wong reached adulthood, he was dispatched by the Ancient One to the US to serve his latest disciple, Doctor Stephen Strange. It was an inspired pairing. Wong would become Strange's martial arts instructor, mystical advisor, and in time, one of his closest friends.

Over the years, Wong has frequently been drawn into Strange's cosmic—and dangerous—adventures. He has been turned into a vampire by Dracula himself (later restored to normal by his mystic master), kidnapped by alien sorcerers and held in a dimension ruled by the Shadowqueen, and almost killed by a vast array of otherworldly threats.

Whatever challenges Doctor Strange's exploits have thrown Wong's way, he has always dealt with them with his characteristic calm and focus... and complete loyalty to the Master of the Mystic Arts.

◄ **New associates**
When Strange moved in with the New Avengers, Wong also arrived as their housekeeper—equipment in tow.

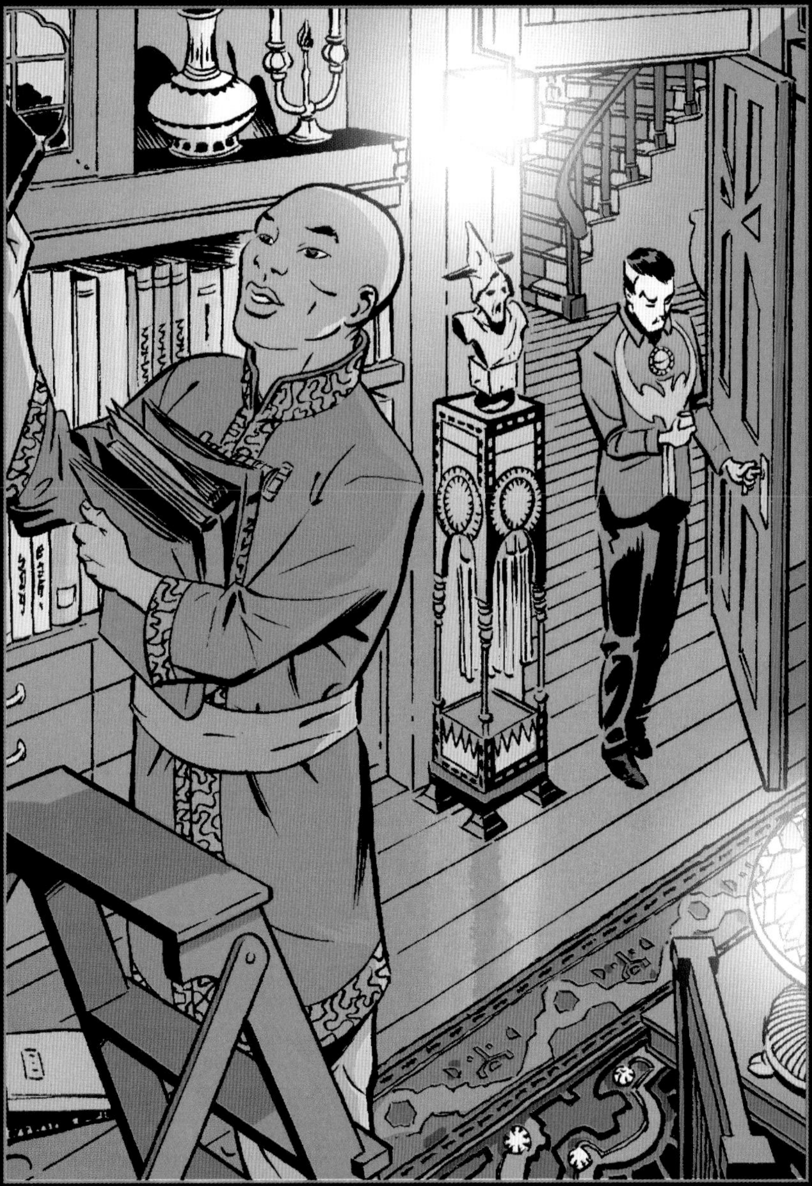

▲ ***Valued assistant*** Meticulous and organized, the faithful Wong ensures that Doctor Strange is able to focus solely on his mystical endeavors.

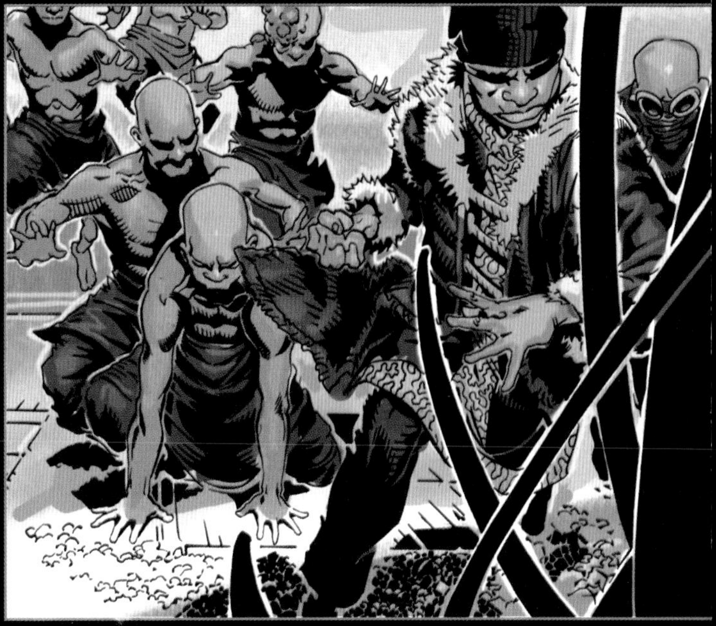

The Secret Disciples of Strange
Wong trained a sect of monks to take the physical strain of using magic off of Doctor Strange. Unbeknown to Strange, his pain is transferred to these Disciples, so that he may continue using magic unhindered.

"FORGIVE ME, BUT THE OATH I SWORE TO PROTECT MY MASTER OVERRIDES ALL OTHER DIRECTIVES... EVEN DOCTOR'S ORDERS"

Wong

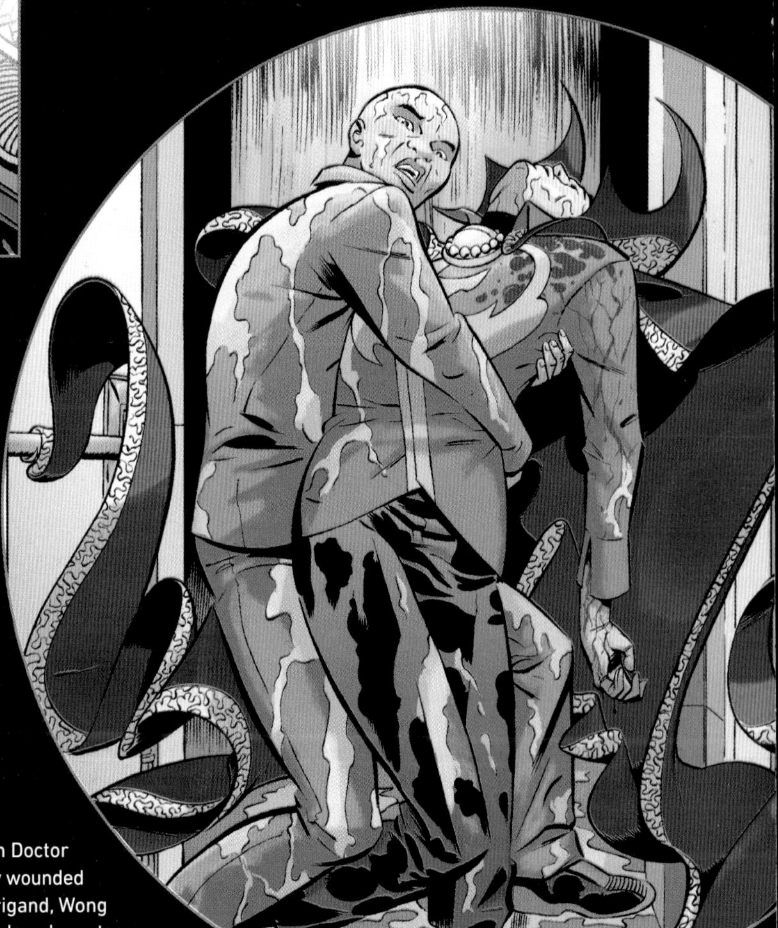

▶ ***A close call*** When Doctor Strange was severely wounded by a thief named Brigand, Wong rushed to save his beloved master.

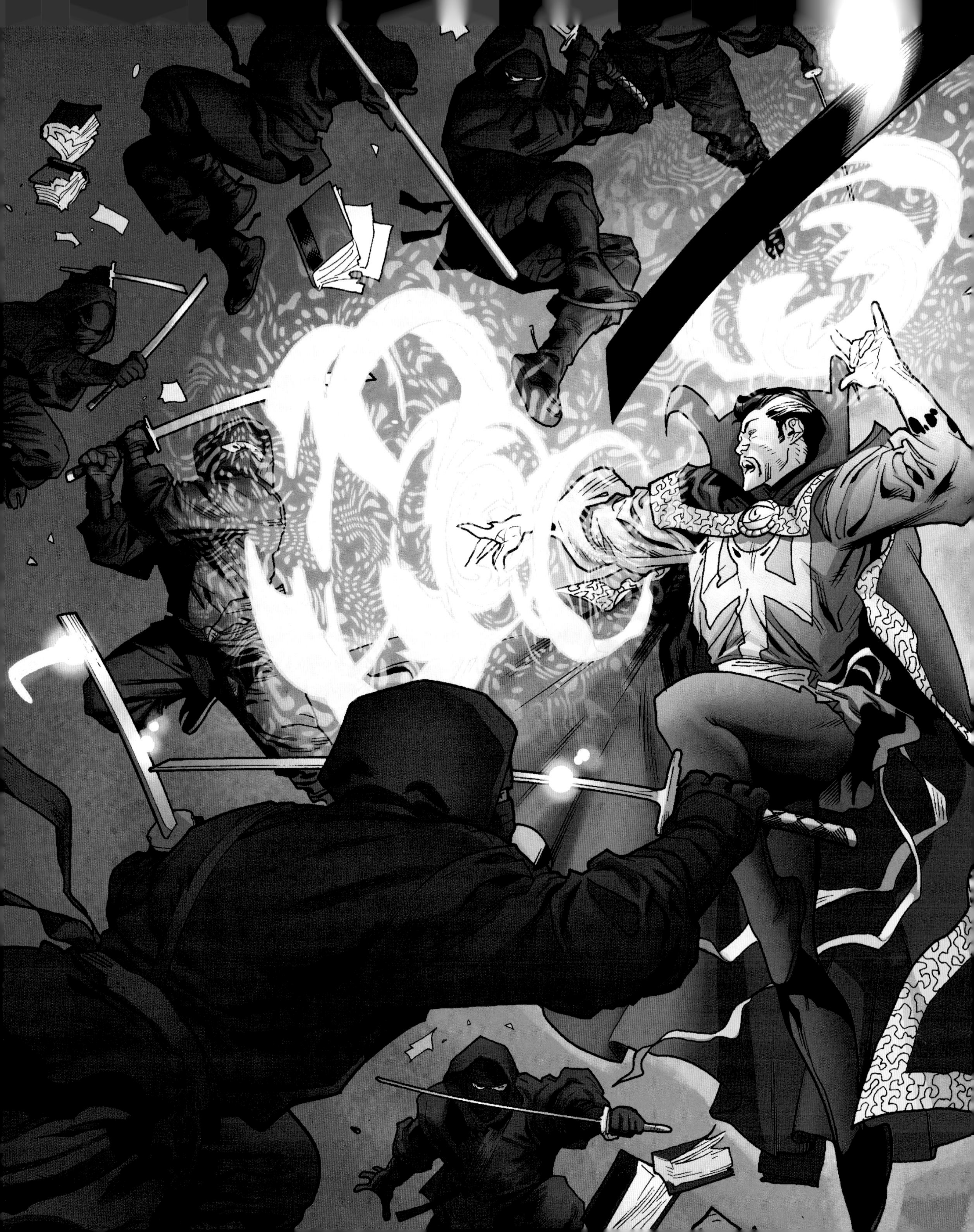

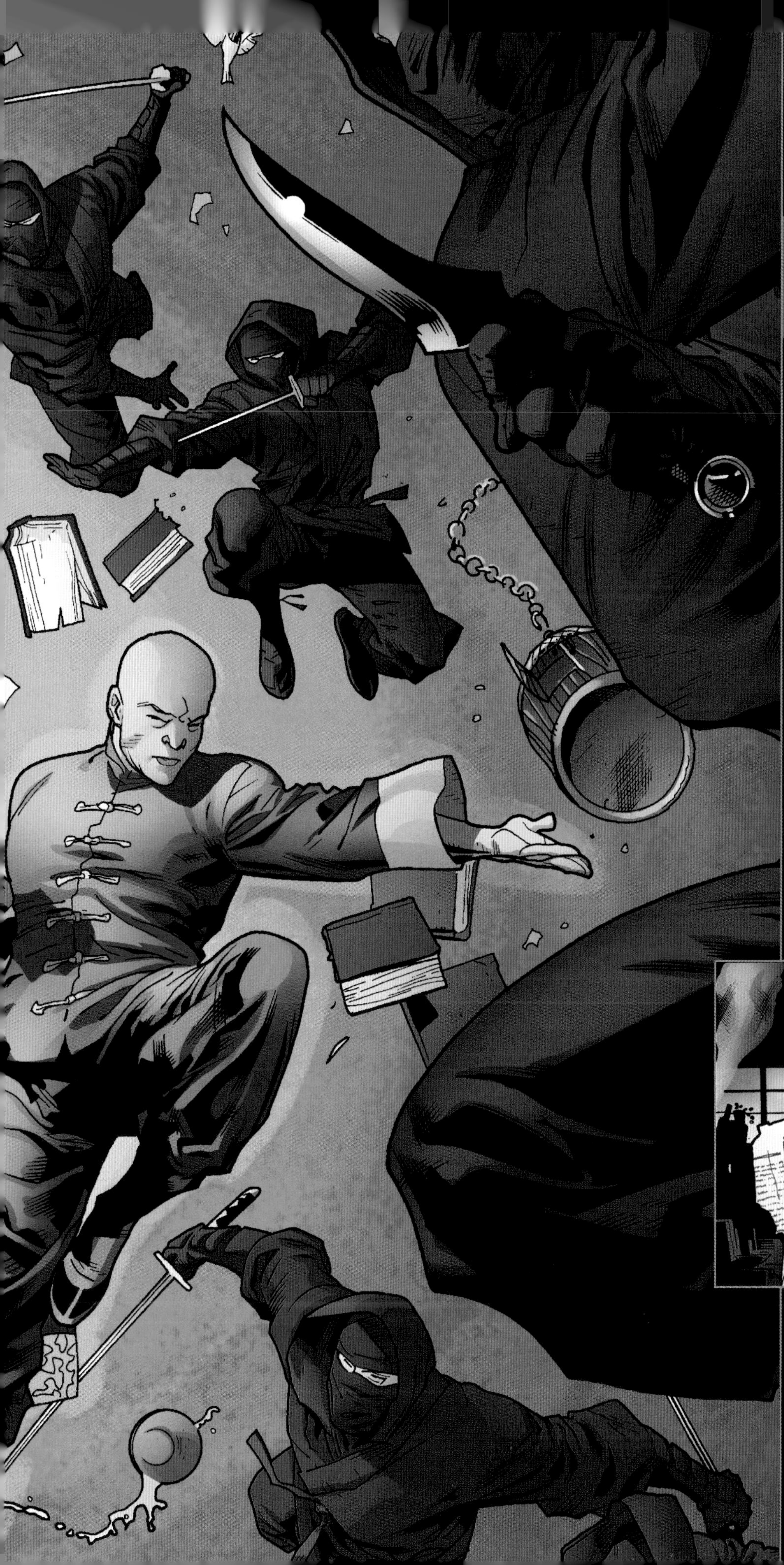

◀ ***Hand to hand combat*** The Hand, a criminal order of mystical ninjas, is feared and respected for its fighting prowess. But that didn't stop Doctor Strange and Wong from taking them on.

HAND OVER FIST

Doctor Strange and his faithful friend, Wong, have fought alongside each other many times. On one occasion, years ago, the pair traveled to Japan to confront the sorcerer Mister Rasputin, who was attempting to obtain the Eye of Agamotto. When Doctor Strange and Wong arrived, Rasputin was in the process of hiring the mystical criminal organization, the Hand, to kill Doctor Strange. An almighty battle ensued—one in which Wong, with his considerable martial arts skills, played as big a part as Strange.

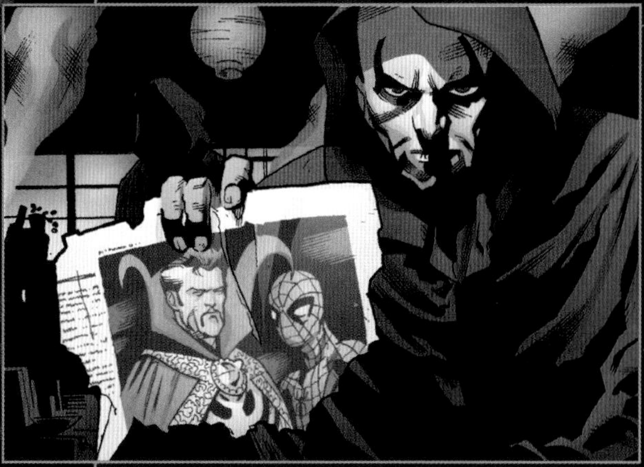

Mister Rasputin

The first time Doctor Strange encountered Mister Rasputin—alias Pavel Plotnick—he almost met defeat when Rasputin shot him. Strange recovered and vanquished his foe, leading to a lasting enmity between them.

SPIDER-MAN

Doctor Strange initially avoided contact with the thriving superhuman community in his native New York. However, his mystical adventures soon found him working alongside a particular youthful, wise-cracking wall-crawler, Spider-Man. Although a very different personality to Strange, Spider-Man would not only become a regular ally of the Sorcerer Supreme, but also a true and trusted friend.

A MAGICAL WEB

Peter Parker's life changed in an instant when he was bitten by a radioactive spider while visiting a science exhibit. Discovering he had gained amazing abilities, Peter initially wanted to use his new powers for profit, bu the murder of his beloved Uncle Ben made Peter solemnl swear that they would only be used to help those in need

Early in his crimefighting career, the young hero met his fellow New Yorker, Doctor Strange, during a battle with Baron Mordo. Strange was greatly impressed when the wall-crawler helped rescue several people from a mystical dimension. Spider-Man implored the sorcerer to make them forget the trauma of the experience—even though that mean them forgetting the bravery of the publicly-mistrusted hero.

After becoming friends, the seemingly mismatched pair later joined forces to combat the evil wizard Xandu, who had manipulated Spidey into attacking Doctor Strange to restore the Wand of Watoomb. The duo fought Xandu is his own alternate realm, finally defeating him.

Over the years, Doctor Strange and Spider-Man have fought and overcome ever-greater threats together. These have included the formidable pairing of Doctor Doom and Dormammu, who planned to unleash the devastating magical phenomenon, the Bend Sinister, on mankind.

Even in tumultuous moments, the sorcerer has maintained his early promise that "the friendship of Doctor Strange will be yours, whatever befalls!"

◄ *Battle partners*
Doctor Strange and
Spider-Man find that
their unique abilities perfectly
complement one another.

▲ *Air travel* When swinging from his webs, Spider-Man has no problem keeping up with Strange's flights across the city.

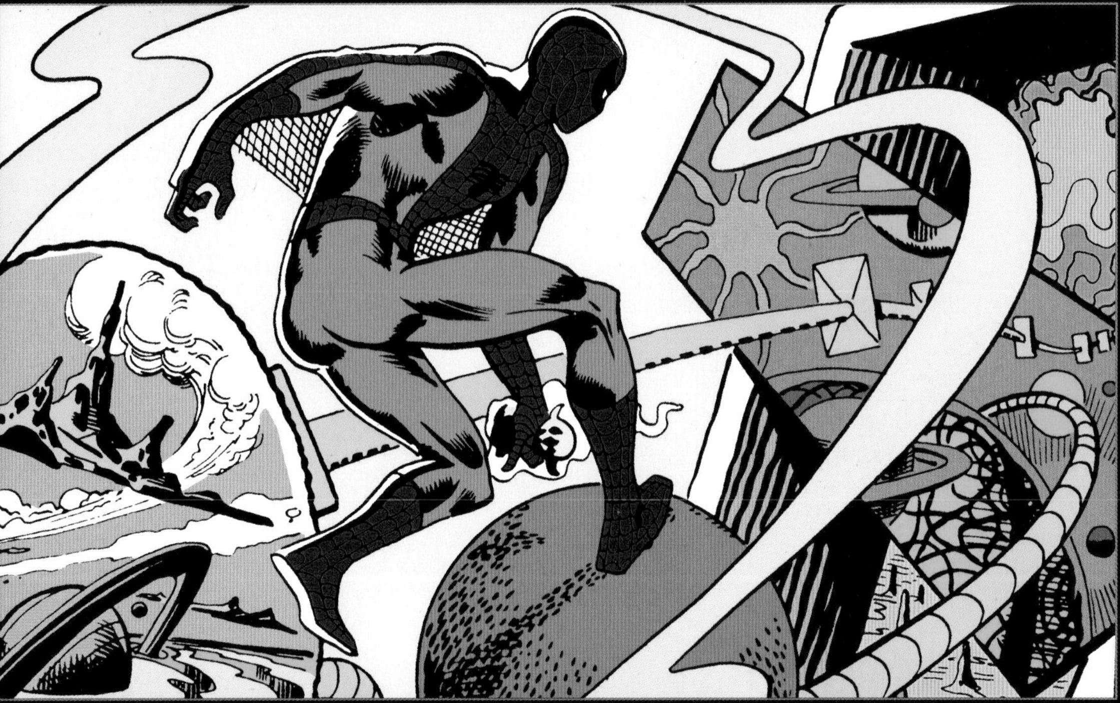

◀ ***Out of this world*** Spider-Man's first encounter with Doctor Strange also led to his first experience of an otherworldly dimension.

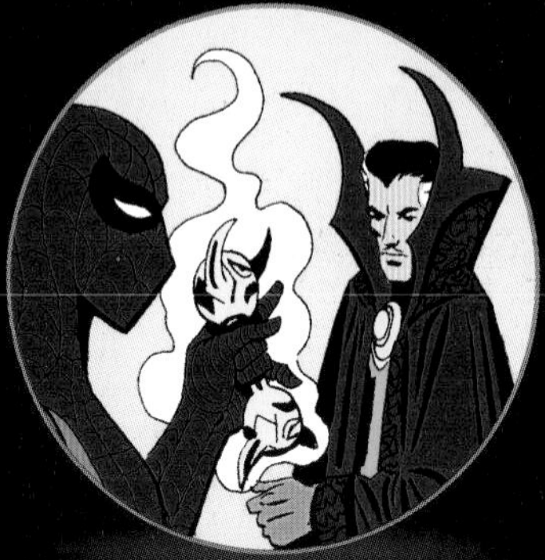

Irresistible artifact

During their battle with Xandu, both Doctor Strange and Spider-Man fell under the influence of the mystical Wand of Watoomb.

"MAY THE VISHANTI WATCH OVER THEE!"

Doctor Strange

"MAY YOUR AMULET NEVER TICKLE!"

Spider-Man

A helping hand

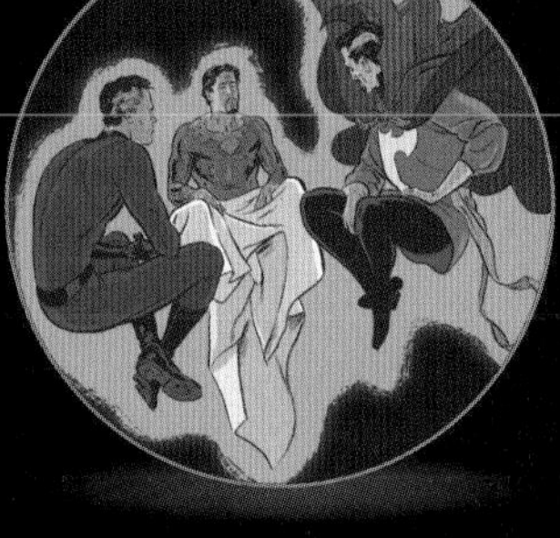

When Spider-Man announced his identity to the world, it was Doctor Strange, along with Mr. Fantastic and Iron Man, who achieved the means to erase the event from people's memories.

Seeking counsel

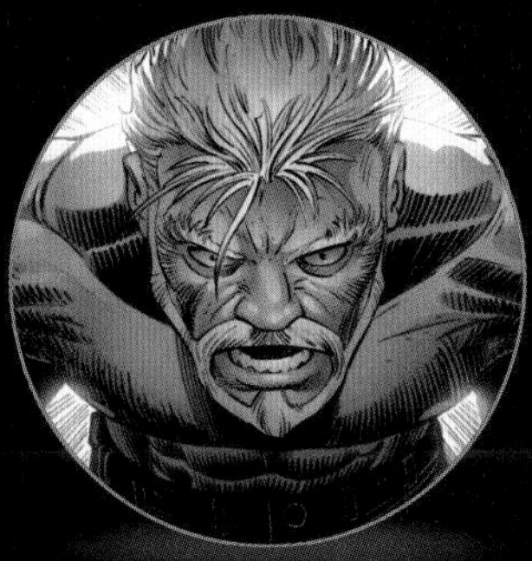

Spider-Man has come to depend greatly on Doctor Strange's knowledge—no more so than when a mysterious stranger, Ezekiel, claimed that Spidey's powers were based in magic, rather than the bite of an irradiated spider.

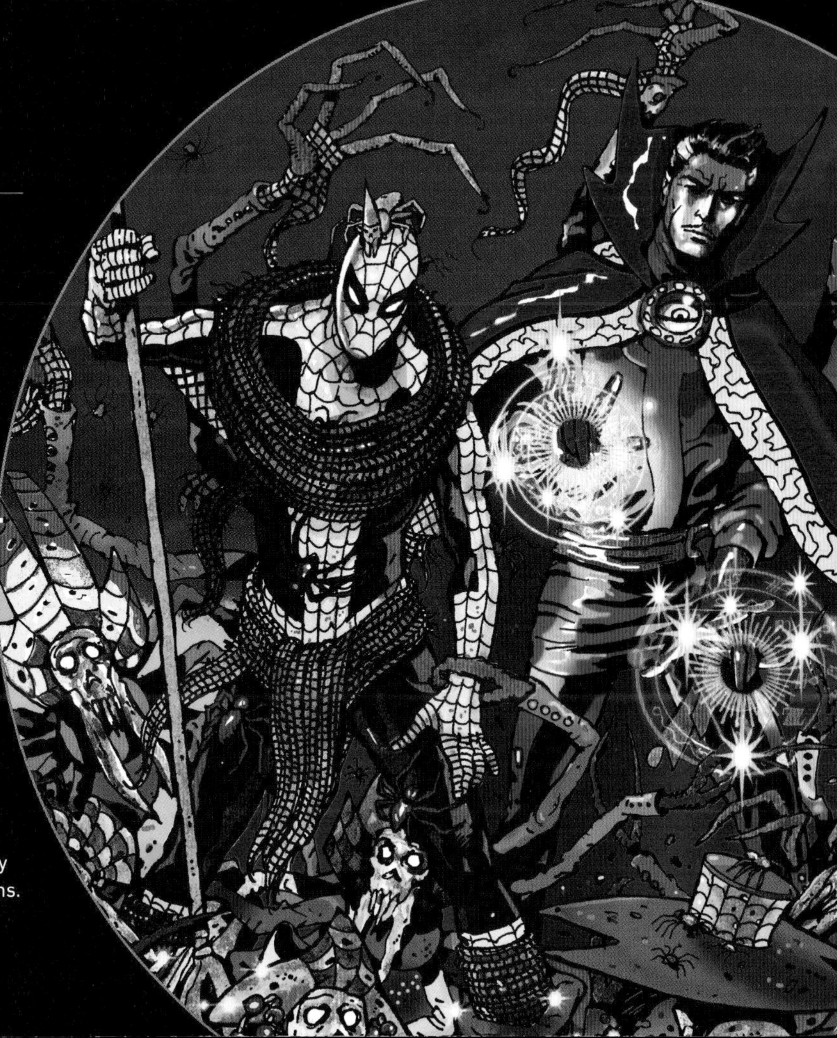

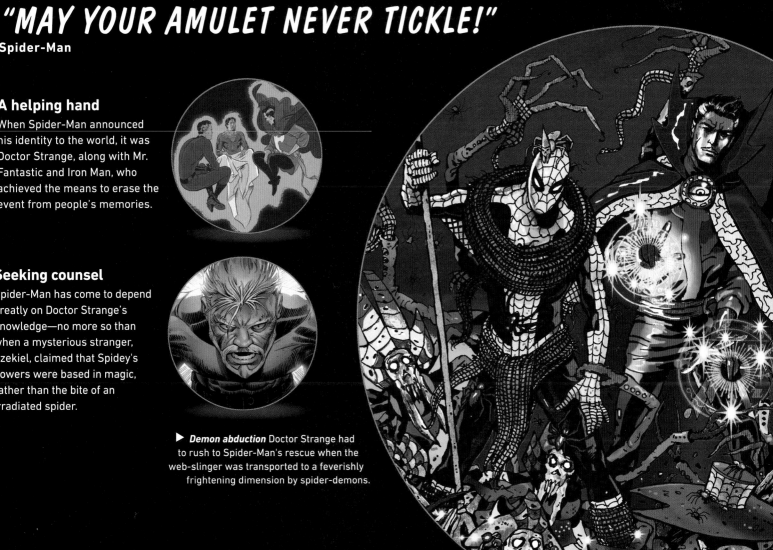

▶ ***Demon abduction*** Doctor Strange had to rush to Spider-Man's rescue when the web-slinger was transported to a feverishly frightening dimension by spider-demons.

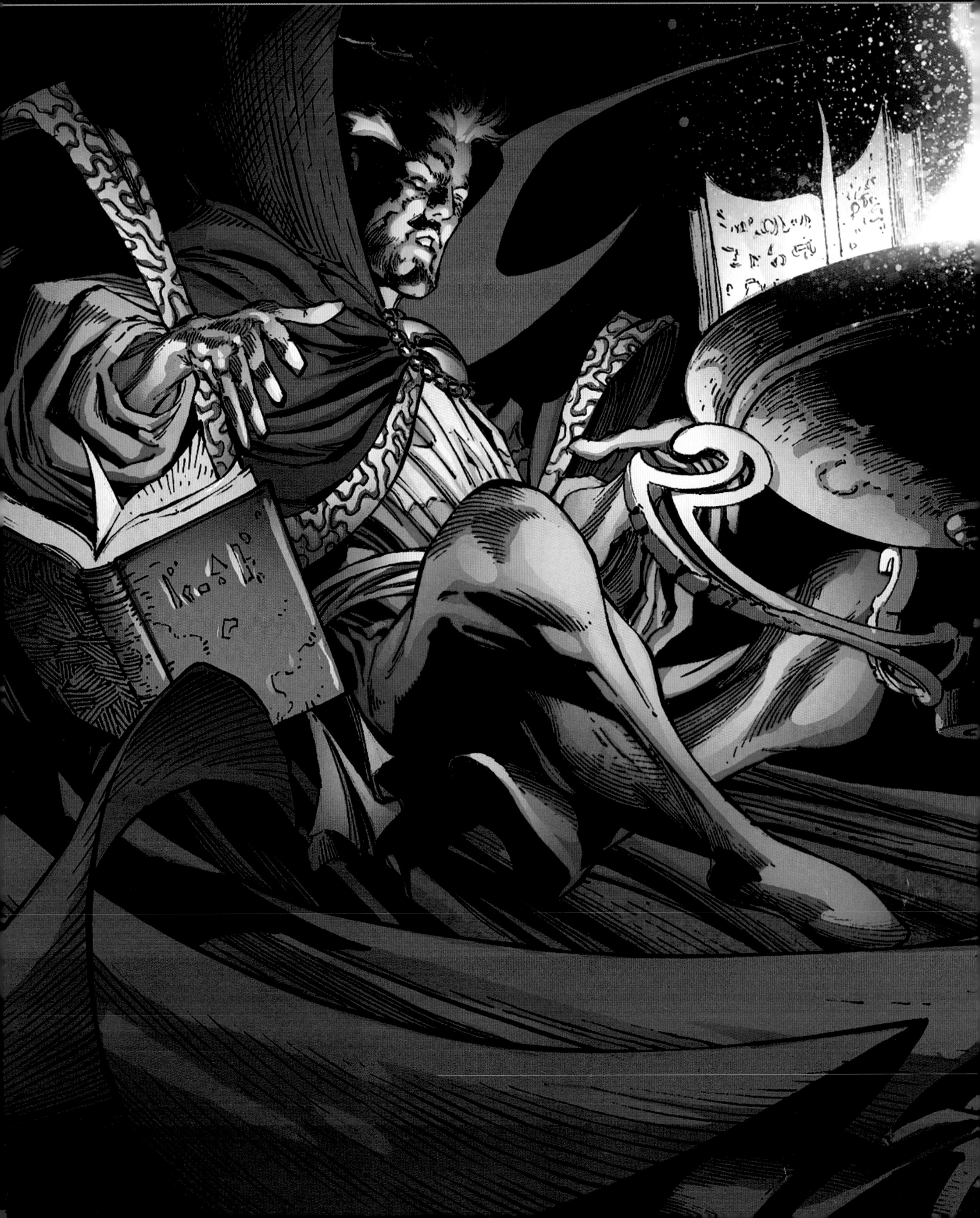

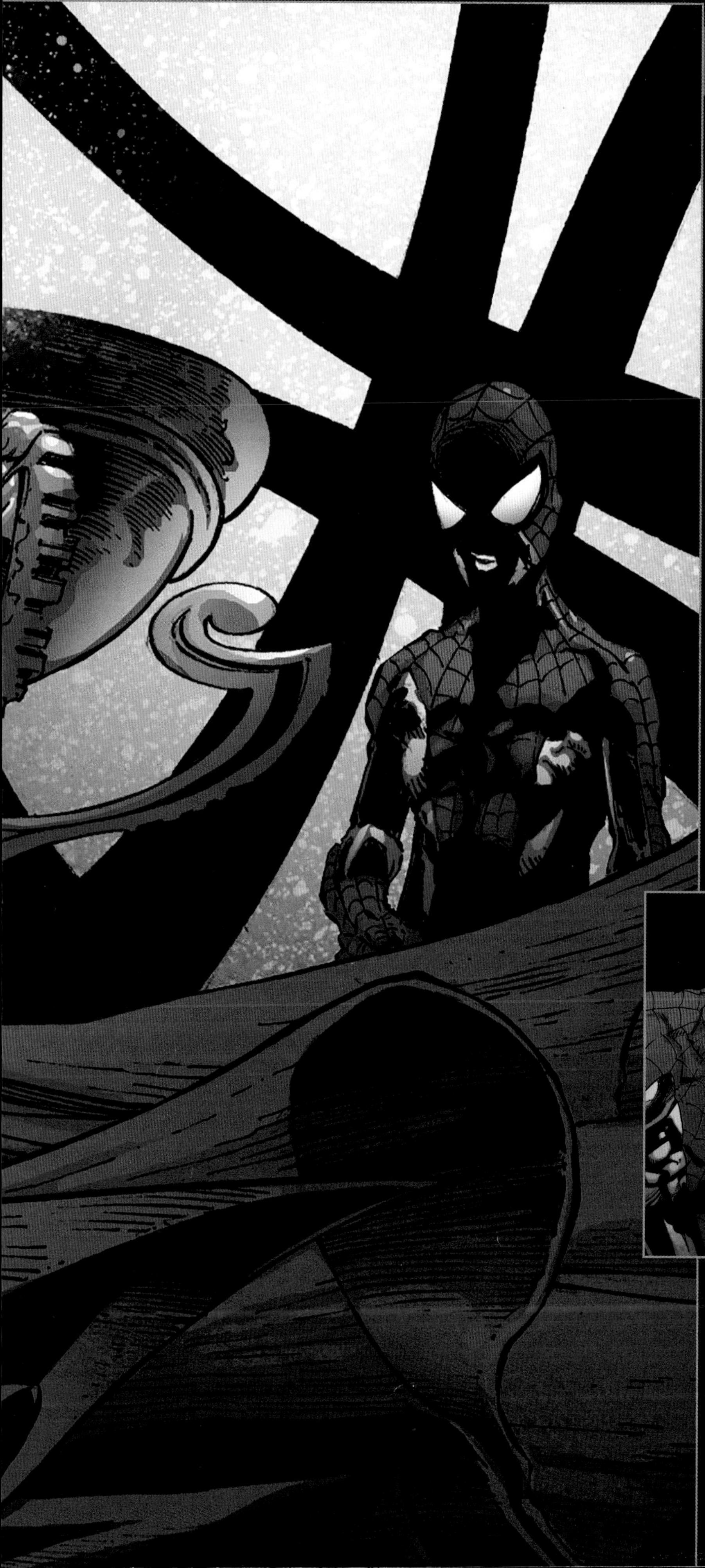

FRIEND IN NEED

Doctor Strange and Spider-Man's friendship faced its greatest test when Peter Parker's Aunt May was shot and lay dying in hospital. With all medical options exhausted, the Sorcerer Supreme used the Hands of the Dead to send Peter through time and space to consult his friends—and even his enemies—on a possible remedy. The answer was always the same: there was no saving May. In the end, Peter was forced to resort to more drastic measures, and made a diabolical deal with the demon Mephisto for May's life.

◀ ***Beyond helping hands*** Spidey pleads with Doctor Strange to save Aunt May's life, but even the Sorcerer Supreme's powers were not enough.

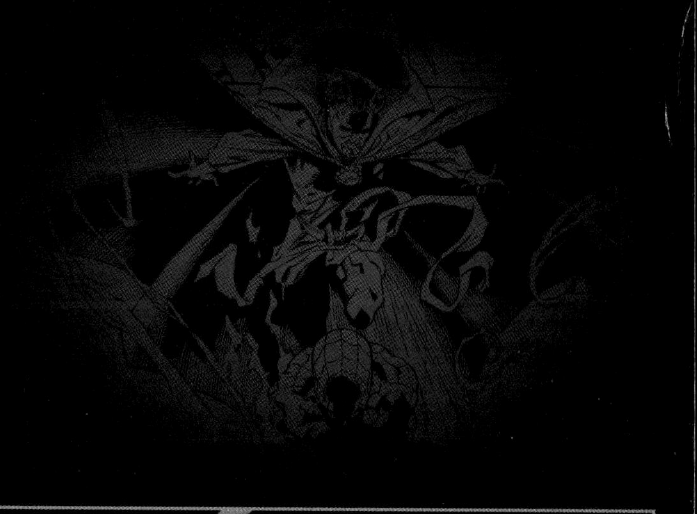

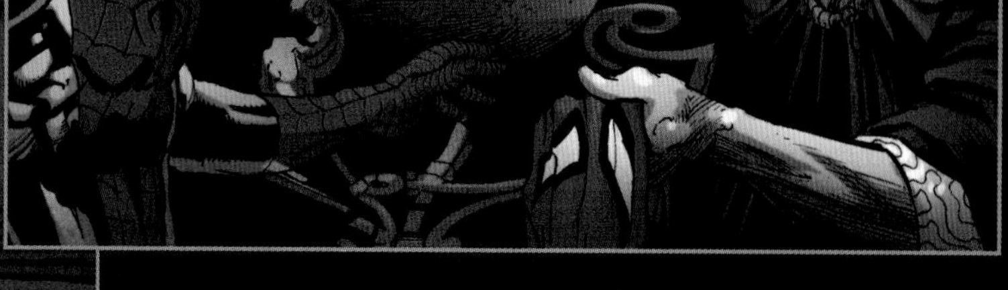

Desperate times...

In desperation, Peter Parker took control of the mystical Hands of the Dead and tried to prevent his Aunt May from being shot in the first place. When his quest through time failed, Doctor Strange advised him to go and be with his beloved aunt.

DOCTOR DOOM

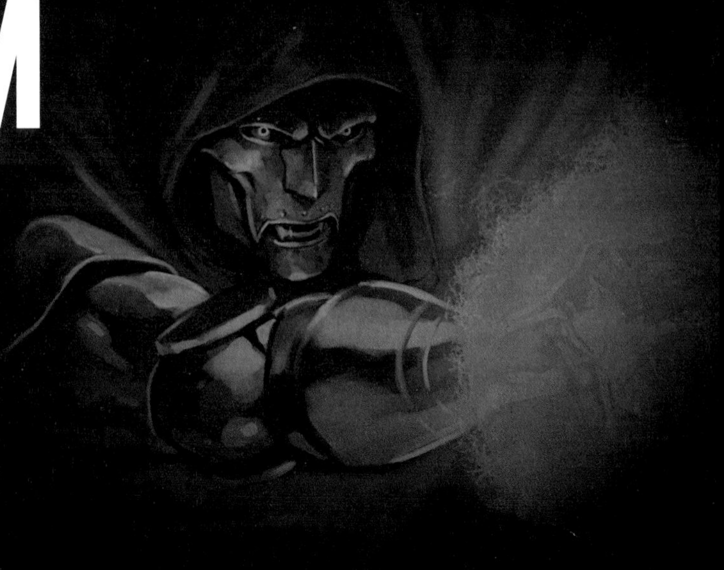

Possessed with a brilliant, if twisted, mind, and a steely resolve, the masked monarch Doctor Victor von Doom is a force to be reckoned with. As well as being a genius in technology, strategy, science, and time travel, Doom has developed great skills in the mystic arts. Many consider him a ruthless, power-hungry foe, but Doctor Strange has been willing to work with him on more than one occasion. However, Doom's deceitful nature makes him difficult to trust.

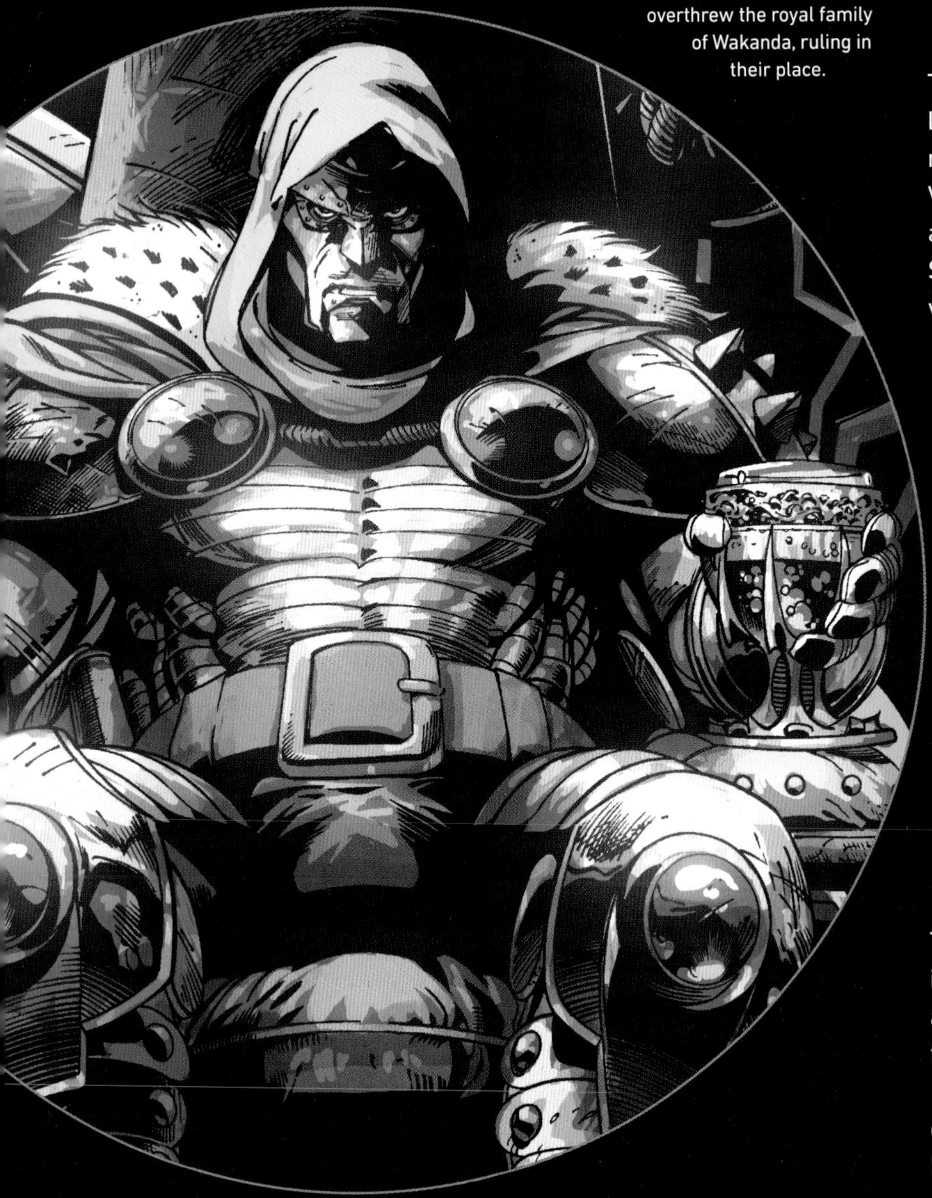

▼ ***Taking the throne*** Doom once overthrew the royal family of Wakanda, ruling in their place.

THE DREADED DICTATOR

The man who would come to rule the small country of Latveria with an iron fist came from humble beginnings, marked by tragedy. Born in an Eastern European village, Victor von Doom was raised by his physician father, Werner, and his doting mother, Cynthia, who was also a witch. Seeking more power to fight the persecution she and her villagers faced from the brutal Baron who governed them, Cynthia made a bad bargain with the demon Mephisto. The deal led to her death and her soul being trapped in Hades. Victor fled with his father, but Werner later died. The grieving orphan swiftly vowed terrible vengeance on the world that robbed him of his parents.

Victor taught himself witchcraft after finding his mother's occult artifacts, and became immensely skilled in magic and science. Winning a scholarship to study in the US, the young Victor met his future nemesis, Reed Richards, aka the hero, Mr Fantastic.

Desperate to rescue his mother's soul, Doom created an inter-dimensional device that Richards warned him was built on a grave miscalculation. Victor dismissed his rival's concerns, but the machine exploded on activation, seriously scarring Victor's face.

Broken and desperate, Victor found a secret order of Tibetan monks who took him in, healed him, and trained him in their mystic arts. They also fashioned the metal mask and armor that would hide his disfigurement and form his fearsome identity. As gratitude, he slaughtered them all.

Victor returned to Latveria as Doctor Doom, seizing control of his former homeland and fervently dedicated his life to freeing his mother... and ruling the planet.

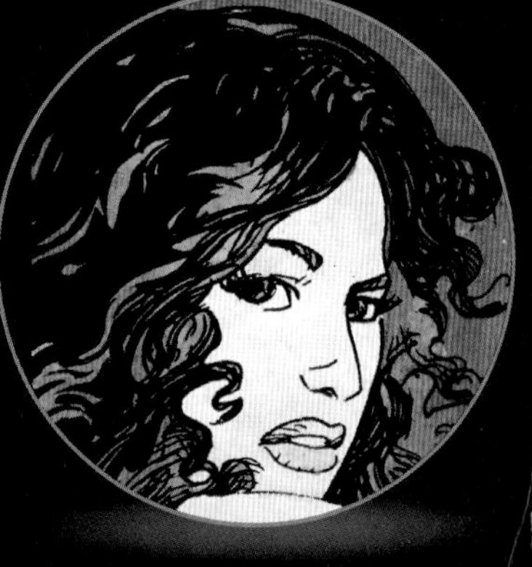

A diabolical deal

Cynthia von Doom's dying wish was for her son to never use black magic. Victor, however, had other ideas and struck a deal with Mephisto. Once a year, he could challenge the Dark Lord for his mother's soul. On one occasion, the demon offered to release her—in exchange for Doctor Strange's soul!

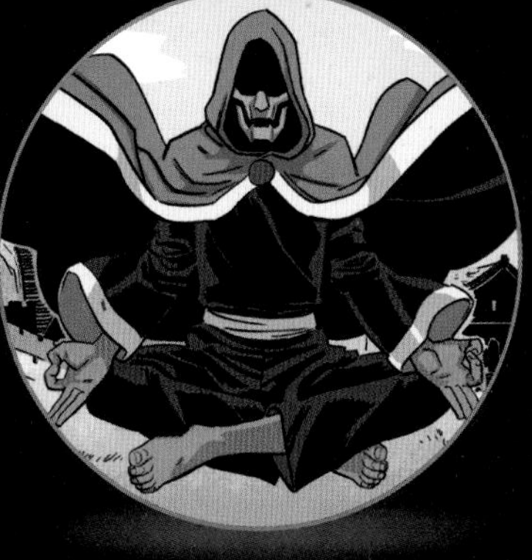

Mahatma Doom

Doom thought he had killed all the monks who rejuvenated him, but one survived. To atone for the evil his order had unwittingly revived, the last monk adopted Victor's name and appearance, becoming a magical force for good—Mahatma Doom.

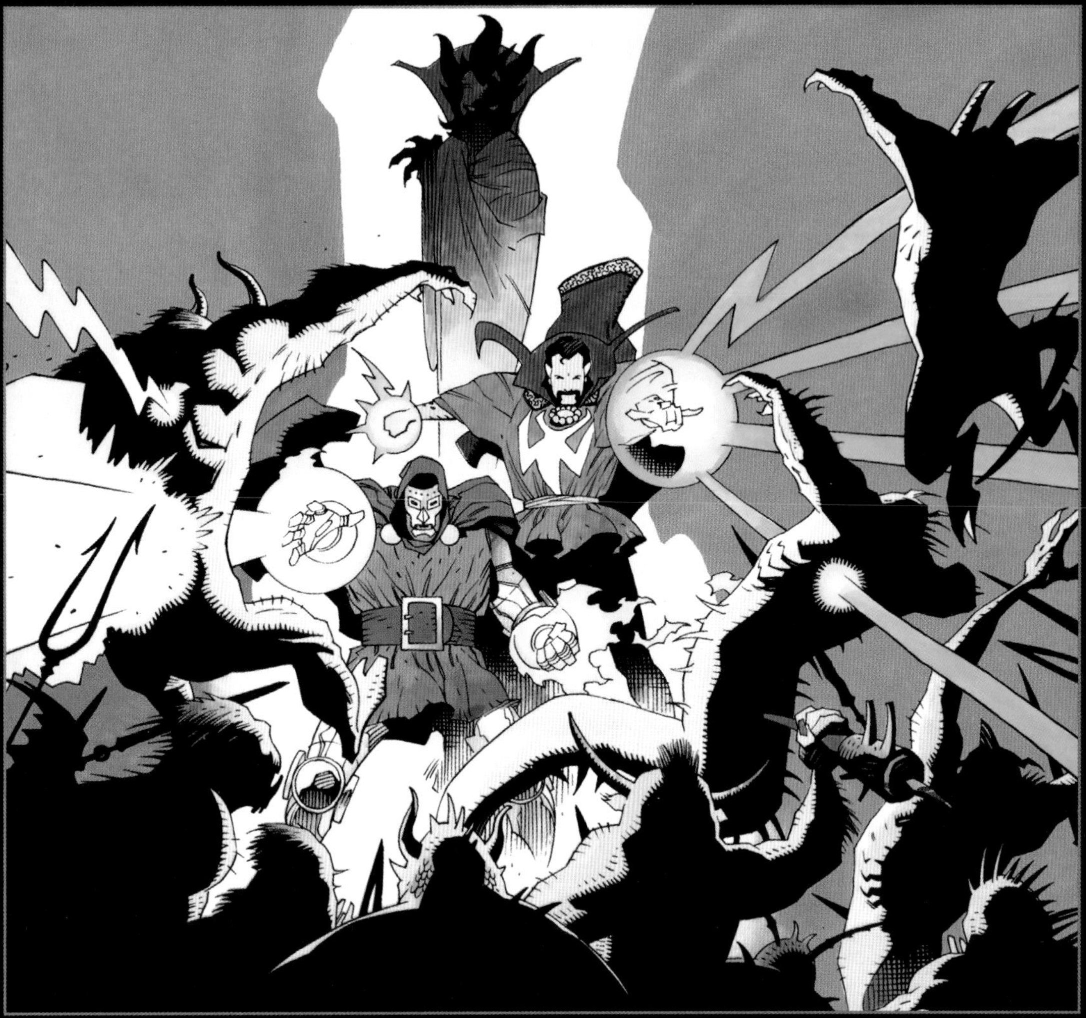

▲ ***Strength in unity*** Doom once enlisted Doctor Strange's help in his annual challenge to free his mother from Mephisto's clutches. The Doctors' combined might saw off all manner of demonic attacks, and together they finallly liberated Cynthia von Doom's soul.

"PAIN? PAIN IS LIKE LOVE, LIKE COMPASSION! IT IS A THING ONLY FOR LESSER MEN. WHAT IS PAIN TO DOOM?"

Doctor Doom

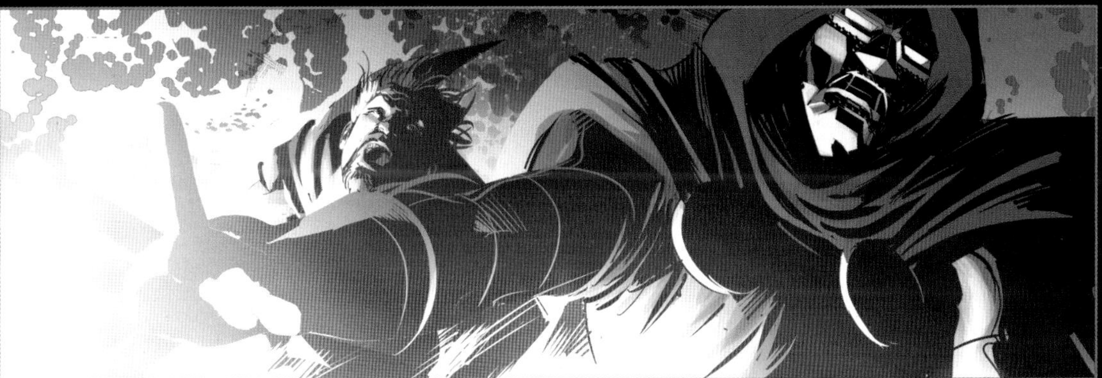

A new world order

Doctor Strange looked on in shock as Doom harnessed the cosmic powers of the near omnipotent Beyonders to salvage several realities from the aliens' multiverse-destroying experiment. By merging these realities together, Doom created a new planet named Battleworld, under his dominion.

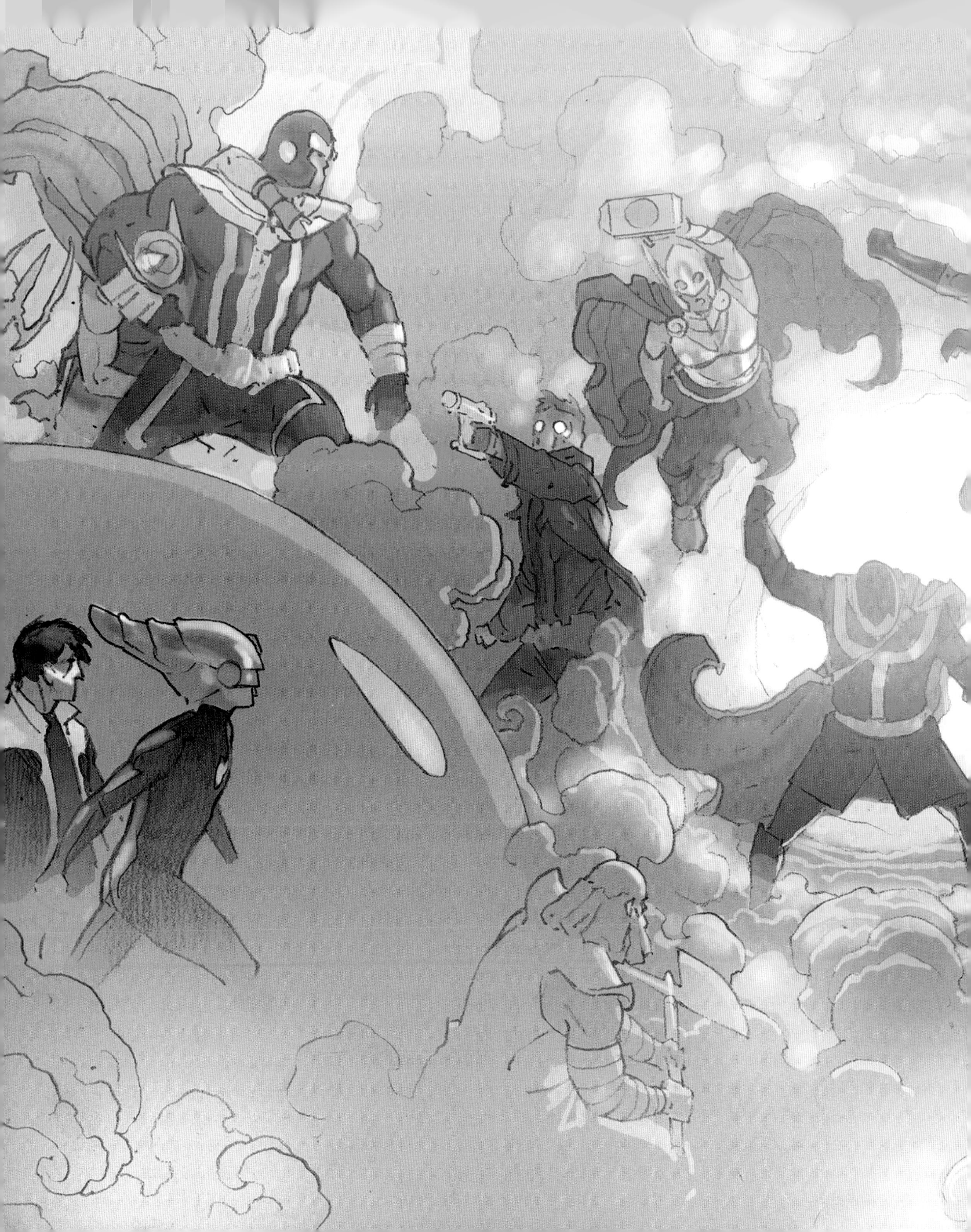

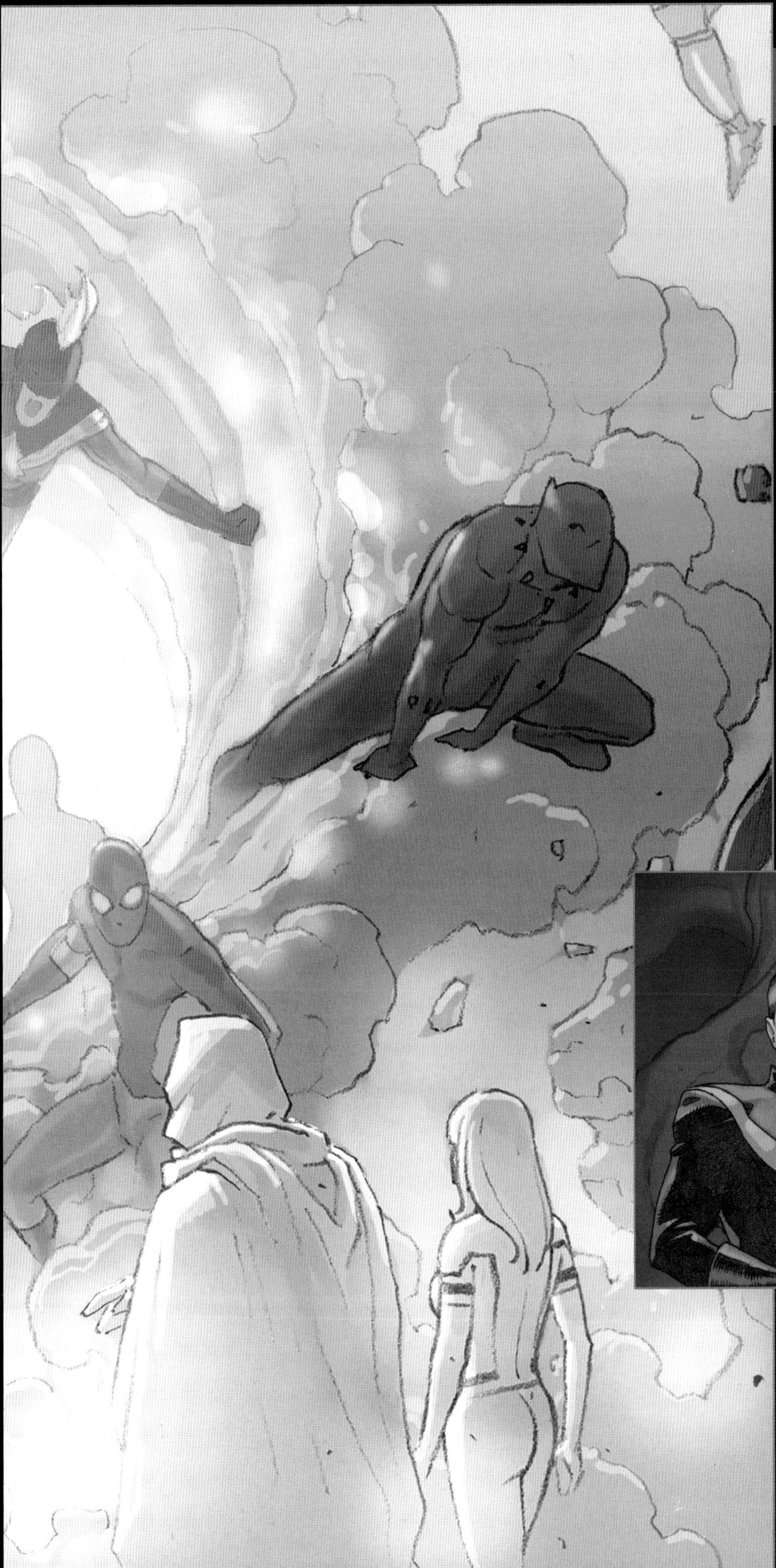

GOD DOOM

After Doctor Doom, Doctor Strange, and the Molecule Man salvaged what they could following a multiversal cataclysm and formed Battleworld, Doom became ruler of this patchwork planet. The reign of "God" Doom was threatened, however, when survivors from Earth—including Spider-Man and the Black Panther—arrived on Battleworld. Doctor Strange, now known as the Sheriff of Agamotto, sided with the heroes when they challenged Doom's rule—and paid dearly when he helped them escape the despot's wrath.

◀ ***To defy a god*** Besides Strange, Doom was opposed by Thanos, Star-Lord, Thor, Captain Marvel, and others.

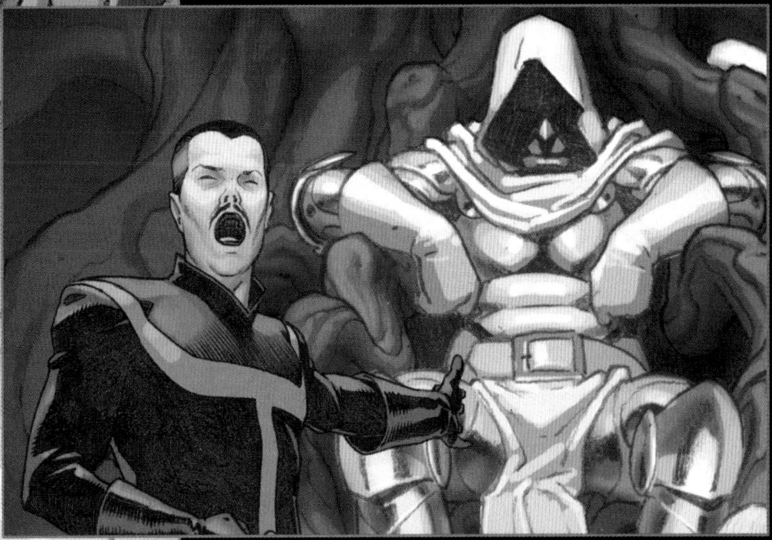

I am the Law
As the Sheriff of Agamotto, Doctor Strange was Doctor Doom's right-hand man on Battleworld. When disputes between the Barons of the various realms of Battleword arose, it was Strange's job to resolve them.

POWERFUL FRIENDS

While Doctor Strange is the Sorcerer Supreme of Earth, there are a great many other sorcerers—both good and evil—on the planet and beyond. Doctor Strange has found numerous magically endowed allies, some of who have become disciples, others who have themselves been deemed worthy to hold the title Sorcerer Supreme.

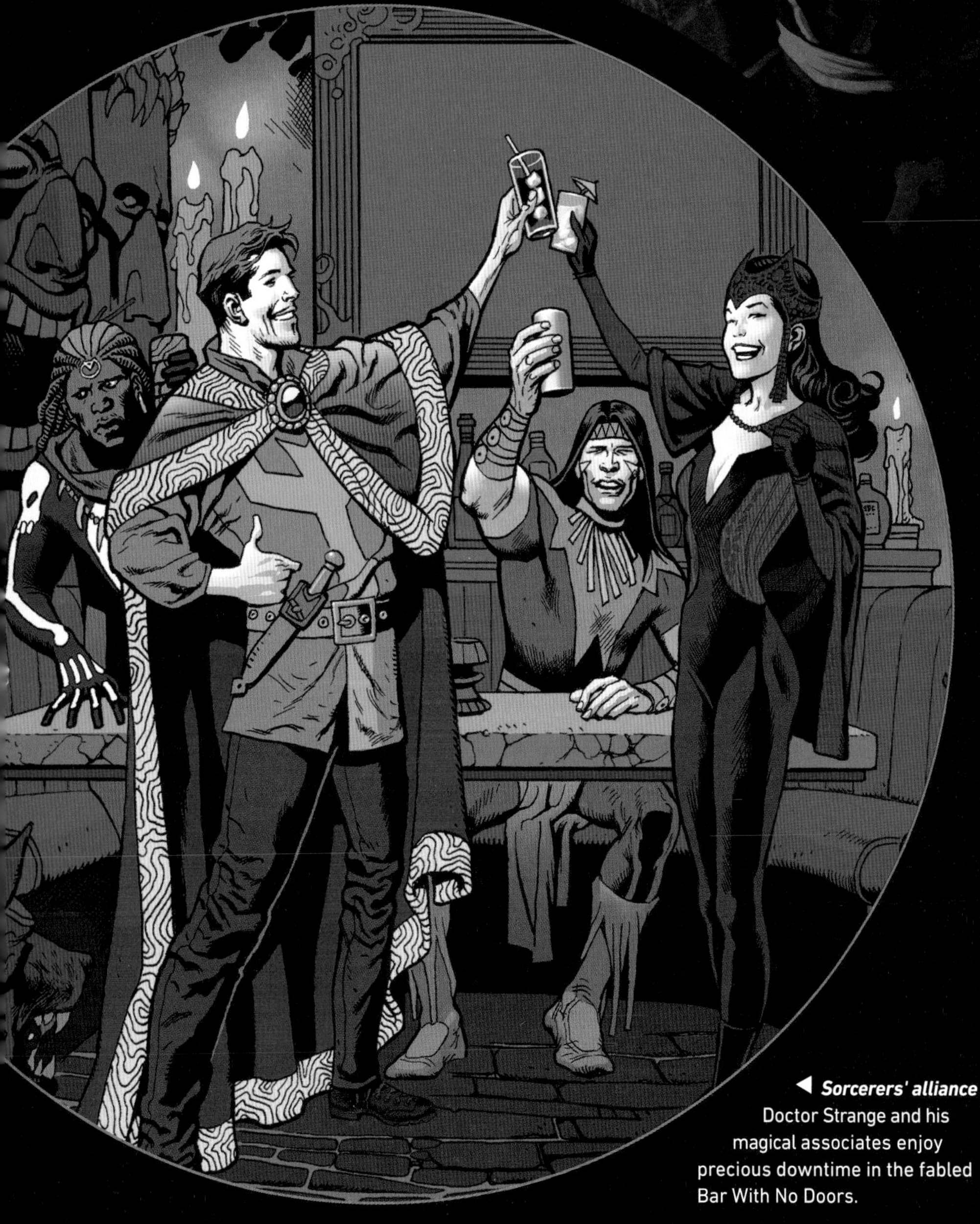

◀ ***Sorcerers' alliance***
Doctor Strange and his magical associates enjoy precious downtime in the fabled Bar With No Doors.

MAGIC MAKERS

Wanda Maximoff, the Scarlet Witch, is the daughter of the feared super villain Magneto and the twin of the Avenger, Quicksilver. This highly skilled sorceress uses Chaos Magic—a form of magic so uncanny and powerful that at one point Doctor Strange doubted its very existence. With her reality-altering hexes, Scarlet Witch can manipulate the very fabric of existence. However, there have been times when her powers developed beyond her control, which have left Strange uncertain as to whether she could be entirely trusted.

Like Doctor Strange, Dr. Michael Twoyoungmen was once a boastful surgeon, until he became the master of native American Sarcee magic, Shaman. He carries a medicine bag which contains a pocket dimension known as the Void, from which he can summon any number mystical objects. Shaman made his name as a member of the Canadian super group, Alpha Flight.

Jericho Drumm abandoned a career in psychology to study the ways of voodoo, succeeding the powerful Papa Jambo as the Houngan Supreme of Haiti. He was henceforth known as Brother Voodoo. After meeting Doctor Strange—when the Sorcerer Supreme freed him from possession by the evil god, Damballah—Brother Voodoo became a close magical associate. The two often worked side by side, until Brother Voodoo eventually succeeded Doctor Strange as Sorcerer Supreme, becoming Doctor Voodoo.

Illyana Nikolievna Rasputina, known as Magik, is a formidable sorceress. Raised in the Limbo dimension by the demon-sorcerer Belasco, Magik became the Sorceress Supreme of that realm. She eventually gained control over Limbo and became Doctor Strange's disciple, developing her powers to ever greater degrees.

Magik's Soulsword

Magik's chief weapon is the Soulsword, which was formed from her own soul after she drew the blade from a pool of Eldritch energy. The more the sword is used, the more powerful and intricate it becomes.

▲ *Switching sides* At first, Scarlet Witch and her brother sided with their father Magneto in his war on mankind. They both later abandoned this cause and joined the Avengers.

"WHAT'S WRONG GUYS? NEED A LITTLE BACK UP?"
Magik

Shaman

Shaman's mystical abilities have a strong connection with nature. The sorcerer can control the elements, and communicate with animals and spirits. He is also adept at shape-shifting and teleportation, and using magic potions to heal the wounded.

▲ *Voodoo mystic* When Brother Voodoo summons the spirit of his deceased brother, Daniel, his powers are doubled. He can also send his spirit to possess others, control elemental forces, and summon mystical creatures.

BROTHER VOODOO

During his time as Sorcerer Supreme, Brother Voodoo, aka Doctor Voodoo, acquitted himself with great honor, battling Dormammu, Doctor Doom, and a zombified Deadpool. His tenure as Earth's protector came to a tragic end when Agamotto of the Vishanti attempted to seize the Eye of Agamotto from him. Doctor Voodoo managed to vanquish Agamotto—at the cost of his own life.

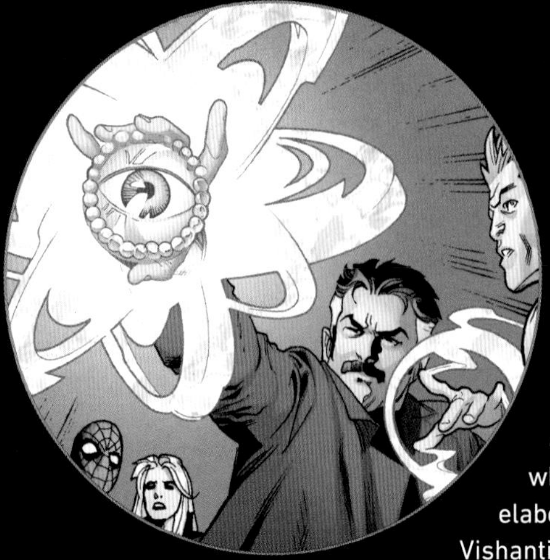

Eye of the beholder
Agamotto used the Eye to possess both Doctor Strange and Daimon Hellstrom. He pitted them against the New Avengers, which was all part of Agamotto's elaborate scheme to usurp the Vishanti, who had cast him out.

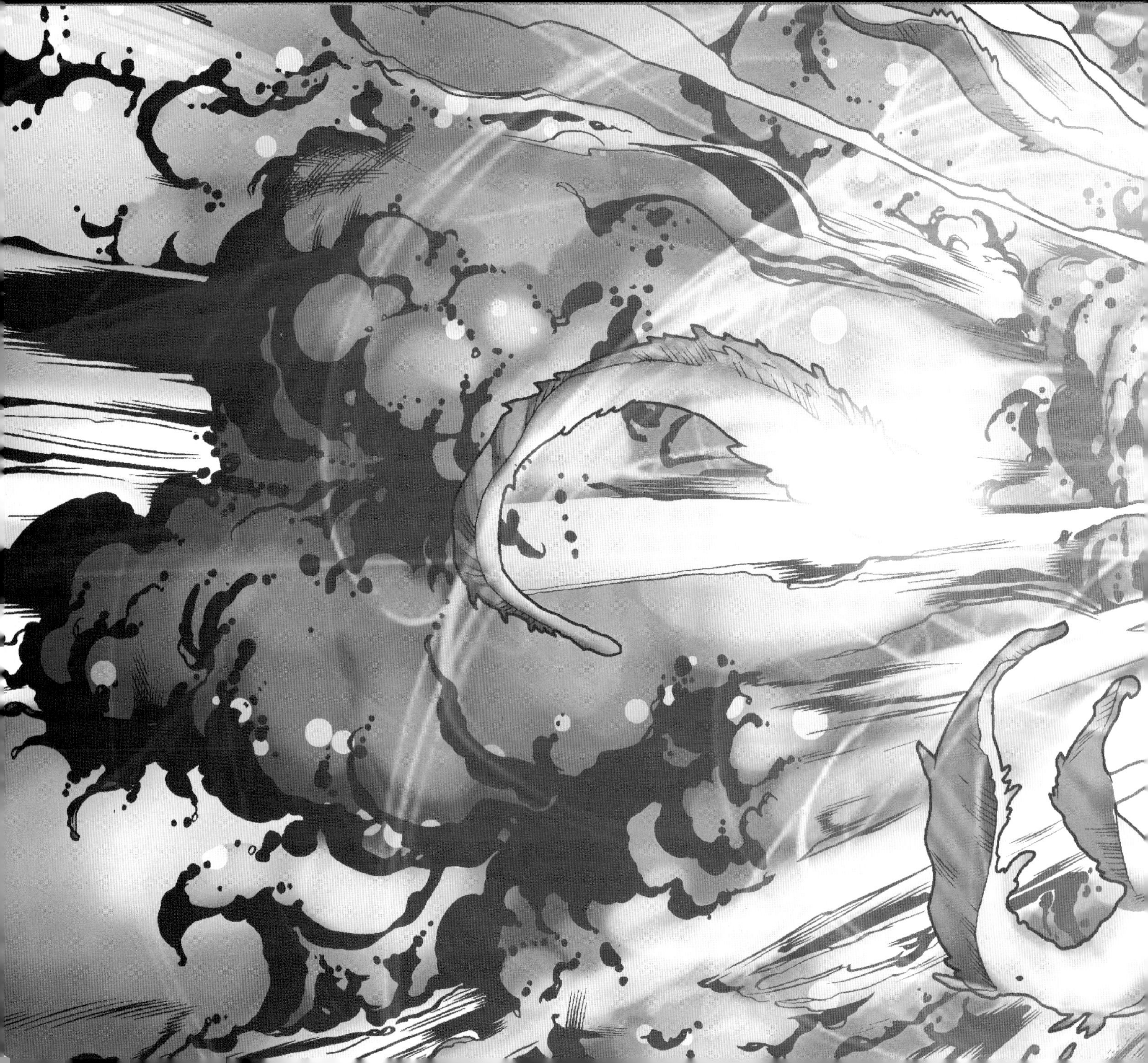

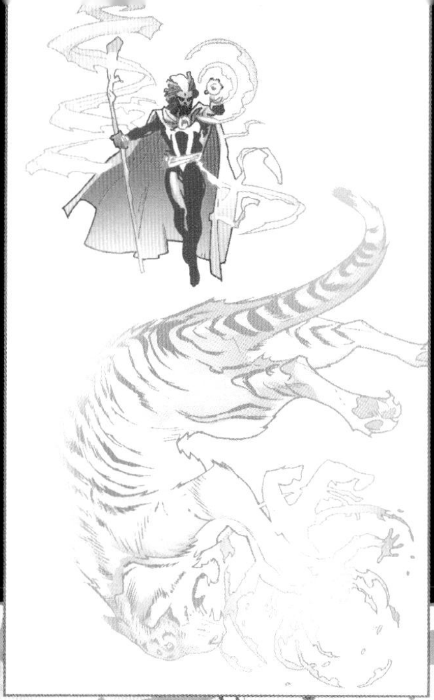

Two against Agamotto

Doctor Voodoo traveled to the Light Dimension to confront Agamotto. Voodoo was joined by the spirit of his deceased brother, Daniel Drumm, and together they fought Agamotto, who assumed many guises, including his deadly tiger form.

▼ ***Fatal reckoning*** In a desperate last-minute assault, Doctor Voodoo destroyed Agamotto, but was killed in the ensuing explosion. He was later resurrected by Doctor Doom, in a deal with a demonic demigod, to take on an evil, rampaging version of the Scarlet Witch.

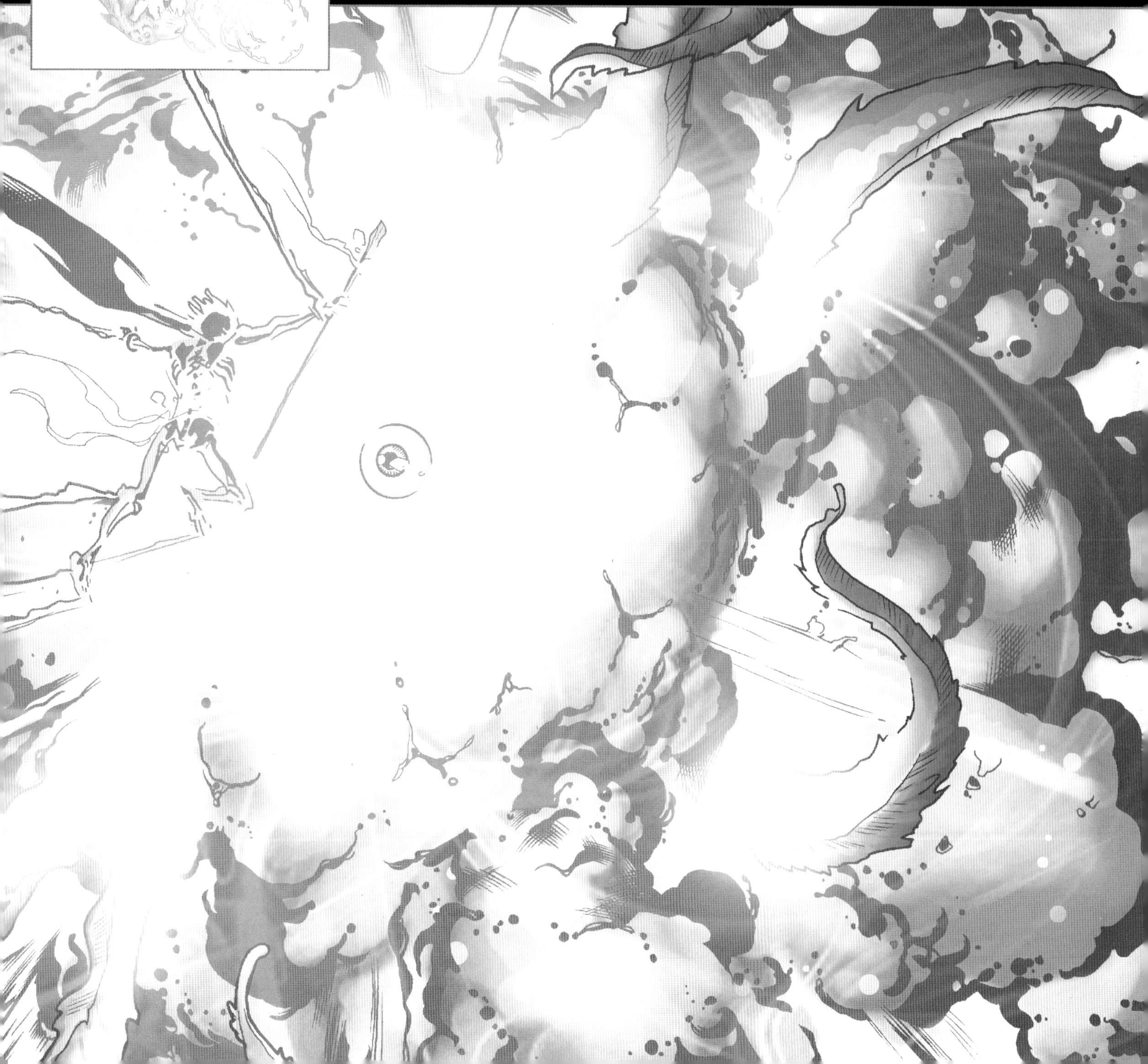

TEAM-UPS

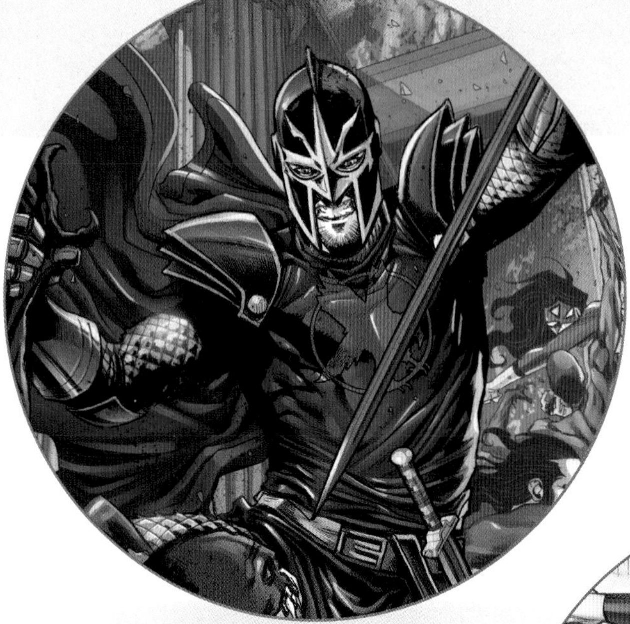

When he first assumed the mantle of Sorcerer Supreme, Doctor Strange assumed he would work alone. In fact, his epic adventures have been shared with many. Super Heroes, mystical beings, average citizens—even a talking duck—have stood shoulder to shoulder with the Master of the Mystic Arts as he negotiated the supernatural.

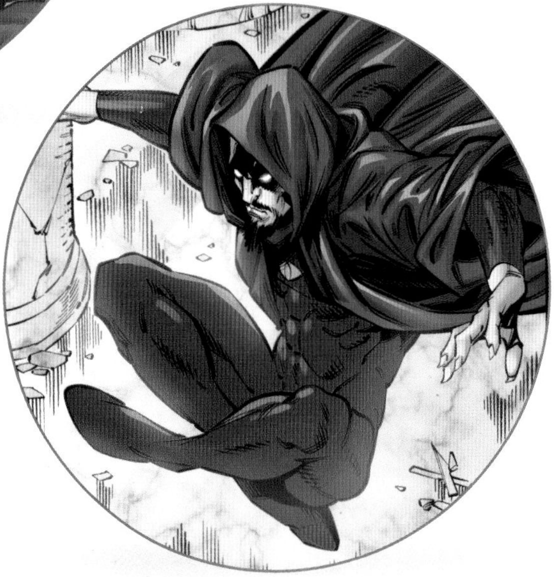

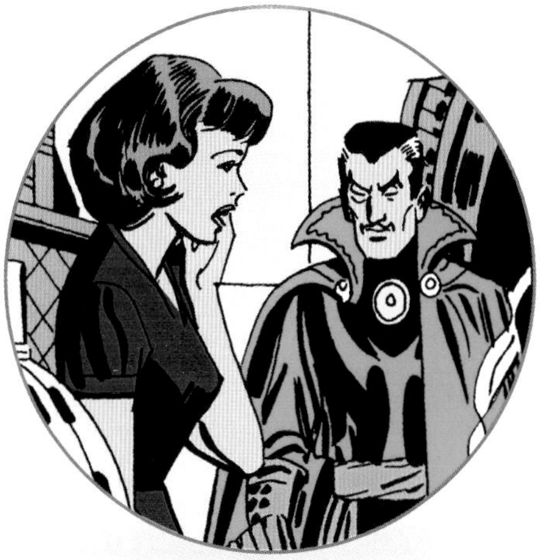

Black Knight

Dane Whitman, the nephew of the villainous Black Knight, Nathan Garrett, took his uncle's name and restored its honor by working with the Avengers. Whitman met Doctor Strange through Victoria Bentley, and together they fought extra-dimensional fiends like Tiboro and Surtur.

Victoria Bentley

The daughter of a wealthy secret sorcerer, British socialite Bentley was a very close associate of Doctor Strange. She aided him in battling many of his most formidable enemies, all the while hiding her love for him.

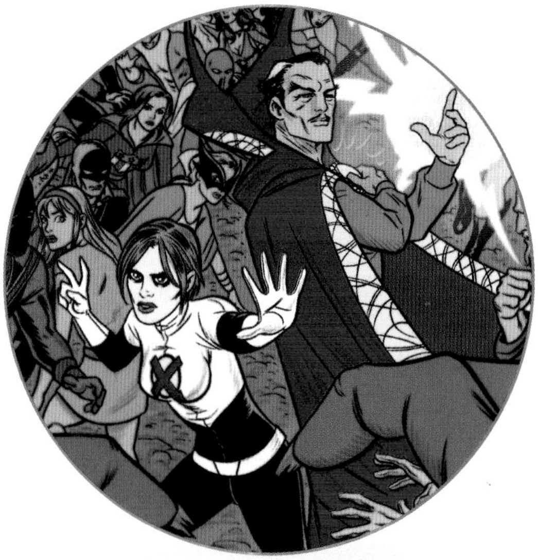

Dr. Druid

Like Doctor Strange, Anthony Druid was taught by the Ancient One. Strange persuaded Dr. Druid to lead the Secret Defenders, but Druid tired of leadership and faked his own death, spiralling into self-destructive behavior.

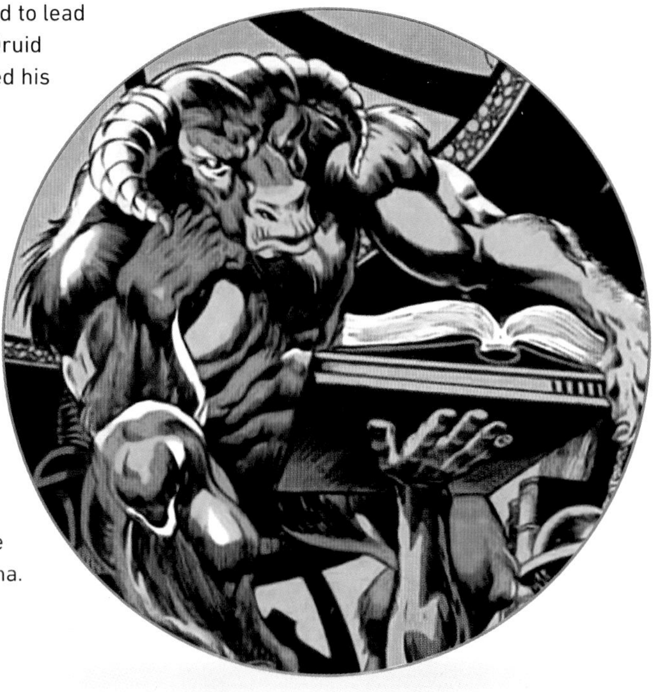

Rintrah

Rintrah is a green-furred minotaur and mystic from the planet V'raal. He met Strange after helping to repair the Cloak of Levitation. Recognizing Rintrah's potential as a sorcerer, Strange sought his aid to fend off the alien wizard, Urthona.

Dead Girl

Physically deceased but kept "alive" by her mutant powers, Dead Girl partnered with Doctor Strange to stop a plan by the Pitiful One to resurrect denizens of the afterlife. To succeed, they enlisted the help of dead heroes in Heaven.

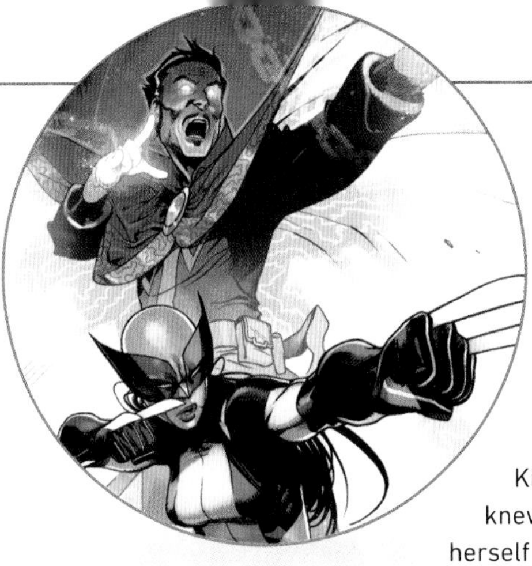

X-23

The female clone of Wolverine, Laura Kinney—codenamed X-23—sought refuge at the Sanctum Sanctorum to hide from Alchemax Genetics, the corrupt corporation that created her. Impressed by Kinney's ingenuity, Strange knew she would distinguish herself as the new Wolverine.

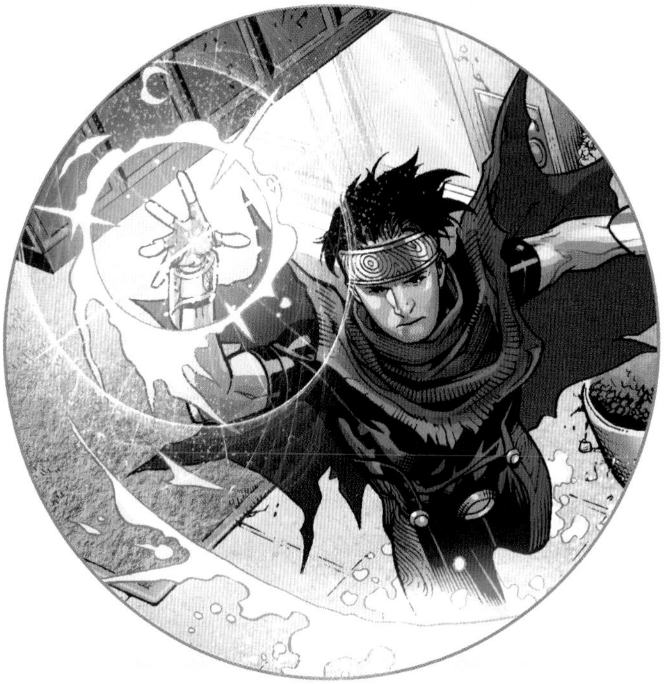

Wiccan

Billy Kaplan may be young, but he is incredibly powerful. The mutant magician put his spellcasting abilties to good use by helping Doctor Strange battle the power-hungry super criminal, the Hood.

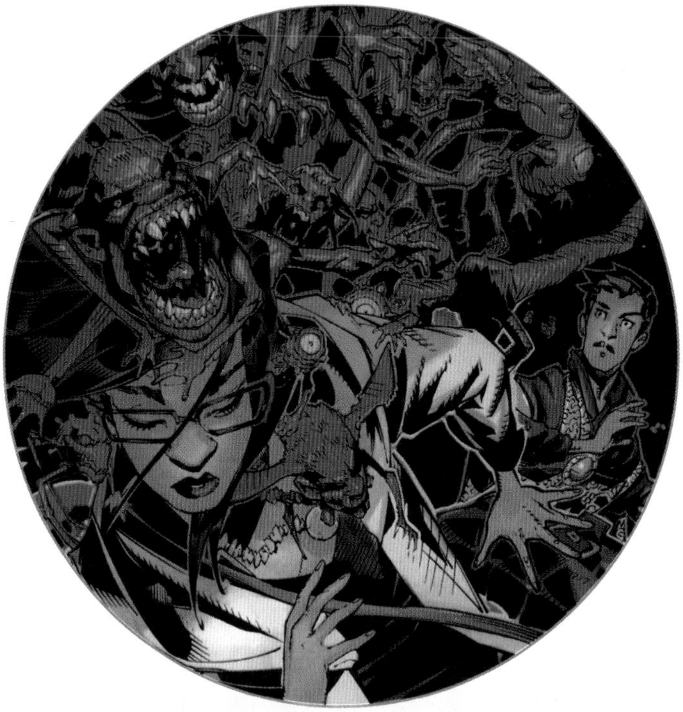

Zelma Stanton

When New York librarian Zelma was infected with malevolent Mind Maggots, she sought help from Doctor Strange. He absorbed the maggots, curing her completely. Strange then offered Zelma a job in his library, which she gladly accepted.

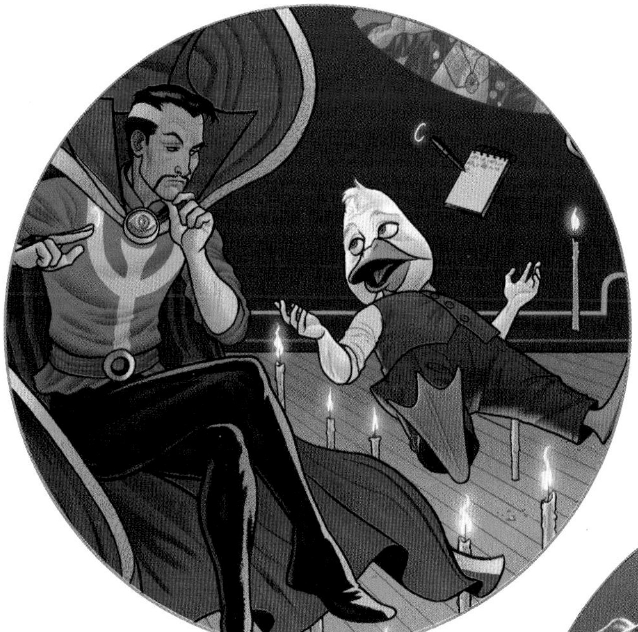

Howard the Duck

Doctor Strange and the talking duck first teamed up with the Defenders. Strange later noticed that Howard possessed some mystical abilities and taught him some spells. He even offered Howard an apprenticeship, but the duck declined.

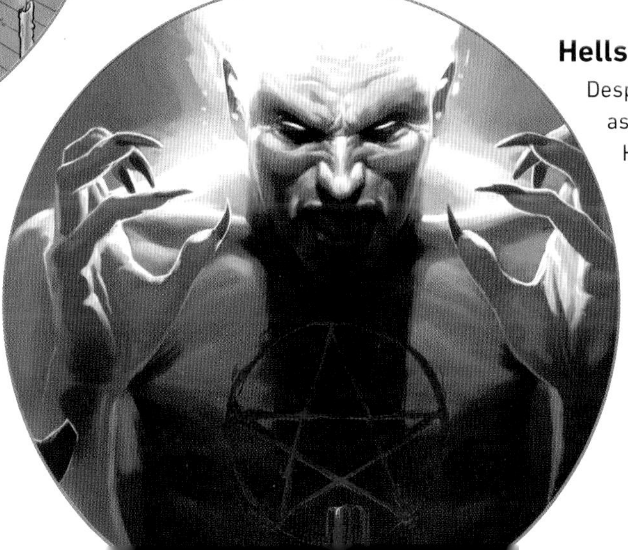

Hellstorm

Despite his dark heritage as a son of Satan, Daimon Hellstrom fought alongside Doctor Strange in the Defenders and, later, the Midnight Sons. Strange has also considered Hellstrom as a future Sorcerer Supreme of Earth.

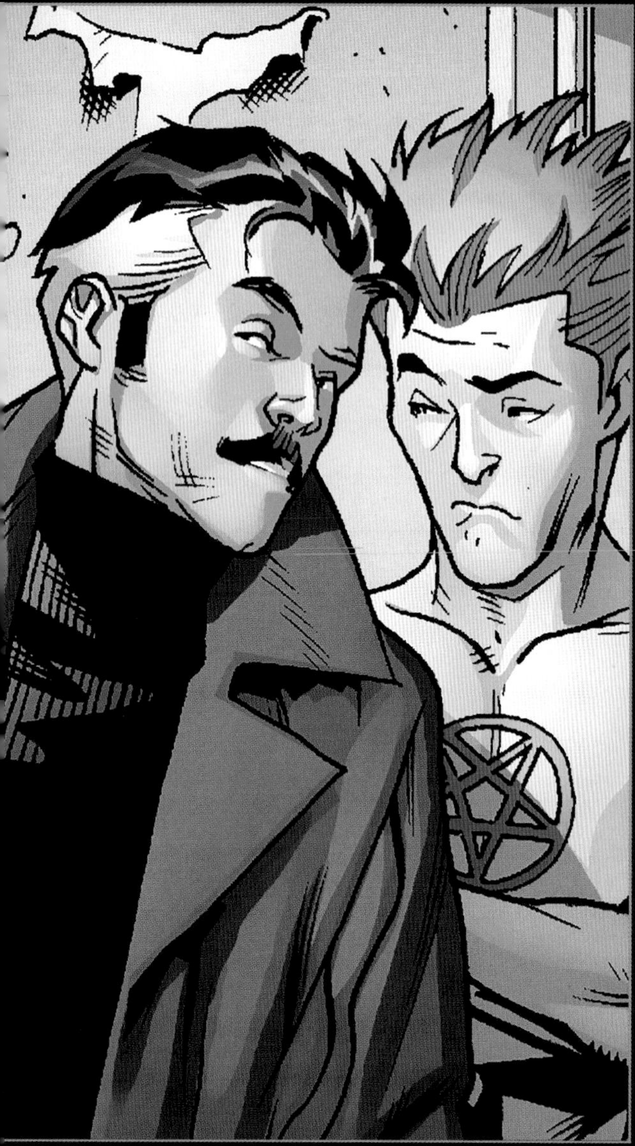

DAIMON HELLSTROM

When Doctor Strange relinquished the title of Sorcerer Supreme after using dark magic to stop the villainous Hood and his crime gang, the Eye of Agamotto sought a worthy successor. Among the first candidates for the role was Daimon Hellstrom, Son of Satan. This provoked a ferocious attack by the Hood, under orders from Dormammu, who wanted the Eye. Doctor Strange and the New Avengers raced to Hellstrom's aid and helped him fend off the Dormammu-empowered Hood. However, the Eye of Agamotto ultimately chose another to be the new Sorcerer Supreme: Jericho Drumm, aka Brother Voodoo.

▶ ***Demonic face-off*** Armed with his trusty soulfire trident, Daimon fearlessly confronts the Dormammu-possessed Hood.

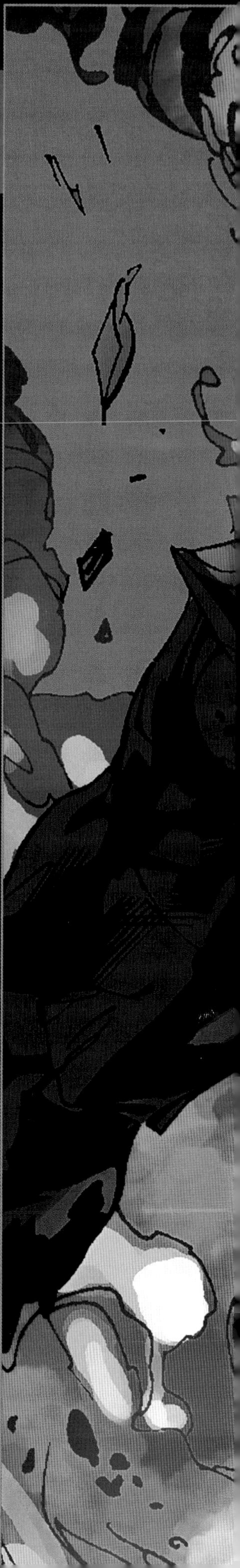

▲ ***Between hero and Hell*** Daimon has a Darksoul—the demonic equivalent of a human soul, which manifests as a pentagram on his chest. Despite this, Hellstrom is a proven hero, as well as a firm friend of Doctor Strange and a valiant member of the Defenders.

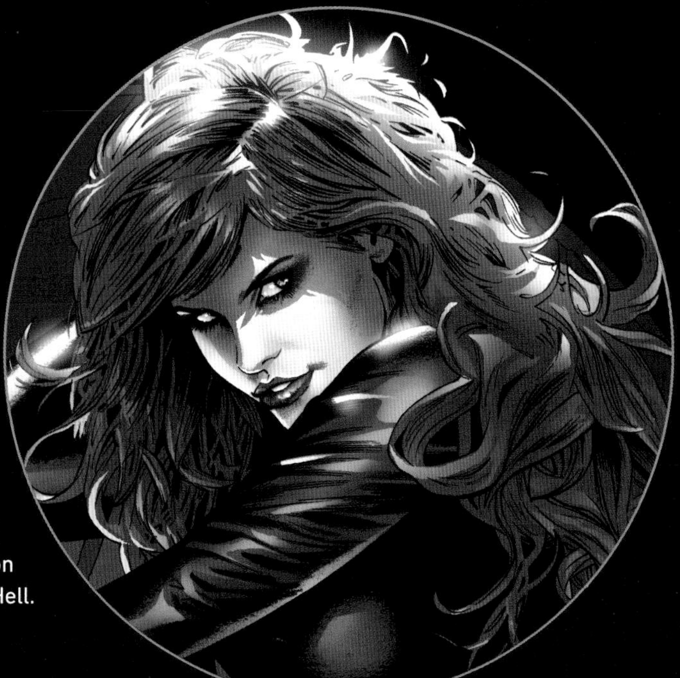

Sibling rivals

Daimon Hellstrom has always struggled with his hellish heritage as the Son of Satan—unlike his sister, Satana. Where Daimon rejected his father's evil ways and tried to follow a noble path, Satana embraced darkness. She is a succubus who feeds on the souls of men, and she longs to rule Hell.

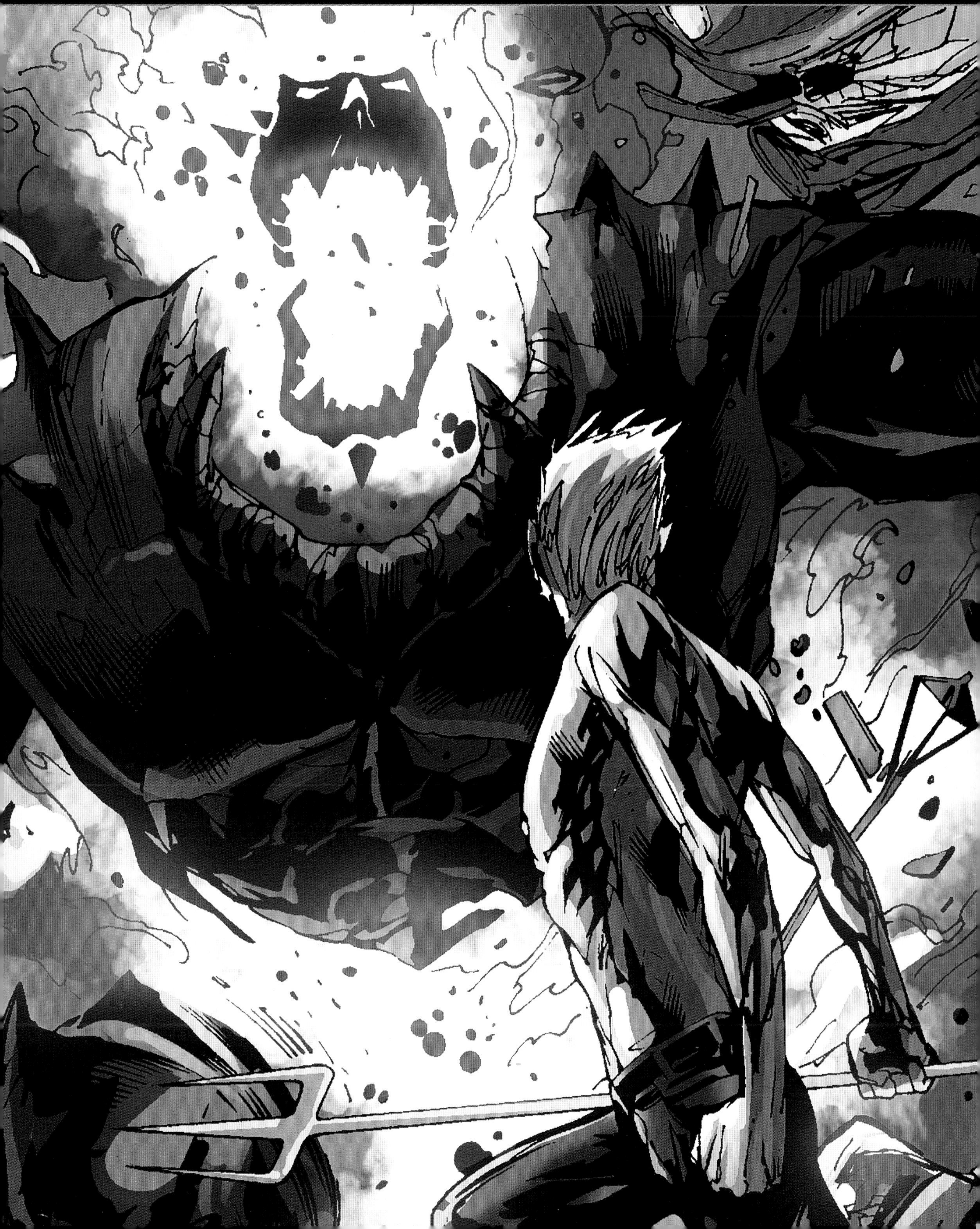

THE DEFENDERS

Dysfunctional and disparate, the Defenders were born of a willful act of manipulation on Doctor Strange's part, when he created an unlikely alliance between himself, Namor, the Hulk, and the Silver Surfer. This affiliation of very different heroes has come together as a last resort—and proven to be mankind's savior—on many an occasion.

The original trio

After their inital battles alongside Doctor Strange, the Hulk and Namor swore that they would never work together again. However, Strange's powers of persuasion ensured that their alliance would continue.

THE "NON-TEAM"

It was the attack of the demon race, the Undying Ones—led by the Nameless One—that brought about the formation of Doctor Strange's team, the Defenders. Strange recruited superpowered outsiders Namor and the Hulk to aid him in protecting Earth from the demonic horde. He later reunited with the reluctant pair to combat alien scientist, Yandroth, and an Omegatron doomsday device.

Victorious, the "non-team" of the Defenders was born. Unlike the Avengers and other Super Hero alliances, the Defenders operated without a charter, rules, a fixed roster, or even a headquarters. Despite this, their ranks grew. Strange's apprentice and partner Clea often aided the team, and the Silver Surfer—who would become a core member—joined after the team assisted the cosmic sky-rider in a conflict with the Warrior Wizard, Calizuma.

◀ *Mystical defense*
Enlisting the aid of other warriors like Iron Fist, the Defenders have become experts in defeating magical and supernatural threats.

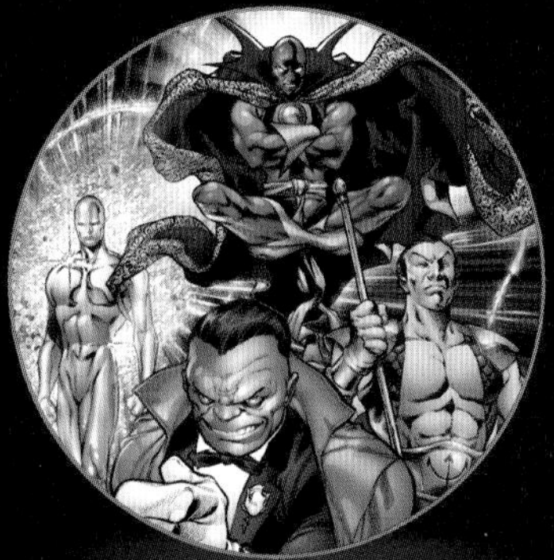

The Order

The Defenders members had to break a curse that caused Doctor Strange, the Hulk, Namor, and the Silver Surfer to lose their humanity and form a new group, the Order. They intended to "protect" Earth by taking control of it.

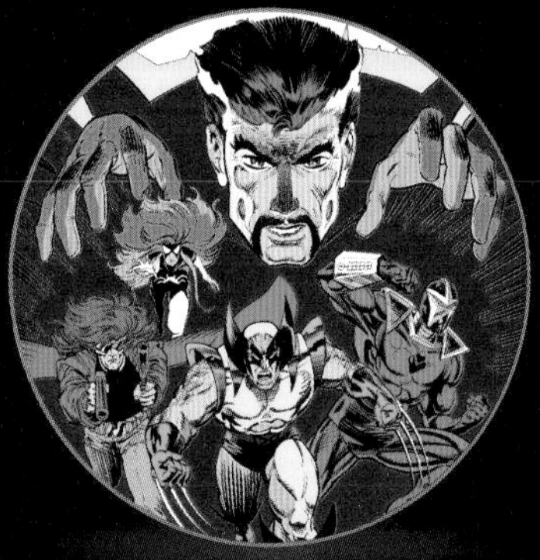

Secret Defenders

When the Defenders disbanded, Doctor Strange set up "The Secret Defenders," with no permanent members, just recruits for special missions. Strange's fellow mystic Doctor Druid took control, but was later corrupted, leading to the group's dissolution.

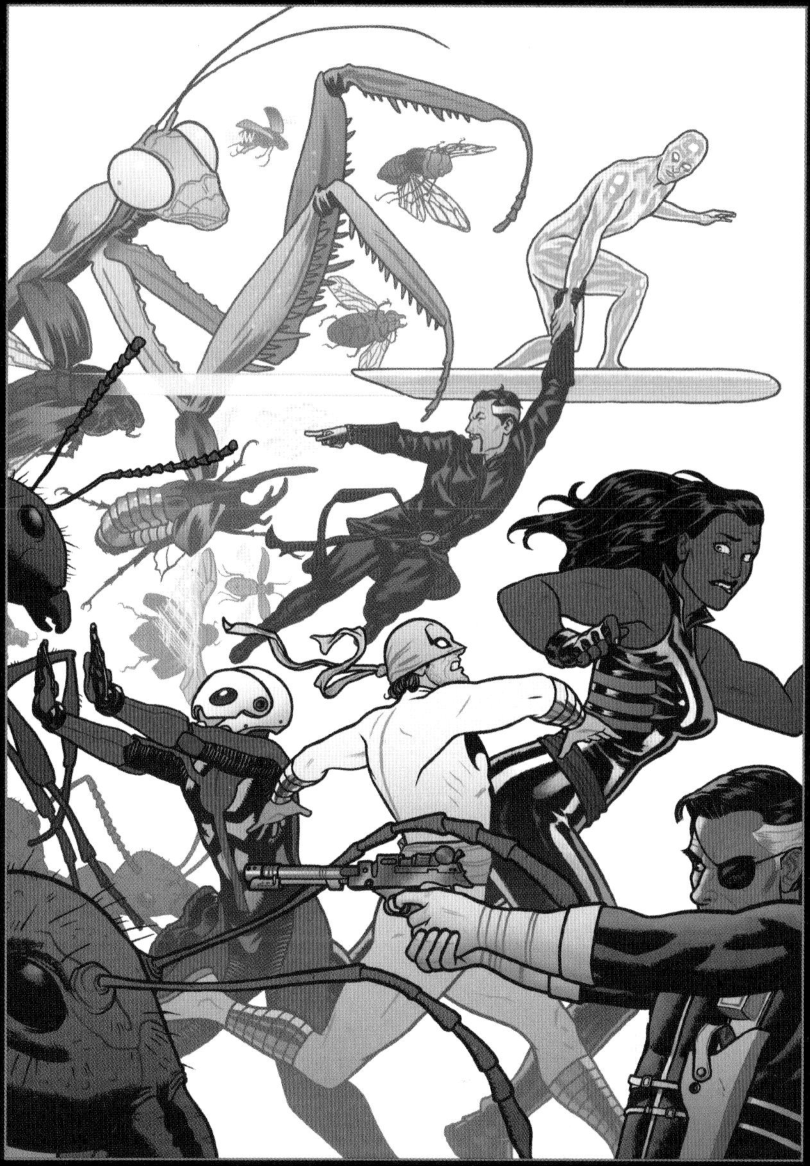

▲ ***Hero recruitment*** More recent members of the team include Ant-Man, Nick Fury, and Red She-Hulk.

"A TRUE DEFENDER NEVER RAISES ARMS AGAINST AN INNOCENT, NO MATTER HOW THEY THREATEN YOU."

Doctor Strange

Despite the group's loose organization, the Defenders have fought and triumphed over the likes of Mephisto, Xemnu the Titan, and the megalomaniacal Headmen. When manipulated by the trickster Loki, they even came into conflict with the Avengers, although the two teams eventually united to defeat Dormammu.

When the aliens known as the Tribunal tricked the core quartet into believing that their continued involvement would destroy Earth, they disbanded, vowing never to return. While the Defenders have repeatedly reformed with different members, these efforts have been marked with the tension that defined the original group, resulting in few lineups lasting very long. However, whenever the Earth faces doom, the Defenders will rise to the challenge.

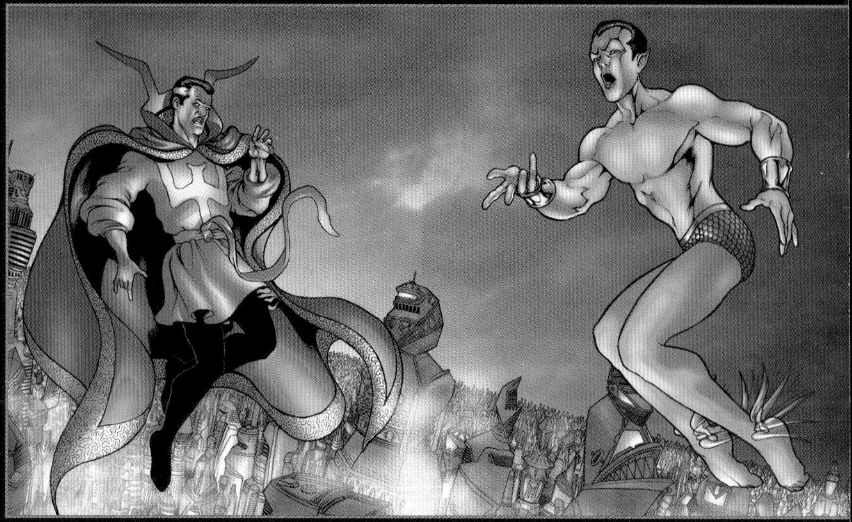

▲ ***A dark world*** The original Defenders reunited in order to stop Dormammu's plan to remake Earth in his own nightmarish image.

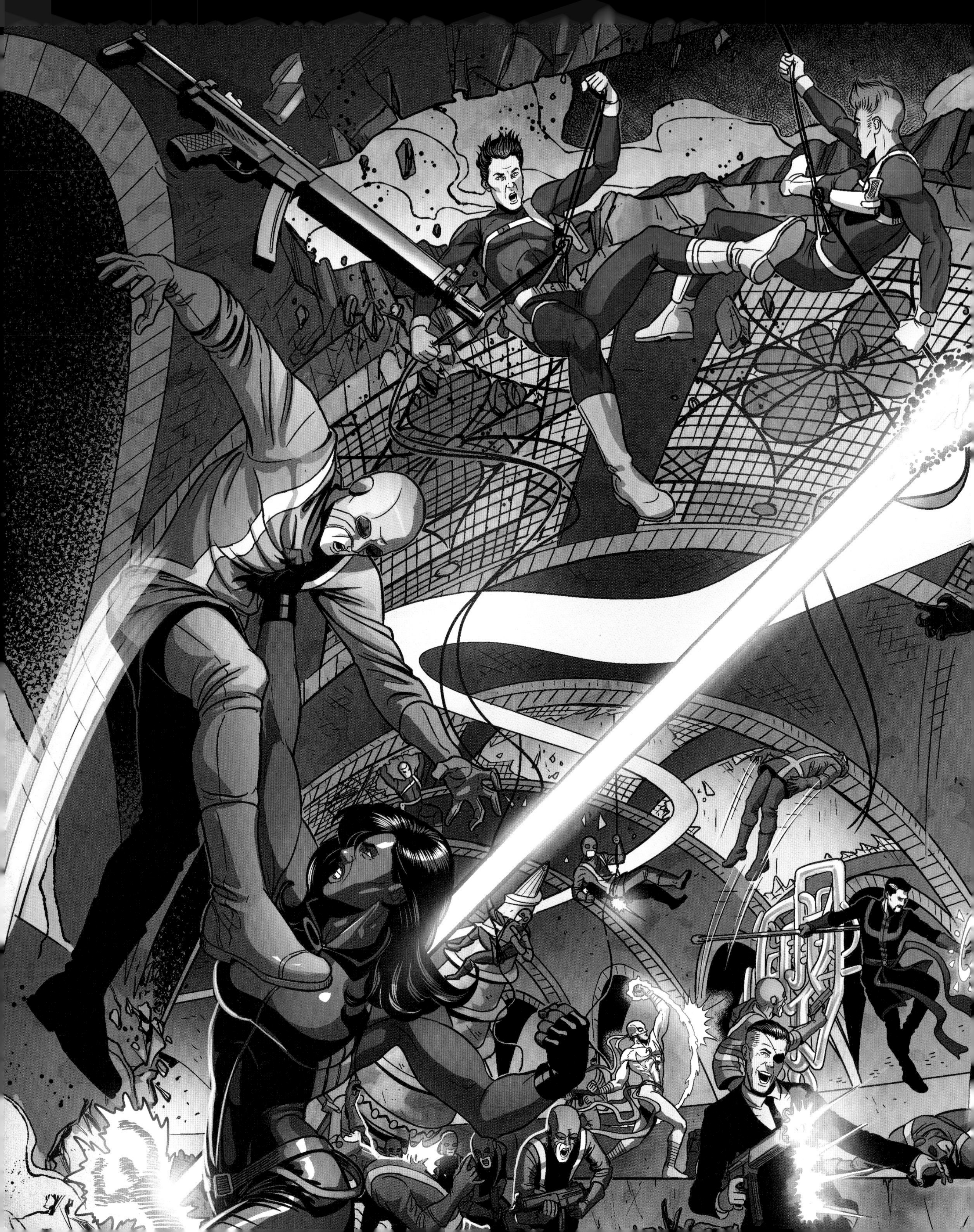

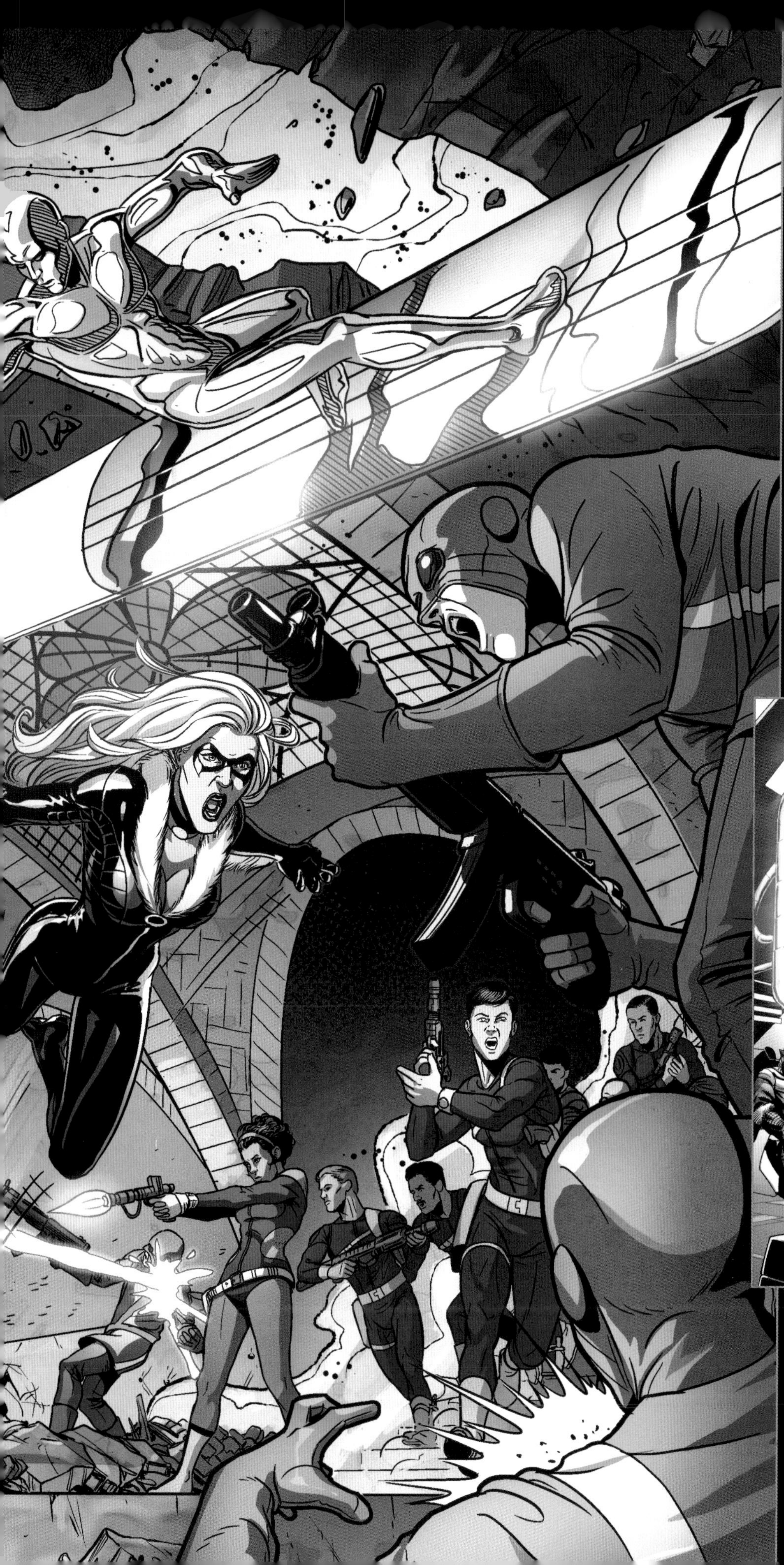

BLAST TO THE PAST

Doctor Strange recruited Namor, Iron Fist, the Silver Surfer, and Red She-Hulk to form a new team of Defenders to protect humanity from the Breaker of Worlds, Nul. Their misson saw them encounter the powerful Concordance devices, which had been built by the superhuman Presters. During the Defenders' battle with the Prince of Orphans, John Aman, the villain used one of the devices to blast the team into an alternate past, where they also faced the evil organization, Hydra.

◀ ***An old foe*** Trapped in time, the Defenders found themselves fighting alongside S.H.I.E.L.D. against dozens of Hydra agents.

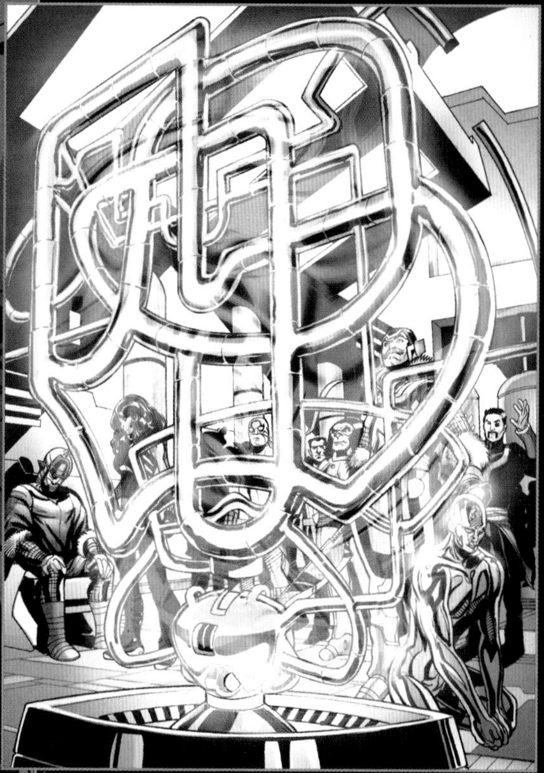

Engineering reality

The power of the Concordance Engine is not something to be taken lightly. This reality-warping weapon is the map of everything in the universe, and has the ability to shape all of space and time.

THE ILLUMINATI

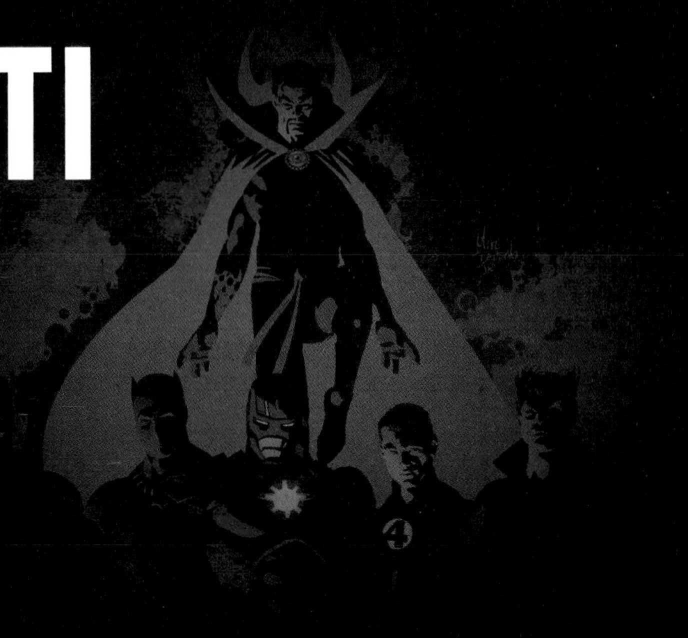

The Illuminati are a clandestine group comprising six of the most influential figures in the superhuman community: Tony Stark, Charles Xavier, Reed Richards, Namor, Black Bolt—and Doctor Strange. Formed in secrecy by Stark, this powerful organization has sought to quietly shape the role and effectiveness of superhumans, and to protect Earth from all manner of terrifying threats.

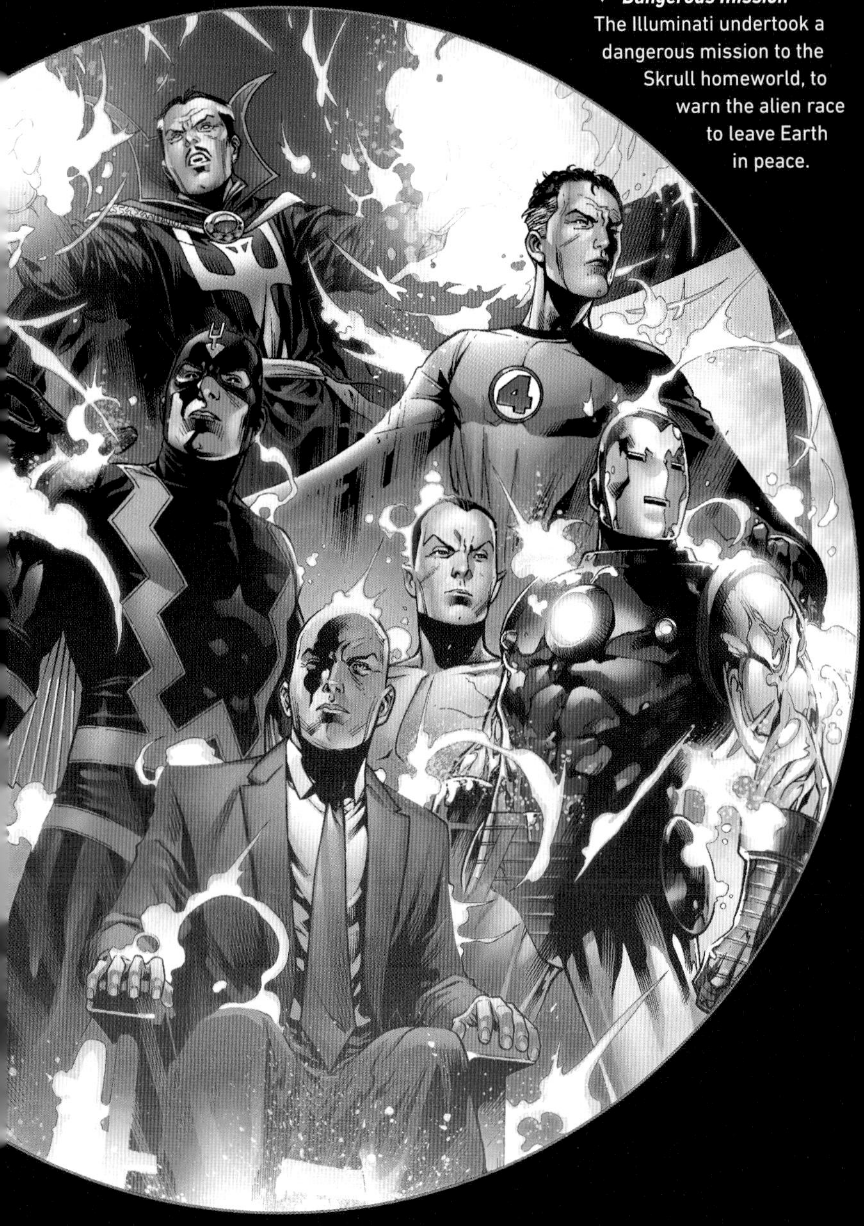

▼ ***Dangerous mission*** The Illuminati undertook a dangerous mission to the Skrull homeworld, to warn the alien race to leave Earth in peace.

THE SECRET GROUP

The Illuminati first came together in the wake of the cosmos-shaking Kree-Skrull War. Stark realized that the malevolent Skrull invaders could have been better repelled using the collective know-how of the group.

This collaboration was originally perceived as a large, overarching group of various teams, but Stark's initial, ominous suggestion of a "superhuman government" was soundly rejected, particularly by Doctor Strange. Their alliance was further refined to be a secret cabal of high influence, with six members meeting regularly to share information. Despite their considerable differences, each figure was chosen because of their specific expertize. Doctor Strange played an important role by contributing his unparalleled knowledge and skills in the mystic arts.

Despite many successful missions working together, tensions between the Illuminati members surfaced on a regular basis, threatening its stability. The group suffered deep fractures when Stark suggested shooting the rampaging Hulk into space to an uninhabited planet. Namor dissented, knowing the Hulk would seek revenge, which he did, on a devastating scale. These constant disagreements led to the organization disbanding on several occasions.

The Illuminati's most significant dispute came with the Superhuman Registration Act. Stark implored his colleagues to support the legislation, but he was met with fierce resistance by all members, except Richards. This once again led to the group's dissolution.

The Illuminati have reunited on occasion, but internal arguments constantly risk upsetting the group's delicate balance of trust and undermining its noble cause.

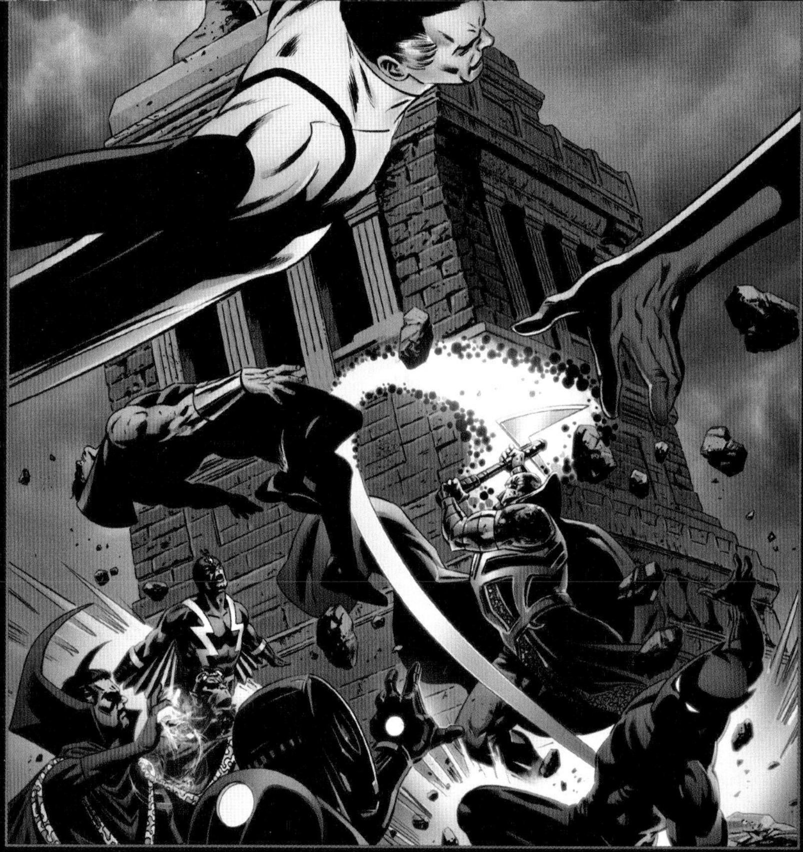

When worlds collide

The Illuminati members used their collective genius to stop the planetary Incursions—collisions between two universes—that threatened the entire multiverse. They strived to find peaceful methods of protecting Earth, but some of their solutions were more controversial.

"WE MADE IT CLEAR THAT IF THEY DO COME AT US, THE FIGHT WILL BE A REAL FIGHT."
Tony Stark

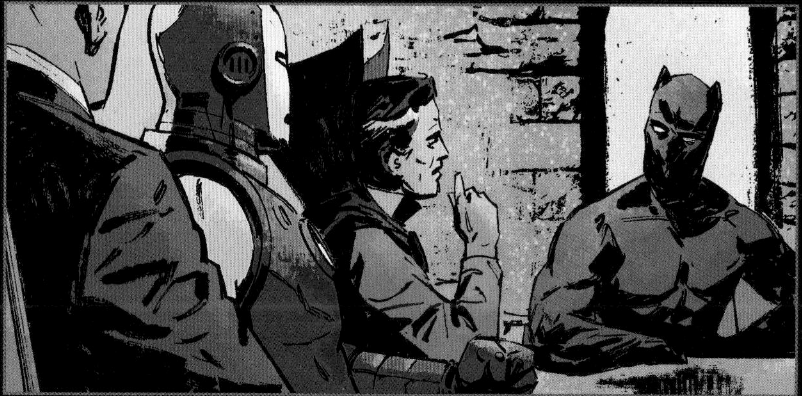

▲ ***Extended membership*** Over time, various other superhumans were asked to join the Illuminati, when the original members felt that they could contribute to the group. New members include Black Panther, Yellowjacket, Captain America, and Beast.

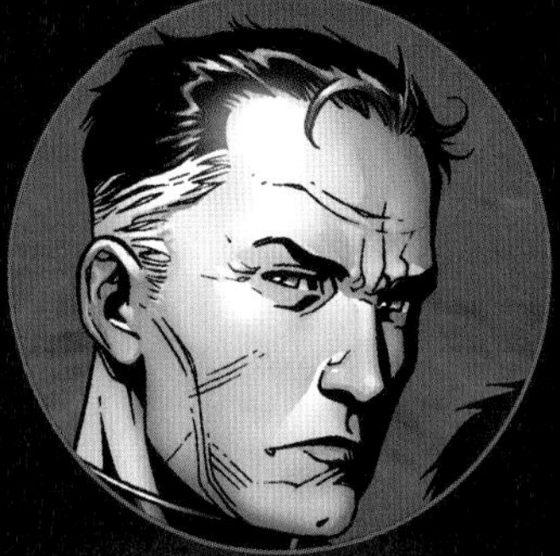

Mr. Fantastic

Reed Richards—also known as Mr. Fantastic—possesses the abiltiy to change body shape. Richards covers all scientific matters.

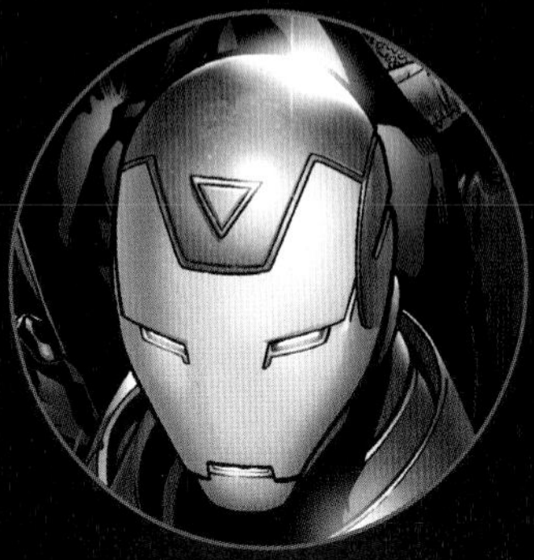

Iron Man

Genius businessman Tony Stark operates as the Super Hero Iron Man. Stark speaks for the Avengers and other heroes in the USA.

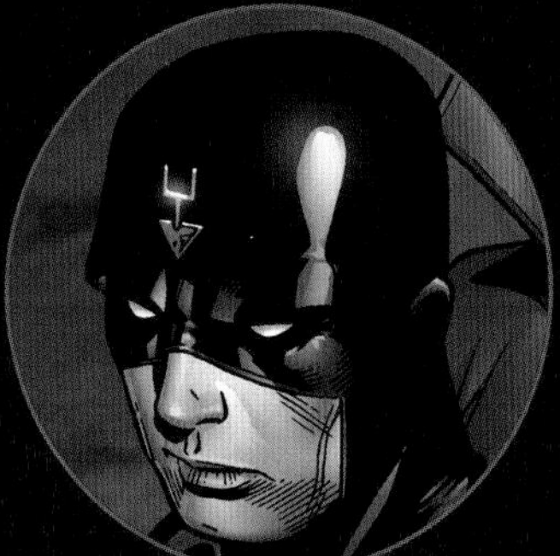

Black Bolt

Superhuman Black Bolt possesses a rarely used but devastatingly powerful voice. He is the ruler and representative of the reclusive Inhumans.

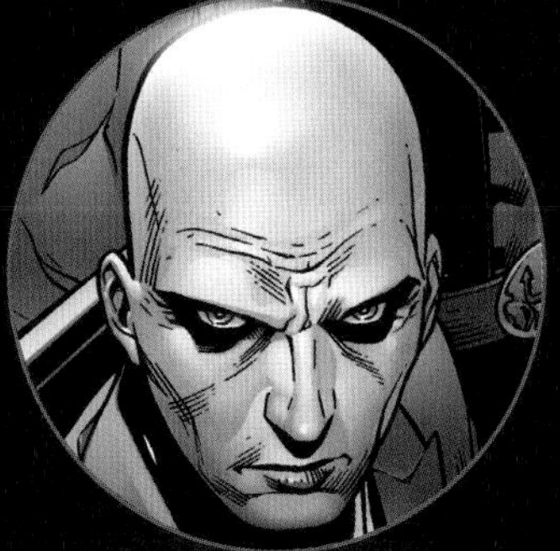

Professor X

Charles Xavier, one of the world's greatest minds and telepaths, speaks for the mutant community.

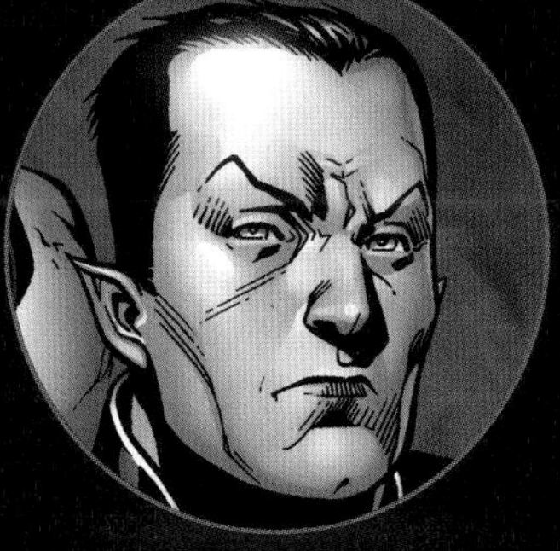

Prince Namor

Namor is regent of the undersea kingdom, Atlantis. Experienced but combative and opinionated, he champions the antihero mindset.

SECRETS AND LIES

The Illuminati's darkest days came when they faced a peril that threatened to bring all of reality to an untimely end. Events known as Incursions—where two alternate Earths clashed in a cosmic survival of the fittest—forced the Illuminati to consider destroying another world to save their own.

Captain America—who was a member at the time—vehemently rejected the idea, making his opposition very clear. Reluctantly, the rest of the Illuminati decided to take more drastic measures to protect their world. At Iron Man's request, Doctor Strange used his magic to erase Captain America's memory of the meeting. Their actions would bring about serious consequences for the group.

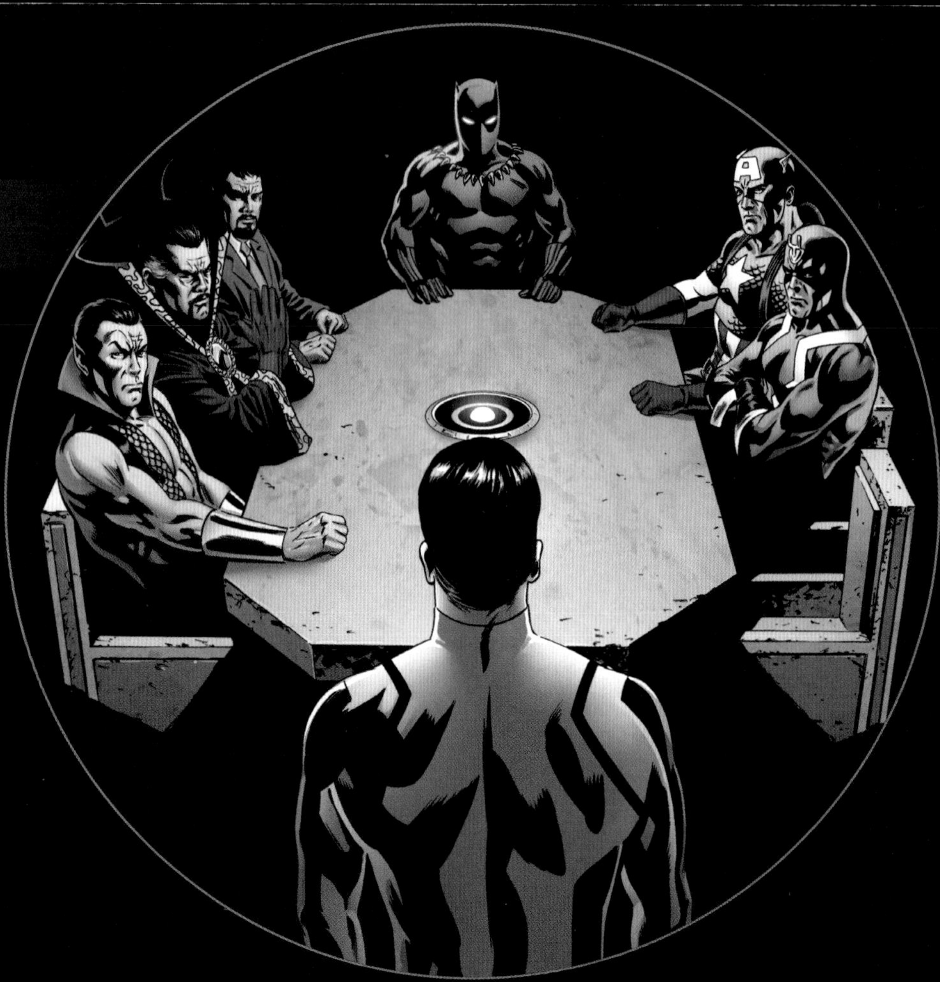

▲ ***Facing disaster*** It was Reed Richards who informed the assembled Illuminati of the grim threat of Incursions—and of the stark choices they faced.

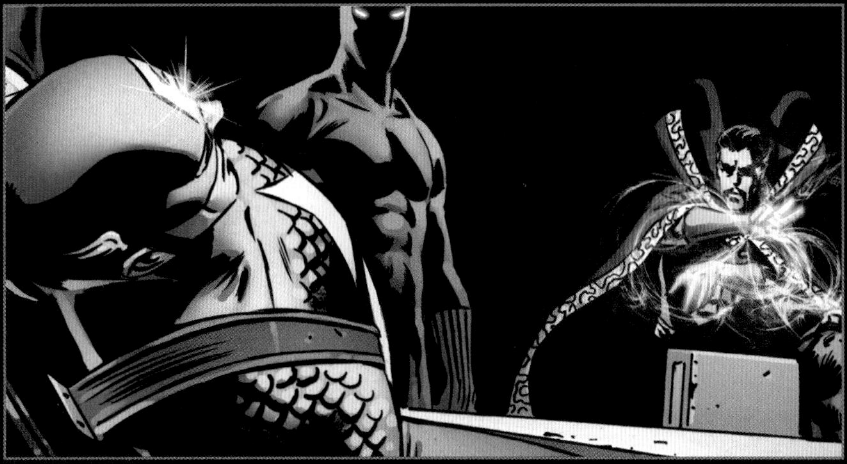

To forget...

"You were never here," intoned Doctor Strange as he wove the spell of forgetting. "You will remember none of this." For a time, the enchantment held, as the Illuminati used ever more extreme means to stop the Incursions.

...but not forgive

Eventually, Captain America did recall what Strange and his former cohorts had done to him. With fellow Avengers Hawkeye, Thor, and Black Widow, he confronted Tony Stark, leading to a conflict that pitted the Avengers against the Illuminati.

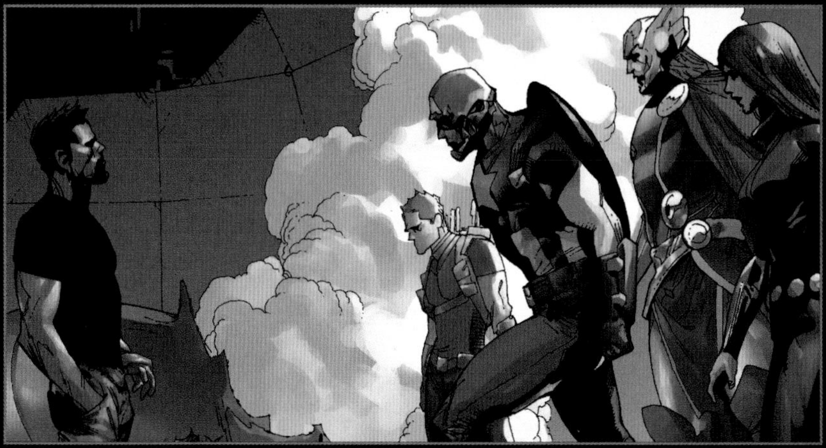

▶ ***Mind wipe*** Captain America paid the price for dissent, with Doctor Strange forcibly purging Cap's mind of the Illuminati's fateful decision.

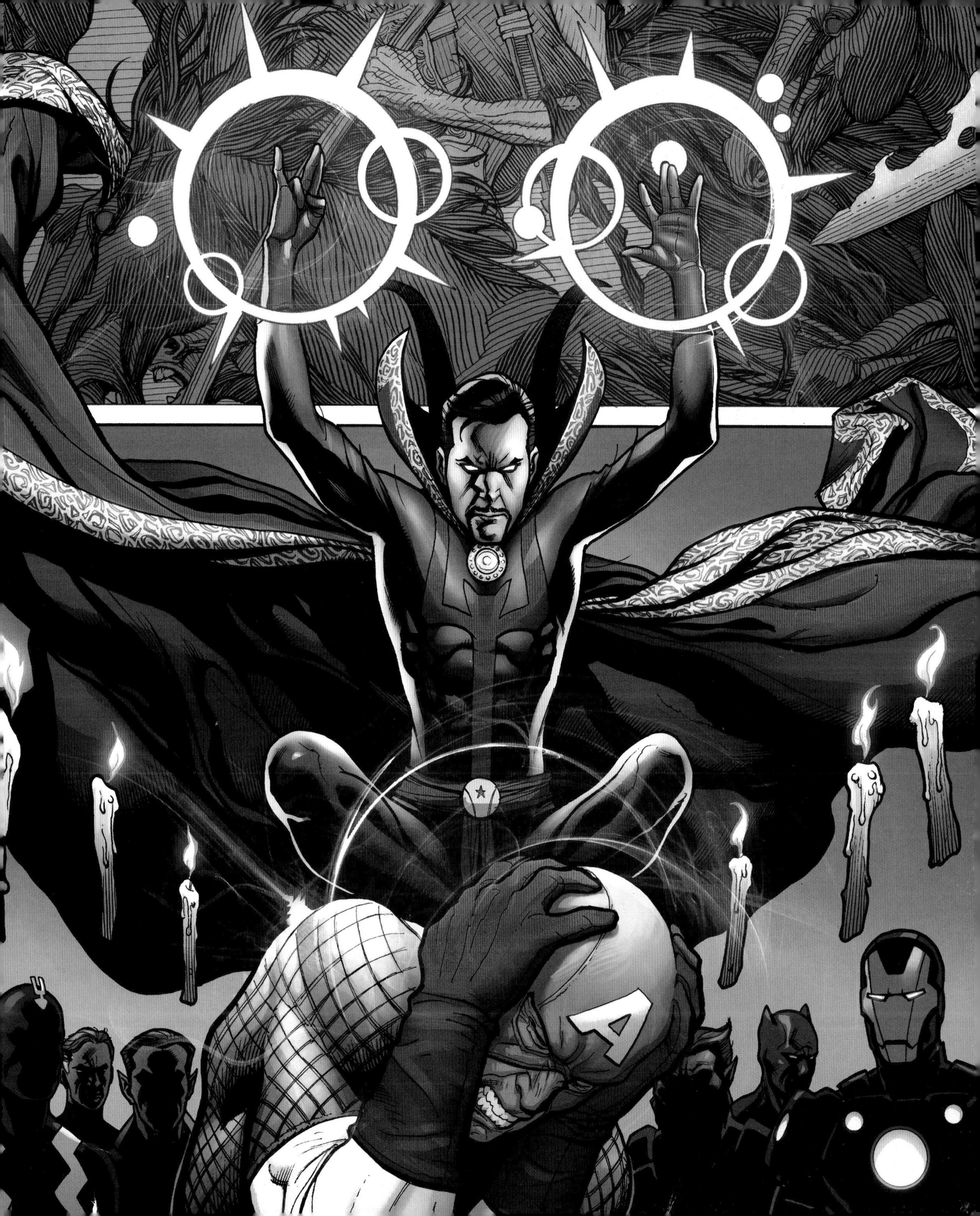

THE NEW AVENGERS

Doctor Strange's involvement with the New Avengers was a long time in the making. During the turbulent events surrounding the Superhuman Registration Act, Strange had been unwilling to take sides. In the aftermath of the Civil War that had followed, he deeply regretted his lack of involvement, and was determined to return to the heart of the action. The formation of a team of New Avengers presented him with the perfect opportunity to do precisely that.

▼ *A changing lineup* The New Avengers roster included heroes such as Jessica Jones, Hellcat, Daredevil, and Iron Fist.

BACK IN ACTION

As a gesture of goodwill, Doctor Strange allowed the renegade Avengers to use his home, the Sanctum Sanctorum, as a base of operations. In addition to his duties as Sorcerer Supreme, he regularly aided them on their missions.

When the New Avengers were attacked by crime boss, the Hood, Strange was able to fool him with an illusion spell, followed by an anti-demon spell that would banish the villain. However, the Hood was determined to take his vengeance and later invaded the Sanctum Sanctorum, forcing Strange to utilize a powerful paralyzing enchantment. Guilt-ridden by his use of such dark magic, Strange felt that he had lost his mastery of mystical arts, and he relinquished the role of Sorcerer Supreme.

However, Strange remained an active member of the New Avengers, passing the mantle of Sorcerer Supreme onto his associate, Jericho Drumm, aka Brother Voodoo. This arrangement continued until a fearsome battle between the New Avengers and Agamotto resulted in the apparent death of Brother Voodoo.

Blaming Strange for setting his brother up to fail, Daniel Drumm took his revenge by possessing the Avengers and using them to attack Strange. To defeat Daniel, a formidable necromancer in his own right, Strange was forced to use dark magic once again. However, this time the Ancient One appeared and absolved his former disciple of his necessary actions, and commended his valor. Doctor Strange was restored to his rightful place as Sorcerer Supreme, and continued to serve the New Avengers in this role.

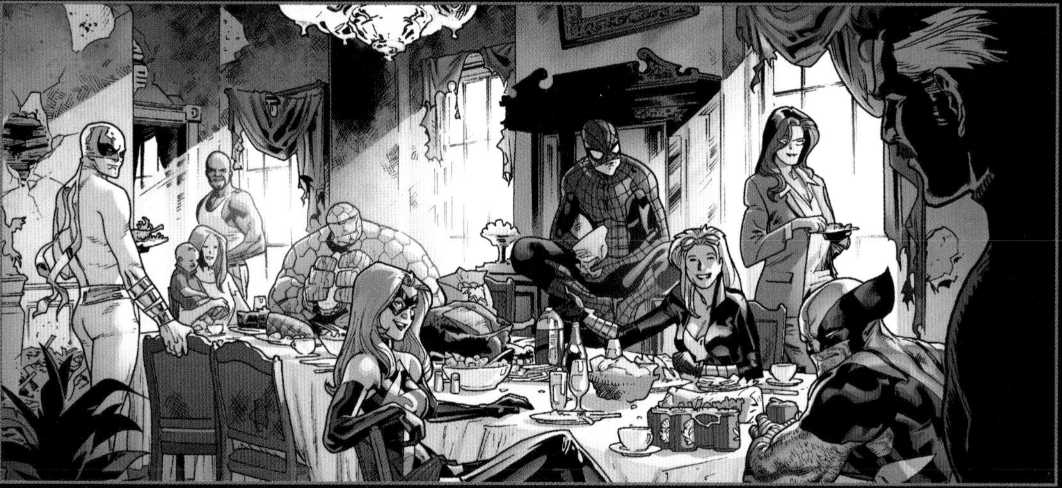

Trusted team
The new team members were carefully selected by Luke Cage. The heroes' shared history made them a close-knit group.

Victoria Hand
Victoria Hand was the scheming Norman Osborn's former right hand woman. She was offered a place on the New Avengers—and a chance of redemption—by Steve Rogers.

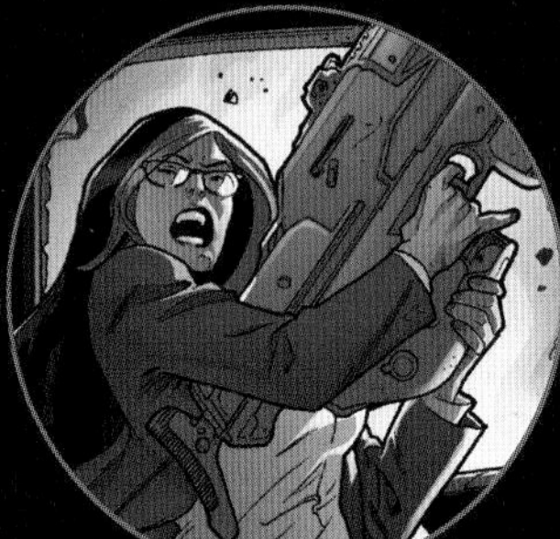

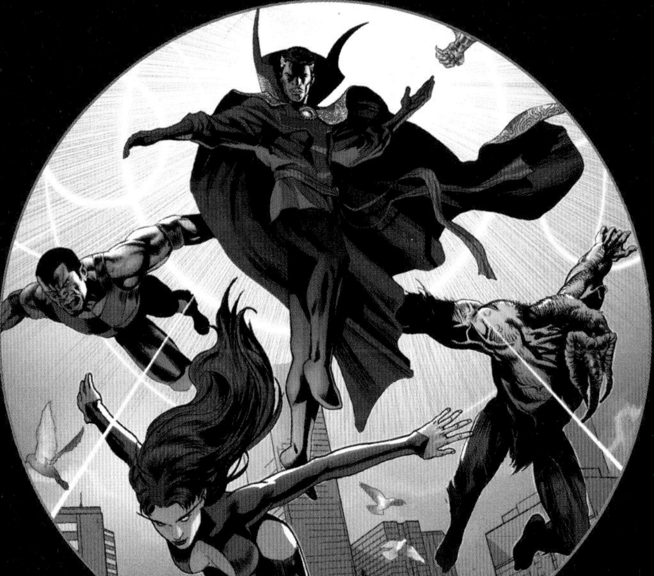

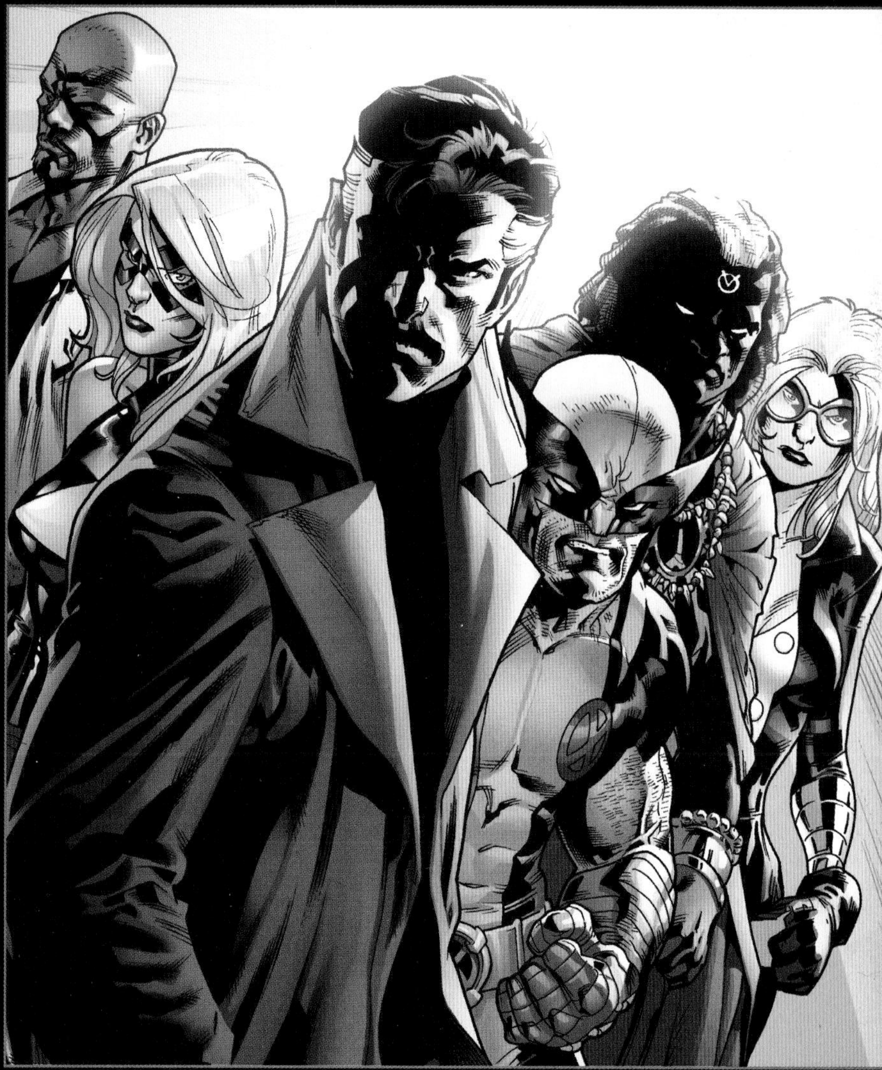

▲ ***A simple look*** After losing the title of Sorcerer Supreme, Doctor Strange no longer wore his mystical attire.

Avengers of the Supernatural
An alien named Mojo, who came from a literally spineless race of beings from the planet Mojoworld, once forced many heroes—including Doctor Strange—to become the Avengers of the Supernatural. They were brainwashed into taking part in his warped reality show, "Martian Transylvania Super Hero Mutant Monster Hunter High School."

"ALL OF US, WE GOT HISTORY."
Luke Cage

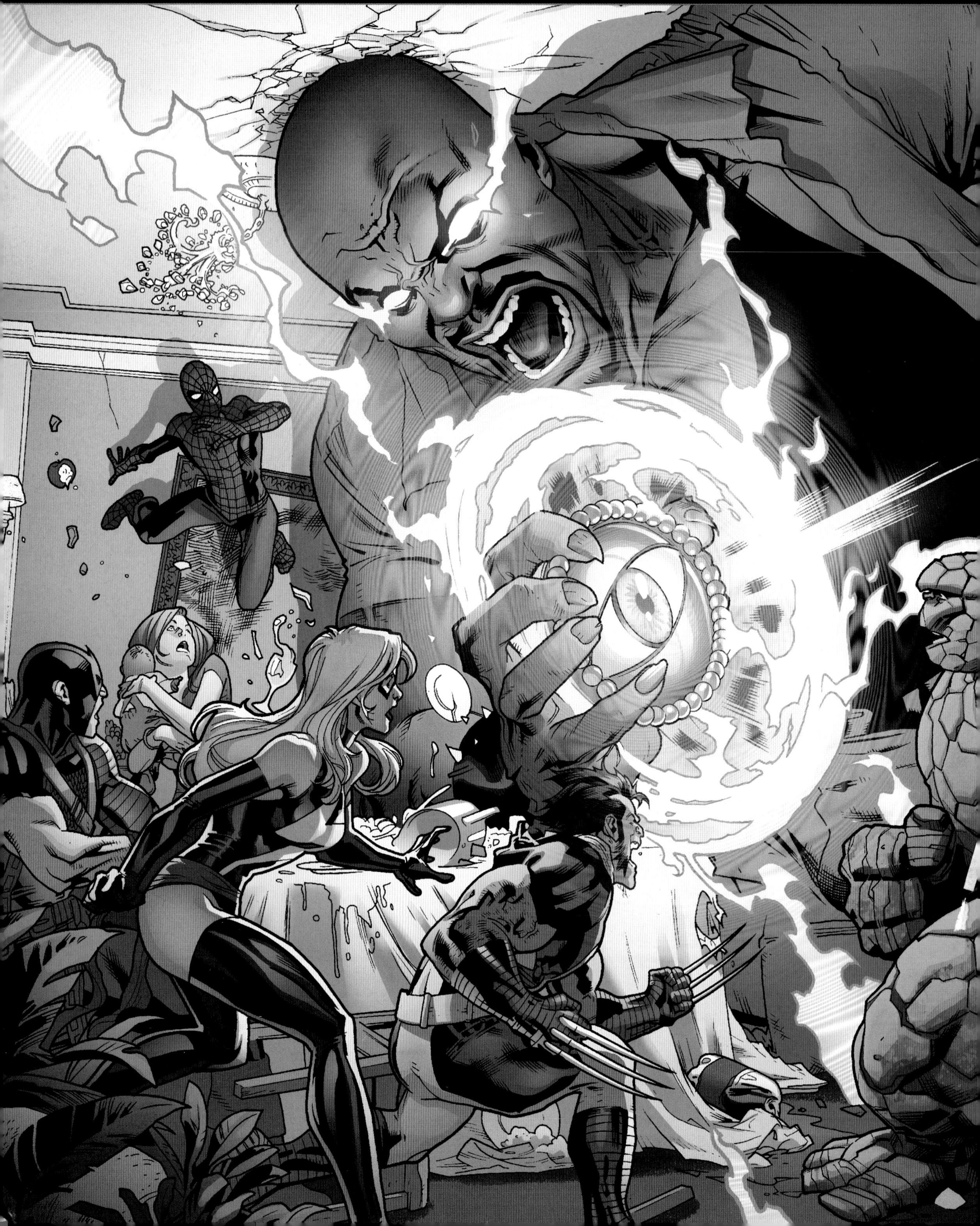

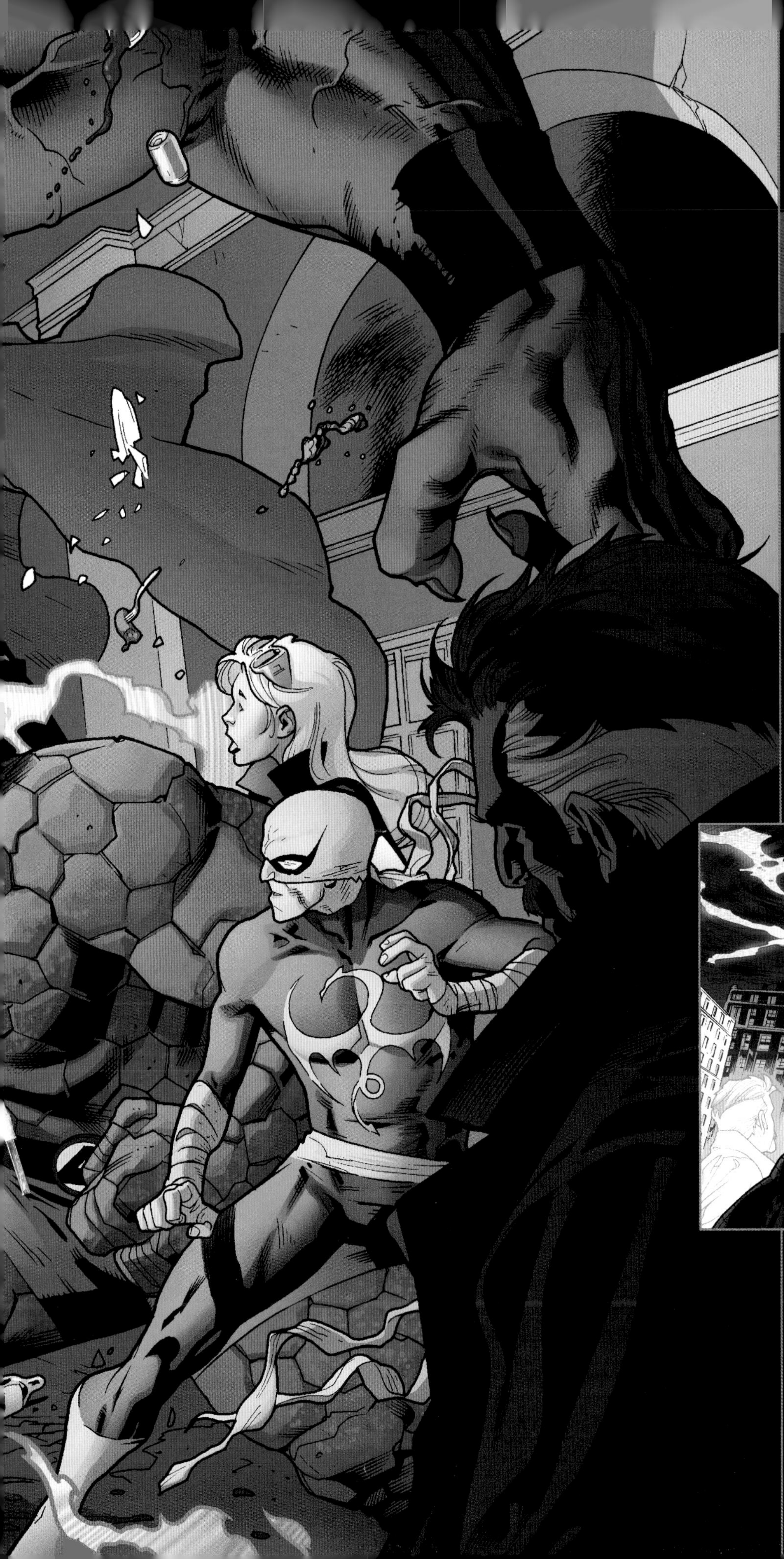

◀ ***Power Man possessed*** After the Eye of Agamotto materialized in his hand, Luke Cage grew to a monstrous size.

AVENGING AGAMOTTO

The New Avengers faced a deadly threat from within when Doctor Strange, Daimon Hellstrom, and the team's leader, Luke Cage (alias Power Man), were each possessed. At first it was believed a demon had gained control of them through the Eye of Agamotto. However, it soon became clear that it was Agamotto himself, who was trying to reclaim the Eye. Luke Cage wrecked Avengers Mansion and rampaged across New York's Central Park before his teammates rescued him from Agamotto's clutches.

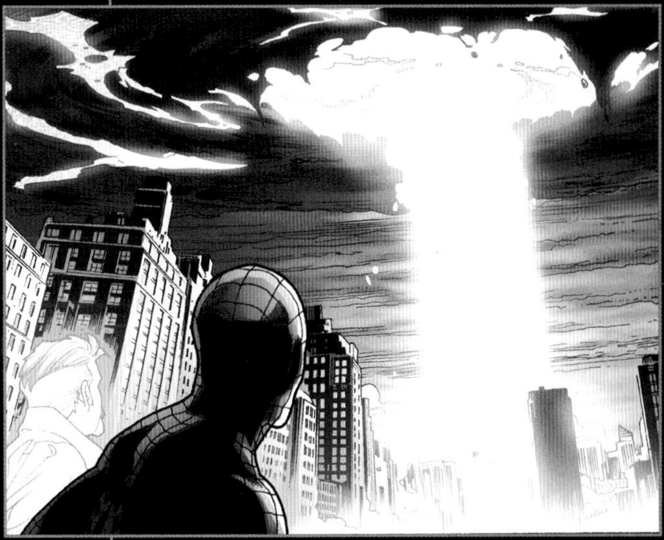

Skies rent asunder
Agomotto's attack tore a dimensional hole in the sky above New York, unleashing a wave of demonic entities on the city. It was up to Doctor Strange, Spider-Man, and the rest of the New Avengers to fend them off.

SUPERNATURAL STRANGE

Doctor Strange has been most commonly associated with the Defenders, various incarnations of the Avengers, and other Super Hero teams. However, he has also had dealings with two groups that are firmly rooted in the supernatural: the Midnight Sons and the Black Priests.

Blade

Eric Brooks operates as the vampire hunter Blade. This vampire-human hybrid possesses all the strengths of the night creatures, but none of their weaknesses— except a thirst for blood.

Ghost Rider

Both motorcyle-riding, chain-wielding versions of Ghost Rider are forces to be reckoned with. These hellfire flaming skeletons can inflict great pain on their enemies.

Morbius

As a pseudo vampire born of science, Michael Morbius possesses superhuman strength and speed as well as the power of hypnosis.

▲ *Supernatural attack* Doctor Strange leads the Midnight Sons into battle against dark and unnatural forces.

MYSTICAL DEFENSE

Intending to form a firm line of defense against Lilith, the Mother of Demons, Doctor Strange gathered together a formidable alliance of supernatural heroes, all reputed to have had a "taste of damnation." The Midnight Sons were made up of the Living Vampire Morbius, the mystic hunting Nightstalkers (led by Blade), and the Darkhold Redeemers, while the leaders of the team were the first two incarnations of Ghost Rider—Johnny Blaze and Daniel Ketch.

Strange initially tricked them all into coming together when Lilith staged an invasion of Greenland. The fractious group initially displayed great animosity toward each other, and almost all resented Strange's manipulative tendencies.

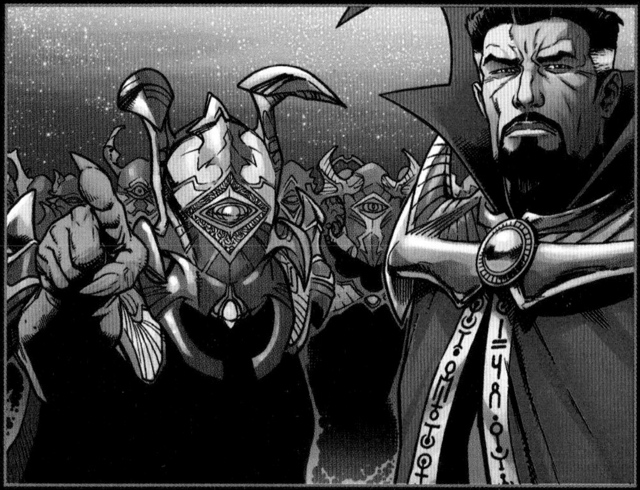

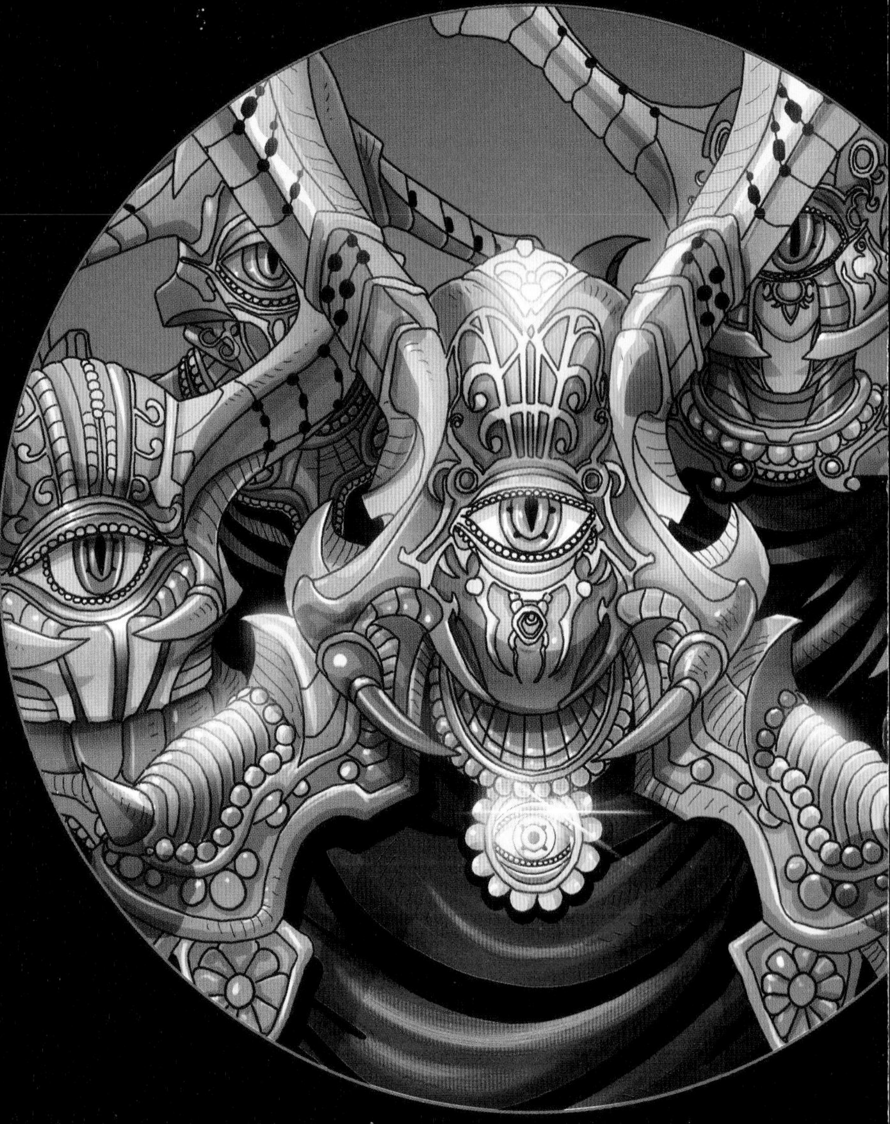

Dark deeds

Having mastered the Black Priests' brand of mystical power, Doctor Strange offered to join their priesthood. The New Avengers were shocked to learn that Strange had become the group's leader, thanks to his formidable skills at sorcery. Despite his intention to save the multiverse, the Black Priest's controversial actions brought Strange into conflict with his fellow heroes.

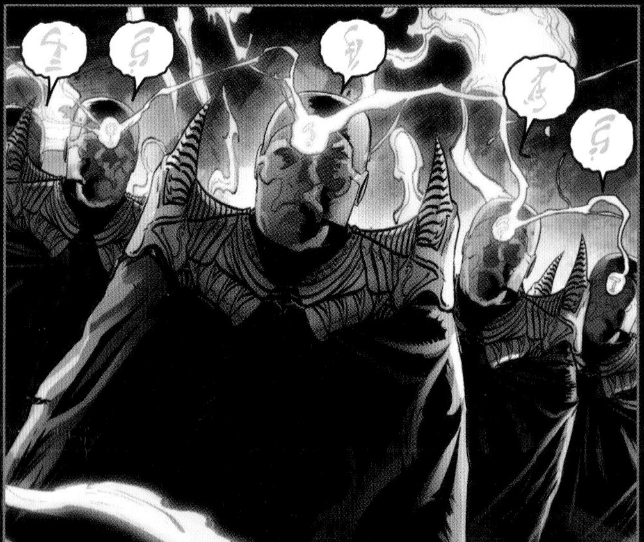

◀ ***Secret language*** The Black Priests are able to use a confounding yet potent language of symbols that is capable of distorting reality.

▲ ***Second sight*** The Black Priests may not possess eyes, but their elaborate headwear does.

Doctor Strange's involvement with the Black Priests came with greater risk than his association with other groups. The Black Priests are an assembly of unfathomable beings from another reality, who possess tens of thousands of interlinked minds. They are involved in the Game of Worlds, in which "intrusive" Earths are eradicated as part of a greater effort to stabilize the multiverse. Anyone standing in their way by trying to save their own universe is swiftly destroyed.

Following the public exposure of the Illuminati, Doctor Strange joined the Black Priests in a last-ditch attempt to save the multiverse.

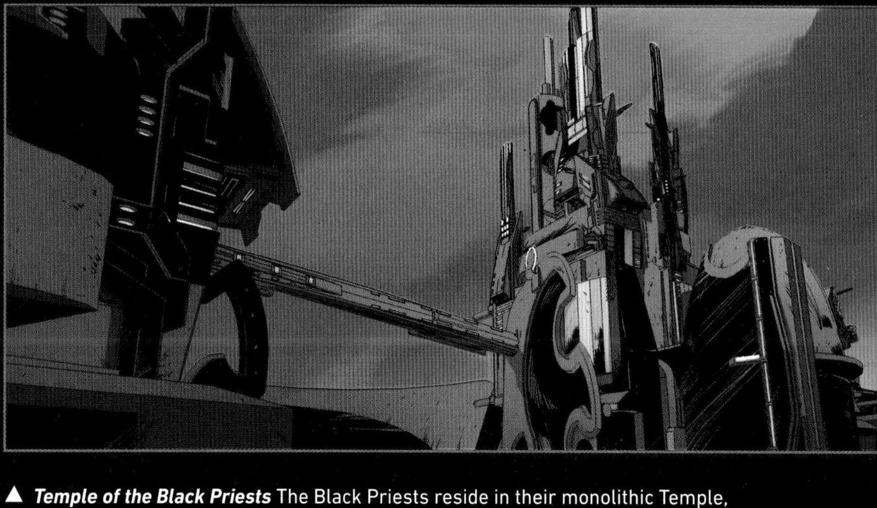

▲ ***Temple of the Black Priests*** The Black Priests reside in their monolithic Temple, which is located in the void between destroyed universes.

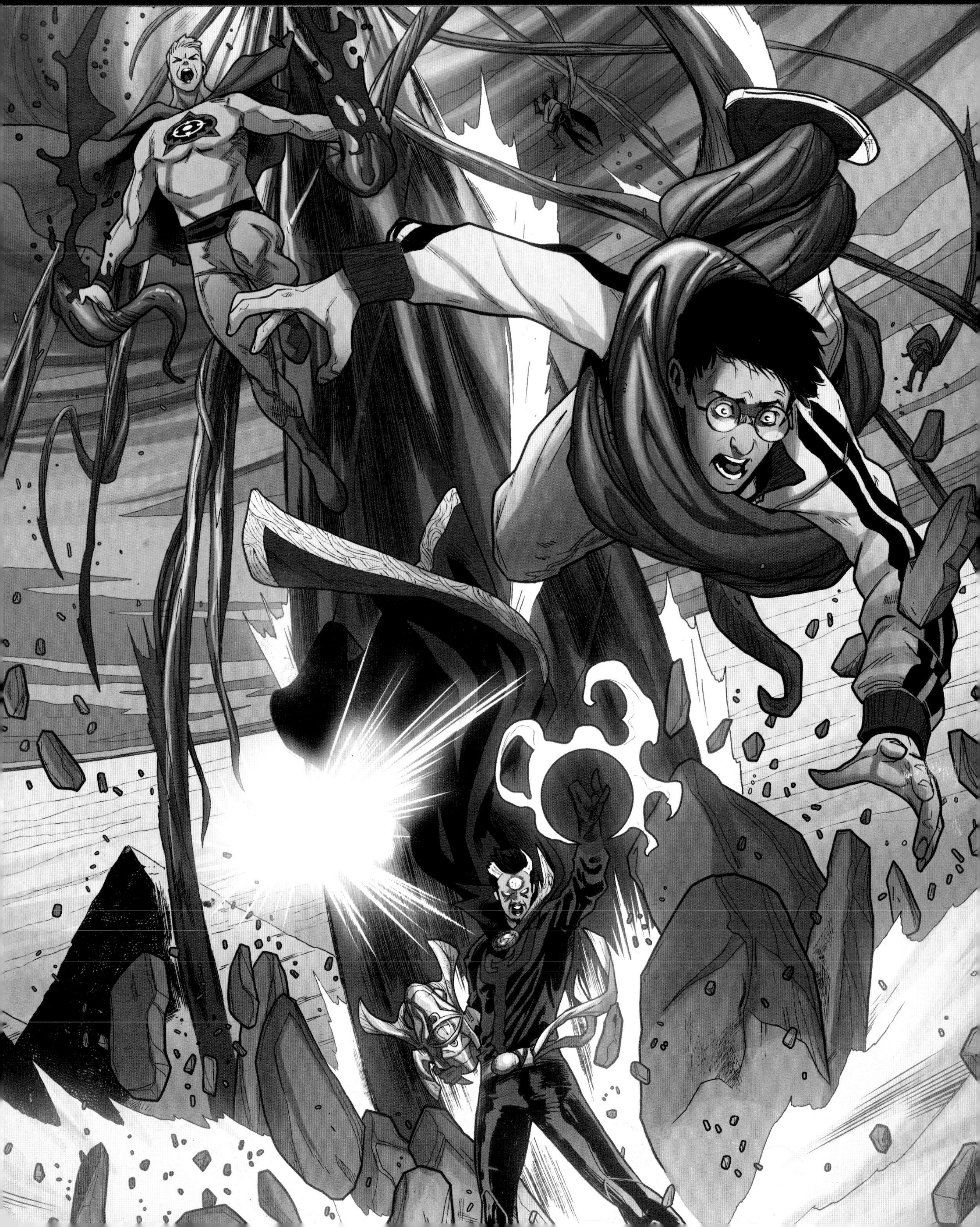

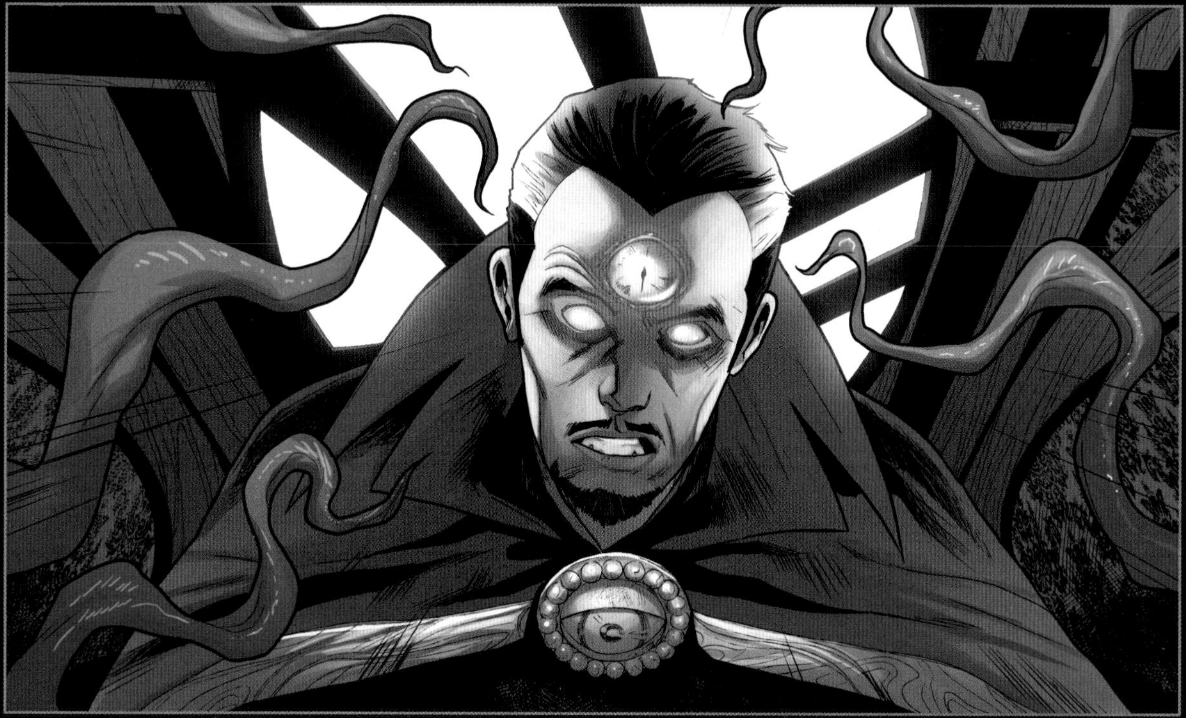

◀ ***Price to pay*** The tentacled horror Doctor Strange brought forth in his bid to save the world cost him his very soul.

THE BLACK PRIESTS

In his desperate efforts to find a solution to the dire threat of the Incursions—universal cataclysms where alternate Earths collided—Doctor Strange turned to dark magic. To protect his own world, he summoned a demonic entity and unleashed it on the Earth of another dimension. The heroes of that planet, the Great Society, were overwhelmed, and it was left to Strange's Illuminati brethren to destroy the beast that had possessed him.

Doctor Strange subsequently sought out the mysterious, alien Black Priests, becoming their leader to destroy enough unstable alternate Earths that the rest of reality might be saved.

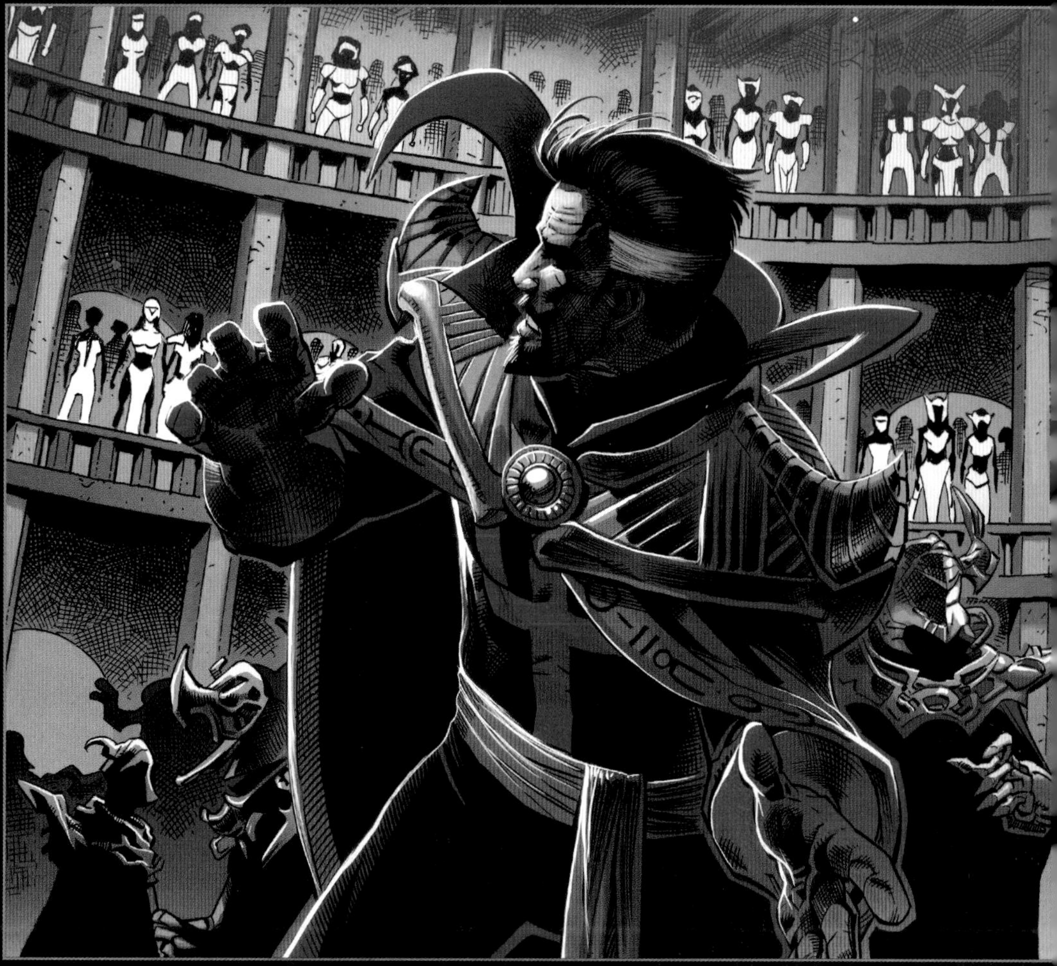

◀ ***Society's ills*** Sun God, the Norn, and the other heroes of the Great Society were no match for Doctor Strange's demonically enhanced powers.

Of priests and swans

The sworn enemies of the Black Priests were the Black Swans, whose leader, Rabum Alal, seemingly sought the end of everything. In a final confrontation with the Swans, the Black Priests were wiped out, and Doctor Strange was brought before Rabum Alal, who stood revealed as Doctor Doom.

CHAPTER 3
ENEMY MINE

Beyond our world, there are dark dimensions where evil beings of unimaginable magical might lurk. Harboring an unquenchable thirst for more power, these entities prey on the souls of humanity. Monsters, wizards, and demons like Dormammu, Mordo, Nightmare, and Mephisto seek dominion over all existence. But one man has thwarted their schemes time and time again—the Sorcerer Supreme. Now these evil beings' hatred of Earth's protector fills them with one burning desire—the absolute destruction of Doctor Strange!

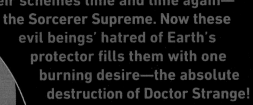

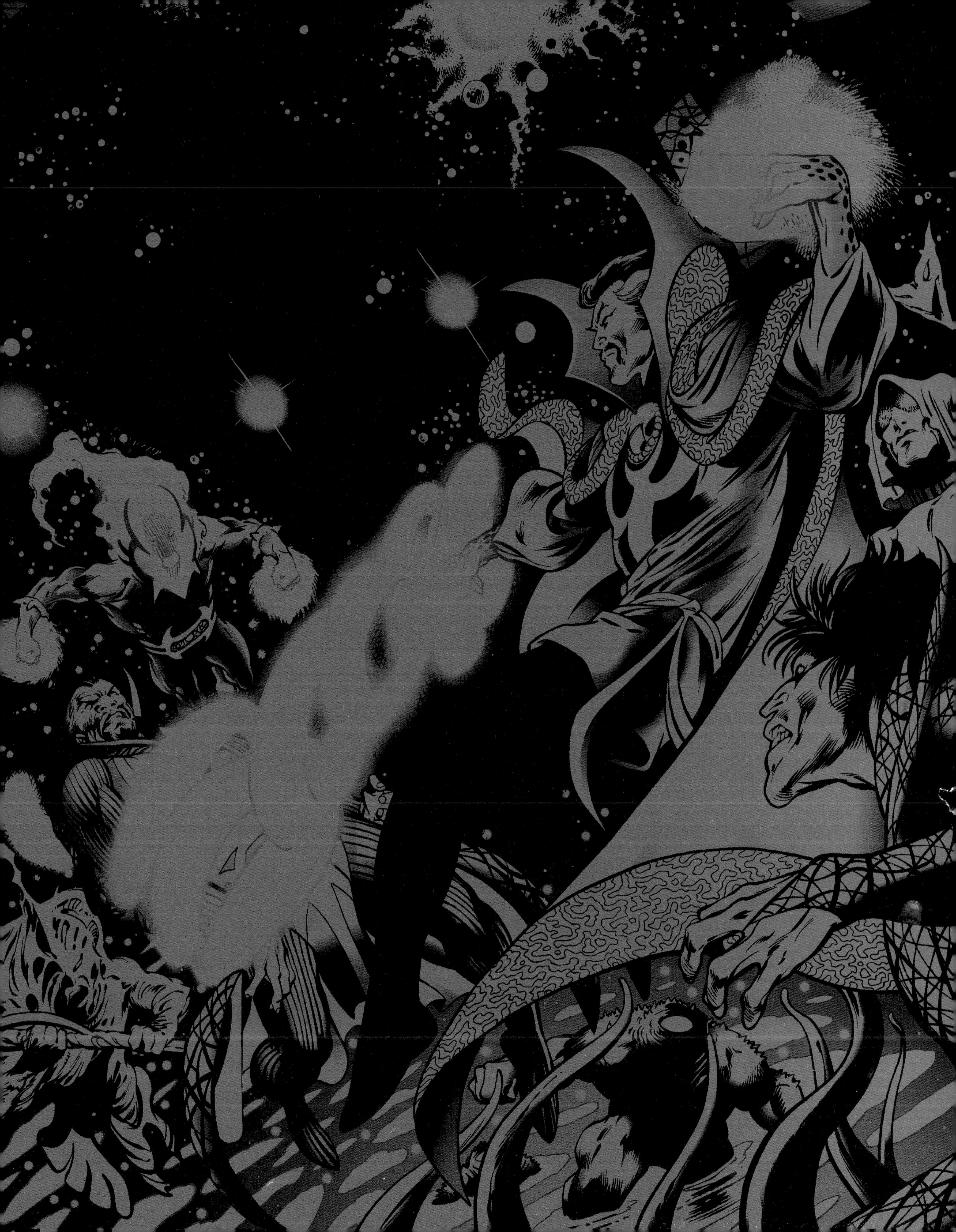

DORMAMMU

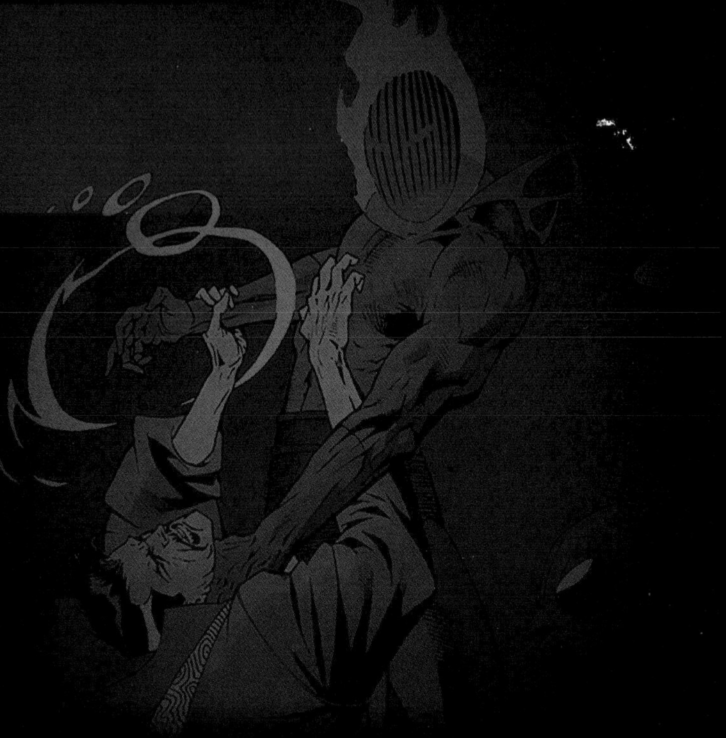

Known as the Dread One, Dormammu is an ancient and powerful extra-dimensional being made partly of mystical energy. He is the sovereign ruler of the Dark Dimension, from where he seeks to bring ever more realms under his control—especially Earth! Doctor Strange considers him to be one of the greatest threats to life in the universe.

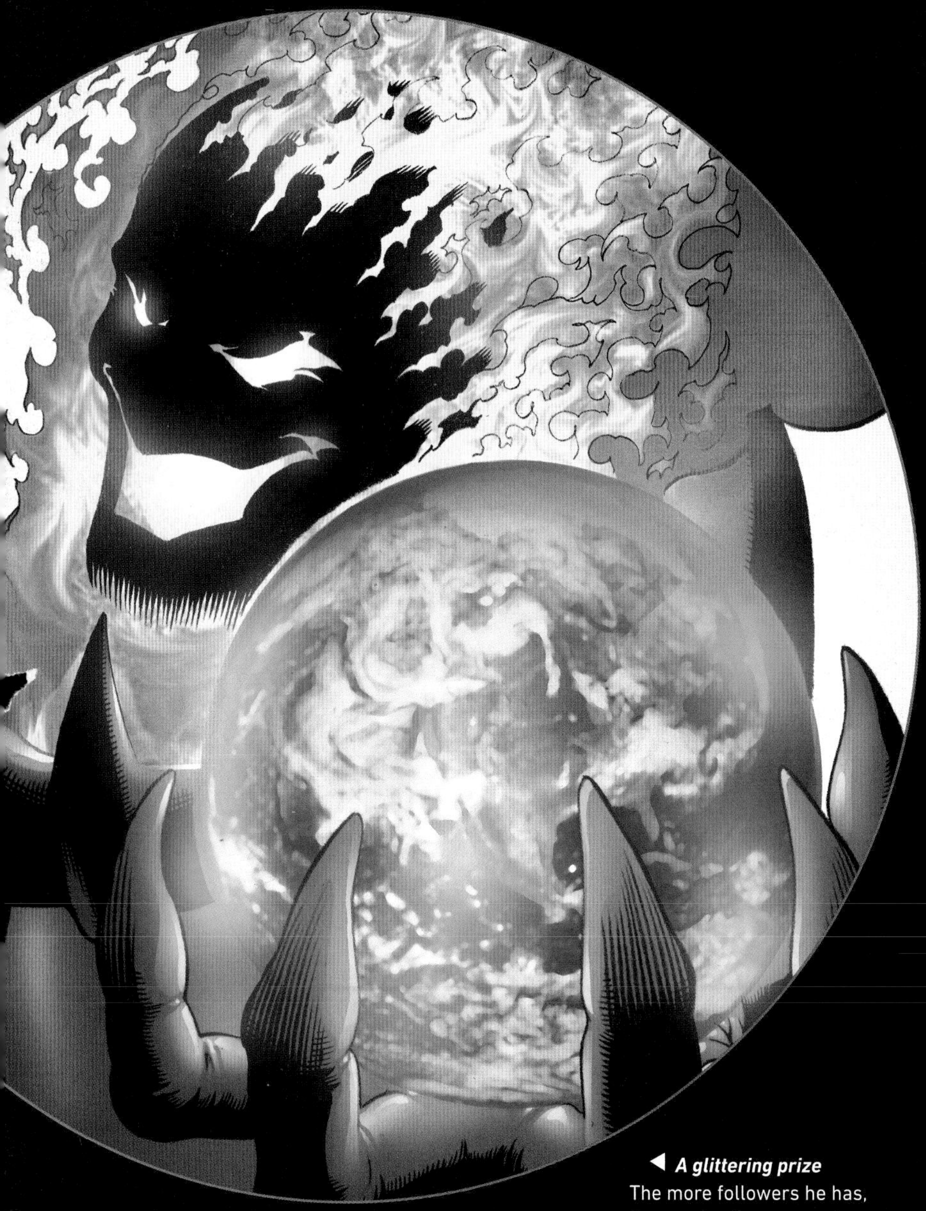

◀ ***A glittering prize***
The more followers he has, the greater Dormammu's power becomes, making Earth a prize to be won.

FIERY FIEND

At some point in the very distant past—at least in the way that humans perceive time—Dormammu and his sister, Umar, were driven from their home dimension, Faltine. The Faltines were a race of beings comprised of pure mystical energy, and the two siblings were found guilty of craving and experimenting with their own physical matter, as well as slaying their father. These acts were considered unacceptable by the Faltines.

After wandering for an unknown length of time, the banished siblings discovered the Dark Dimension. Becoming the advisor to Olnar, king of the Mhuruuks—the magically skilled people of the Dark Dimension—Dormammu cunningly encouraged the king's dreams of conquest. He helped the king overthrow several other dimensions, until they came to the realm of the Mindless Ones. The fugitive Faltines maneuvered Olnar into unleashing these unstoppable beings of destruction, who overwhelmed the Mhuruuk forces, even killing the king. Dormammu and Umar then drove back the Mindless Ones, erecting a mystical barrier to protect the Dark Dimension.

With Umar weakened by the battle, Dormammu claimed the Dark Dimension throne for himself. He reverted to his original energy state and merged with the realm's magical energies to become a flaming being with near-godlike power. He has often sought to subjugate the human world and bring it under his control, which led to early conflict with the Ancient One and his disciple, Doctor Strange.

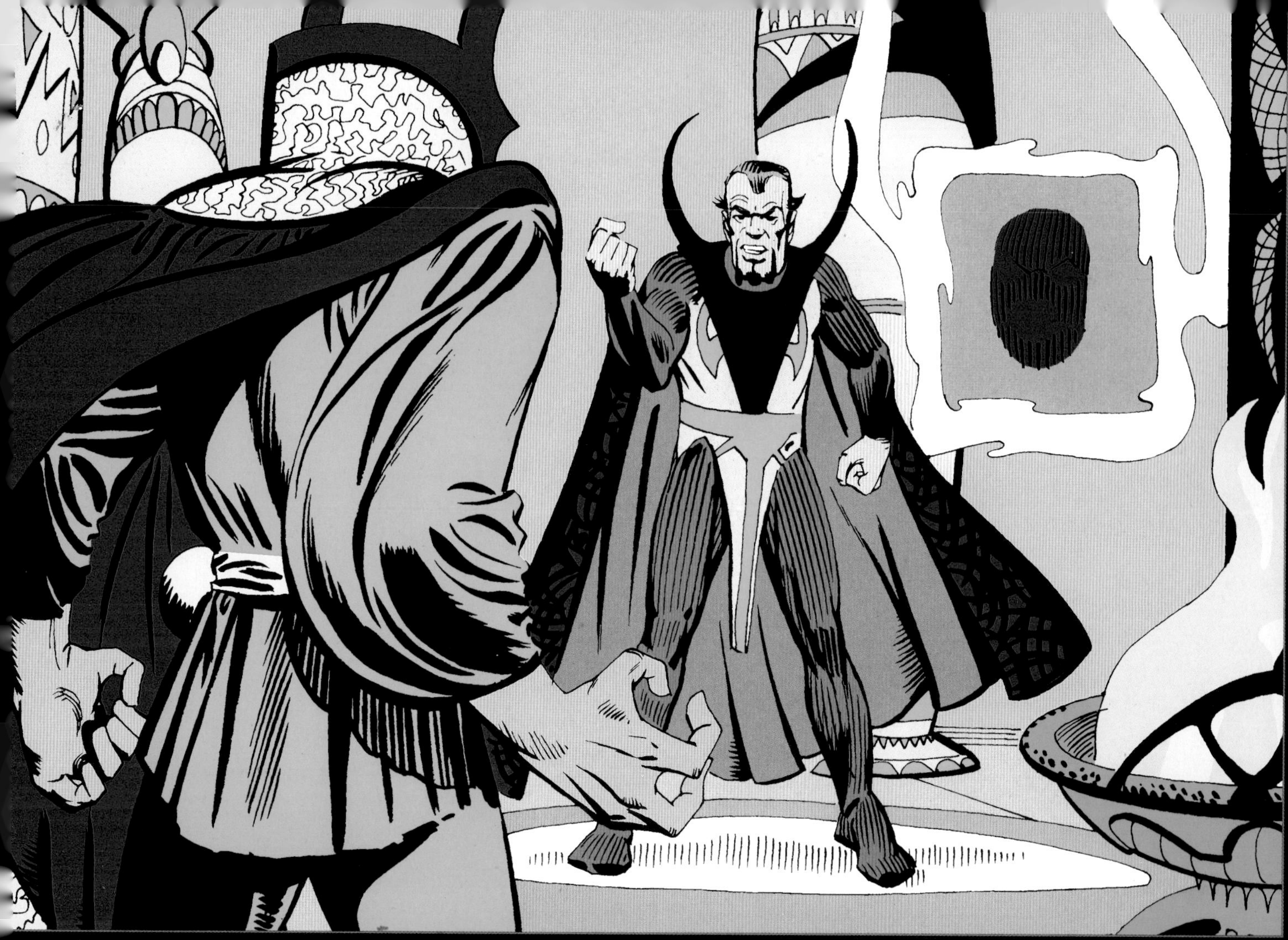

▲ ***Dormammu's dominion*** Because he weakens when away from the Dark Dimension, Dormammu often uses human agents, such as Baron Mordo, to carry out his plans in the Earthly realm.

"MERCY? BAH! THAT IS A WORD FOR HUMANS—NOT THE DREAD DORMAMMU!"

Dormammu

Flames of Faltine

The Flames of Faltine are a mystical form of energy granted by the Faltine race. They power Dormammu, but can also be called upon by master magicians such as

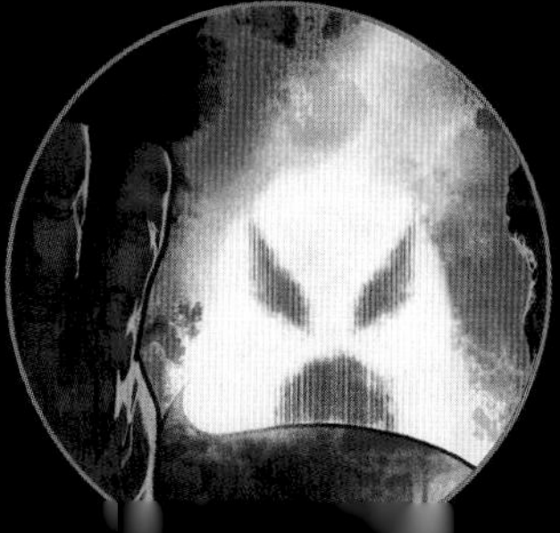

Mindless Ones

Dimwitted but powerful and seemingly endless in number, the Mindless Ones' ability to cause untold destruction and chaos is feared even by

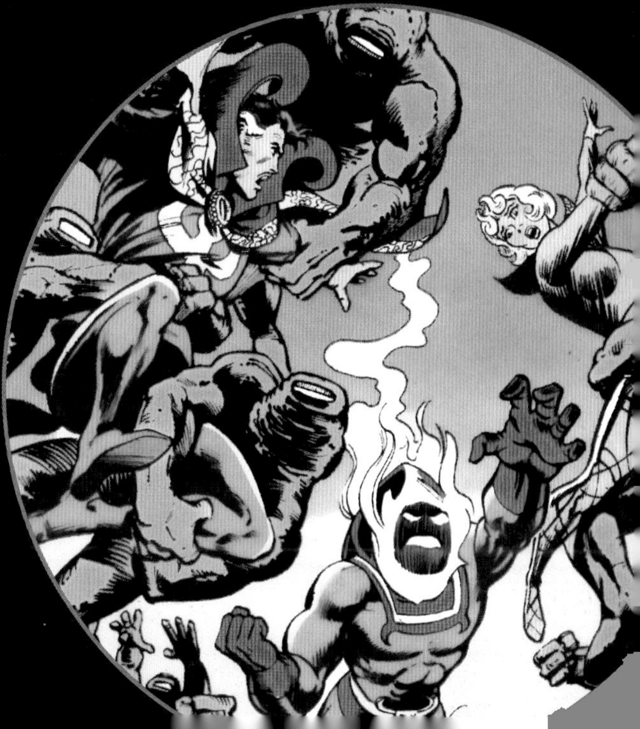

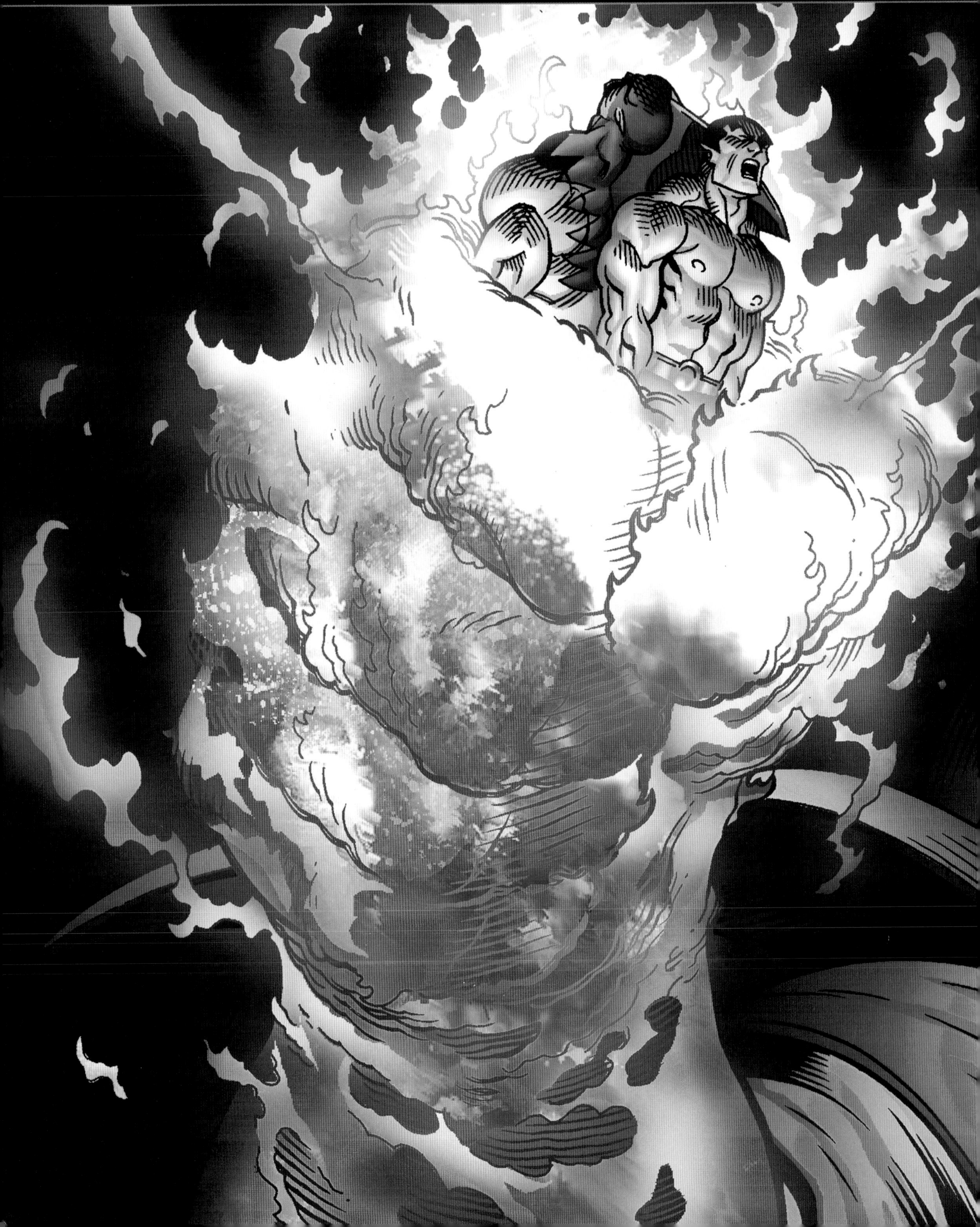

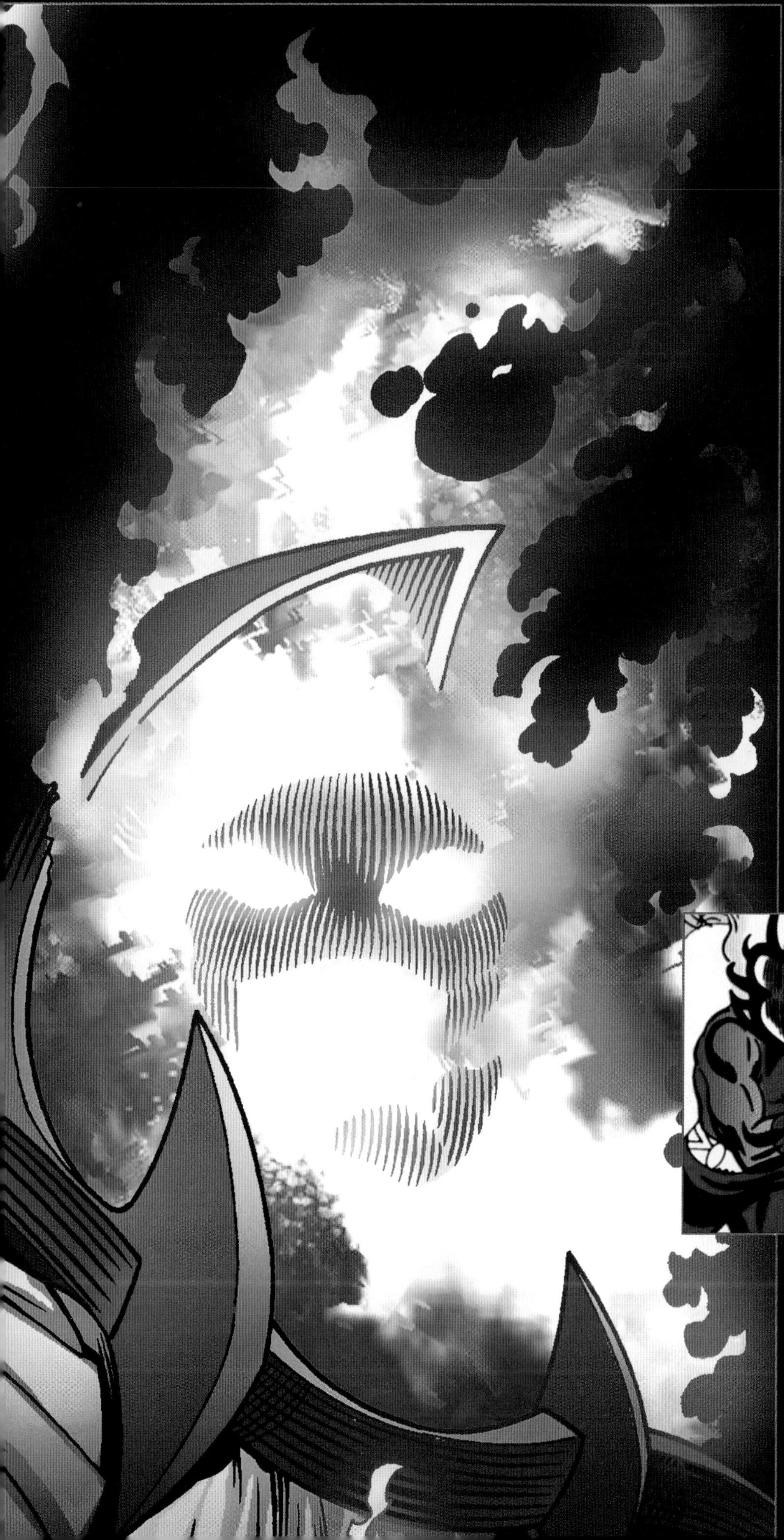

◀ ***Dark designs on Earth*** Dormmamu used all his might on the Sub-Mariner and Tiger Shark in order to make them show him the way to Earth.

THE DREAD ONE DEFEATED

Time and again, Dormammu has set his sights on Earth only to be repelled by its heroes and champions. Despite his incredible power and cunning, he has failed due to his own impatience and arrogance, the quick wit of his opponents, or betrayal by his allies. He has even been bested in straightforward physical combat by Doctor Strange. On one occasion, Dormammu tried to force the Sub-Mariner and the villain Tiger Shark, who had been unwittingly thrown into the Dark Dimension, to show him the way to Earth. They withstood his fiery might and fury, thwarting Dormammu once more.

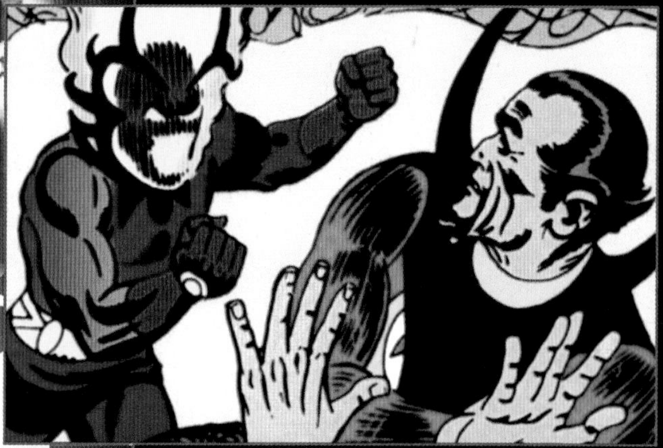

Twisted honor

During a fight with Doctor Strange, Dormammu's sense of honor was offended when his servant, Mordo, struck Strange down from behind. Dormammu both punished Mordo and conceded defeat to his opponent... for a short time.

BARON MORDO

Cunning and iron-willed, Karl Amadeus Mordo
was born with the ability to harness the
mystical energies flowing in his veins.
From an early age he practiced the black
arts under the watchful eyes of his family.
Eventually, Mordo set out in search of greater
knowledge to further his own ends—a path
that led him to becoming Doctor Strange's
bitter enemy and sworn rival.

◀ *Mystic might* Baron Mordo is
one of the few mortals who wields
enough magical might to take on
the Earth's Sorcerer Supreme.

MALEVOLENT MAGICIAN

Baron Mordo possesses skills and knowledge of
the mystical arts and the occult comparable to those
of Doctor Strange. He can cast spells and call upon
ancient entities and other-dimensional beings for a
variety of abilities, including levitation, mind reading,
and mind control. He can open gateways to other
realms, and discharge deadly mystical bolts of energy
at his enemies. Mordo is able to separate his astral
form from his living body, and project it through time,
space, and even into other dimensions. Though he is
intangible in this form, he continues to possess most
of his magical prowess.

However, unlike Doctor Strange, Mordo uses his
abilities only for gain and the accumulation of ever
more power. To amplify his might, he has allied himself
with evil entities such as Dormammu and Satannish.
But despite this additional power, Mordo and his
powerful dark masters have frequently been outwitted
by Doctor Strange and his allies.

Baron Mordo also possesses martial arts skills, as
well as training in other physical disciplines necessary to
master magic. Through a combination of his indomitable
will, mystical knowledge, and physical strength, he has
survived many battles that might have defeated a lesser
man. He has even survived death itself!

Evil Eye
From the beginning, Baron Mordo and Doctor Strange clashed.
Before he became an apprentice, Strange tried to reveal
Mordo's treachery to the Ancient One, but was stopped by the
magician's hypnotic Evil Eye.

Dormammu

Though often uneasy, alliances with Dormammu increase Mordo's powers many times over—yet they are still never enough to defeat Doctor Strange.

Astrid Mordo

Much like her father, Astrid Mordo has an aptitude for the dark arts as well as an insatiable thirst for power. However, unlike him, she is more insane than evil.

"ONCE I HAVE DESTROYED YOU—ALL OF MANKIND SHALL CALL MORDO MASTER!"
Baron Mordo

▲ *Ancient enmity* Baron Mordo has often marshaled dark forces in his attempts to defeat his lifelong enemy, Doctor Strange.

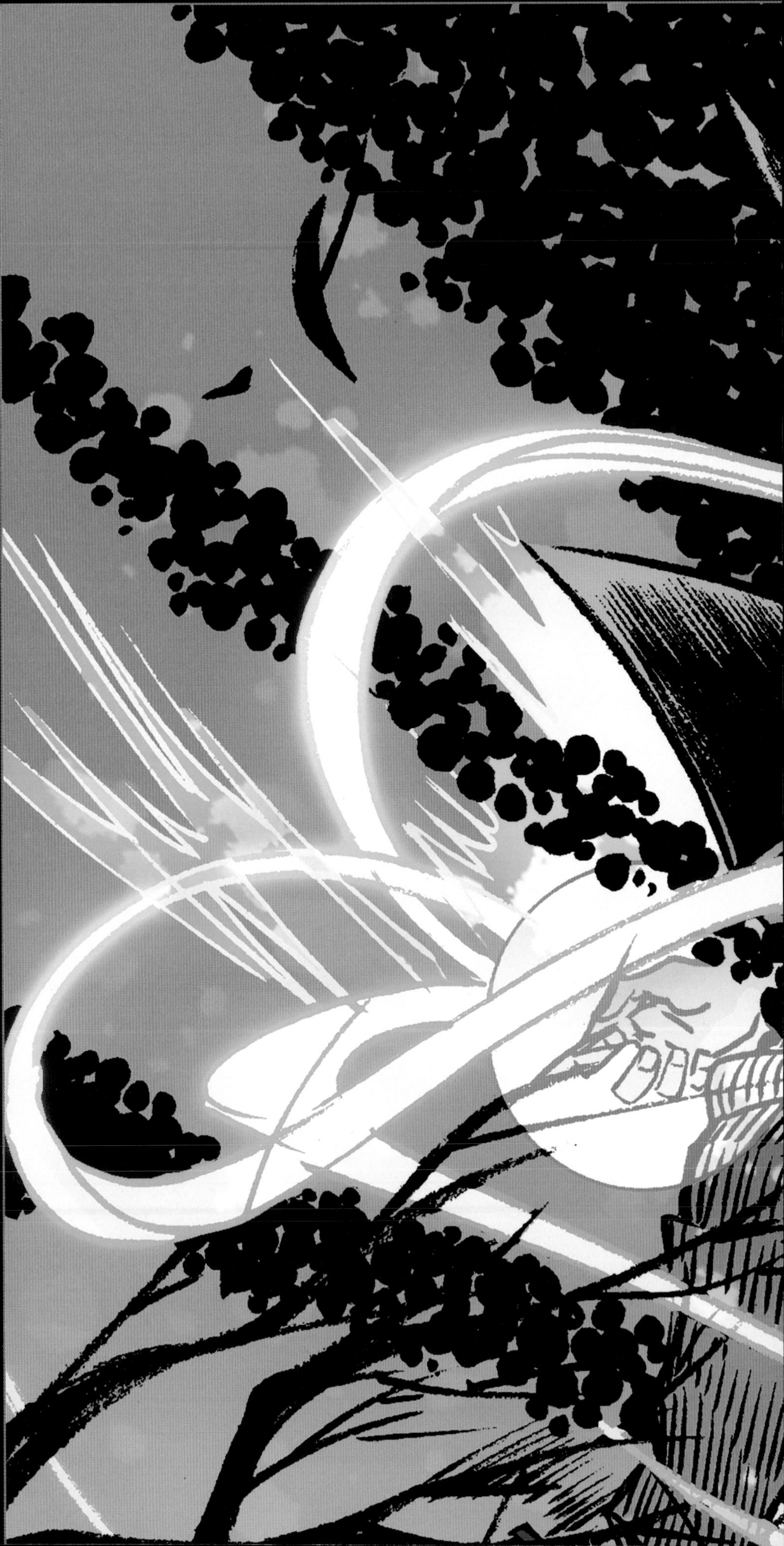

▶ ***Mordo unleashed*** Once Doctor Strange and his friends had obtained the three rings of power, Mordo made his presence known.

QUEST FOR POWER

Whilst still an apprentice to the Ancient One, Doctor Strange embarked on a globetrotting quest to locate three mystical rings of power. Accompanied by Wong—his fellow pupil and soon-to-be firm friend—and museum director Sofia di Cosimo, Strange found the last of the rings at London's British Museum, only to be attacked by Mordo. In the ensuing battle, Mordo tapped into the rings' energy to open a doorway to his master Dormammu's realm. But with Sofia and Wong's help, Strange was able to close the portal and defeat Mordo.

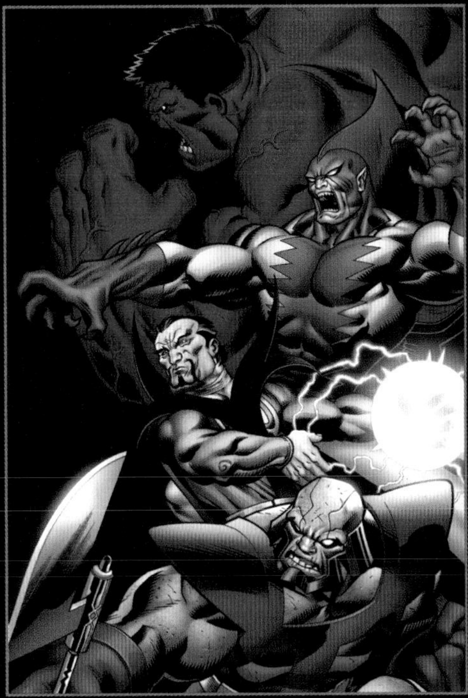

The Offenders
Mordo has sometimes teamed up with other villains, such as Red Hulk and Tiger Shark, in the group known as the Offenders.

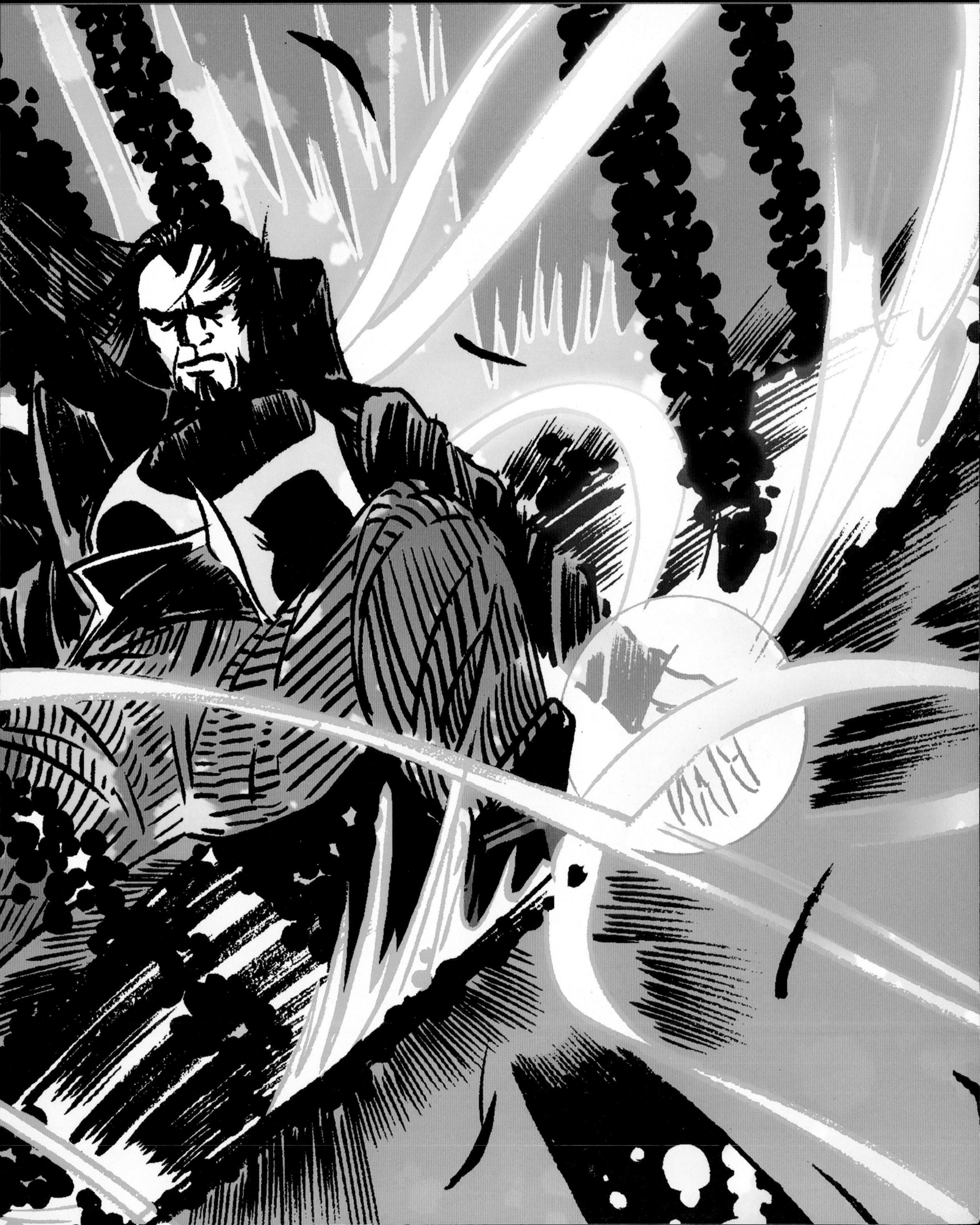

NIGHTMARE

As Lord of the Nightmare Realm, the demon Nightmare gets his power—indeed his very existence—from tormenting sleepers with their deepest fears and darkest secrets. Never content with invading the nighttime world, Nightmare has long sought to extend his influence beyond his dream domain in the hopes of fulfilling his own ambitious and frightening fantasies.

▲ *Mystic prod* Nightmare sometimes uses a mystical staff to channel his power, as well as to control the spinybeasts.

◀ *Dreamstalker*
Nightmare often rides his black steed, Dreamstalker, through the labyrinthine world of dreams.

DEMON DREAMER

Wherever there are dreamers there will be nightmares—and where there are nightmares there is the chalk-white demon Nightmare. No living thing that dreams is completely beyond his influence. Whether it be regular humans, superhumans such as the Hulk, gods like Thor, or even cosmic beings such as Eternity—all are prey for Nightmare. Able to extract psychic energy from the dreaming world, Nightmare controls his realm with absolute authority, and is capable of reshaping it at will to fit his schemes. While he normally draws on the negative psychic energy produced by bad dreams, he sometimes ensnares particular individuals' astral forms for special torments, or to induce nightmares that influence their actions in the waking world.

Like many denizens of the other dark dimensions, Nightmare has sought to increase his power in various ways. He has allied himself with beings such as the ancient Shuma-Gorath, often acting as the tentacled horror's servant in exchange for increased magical abilities. And when the Dweller-in-Darkness brought together a cabal of evil beings called the Fear Lords, Nightmare joined in their plan to heighten the world's fear and horror so that they could all feed off the increased potency of despair and dread.

Though he has always been defeated, Nightmare remains one of Doctor Strange's slyest and most dangerous foes, thanks to his ability to manipulate the living world quietly from the shadows.

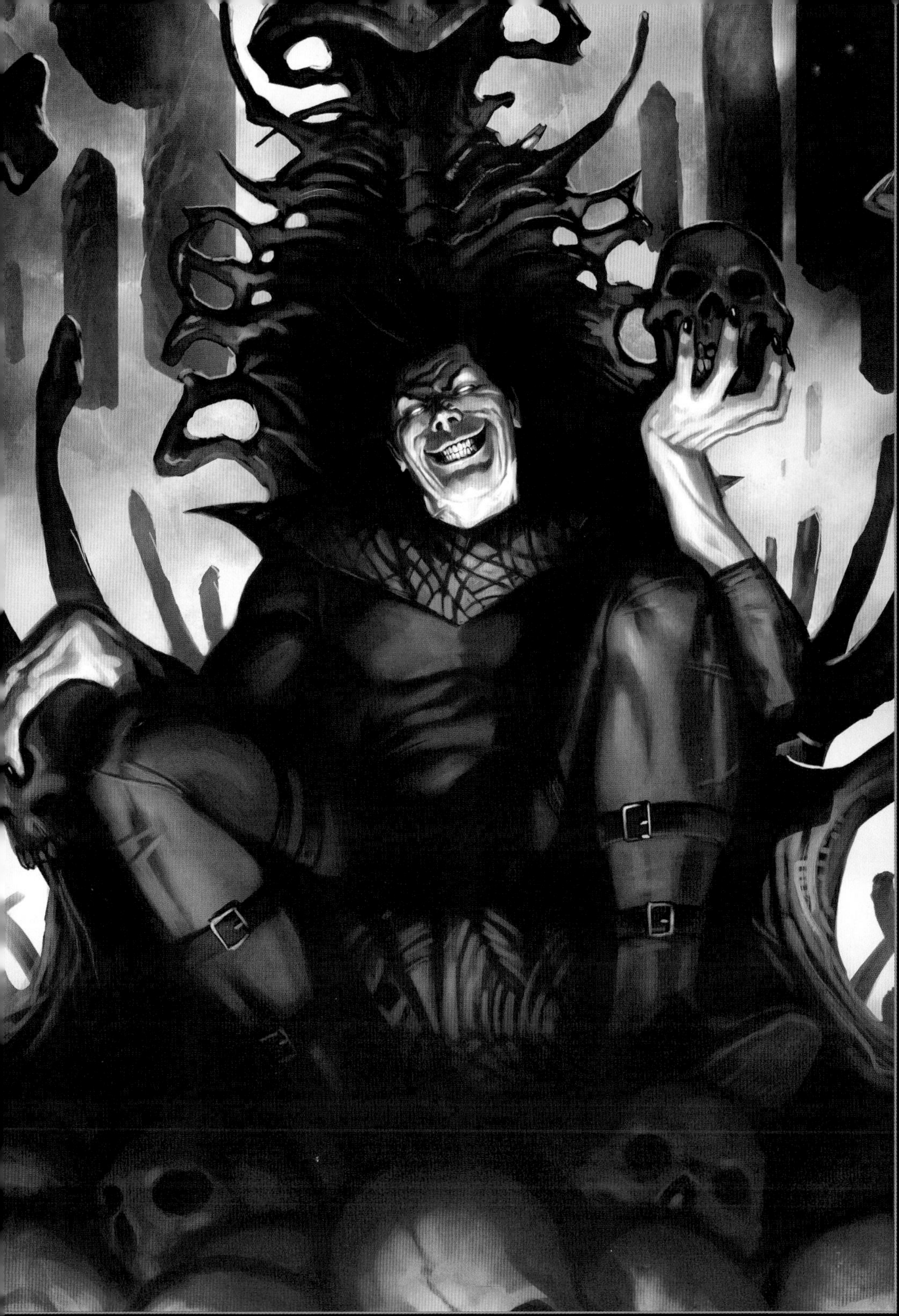

▲ ***Nightmare's realm*** Nightmare is the absolute ruler of the Dream Dimension.

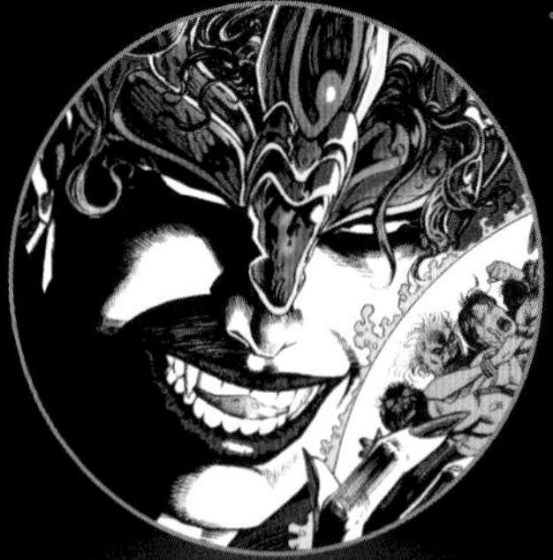

Dreamqueen
The ruler of Liveworld, Nightmare's daughter, Dreamqueen, is a succubus capable of altering perception and casting powerful illusions.

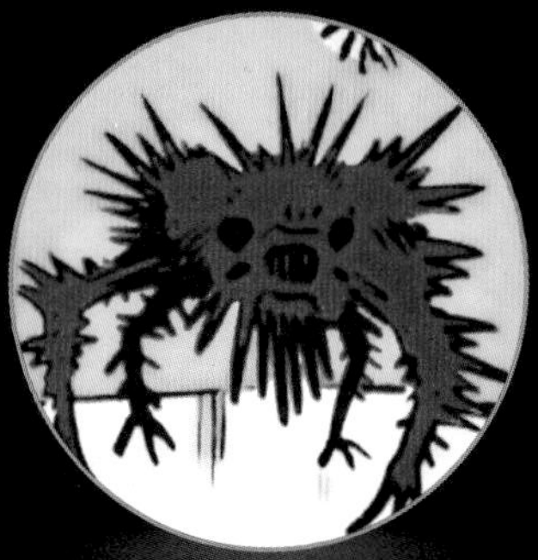

Spinybeast
Employed by Nightmare, the spinybeasts are four-legged creatures covered in sharp spines that are deadly to the touch.

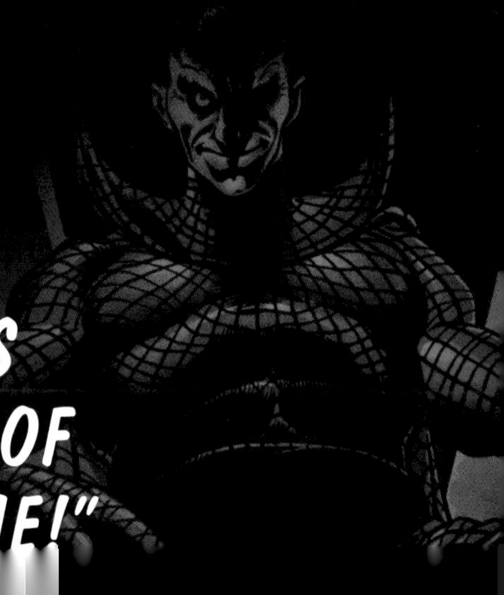

"IN THE SHADOWS UNDER EVERY CHILD'S BED...IN THE SUBCONSCIOUS RECESSES OF EVERY HUMAN HEAD... YOU WILL FIND ME!"

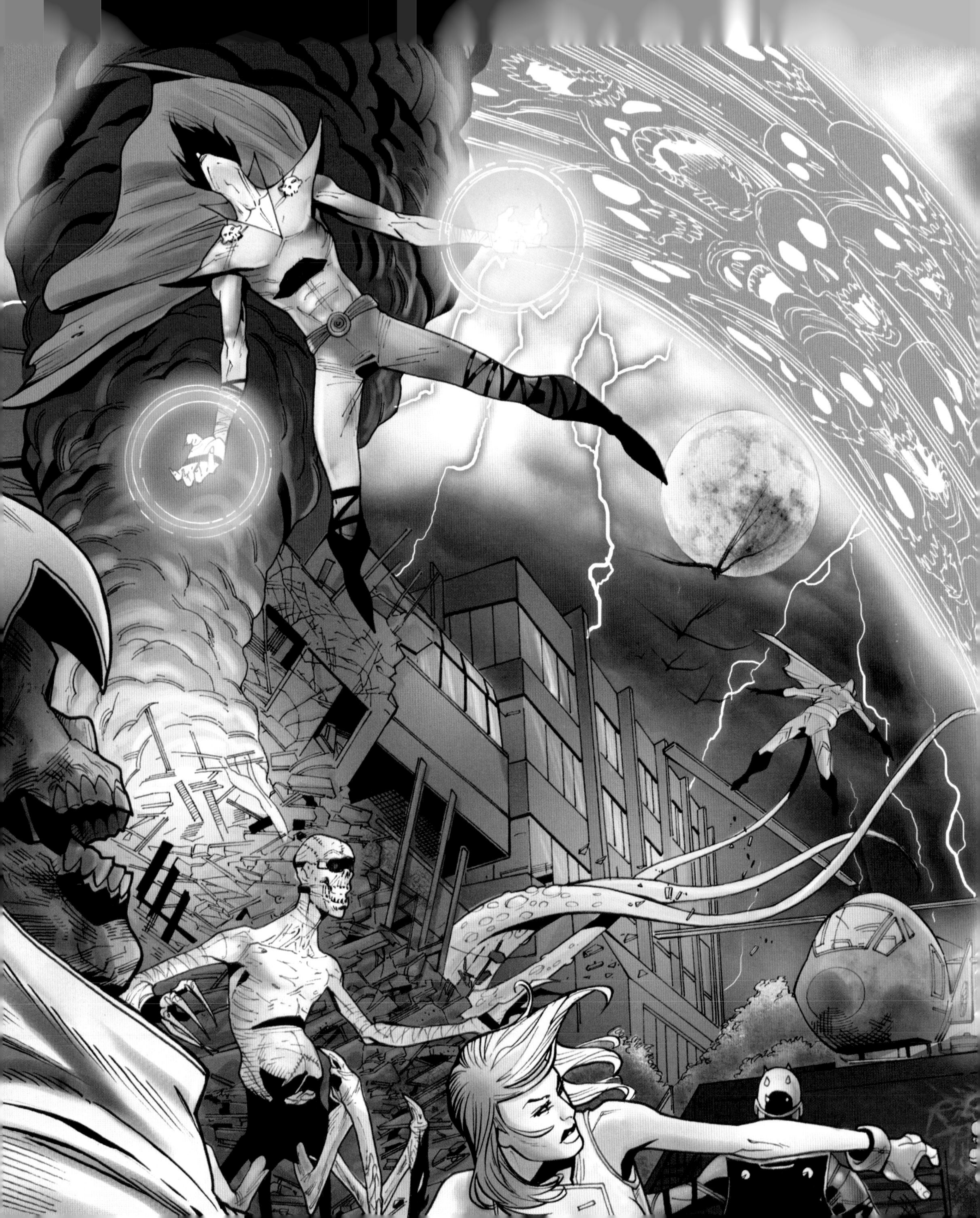

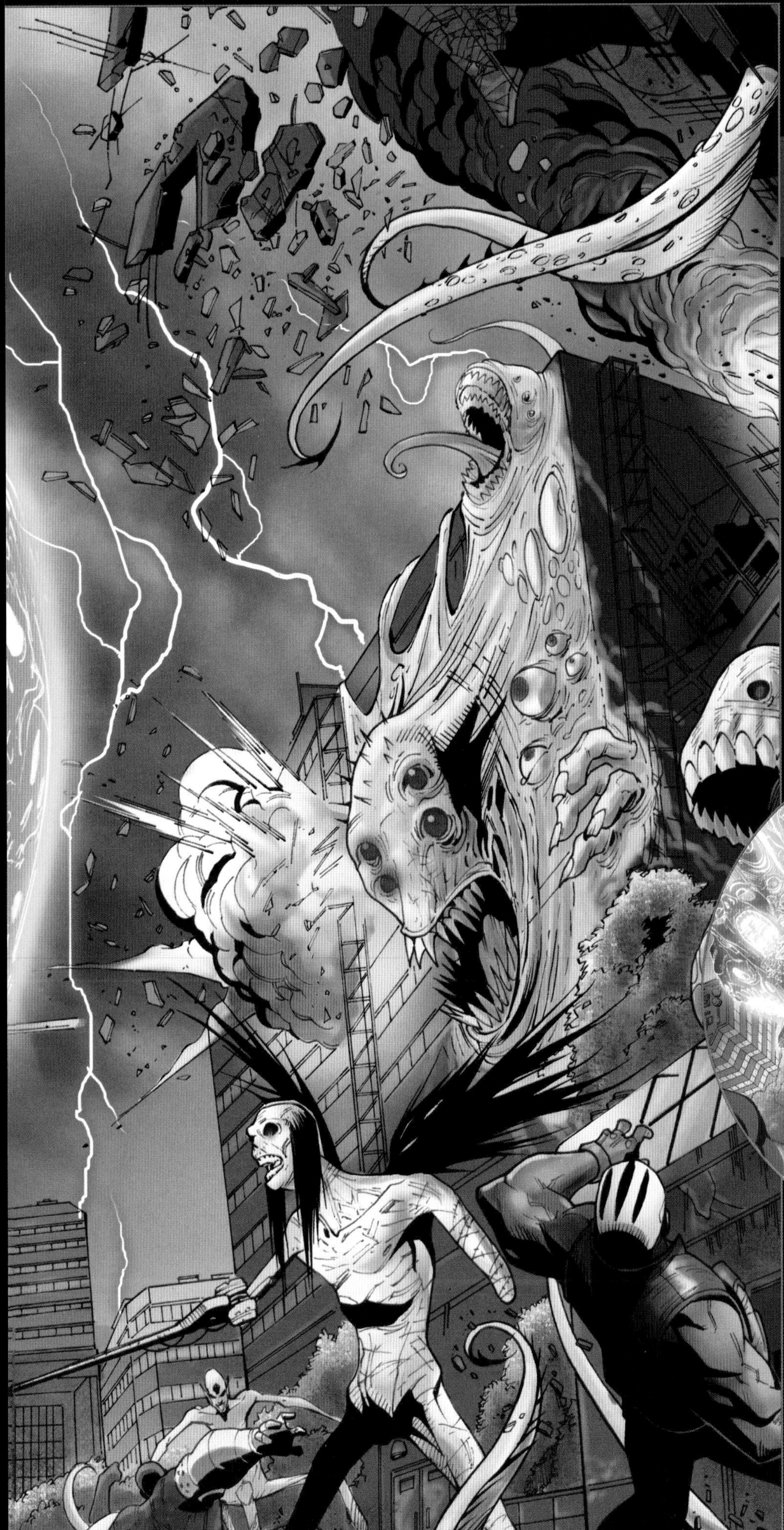

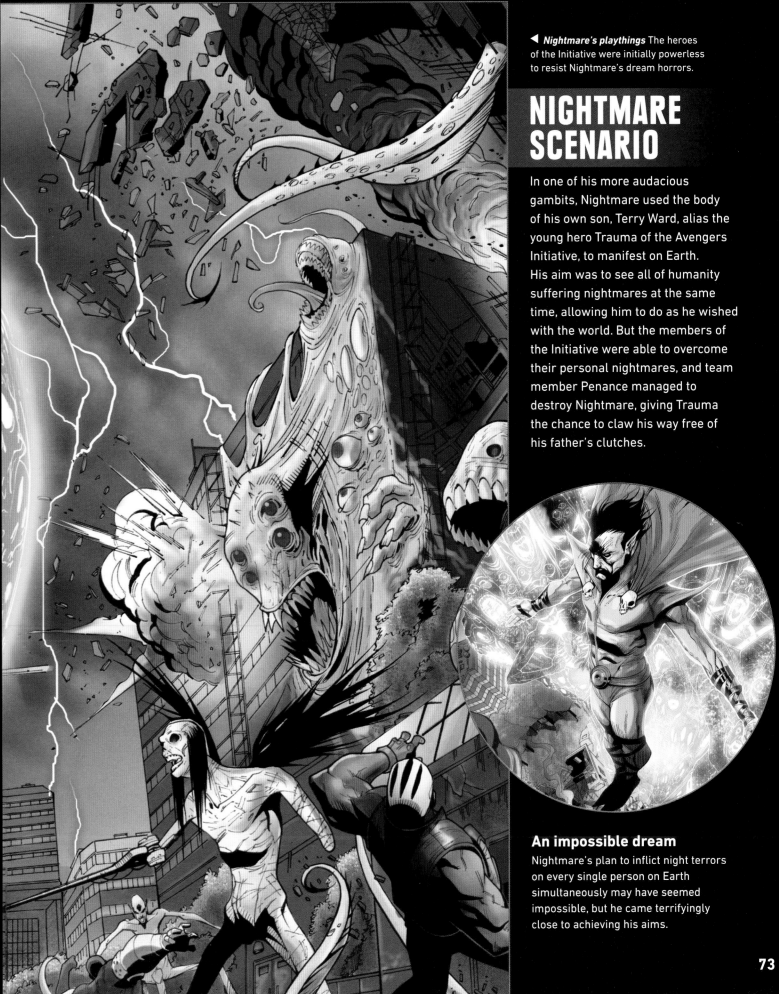

◀ ***Nightmare's playthings*** The heroes of the Initiative were initially powerless to resist Nightmare's dream horrors.

NIGHTMARE SCENARIO

In one of his more audacious gambits, Nightmare used the body of his own son, Terry Ward, alias the young hero Trauma of the Avengers Initiative, to manifest on Earth. His aim was to see all of humanity suffering nightmares at the same time, allowing him to do as he wished with the world. But the members of the Initiative were able to overcome their personal nightmares, and team member Penance managed to destroy Nightmare, giving Trauma the chance to claw his way free of his father's clutches.

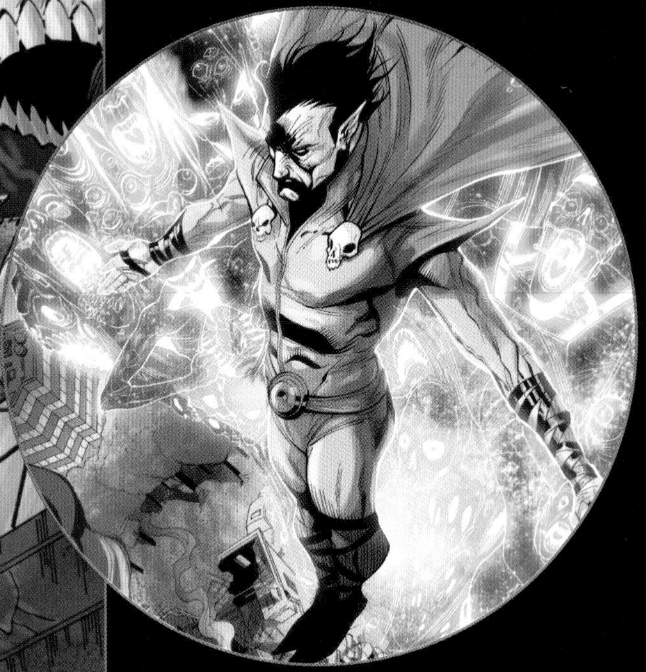

An impossible dream
Nightmare's plan to inflict night terrors on every single person on Earth simultaneously may have seemed impossible, but he came terrifyingly close to achieving his aims.

MEPHISTO

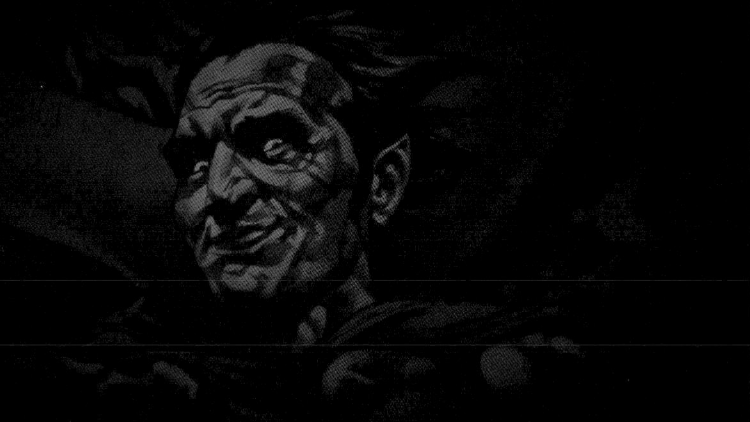

More devious by far than other demonic beings—of which there are many—Mephisto is the most like the singular entity that the general population of Earth thinks of as "the Devil." The fact that he often seeks to buy or bargain for mortal souls to torment in his fiery realm strongly supports this view.

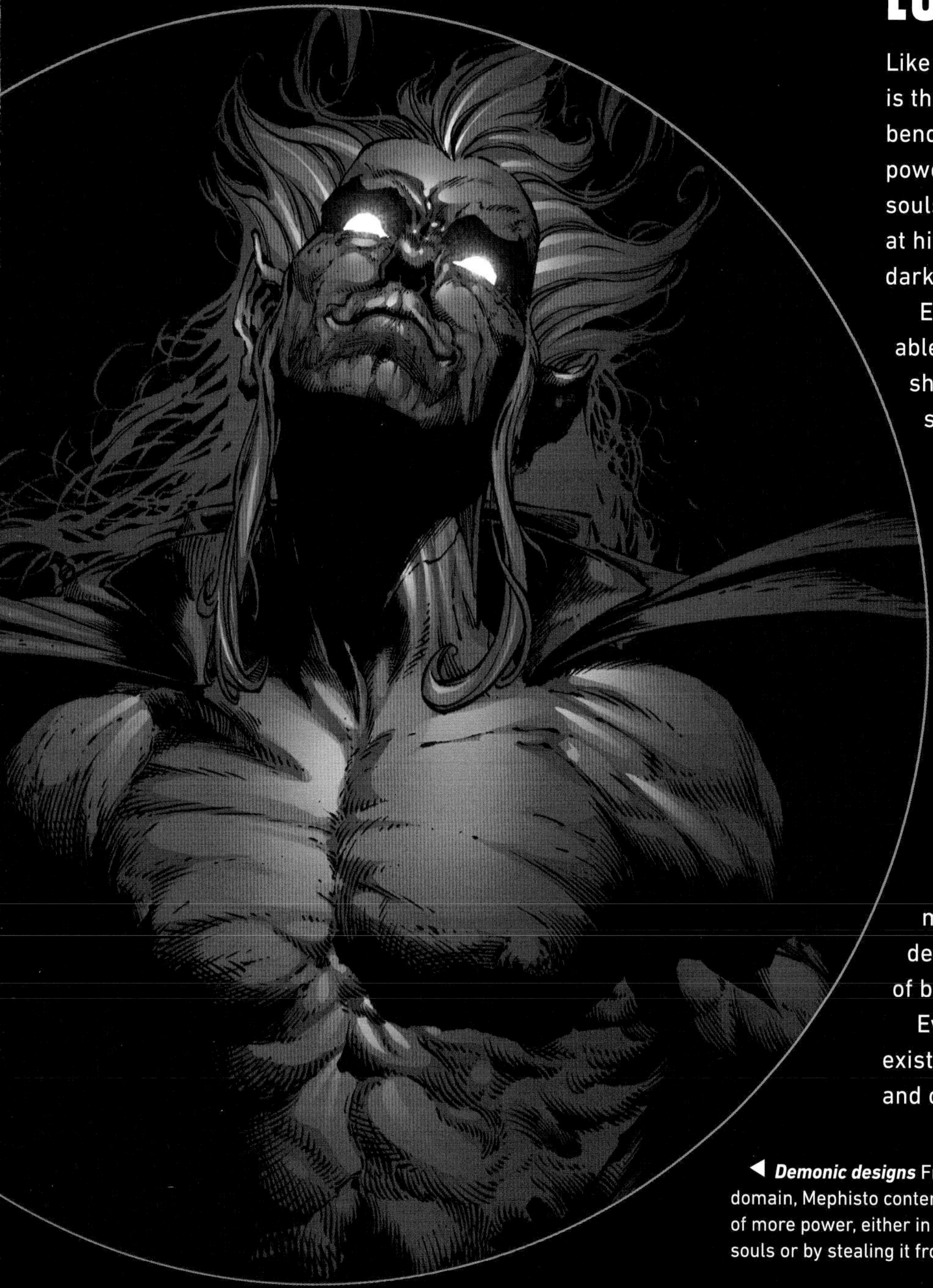

LOATHSOME LORD OF LIES

Like the other demons known as Hell-Lords, Mephisto is the sovereign of his own region of Hell. He is able to bend the very fabric of its reality to his will, but his powers have their limitations. He is dependent on the souls trapped in his domain of eternal suffering to be at his full power, and he can weaken if away from his dark home world for too long.

Even so, Mephisto is a formidable adversary. He is able to travel between dimensions, change his size, shape, and appearance, enhance his physical strength well beyond that of Earth's mightiest heroes, and use mystical energy offensively and defensively. He is also a shrewd liar and manipulator as well as a master of deception. It is entirely possible that many of Mephisto's most terrible feats are actually illusions that trick his opponents into thinking he is more powerful than he actually is.

Mephisto has had numerous conflicts with Earth's heroes, as well as with cosmic entities such as Galactus. For years, Mephisto was consumed with a burning desire to capture the noble soul of Galactus's herald, the Silver Surfer to boost his demonic power. However, despite his many machinations, he has seemingly been defeated in every encounter, sometimes to the point of being utterly destroyed.

Even so, as Doctor Strange knows, so long as evil exists, Mephisto will always be able to reform himself, and can never truly be beaten.

◀ ***Demonic designs*** From his hellish domain, Mephisto contemplates the acquisition of more power, either in the form of human souls or by stealing it from his fellow demons.

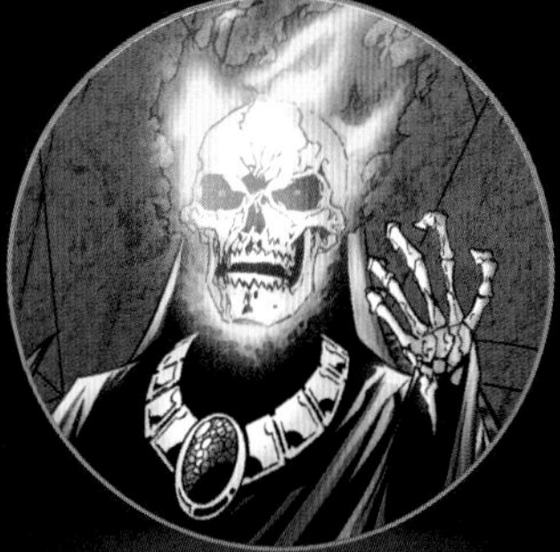

Zarathos

Zarathos was a powerful demon and rival of Mephisto. After Mephisto defeated him, he forced the demon to serve him for many centuries. He bound Zarathos to mortal beings, creating such entities as Ghost Rider.

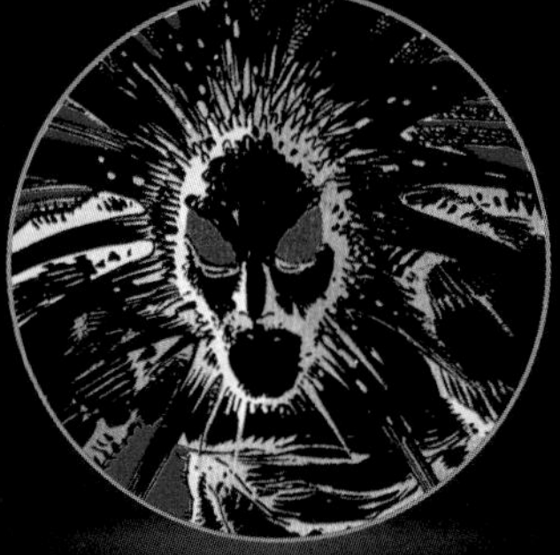

Blackheart

While the exact demonic parentage of Daimon Hellstrom may be debatable, the rebellious and evil Blackheart is truly the son of Mephisto.

"MY DOMINION OVER THE EARTH GROWS GREATER EACH DAY!"
Mephisto

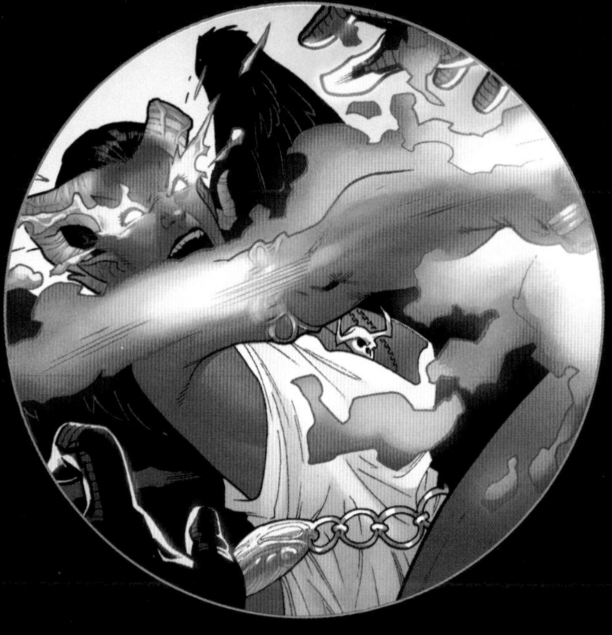

The devil's daughter

Mephisto also has a daughter, Mephista, who first came to the attention of Doctor Strange when she was sent to retrieve the soul of Baron Mordo.

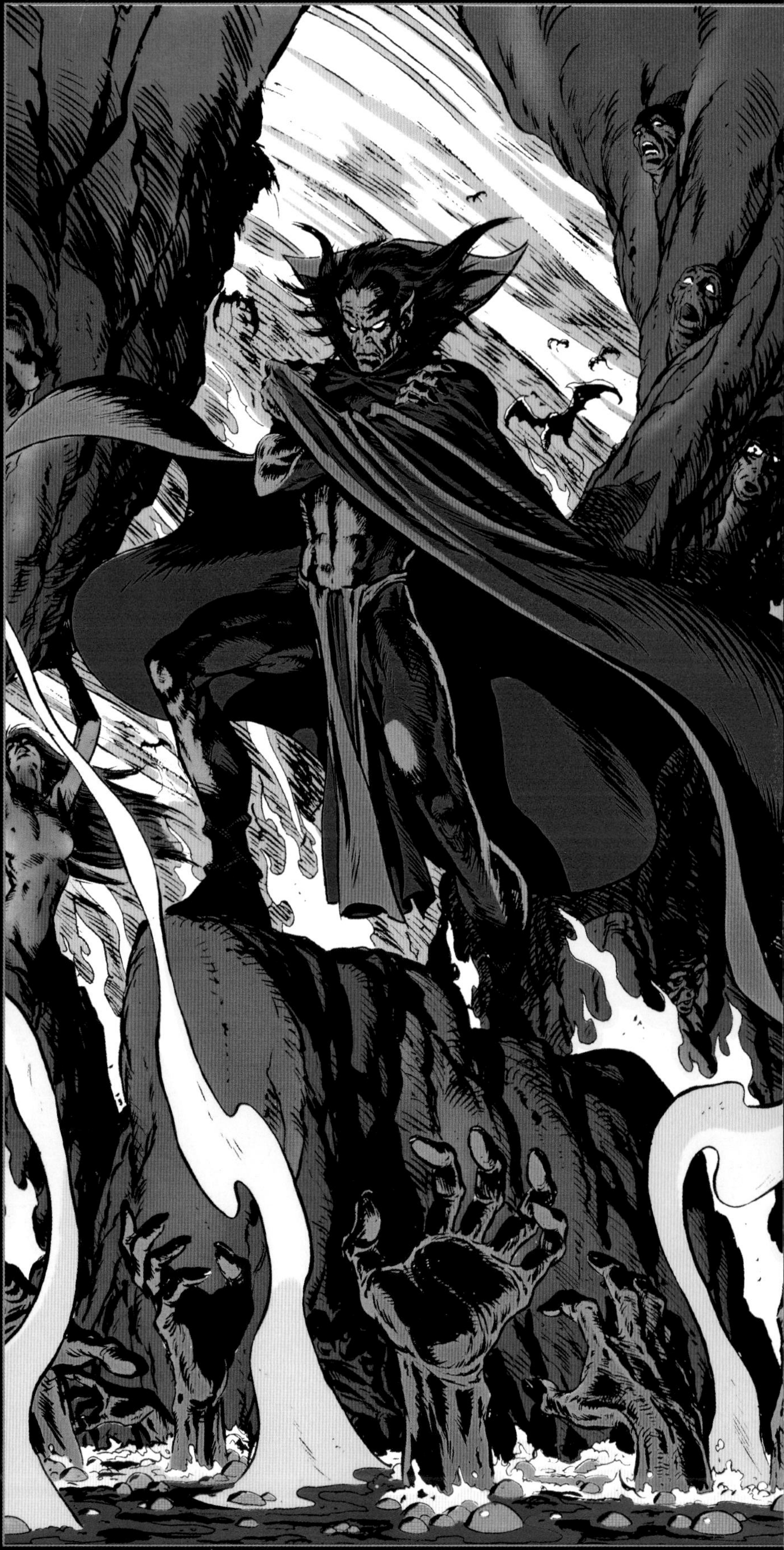

▲ ***To the devil his due*** Dependent on trapped souls in his dimension and worshippers on Earth as a source of power, Mephisto is forever eager to welcome willing new mortals into his clutches.

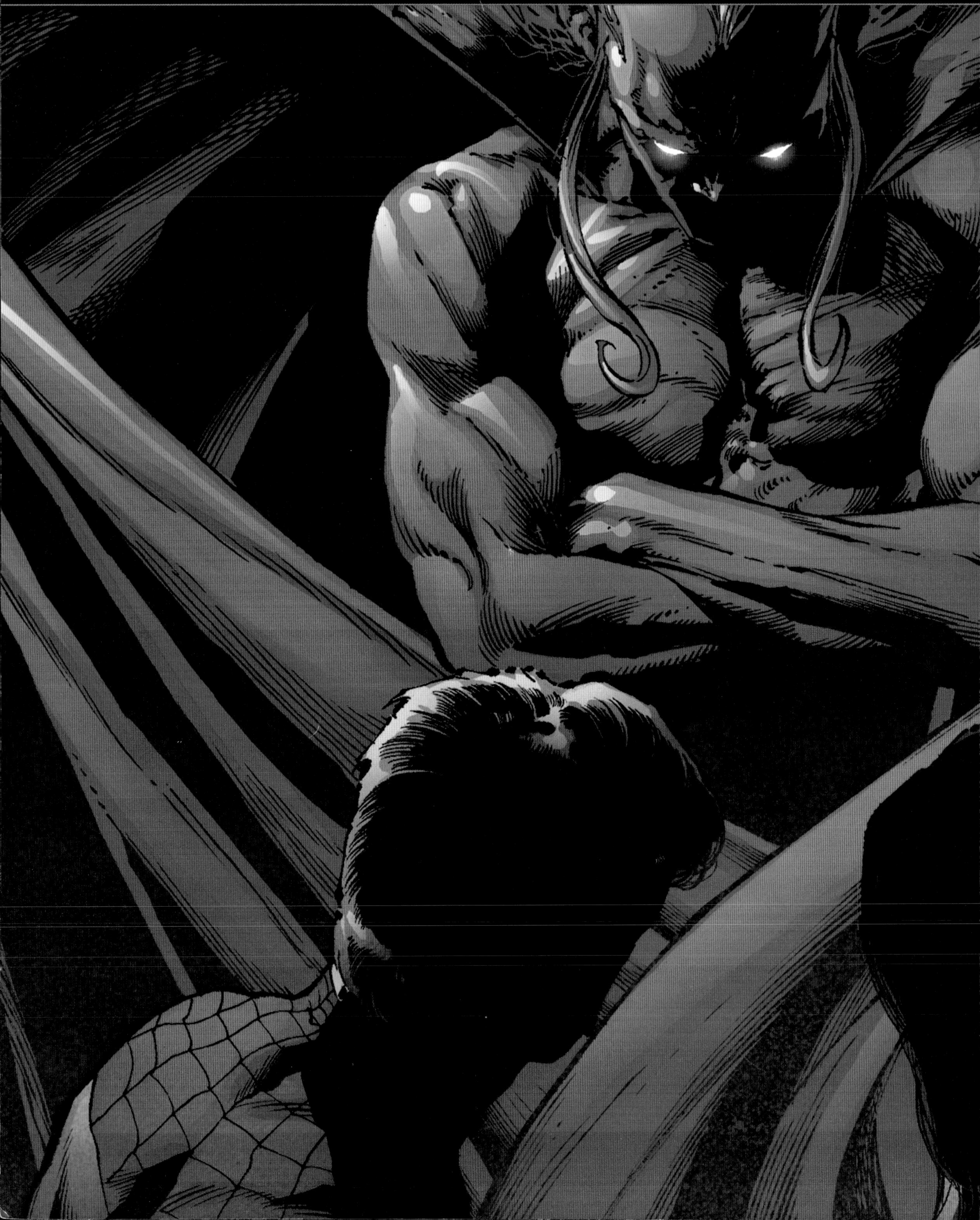

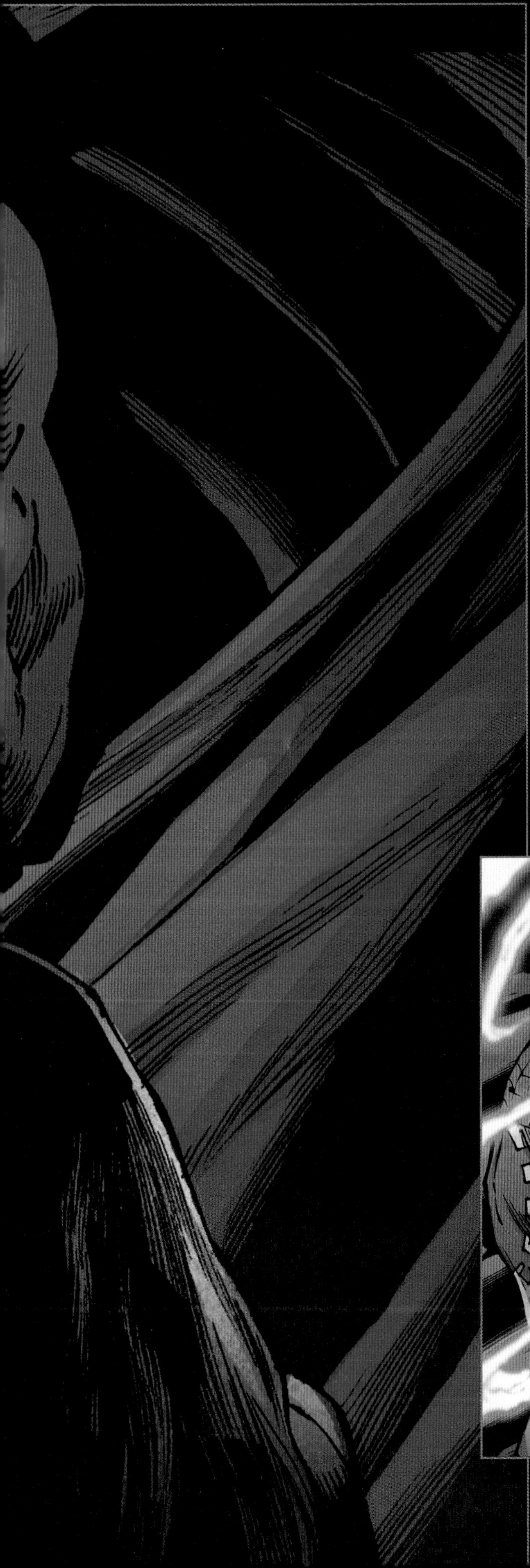

◀ ***Mephisto triumphant***
The bargain that Peter Parker struck with Mephisto cost Peter his marriage and his happiness... and a part of his soul.

DEAL WITH THE DEVIL

Desperate to save the life of his Aunt May, who had been shot when his double life as Spider-Man had been exposed, Peter Parker sought Doctor Strange's help. When Strange advised him to let his aunt go, Peter turned instead to Mephisto. The demon demanded a high price for May's survival—Peter's happiness, in the shape of his marriage to Mary Jane Watson. Both Peter and Mary Jane agreed to the terms, forever altering their lives, and for once Mephisto got precisely what he wanted: the malicious pleasure of being able to listen to a sliver of Peter's soul screaming for all eternity.

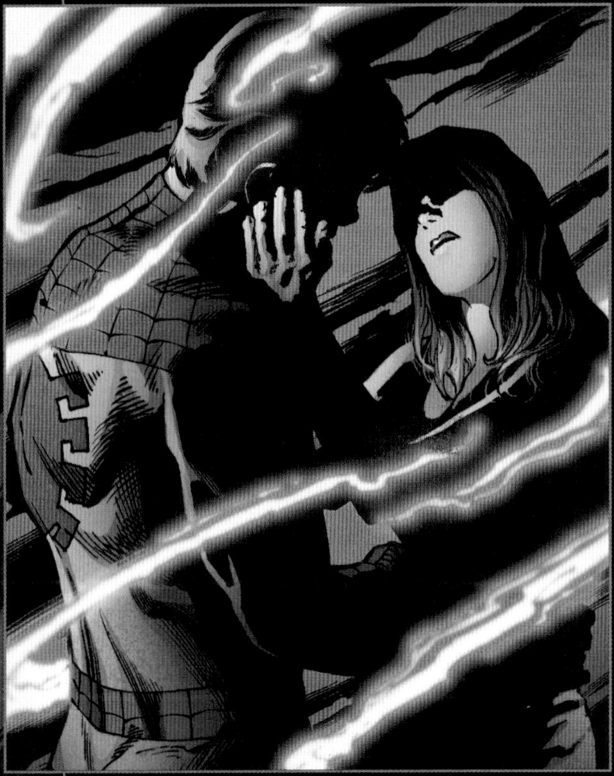

Faustian pact
While humans often sign away their souls to beings like Mephisto in exchange for wealth, power, or immortality, Peter Parker's goal was far more noble.

IN THE SERVICE OF EVIL

Doctor Strange's enemies come in many forms and from many dimensions. Some are humans who started out with the best of intentions, but found themselves on dark paths. Others chose the road to ruin and damnation from the outset. Others still were things born on distant worlds. As Sorcerer Supreme, Strange must keep ever vigilant against his many foes—old and new—and stop the forces of evil from taking over the world.

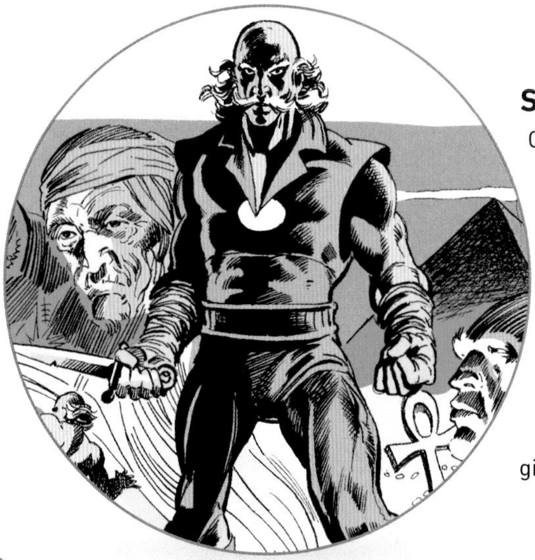

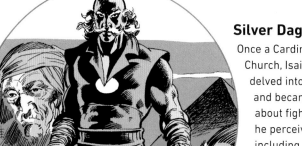

Silver Dagger

Once a Cardinal for the Church, Isaiah Curwen delved into the dark arts and became fanatical about fighting everything he perceived to be evil, including Doctor Strange and his allies. He strikes with the holy water-dipped silver daggers that give him his name.

Dweller-in-Darkness

The Dweller-in-Darkness is an ancient demonic entity that feeds on the fear of sentient beings. He is an old foe of the mystic being Agamotto, and by association, the Sorcerer Supreme.

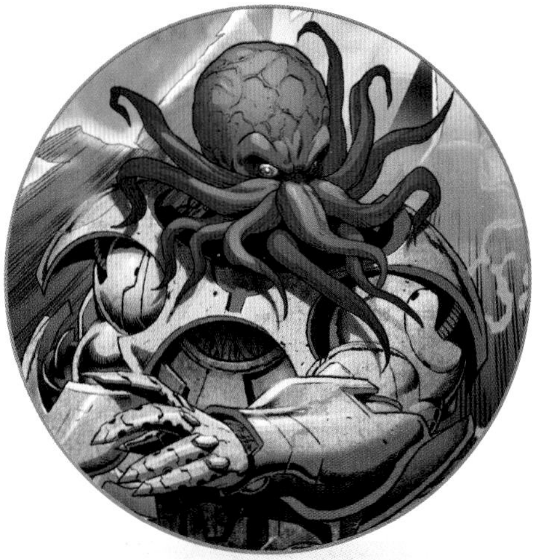

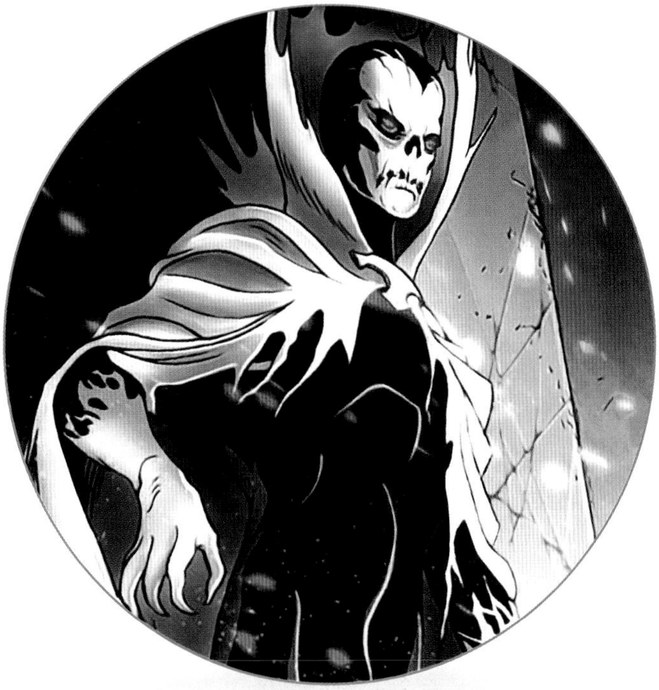

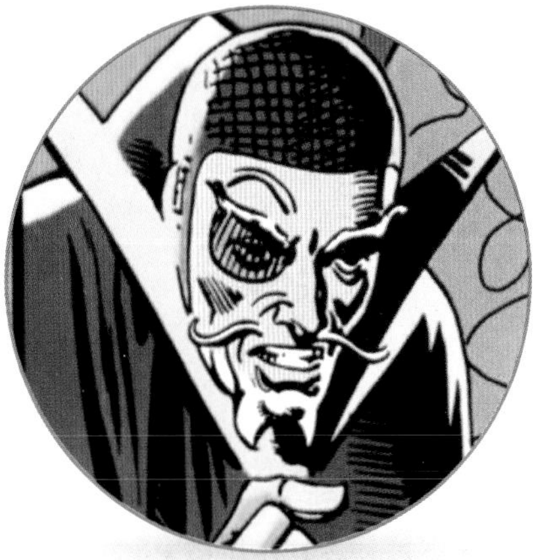

Xandu

Xandu is a talented sorcerer who became mentally unhinged. He has spent much of his misguided career trying to revive the woman he accidentally put into a deathlike trance.

D'Spayre

Created by the Dweller-in-Darkness to be his agent on Earth, D'Spayre preys on human fear and helplessness. He came close to defeating Doctor Strange, until the Sorcerer Supreme saw through D'Spayre's elaborate deception.

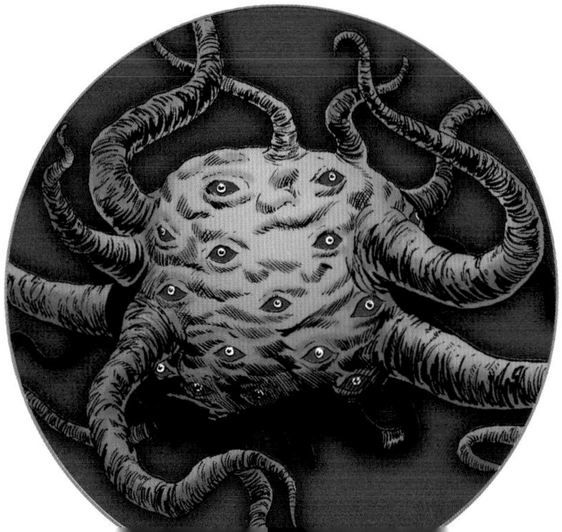

Null the Living Darkness

An enemy of Doctor Strange and the Defenders, Null the Living Darkness was a demon formed from the negative aspects and emotions of the S'Raphh, a race of angel-like beings.

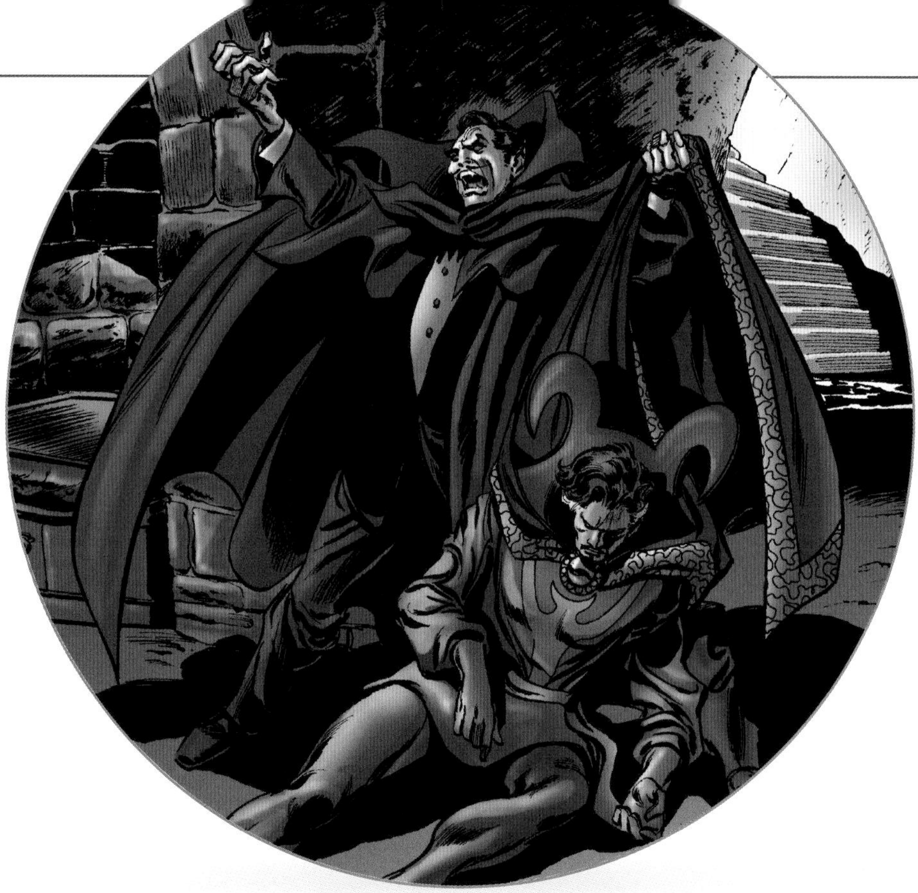

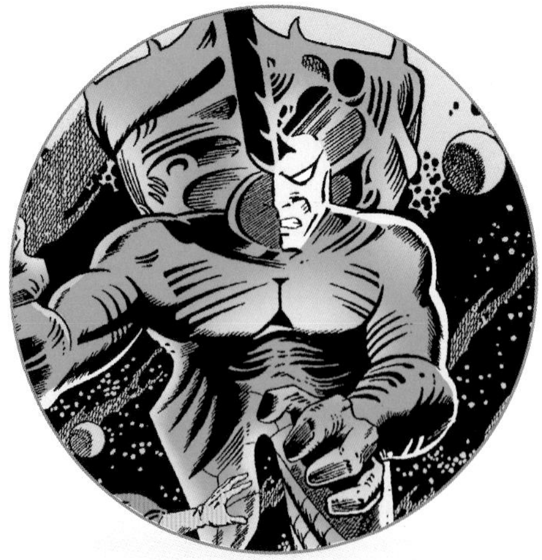

Nebulos

Nebulos was a sinister extradimensional entity who became too powerful, and was opposed by the Living Tribunal. Doctor Strange helped the Tribunal defeat Nebulos.

Dracula

The Lord of the Vampires, Dracula feasted on humanity for hundreds of years. He and the other vampires were destroyed—at least temporarily—when Doctor Strange used the Montesi Formula, a spell found in the magical tome the Darkhold, to banish them from Earth.

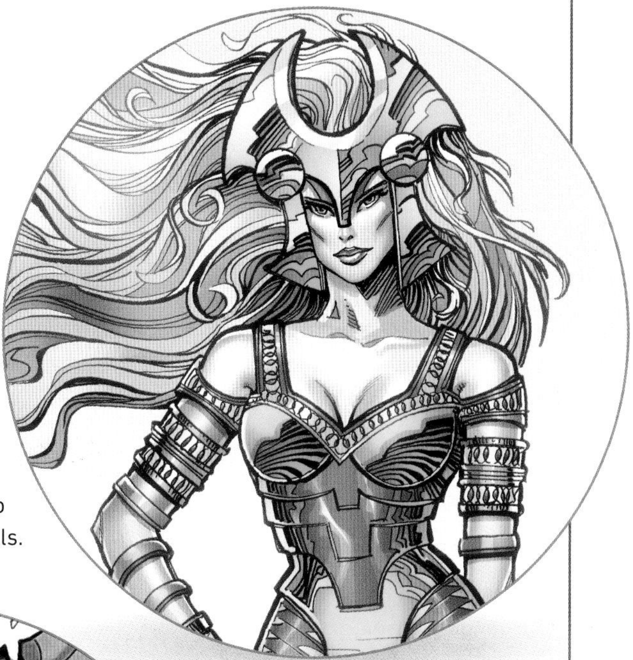

Enchantress

The Enchantress is a powerful Asgardian sorceress who is incredibly accomplished at manipulating emotions. She is able to break the strongest of wills.

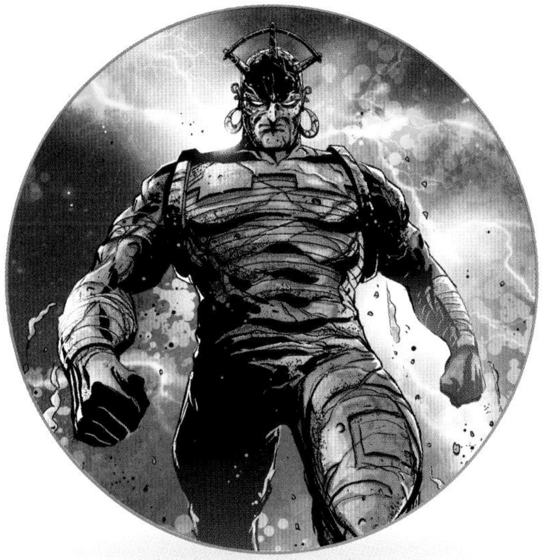

Tiboro

Once a Peruvian wizard, Tiboro became a godlike wizard after being banished to his own realm, the Sixth Dimension.

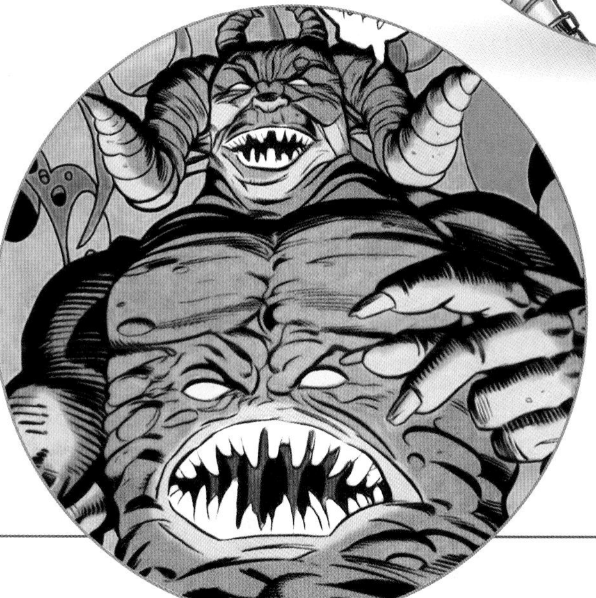

Satannish

Satannish is a demonic being whose power rivals most of the other Hell-Lords. He usually prefers to operate through human agents who have sold him their souls.

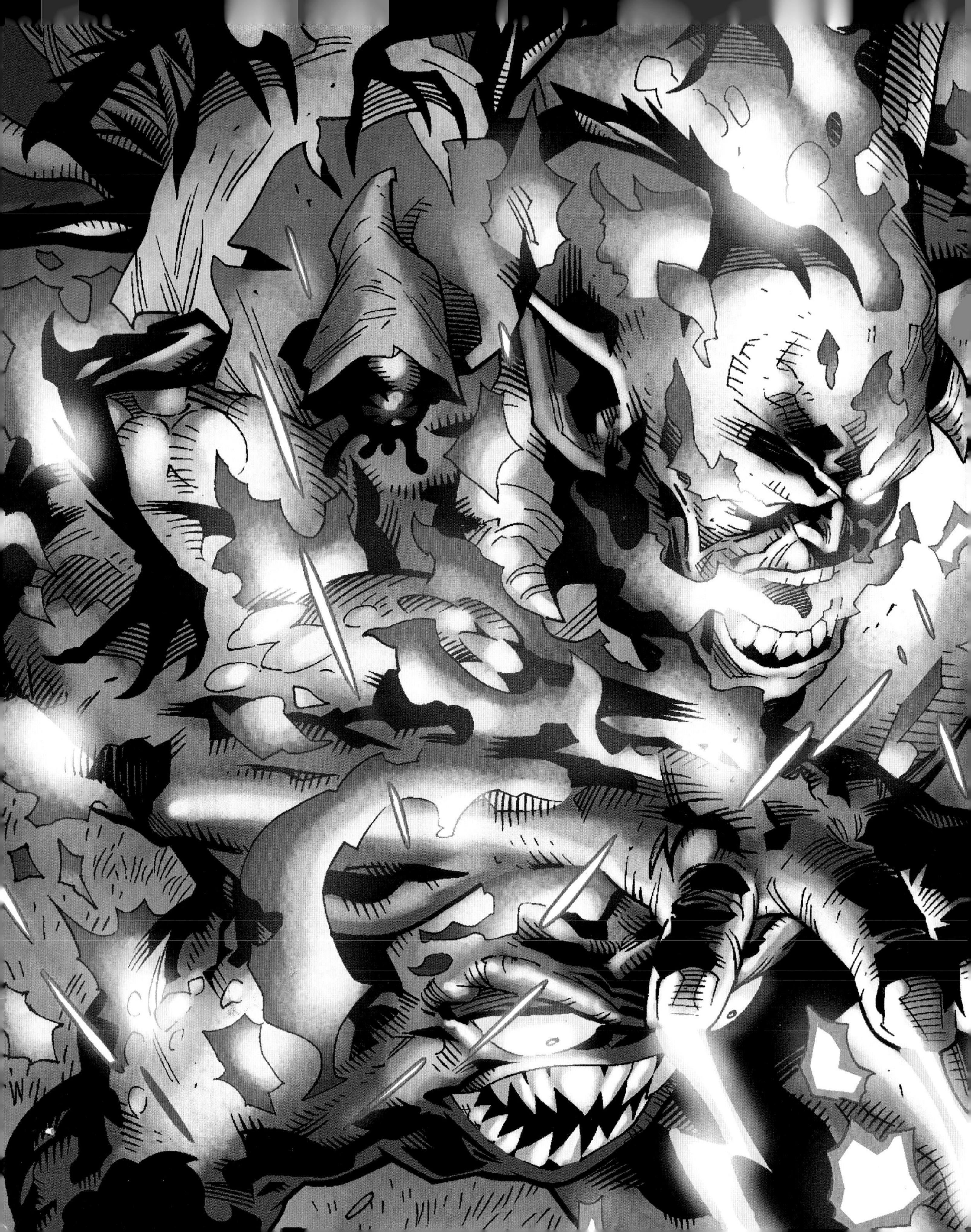

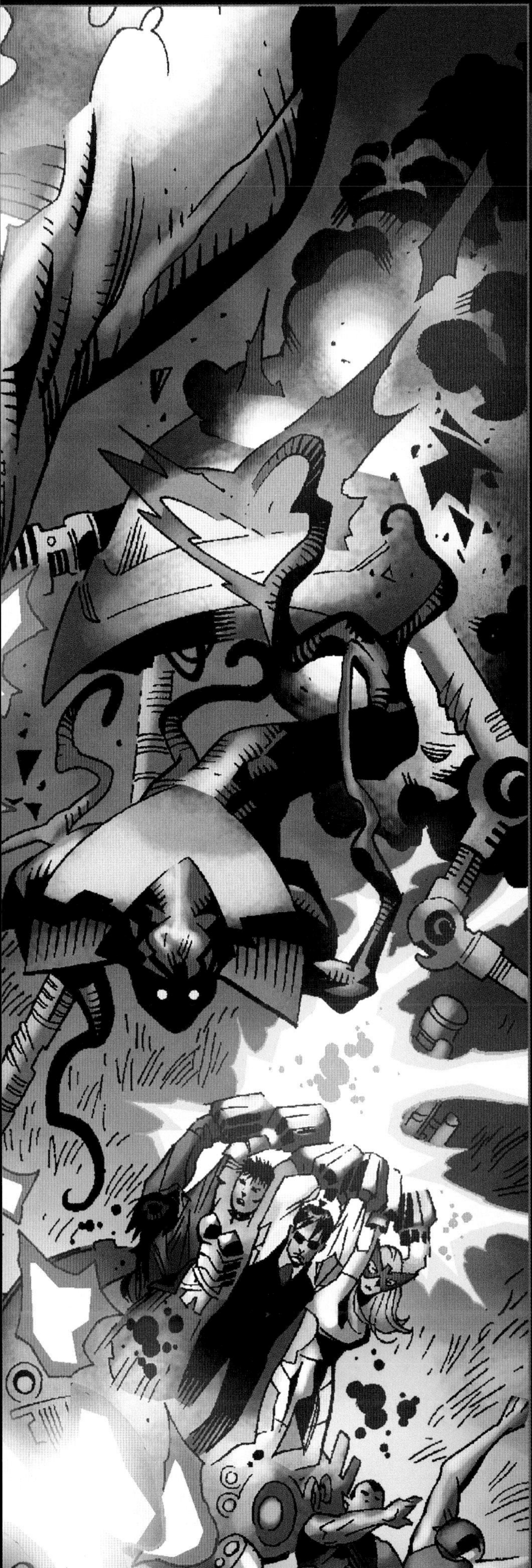

SATANNISH

Satannish is a monstrous, fiery Hell-Lord with power second only to Mephisto's. Coveting the souls that inhabit the Earthly domain, Satannish forever schemes to rule humanity. Yet, sometimes, his evil intent has worked in favor of this world. When the alien Skrull race tried to take over the mystical realm of Avalon in Britain, from where they could seize control of Earth's magic, Satannish eliminated their entire invading force with a single spell. He then cast a barrier to prevent their return and ensure that one day the Earth would be his and his alone.

◀ ***The demon's fury*** Satannish unleashes his wrath upon the unwitting alien interlopers into his domain.

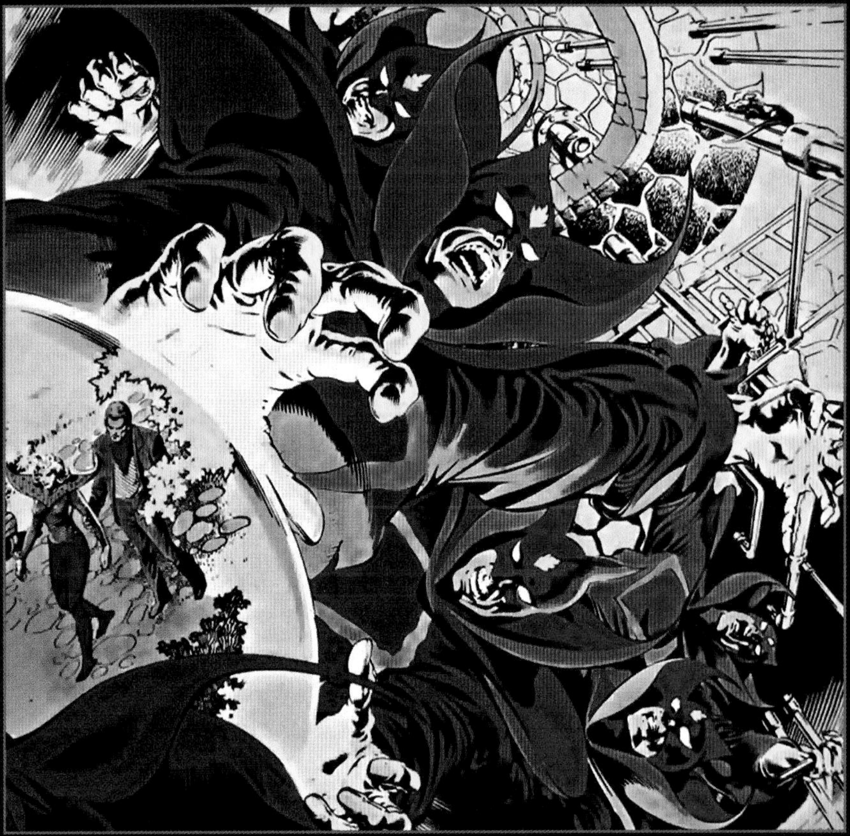

Sons of Satannish

The Sons of Satannish is a dangerous cult of minor wizards and magical dabblers who have banded together to use their combined talents in the quest for greater power. Operating furtively in the shadows, they are dedicated to the worship of the demon Satannish and are a threat to Doctor Strange and his allies. In the past, the Sons of Satannish have kidnapped Clea, tried to steal The Book of the Vishanti, and unleashed deadly demons.

ENTITIES, OLD AND EVIL

Some evils come and go, while others linger and spread. Ancient things like the tentacled terror Shuma-Gorath have existed for billions of years in countless dimensions. It has feasted on humankind in body and soul since the Earth was new. Other entities, such as Chthon, have proven to be a source of dark magic and sinister knowledge, tainting the world down through the ages.

◄ *Primeval horror* One of the Old Ones, Shuma- Gorath is an extradimensional being who has sought to conquer Earth and other realms for millennia.

CALL UPON THE EVIL ONE

Long ago, when ancient, powerful entities and corrupted gods were at war, the being known as Mother Nature created a son—a new, godlike super being—to oppose them and save the Earth. One of the warring Elder Gods was Chthon, who was turning increasingly demonic due to his pursuit of dark magic. Knowing that he could not win against Mother Nature's champion, Chthon set down all of his terrible knowledge on indestructible pieces of parchment for future generations to find.

Though Chthon did survive, he was banished to another dimension. However, his influence has continued to be felt on Earth as practitioners of black magic have turned to his writings and invoked his name in the quest for more power.

In recent times, Mordred the Mystic freed Chthon from his exile. The Elder God has clashed with Earth's heroes as he attempts to be fully reborn into this reality—but has been thwarted by Doctor Strange and his allies.

▲ *Dawn of the gods* The Elder Gods, including Chthon, sprang forth from the primordial energies of a newly formed Earth.

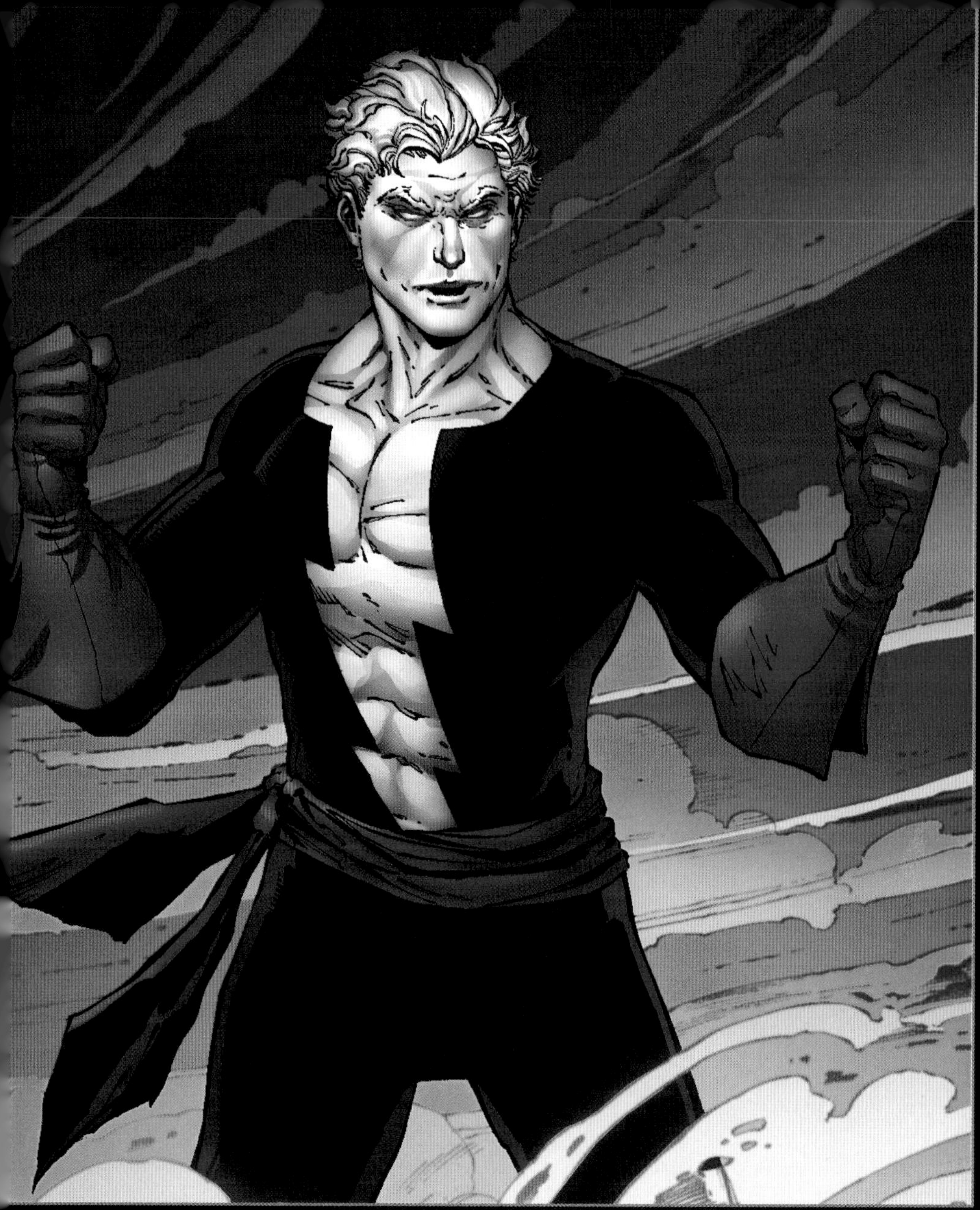

▲ ***Silver nemesis*** Mordred the Mystic opened a gateway between dimensions allowing Chthon to return to Earth and possess the body of the hero Quicksilver.

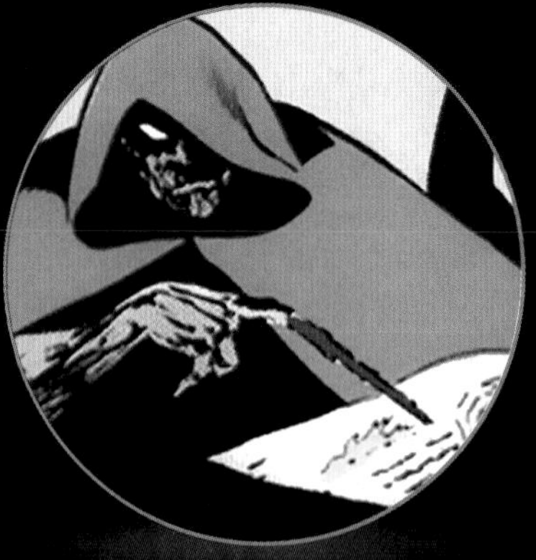

Scrolls

What Chthon wrote down on ancient scrolls would become the basis for black magic, and eventually lead to the creation of the ominous book, the Darkhold.

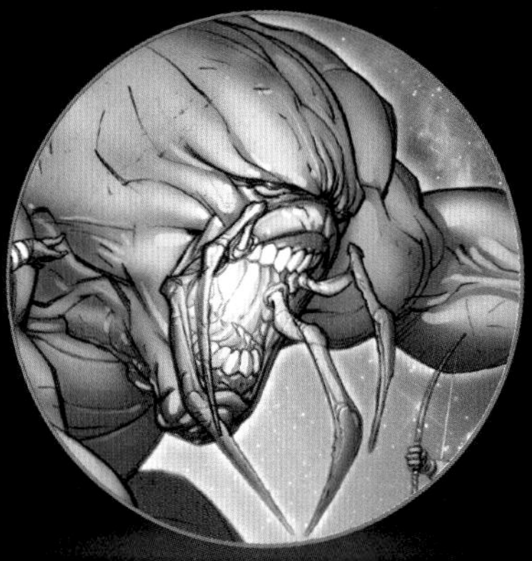

Atum

Atum was created to rid the world of the warring Elder Gods and make way for newer, more benign gods and fledgling humanity.

"THERE IS A WORLD TO UNRAVEL. A REALITY TO DESTROY."

Chthon

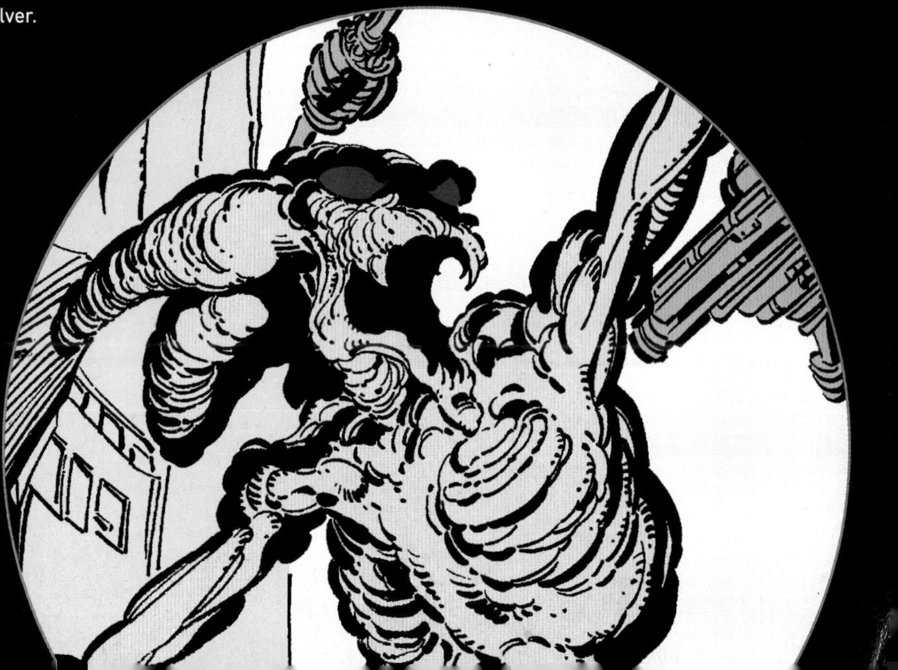

N'Garai

The N'Garai are demons created by Chthon after his banishment. They have troubled humanity for thousands of years.

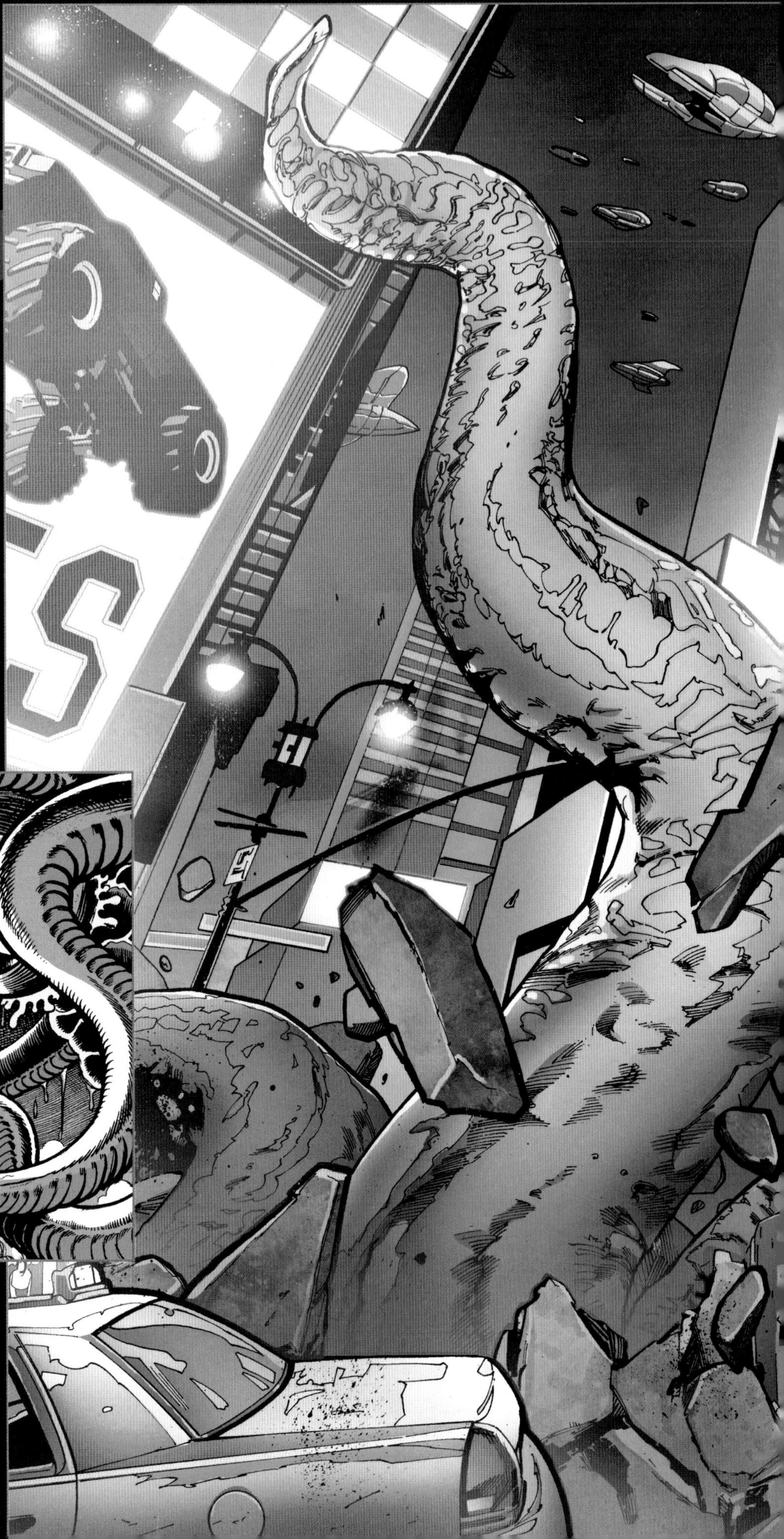

▶ ***Forever evil*** After his long banishment from this dimension, Shuma-Gorath appeared in New York City's Times Square intent on consuming the souls of all those present.

SHUMA-GORATH

Acting on the orders of his master, the evil super-being Thanos, the alien Ebony Maw manipulated Doctor Strange into summoning Shuma-Gorath to New York City. Power Man, White Tiger, and other heroes on hand responded to the threat as the ancient horror took possession of the nearby crowds of people. Power Man channeled his life force into White Tiger, giving physical form to the godlike being that powers her, and together they repelled Shuma-Gorath—at least for the time being.

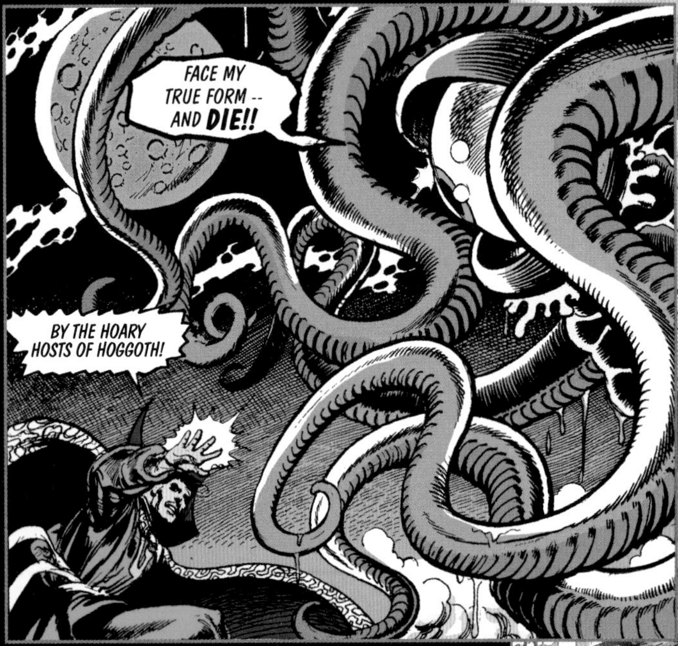
FACE MY TRUE FORM -- AND DIE!!
BY THE HOARY HOSTS OF HOGGOTH!

Fateful decision
In an earlier battle with Shuma-Gorath, Doctor Strange was forced to destroy the Ancient One's ego, which not only stopped the monster, but also freed Strange's master to evolve to a higher state of being.

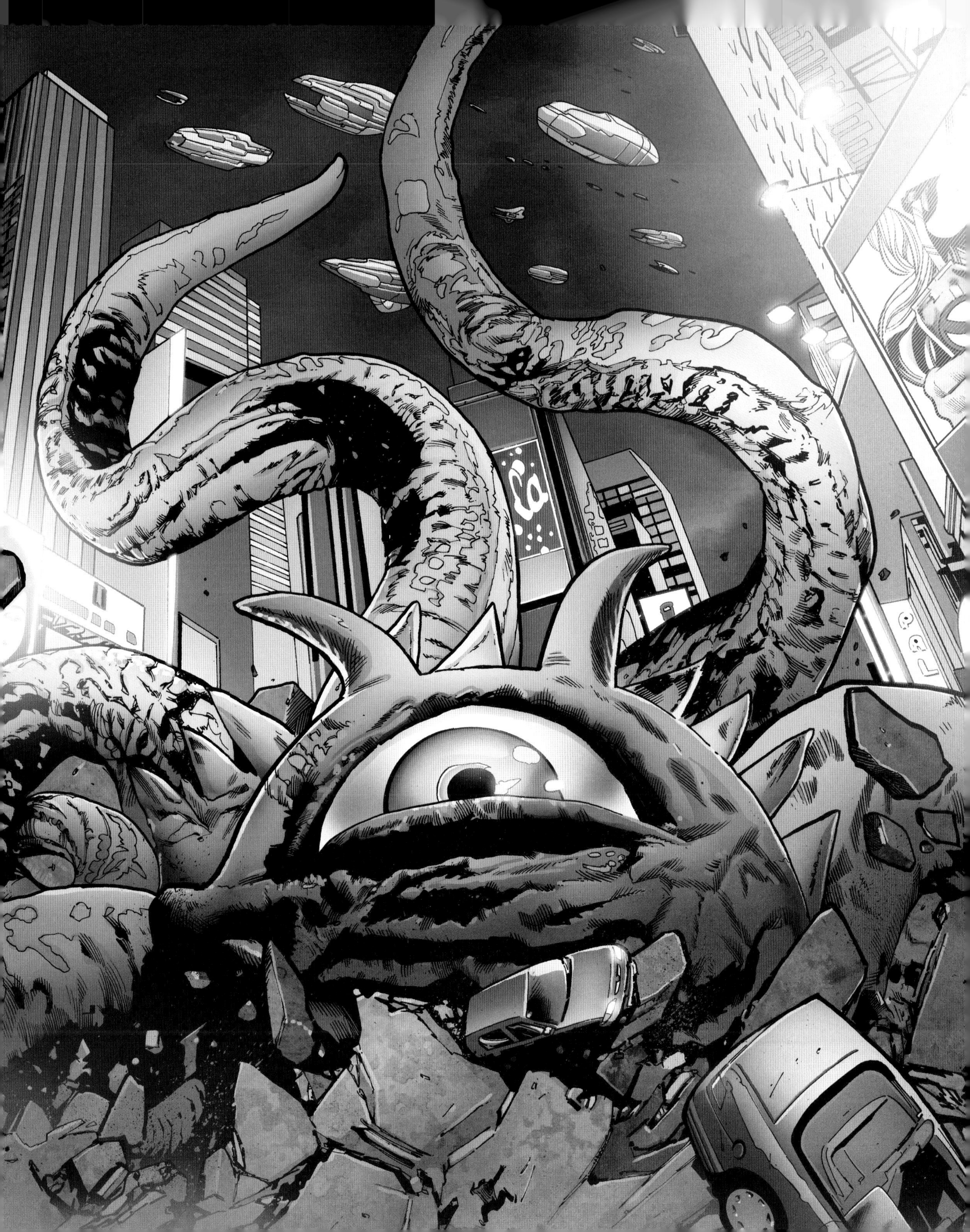

The perils of immortality and time travel dramatically presented themselves to the Sorcerer Supreme in the form of two very different wizards. The mage from the future who would become Sise-Neg traveled through time, amassing magical knowledge and power. Born almost 300 years ago, the conjurer Cagliostro succeeded in unlocking the secret of eternal life. When their paths crossed, Doctor Strange was drawn into a battle for the very existence of life on Earth.

▲ *Cosmic fate* Were some things always meant to be? Wielding the power of a god, Sise-Neg destroyed the Biblical towns of Sodom and Gomorrah as he traveled through time.

POWER INFINITE

Sise-Neg began his life many millennia after Cagliostro was born. He lived in a future where using magic was common but its effects were weak because so many people could tap into the sources of mystical energy. Devising a spell to let him travel back in time without causing the paradoxes that might wipe out his existence, Sise-Neg visited significant magical eras of the past, accumulating ever more power the further back he journeyed.

When he reached 18th century Paris, Sise-Neg took on the guise of a local occultist, Cagliostro, who had just

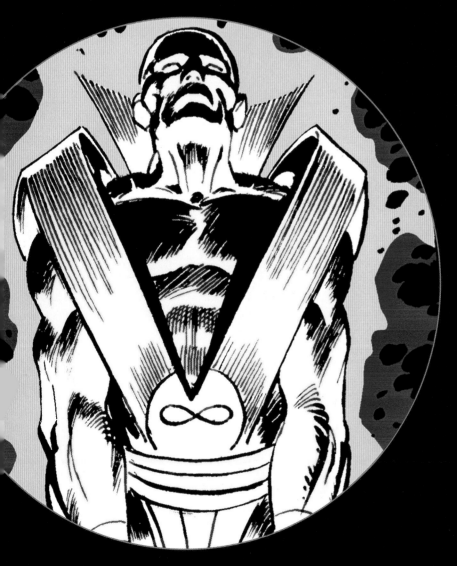

▲ *Revelations* Sise-Neg cast aside his guise as Cagliostro to reveal his true self—a frustrated 31st century magician with an ambitious and ingenious scheme to become a god.

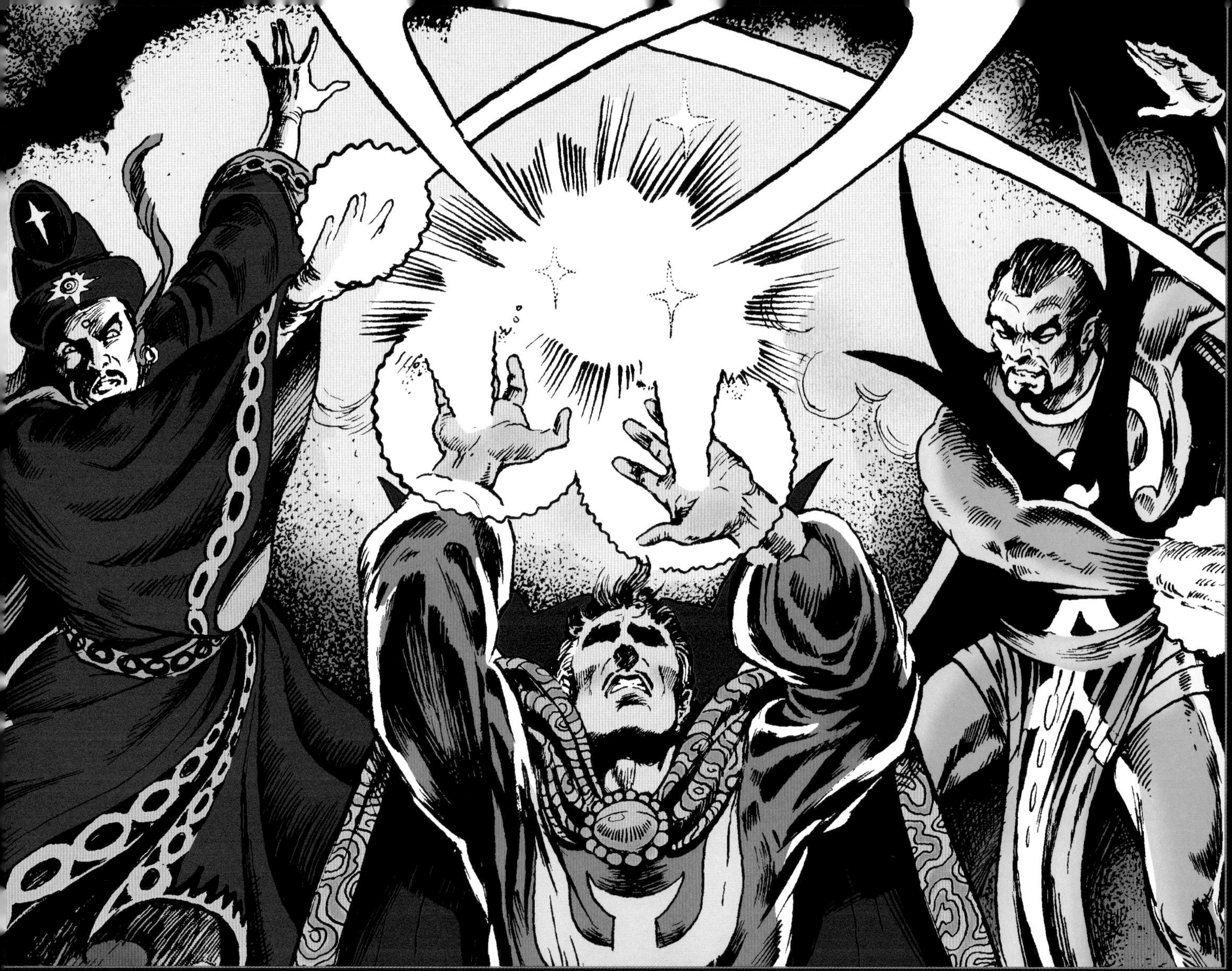

▲ ***Double trouble*** Under attack from both Cagliostro and Baron Mordo—who had come in search of Cagliostro's ime traveling secrets—Doctor Strange was pushed to the farthest limits of his power... and found wanting.

"I HAVE ACHIEVED MY GODHOOD!"

Sise-Neg

departed the city. The real Cagliostro was a schemer and collector of magical ore. His dark explorations had even brought him into conflict with the Lord of the Vampires, Dracula.

Unbeknown to Sise-Neg, Baron Mordo had also sought out Cagliostro. Mordo thought Cagliostro's arcane knowledge might help him defeat the Ancient One and Doctor Strange, so he traveled to the past to learn his secrets. When Doctor Strange learned of the plan, he tracked Mordo to Paris, but instead discovered Sise-Neg. Strange realized that the futuristic sorcerer's time-traveling intentions posed a far greater threat to his world than his old foe, and pursued Sise-neg to the dawn of creation to prevent his plans coming to fruition. Humanity's fate hung in the balance.

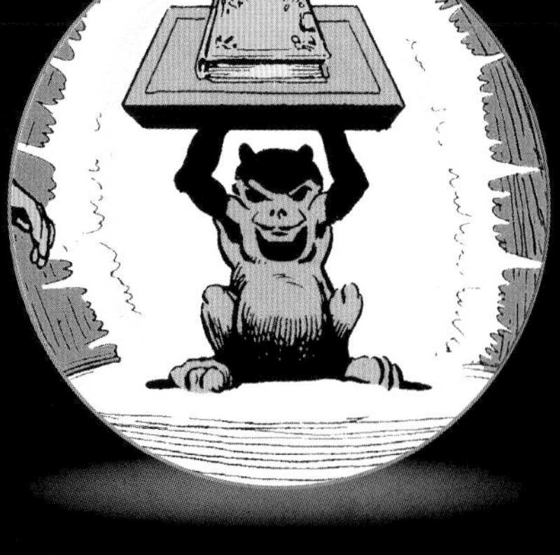

Book of Cagliostro

While impersonating Cagliostro, Sise-Neg added some of his occult knowledge to the mage's tome, the Book of Cagliostro. This book also contains spells from the powerful book of black magic, the Darkhold.

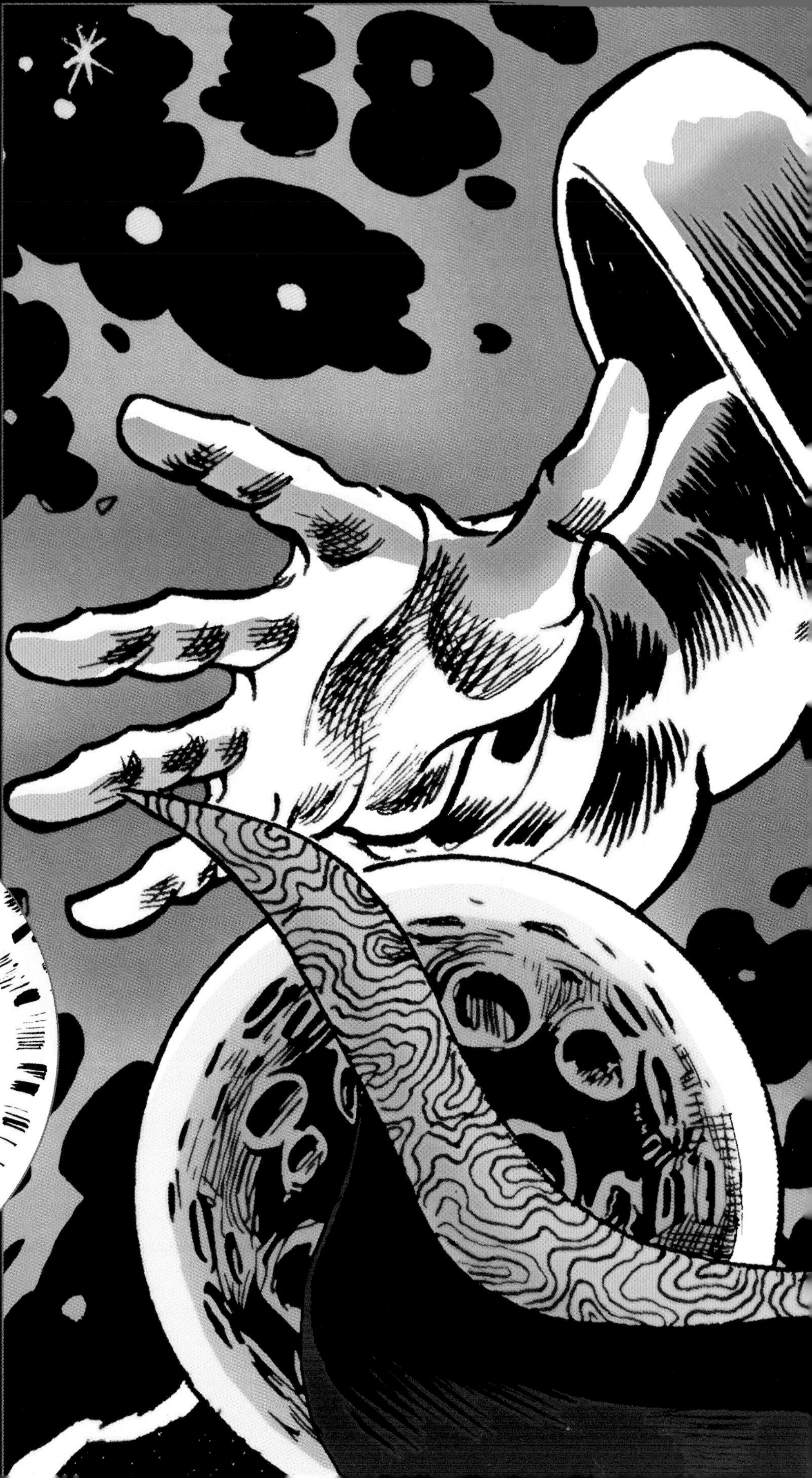

▶ ***Pure magic*** Sise-Neg came to possess all magical energy from the 31st century back to the dawn of creation.

SISE-NEG

The being known as Sise-Neg was once a human sorcerer from the distant future. Realizing that the total amount of mystical energy in the universe was finite, he began traveling backward through time, greedily absorbing magical forces from earlier time periods. Doctor Strange followed him through time, trying to convince the power hungry sorcerer to cease his plan. Ignoring Strange, Sise-Neg would eventually defeat both Baron Mordo and the ancient horror Shuma-Gorath on his way to the beginning of time itself. Having absorbed so much power, Sise-Neg became a godlike entity no longer concerned with his mortal ambitions.

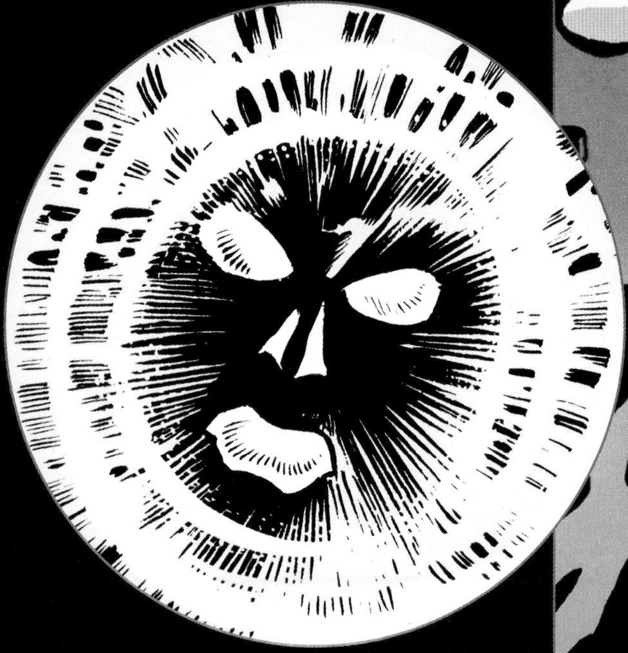

A new understanding

Once Sise-Neg reached godhood, he came to realize that his goal to refashion the universe in his own vision was a foolish and vain one. So he allowed the universe to be created as it should be, and disappeared into the heavens.

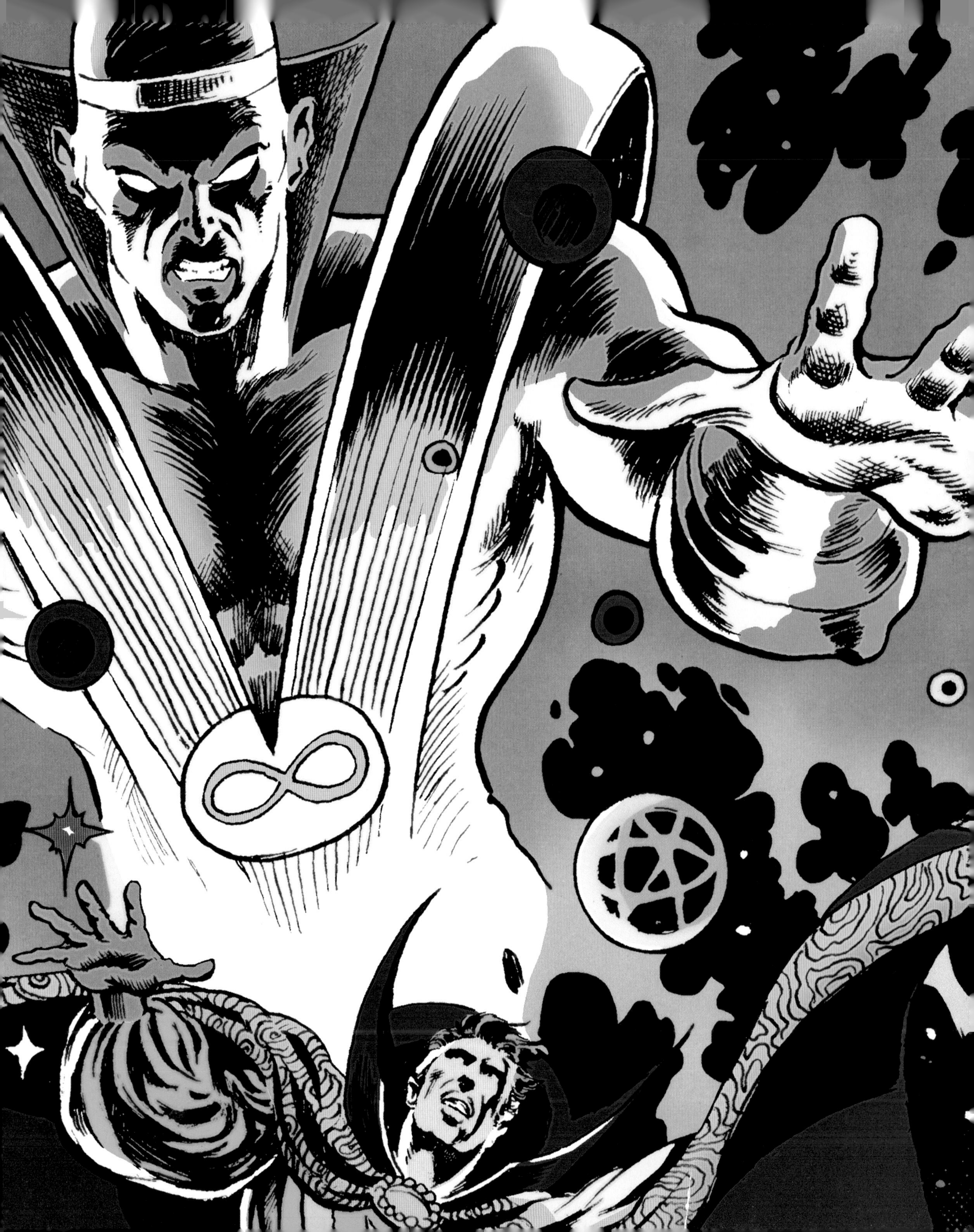

MORGAN LE FAY

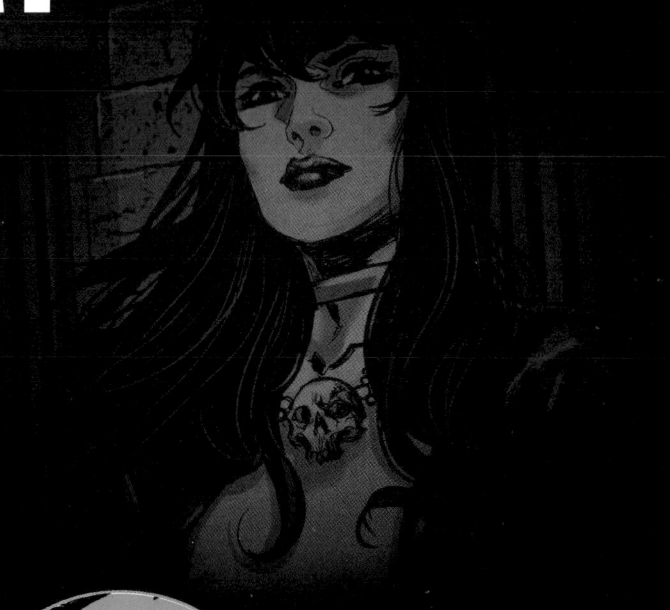

Born during the time of King Arthur and Camelot, Morgan Le Fay became one of the most powerful sorceresses on Earth. Owing to her immortal—and corrupt—nature as well as the time-traveling exploits of both heroes and villains, Le Fay has come into conflict with the forces of both good and evil on several occasions in both the past and the present.

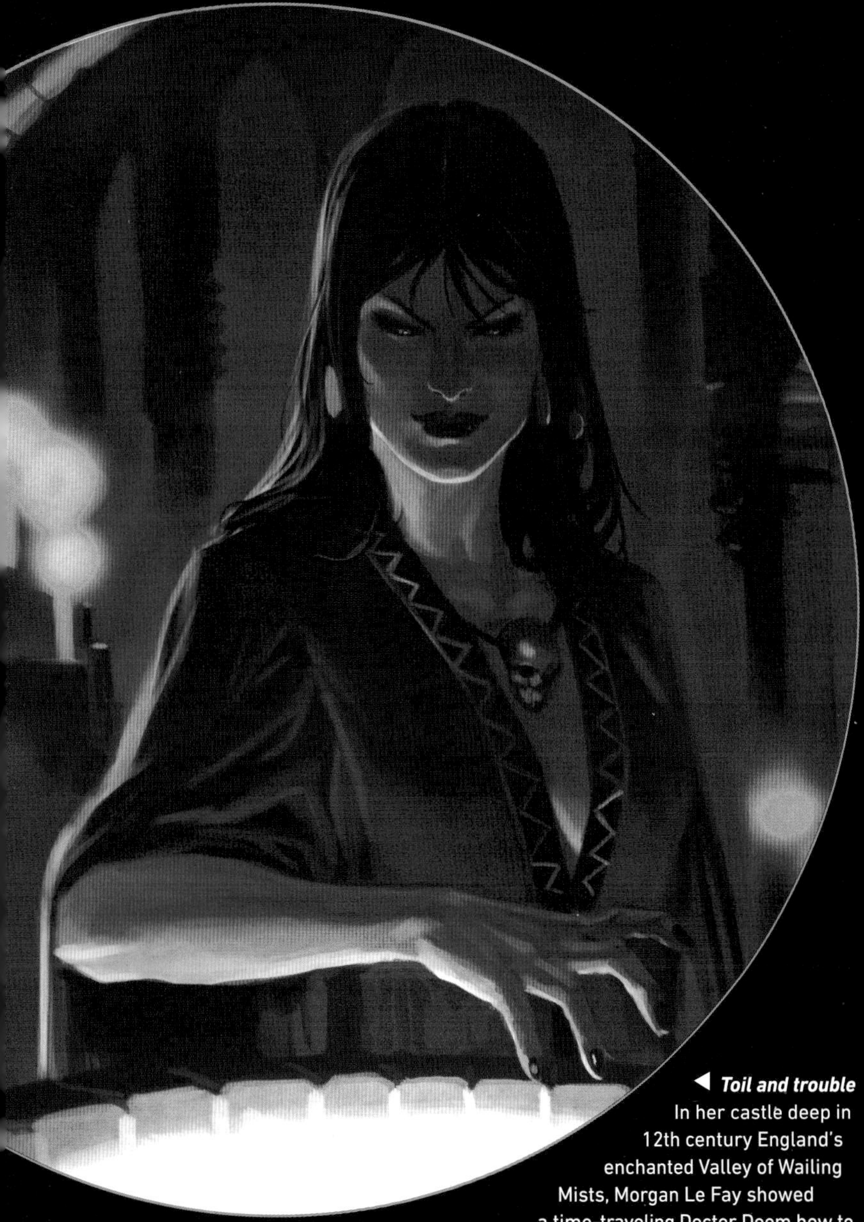

◀ ***Toil and trouble***
In her castle deep in 12th century England's enchanted Valley of Wailing Mists, Morgan Le Fay showed a time-traveling Doctor Doom how to summon an army of unyielding demons.

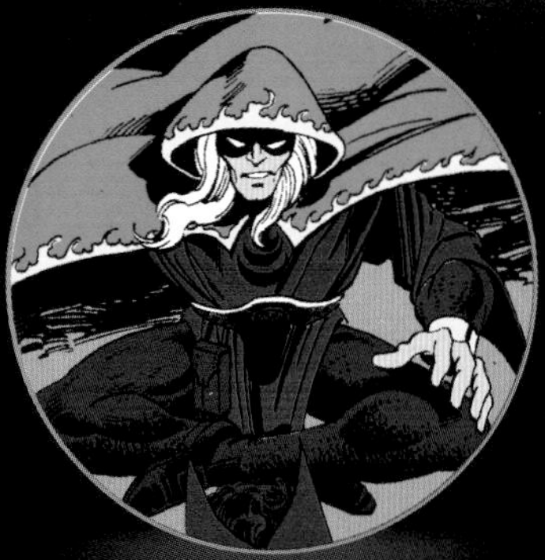

Mordred
Morgan Le Fay's nephew, Mordred the Mystic, was a young sorcerer's apprentice who was forced to sell his soul to Chthon. In return, he became an evil warlock with great magical abilities.

MADAME OF THE MYSTICAL

Part fairie—creatures of natural and very ancient magic—Morgan Le Fay was born in 6th century England, where she often came into conflict with her half-brother, Arthur, the king of the land. Because of her bloodline, she had an affinity for magic, and she sought ever more ways to increase her occult knowledge and might. This led her to pursue the dark writings of the Elder God Chthon; she may even have helped fashion this forbidden learning into the much sought-after book of magic known as the Darkhold. Even at this time, Le Fay was powerful enough to summon Chthon himself, but realizing that the Elder God was uncontrollable, she was forced to bind him safely away in a mountain—at least for a time.

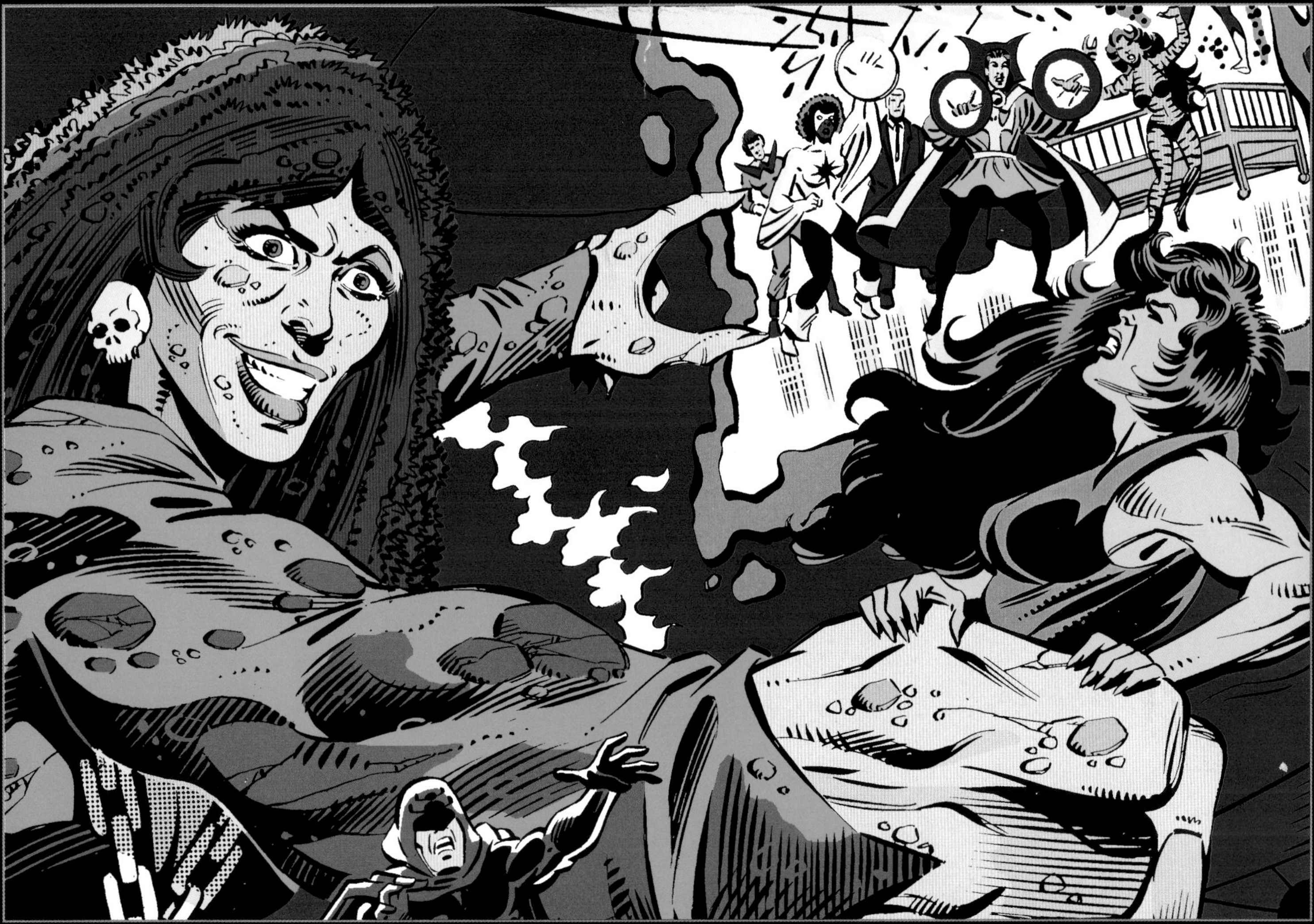

▲ ***Sworn enemy*** Doctor Strange's actions against Morgan Le Fay in aid of the Avengers led her to vow vengeance on him.

"I WILL AGREE TO HELP YOU. FOR A PRICE."

Morgan Le Fay

Morgan Le Fay's lineage makes her virtually immortal, which has given her ample time to continue her study and perfect the dark arts. Like most magical experts, she is able to astral project her spirit in both time and space. She can also travel physically in time, fire force bolts and raise force fields, turn inanimate objects into monstrous creatures, and perform necromancy—raising the dead! Her one weakness is that she can be hurt by objects made of iron and steel.

Le Fay's schemes have reached into the present, where she has harassed the world's heroes and villains alike, repeatedly clashing with Doctor Strange and his longtime allies, the Avengers.

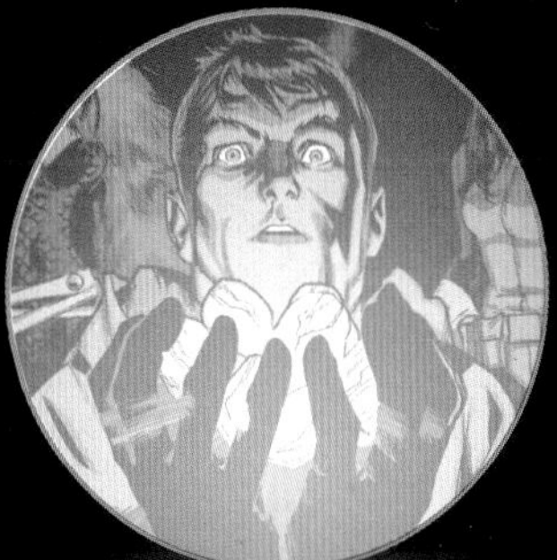

Norn Stones

At times, Morgan Le Fay has used the Asgardian Norn Stones. Channeling great mystical energy, the effect the Norn Stones have is determined by the will and desires of their possessor.

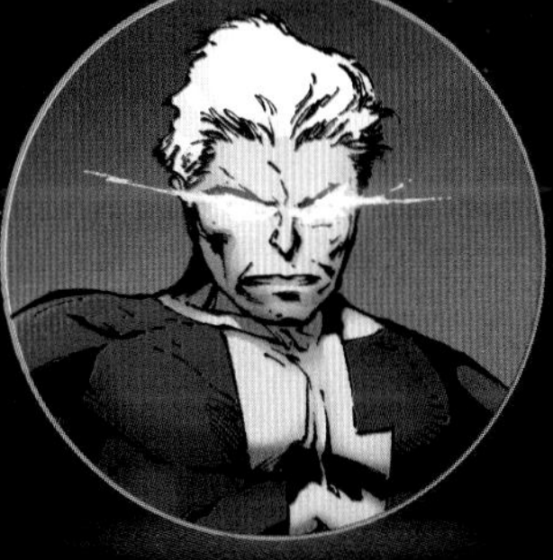

Chthon

The corrupting power of the Elder God Chthon has been an influence on both Morgan Le Fay and Mordred—directly and indirectly—through Chthon's legendary tome of black magic, the Darkhold.

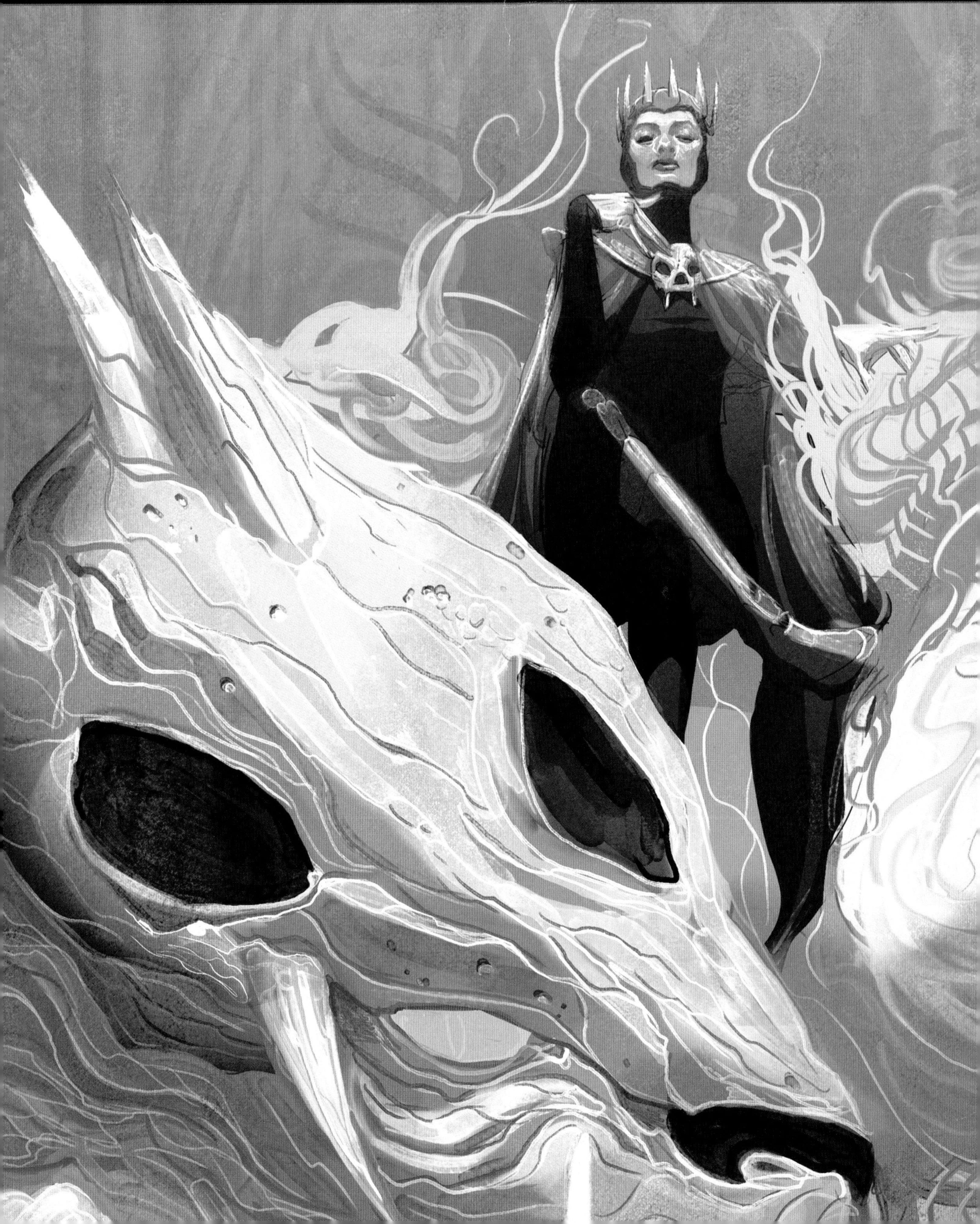

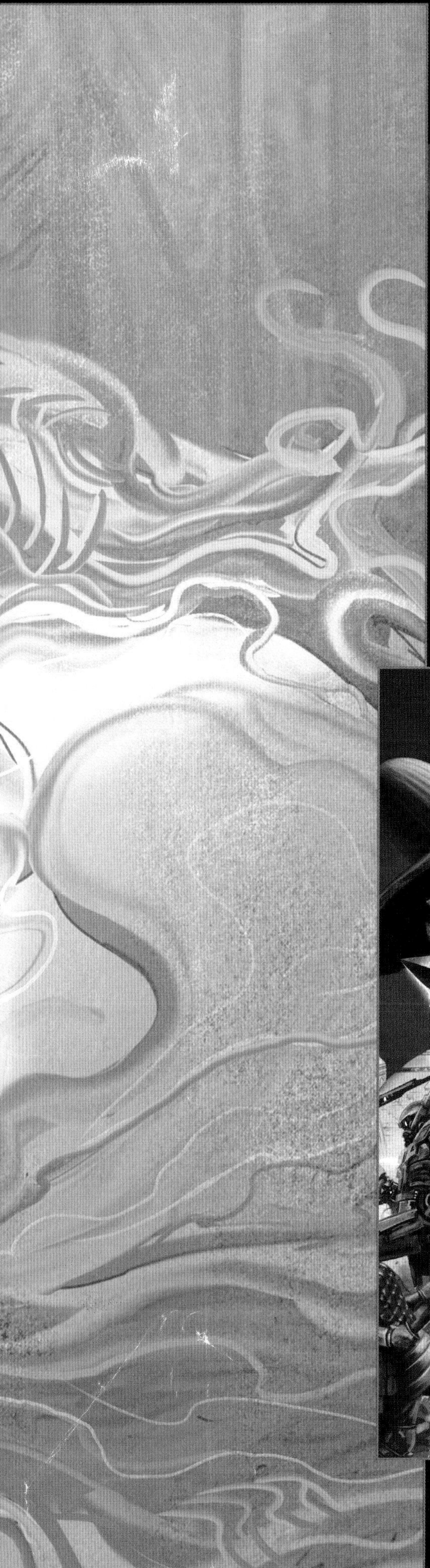

◀ ***Savage sovereign*** Morgan Le Fay is now the ruler of the savage realm Weirdworld, a land of dragons, swords, and sorcery.

WEIRD QUEEN

When all of reality was destroyed in a war with the cosmic beings the Beyonders, Doctor Doom, Doctor Strange, and the Molecule Man forged pieces of countless lost worlds into a patchwork planet known as Battleworld. One region on Battleworld was Weirdworld, a savage domain ruled over by its Baroness, Morgan Le Fay. Battleworld ceased to be when the universe was restored, but Weirdworld lives on as a distinct territory on Earth, with Morgan Le Fay remaining as its ruthless sovereign.

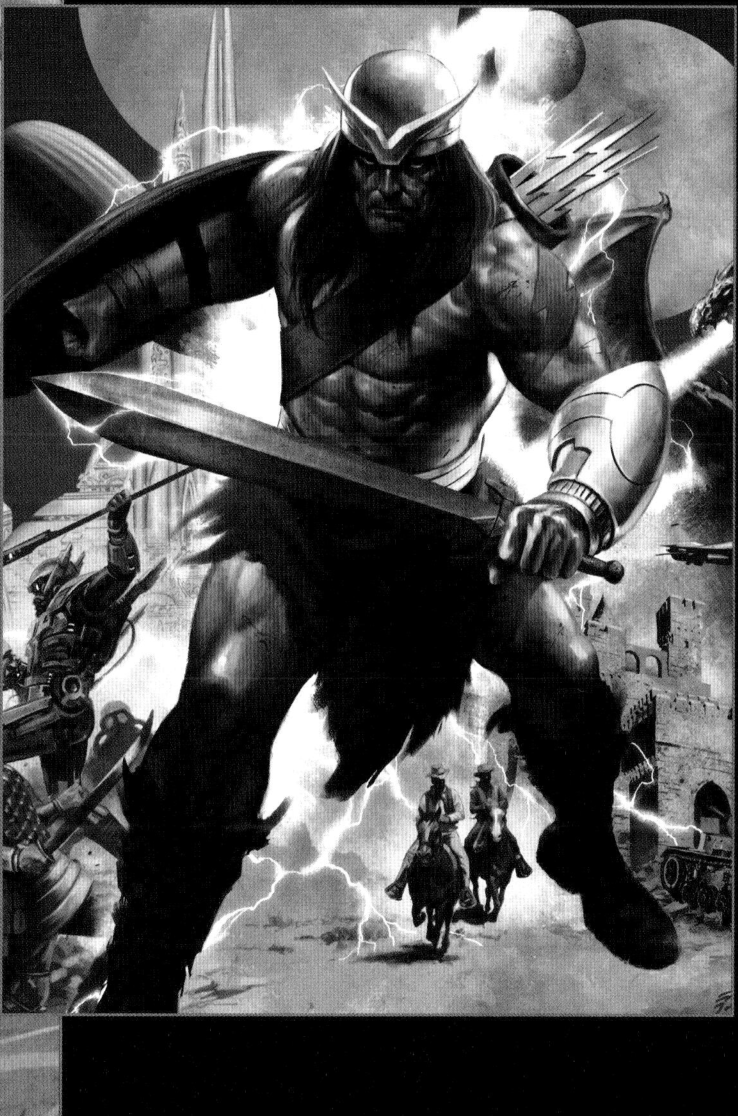

Arkon the Magnificent
The warlord Arkon, whom the Enchantress once tricked into battling Doctor Strange, traveled across Weirdworld in his search for his lost kingdom of Polemachus. He had to deal with ever-scheming Morgan Le Fay along the way.

UMAR

As a member of the Faltine race, Umar was once a being of pure magical energy. Even though she is now bound to her physical form, she is able to effortlessly call upon vast amounts of mystical power. Inclined to evil intentions and always trying to expand her domain, she remains a powerful threat to the human world.

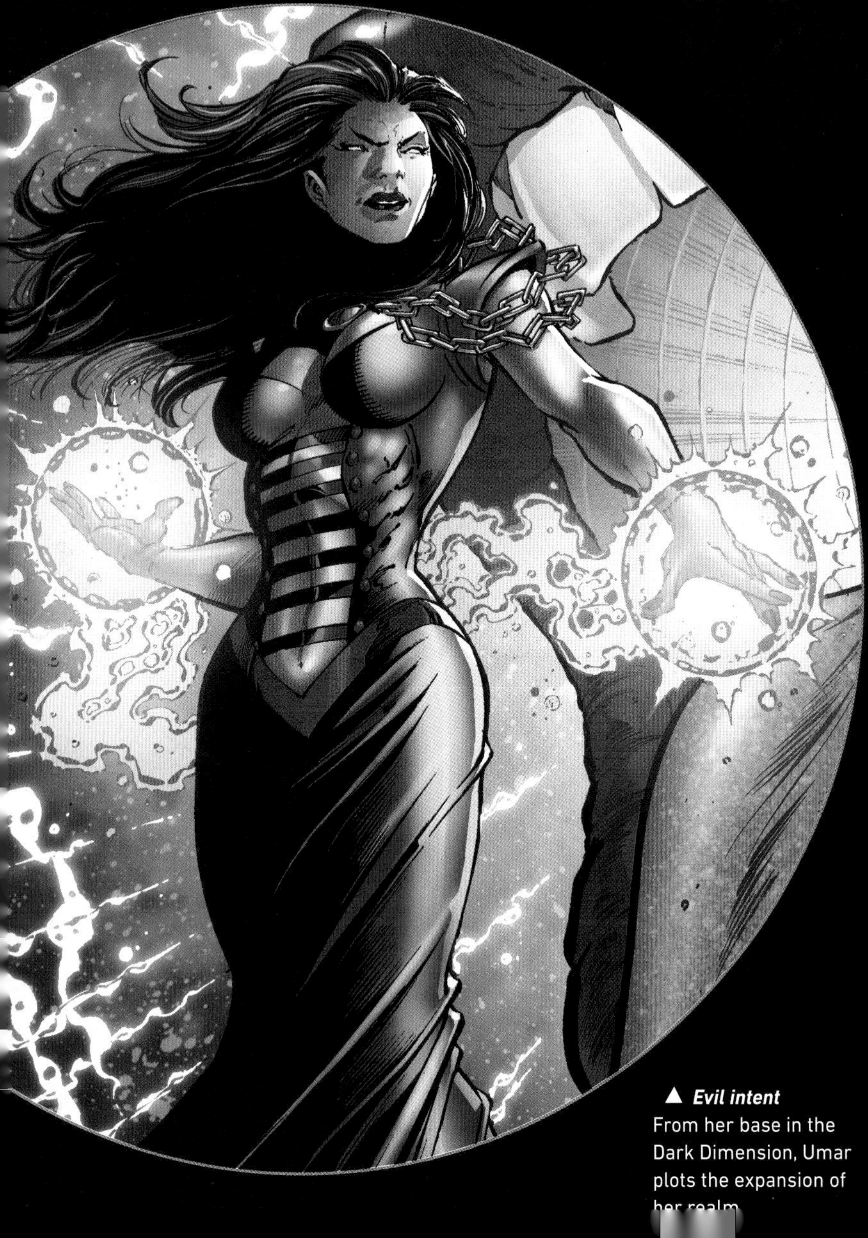

▲ ***Evil intent*** From her base in the Dark Dimension, Umar plots the expansion of her realm.

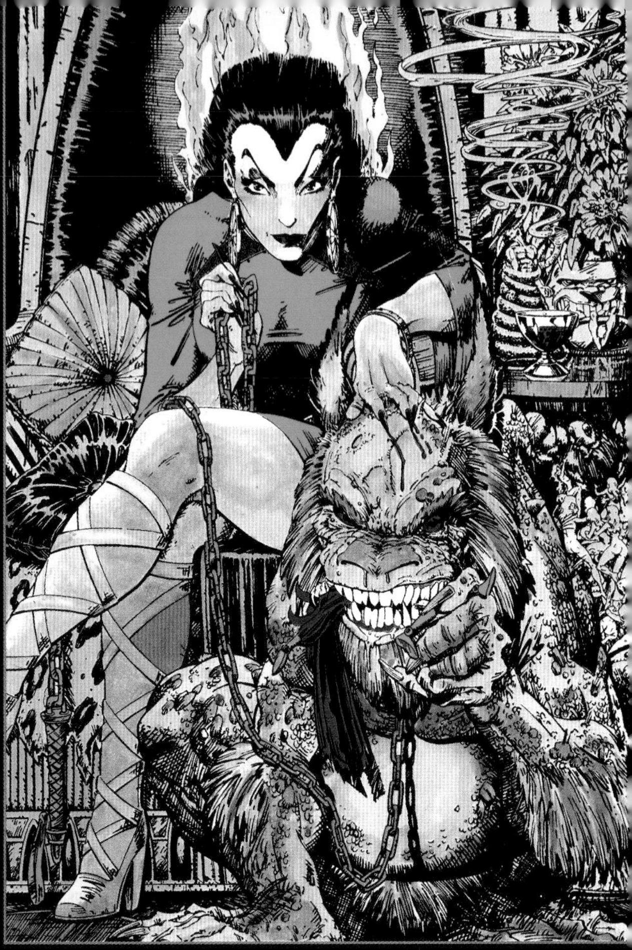

▲ ***Coronet of fire*** The Flames of Regency is a crown of mystical energy that transfers to Umar's head from her brother, Dormammu, during those periods when she reigns over the Dark Dimension.

THE UNRELENTING

Eons ago, when Umar and her brother Dormammu were exiled to the Dark Dimension, they both took on physical forms and became advisors to the Mhuruuk king. At some point, Umar had a child, named Clea, with the Mhuruuk prince—an act that left her unable to revert to her original state of pure magical energy.

Despite this, she retained formidable powers, which she enhanced with the study of spells and occult knowledge, and with the aid of other powerful beings. She became especially skilled at casting illusions and animating inanimate matter. She combined these skills with an array of other abilities, including inter-dimensional travel and the projection of energy bolts and force fields.

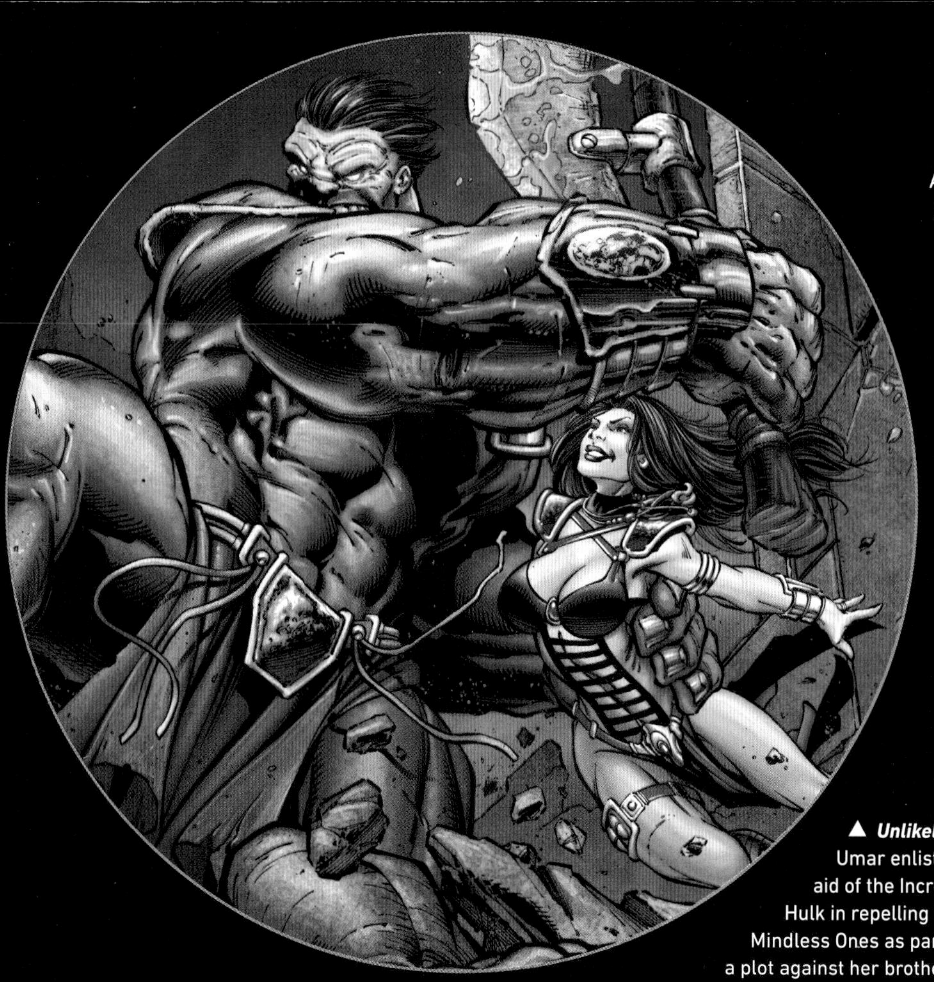

▲ ***Unlikely allies***
Umar enlisted the aid of the Incredible Hulk in repelling the Mindless Ones as part of a plot against her brother.

Clea

As the daughter of the Mhuruuk prince Orini, Clea is the rightful heir to the Dark Dimension. Like her mother, Umar, and her uncle, she can also assume the Flames of Regency.

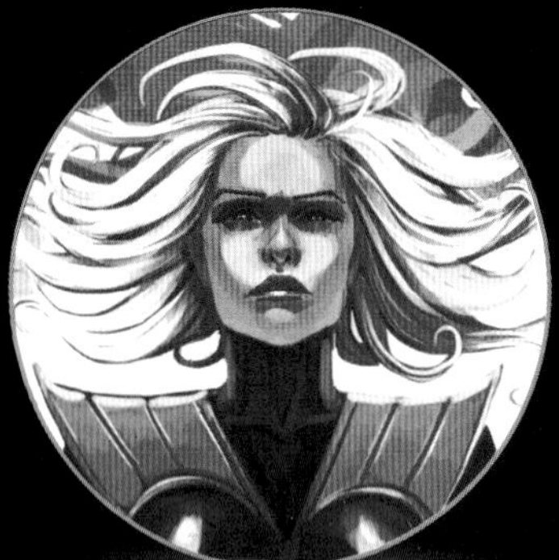

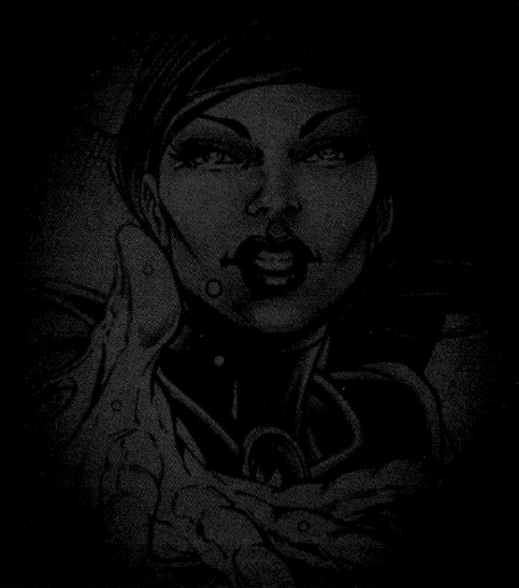

"UMAR IS NOT MERELY AN EVIL FOE—SHE IS EVIL INCARNATE!"

The Ancient One

Fearing that his sister might become a rival, Dormammu imprisoned Umar in another dimension. Ironically, she was set free when Dormammu was himself cast out of the Dark Dimension through the actions of Doctor Strange and the entity known as Eternity.

Taking the throne for herself, Umar sought to ensure that Doctor Strange did not interfere with her own plans. The novice magician was no match for her during that early encounter, and he was forced to unleash the mystical beast Zom to defeat her. But the immortal Umar has returned many times to plague the Sorcerer Supreme. She has even gained cosmic powers—taken from Eternity by her brother—to add to her magical ones.

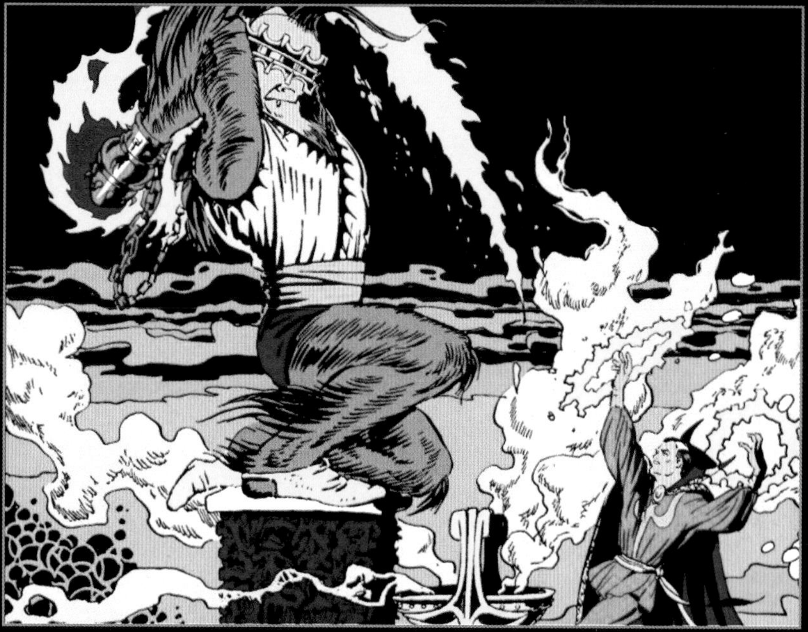

Zom

Zom was once used by Doctor Strange to defeat Umar, and now views Strange, Umar, and her brother as his bitter enemies. He is an immensely powerful mystical beast whose sole purpose is to create chaos and destruction. He was originally stopped and imprisoned by Dormammu and Eternity, who recognized his ability to taint any world with his evil.

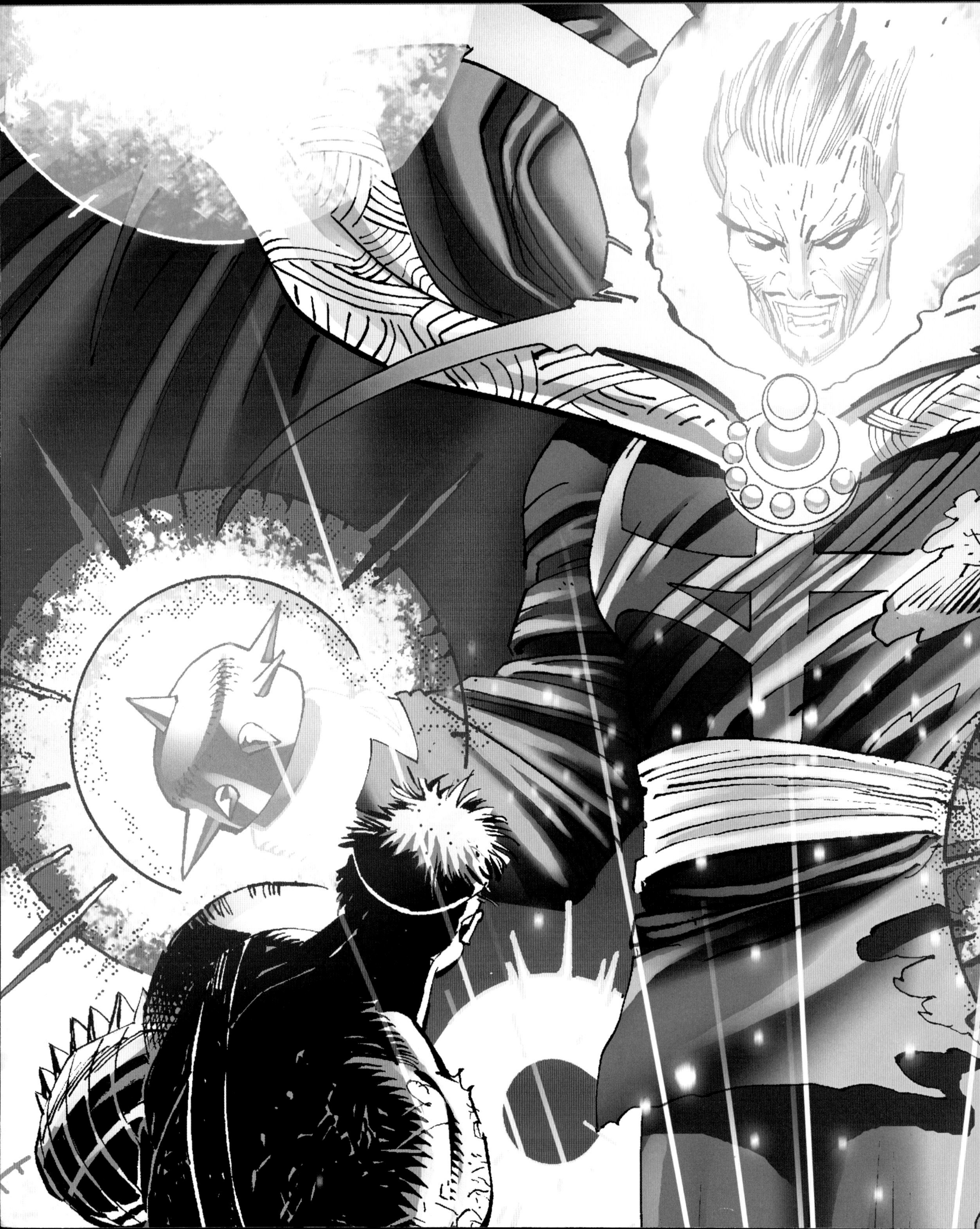

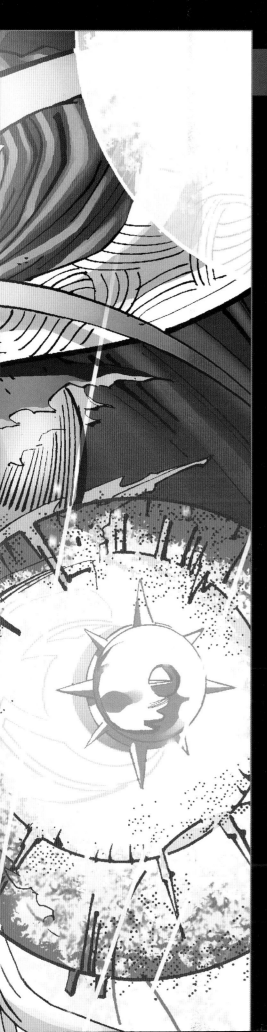

ZOM

The Sorcerer Supreme has mostly been able to keep the Earth safe from the chaos and corruption of Zom. However, when faced with the rampaging Hulk, Doctor Strange was forced to summon Zom and channel the demon's power to stop the green-skinned goliath. However, while Zom's additional power gave Strange the upper hand, the master of the mystic arts realized that in the heat of battle he was losing control of the demon. Deciding the Hulk was the lesser of two evils, Strange let the emerald behemoth defeat him.

◀ *A dangerous gambit* Doctor Strange's attempt to use the power of Zom to fight the Hulk almost resulted in him being overwhelmed!

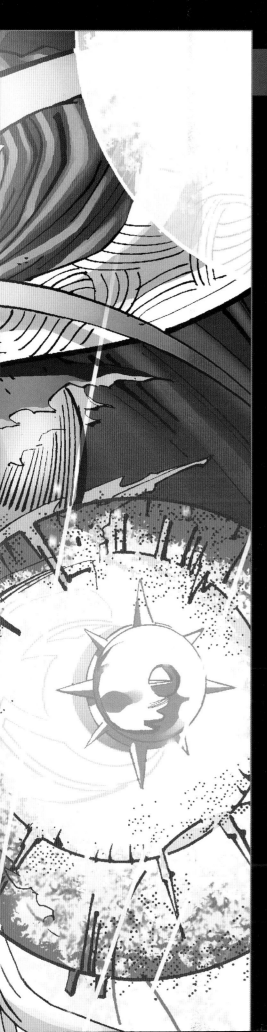

Crown of Blindness

When Doctor Strange first freed Zom to help him defeat Umar, he encouraged the beast to remove the Crown of Blindness he was wearing. However, the Links of Living Bondage shackled Zom's hands to reduce his ability to cause destruction.

THE EMPIRIKUL

Doctor Strange has battled and defeated many mighty foes, but few have been as deadly and seemingly invincible as the Empirikul. Under his watch, this unstoppable army had marched inexorably across all realties on a devastating and single-minded campaign—the death of magic. Now they had reached earth and even the Sorcerer Supreme seemed powerless to stop them.

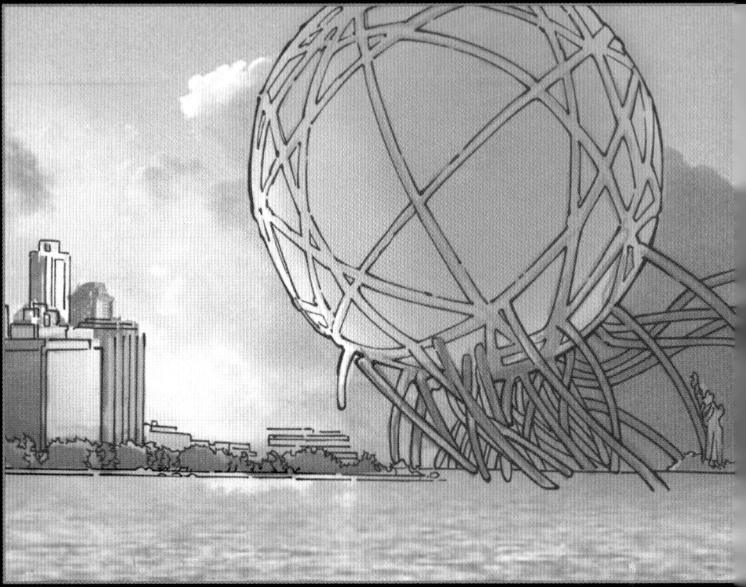

▲ ***Terror from the skies*** The Empirikul descended on Earth, their huge ship casting a dark shadow over New York City.

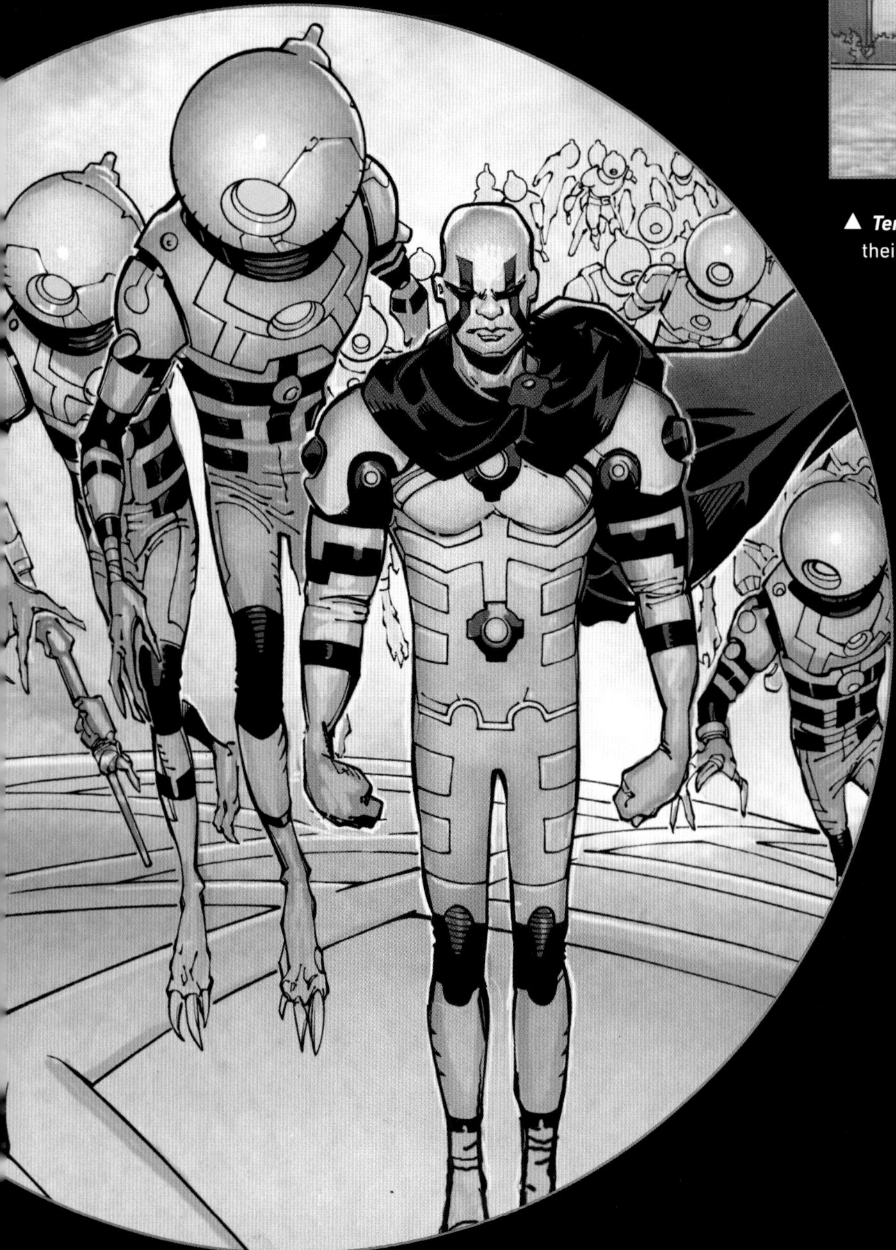

◀ ***A relentless and remorseless enemy*** The Empirikul is an all-conquering force of inter-dimensional beings using super-science to purge existence of all magic users. Leading the way is the murderously zealous Imperator.

THE LAST DAYS OF MAGIC

Like a horde of futuristic Mindless Ones, the terrifying troops of the Empirikul cast their baleful glowing cyclopean eyes on practitioners of magic wherever they find them. Created on a world ruled by mystical forces, these creatures of super-science wield extraordinary power, capable of distrupting and destroying all manner of sorcery. Driven by a fanatical philosophy that magic is an abomination, the Empirikul seek nothing less than the absolute annihilation of magic.

Having eliminated several Sorcerers Supreme and purified their dimensions, the Empirikul set their sights on Earth's magical beings. No-one was safe, from chaos users such as Scarlet Witch and mystics like Shaman and Brother Voodoo, to the demonically-aligned like Daimon Hellstrom and mere channelers of magic such as Iron Fist

Wolves of war
The Empirikul employed ferocious cybernetically enhanced hounds called Witchfinder Wolves to help them hunt down magic users of all kinds.

Shock troops
The Empirikul's cloned Inquisitors examined the battered body of Szandor Sozo, the Sorcerer Supreme of the 13th Dimension—another casualty in their merciless war on magic.

Blood magic
The Blood Monks of the Temple Macabre were the high priests and ruthless enforcers of magic in the Empirikul's home world. They worshipped one of Doctor Strange's oldest foes, Shuma-Gorath.

▲ **When the magic goes** His powers depleted, Doctor Strange was forced to seek out any scrap of magic, mystical weaponry, and even dangerous alliances, to use against the Empirikul.

The Empirikul are led by the Imperator, a righteous man of science, consumed by vengeance. As a child, he was raised by loving parents who dared practice science in a world of magic, watched over by a cruel and ancient god, Shuma-Gorath. When the planet's ruling Blood Monks discovered his parents' heresy, they lay seige to his home. The boy escaped with the help of eyebots, who would become his loyal Inquisitors, but not before he witnessed the murder of his parents. His despair fed his hatred of all things mystical until, as an adult, his need for revenge had become a holy crusade against magic.

As Doctor Strange is one of the most potent wielders of magic ever known, he became the Empirikul's prime target for extinguishing magic's flame on Earth. However, the Sorcerer Supreme wasn't about to go down without a fight.

"OUR HOLY INQUISITION MARCHES ON, MY BROTHERS. PRAISE THE EMPIRIKUL. AND DEATH TO MAGIC."
The Imperator

FIGHT TO THE DEATH

In their dimension-spanning quest to wipe magic from existence, the Empirikul descended on Doctor Strange's Sanctum Sanctorum with overwhelming force. When the Imperator personally assailed the Sorcerer Supreme, Strange could feel an unraveling of the mystical threads binding the world together. In the epic battle that ensued, Strange not only fought for his life, but for the very soul and survival of magic itself!

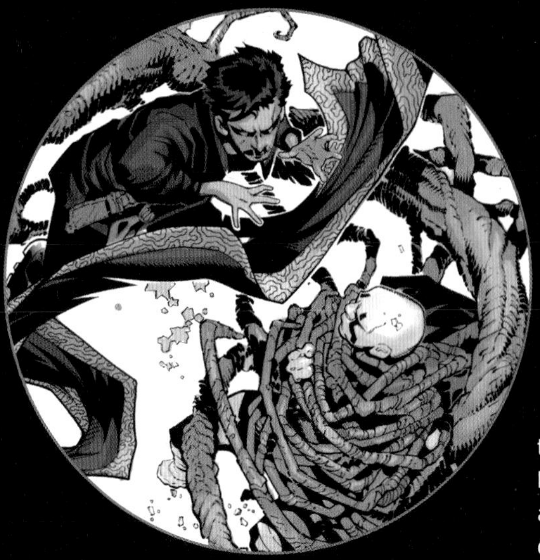

Home invasion
Doctor Strange thought the Empirikul foolish to attack him on home turf, turning the natural environment against his technologically empowered foes. However, he underestimated them and had to virtually drain the Earth of magical energy to aid his struggle.

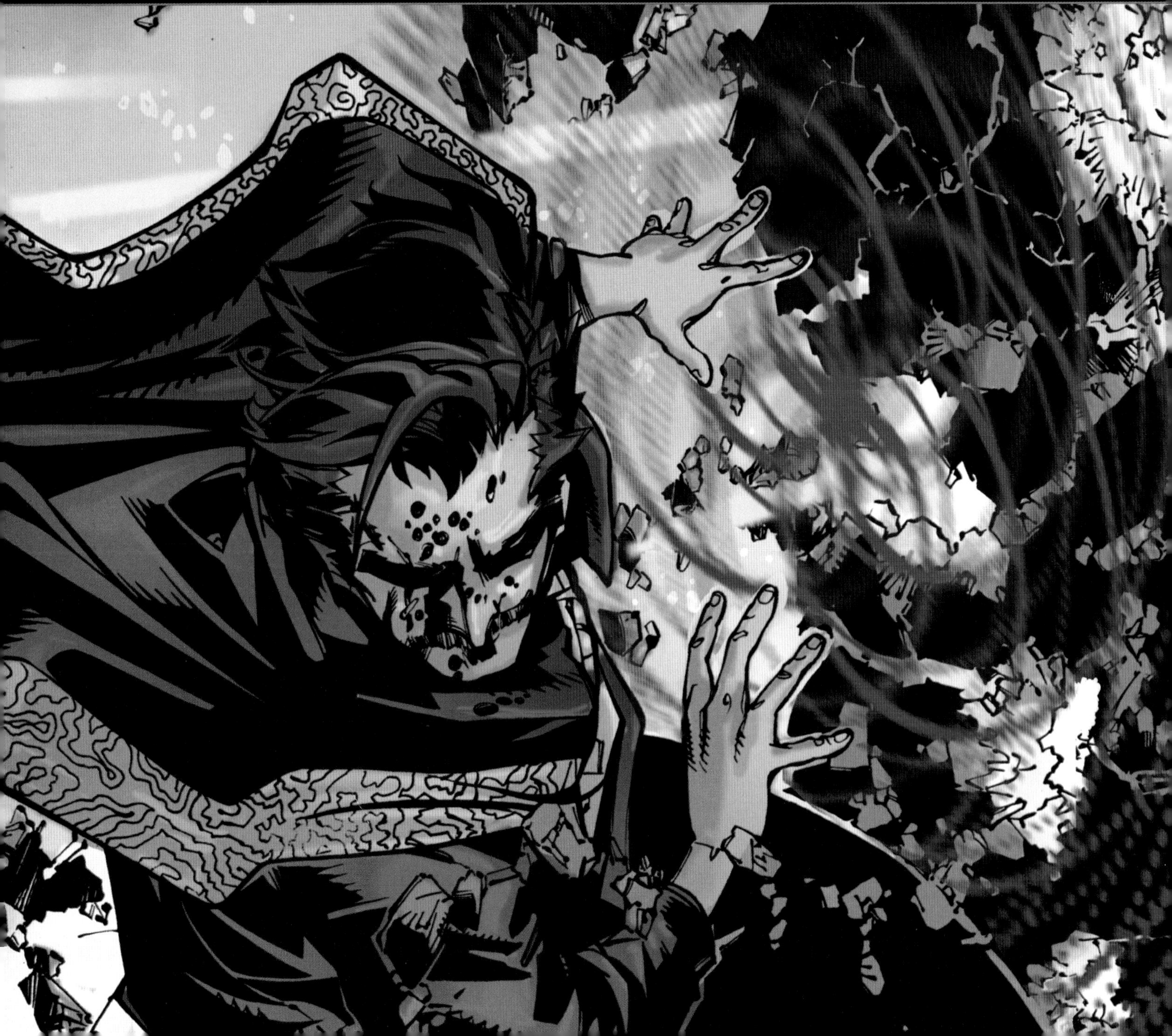

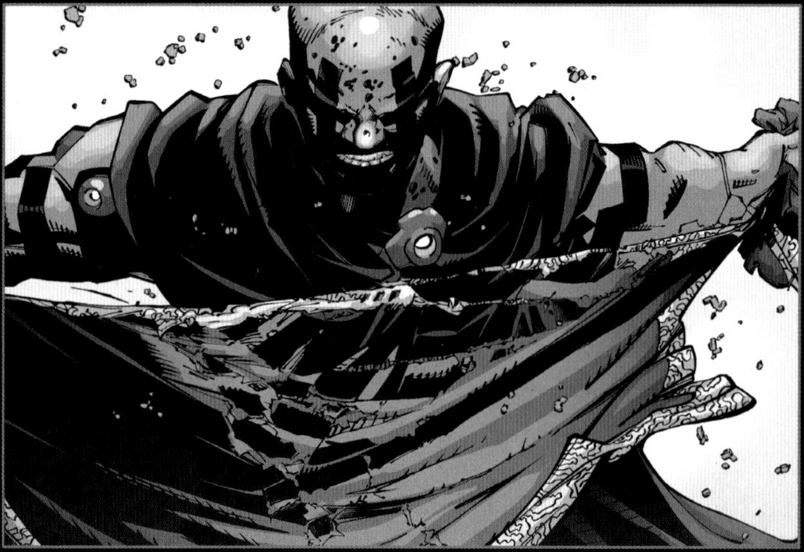

▶ ***Enemy like no other*** The Imperator ripped the Cloak of Levitation asunder, to prove that he was no ordinary opponent.

▼ ***Magic vs science*** When finally confronted by the Empirikul, Doctor Strange found that his magic provided little defense against their super-science.

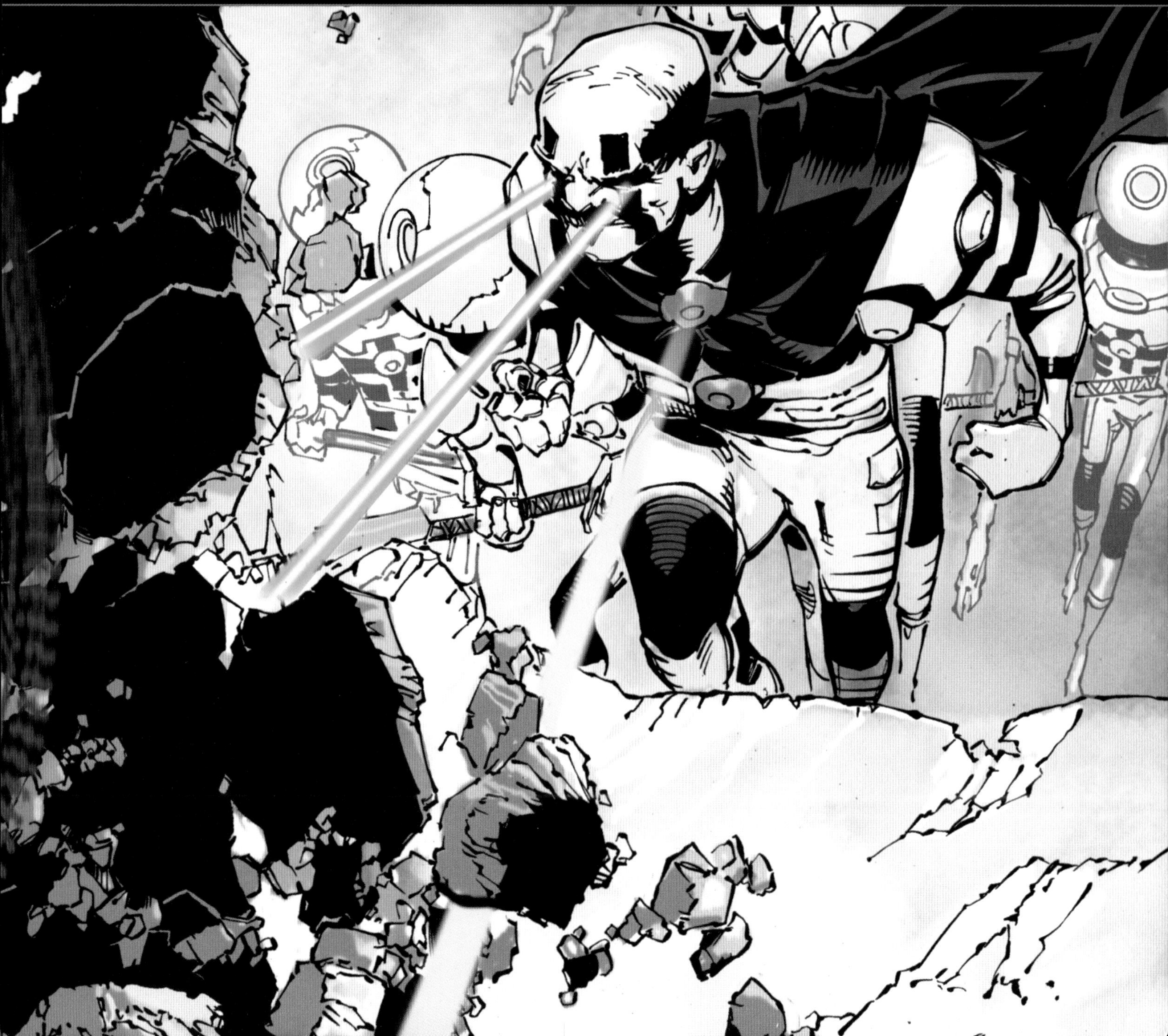

CHAPTER 4

THE ALL POWERFUL

On a scale far beyond that of Doctor Strange, any of the mortal Earthbound heroes, and even entities like Dormammu, are beings who operate on a level that can affect planets, galaxies, and even the universe itself. While all of these beings—with names like Eternity, the Living Tribunal, and the Beyonder—seem to serve some purpose, their otherworldly perspective transcends time, space, and reality as we know it. This can make them appear amoral and uncaring—some might say even godlike.

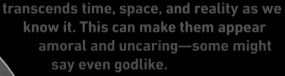

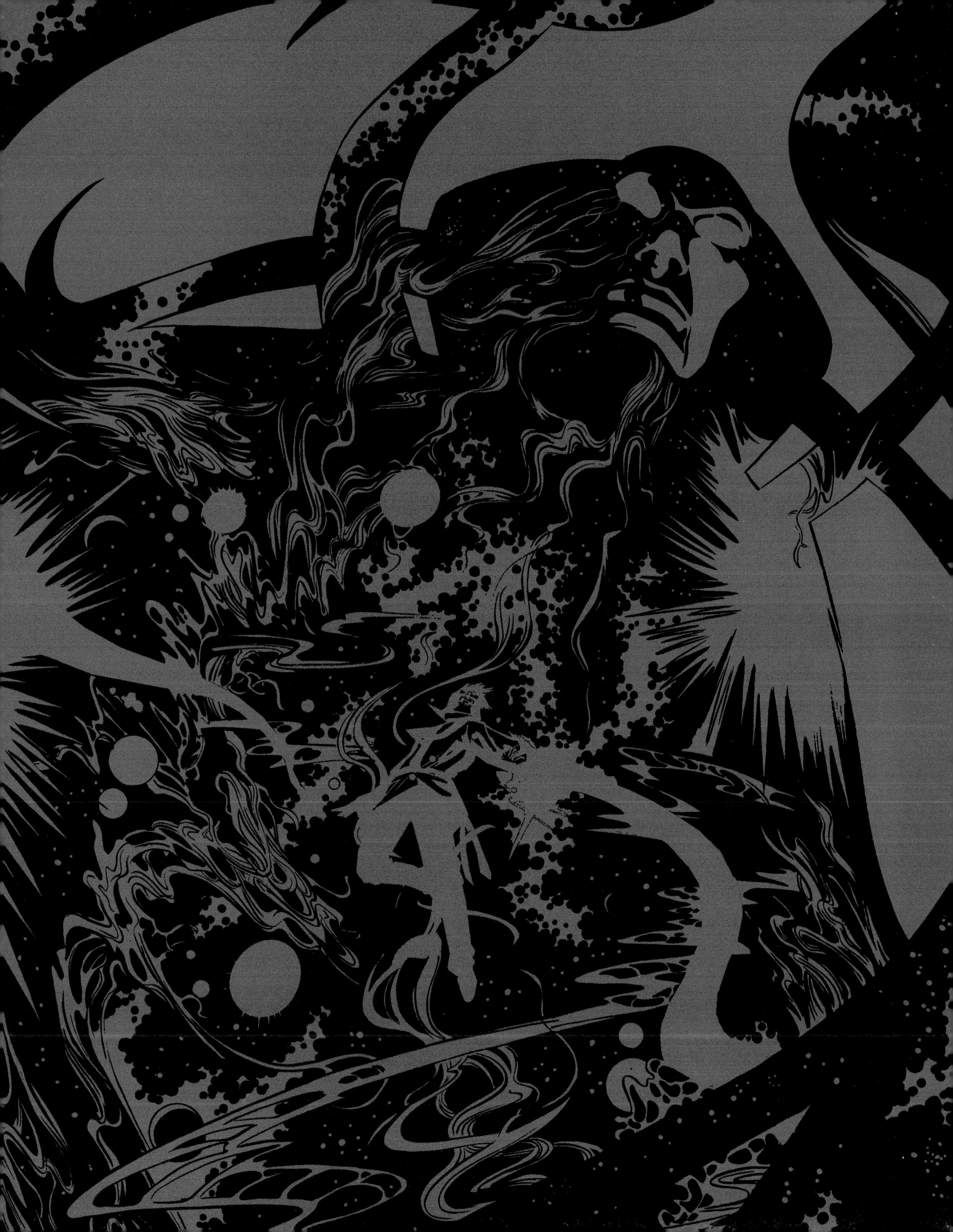

THE VISHANTI

The Vishanti are a trio of extremely powerful mystical beings, named Agamotto, Hoggoth, and Oshtur, who have acted benevolently toward the human race for thousands of years. Through their dealings with human wizards, the position of Sorcerer Supreme was created. It is under their authority that each new Sorcerer Supreme attains the mantle and becomes the Earthly realm's champion and protector.

"BY THE POWER OF ALL-KNOWING VISHANTI, BY THE VISION OF THE ALL-SEEING VISHANTI, I COMMAND YOU—BE GONE!"
The Ancient One

◄ *Three's company* On occasion the Vishanti have appealed directly to Doctor Strange to aid them in their plans.

THE MYSTIC TRINITY

Long before the other Elder Gods—including her sibling, Chthon—met their fate, Oshtur left Earth to explore other realms. At some point in her wanderings she met the being known as Hoggoth, and produced a son named Agamotto. By combining their might, the three became the godlike entity Vishanti—though each also retains their individual personas. They keep a watchful eye on Earth, lending aid and magical energy to its mystics, as well as assistance through a much sought-after tome of spells they created, The Book of the Vishanti. They mostly act through their agent, the Sorcerer Supreme, but in times of great peril they have been known to intervene directly on the side of humanity, even fighting the likes of Dormammu and cosmic world devourer Galactus.

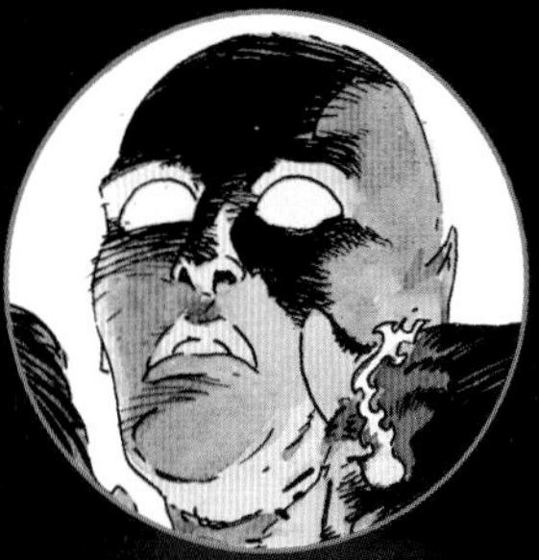

Hoggoth
Like his fellow members of the trinity, Hoggoth can appear in many forms, though most often he chooses that of a wise old man. He is an extremely powerful entity within the realm of magic, and a curious explorer of the cosmos.

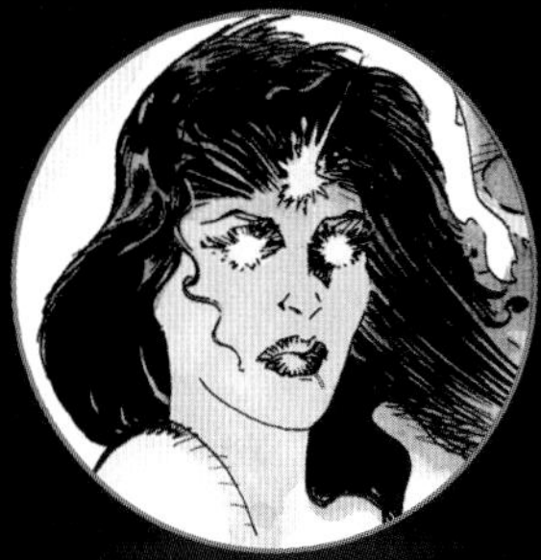

Oshtur
Often assuming the form of a beautiful woman, Oshtur is one of the Elder Gods and the mother of Agamotto. As a force of mystical vitality, she is known for her might, but she is also a fierce defender of logic and reason.

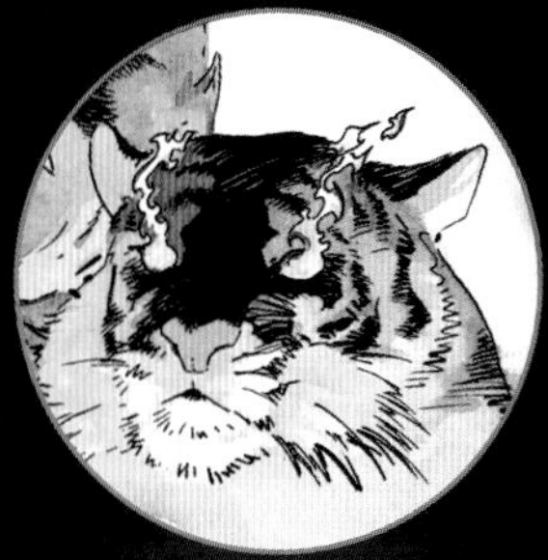

Agamotto
Agamotto has been seen as a caterpillar, a tiger, and in other forms. He was Earth's first Sorcerer Supreme, and his power matches—and possibly exceeds—the combined might of the other two members of the Vishanti.

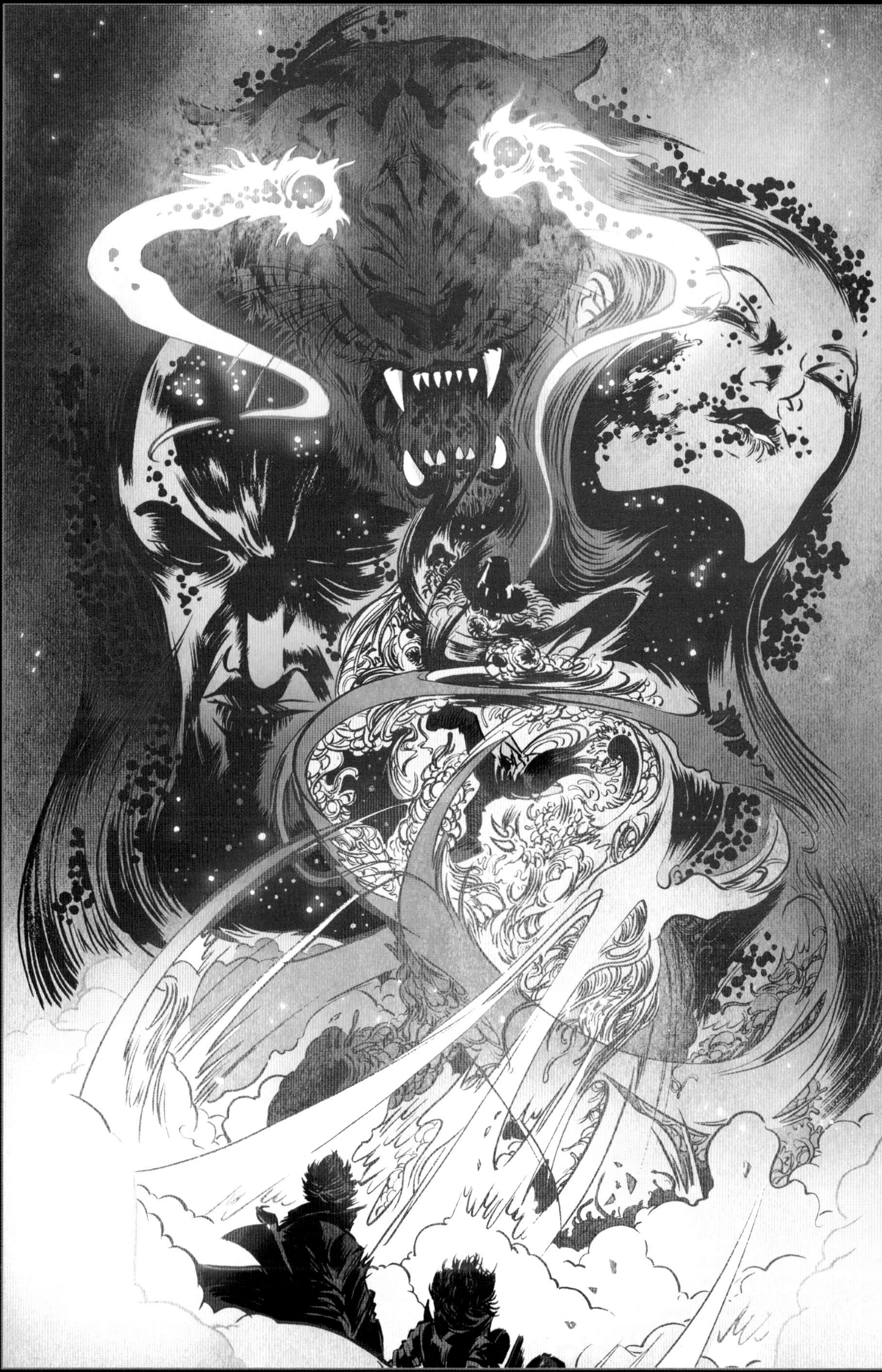

▲ ***Power of three*** Once, while Doctor Strange was an apprentice, the Vishanti intervened to save the life of his friend, Wong.

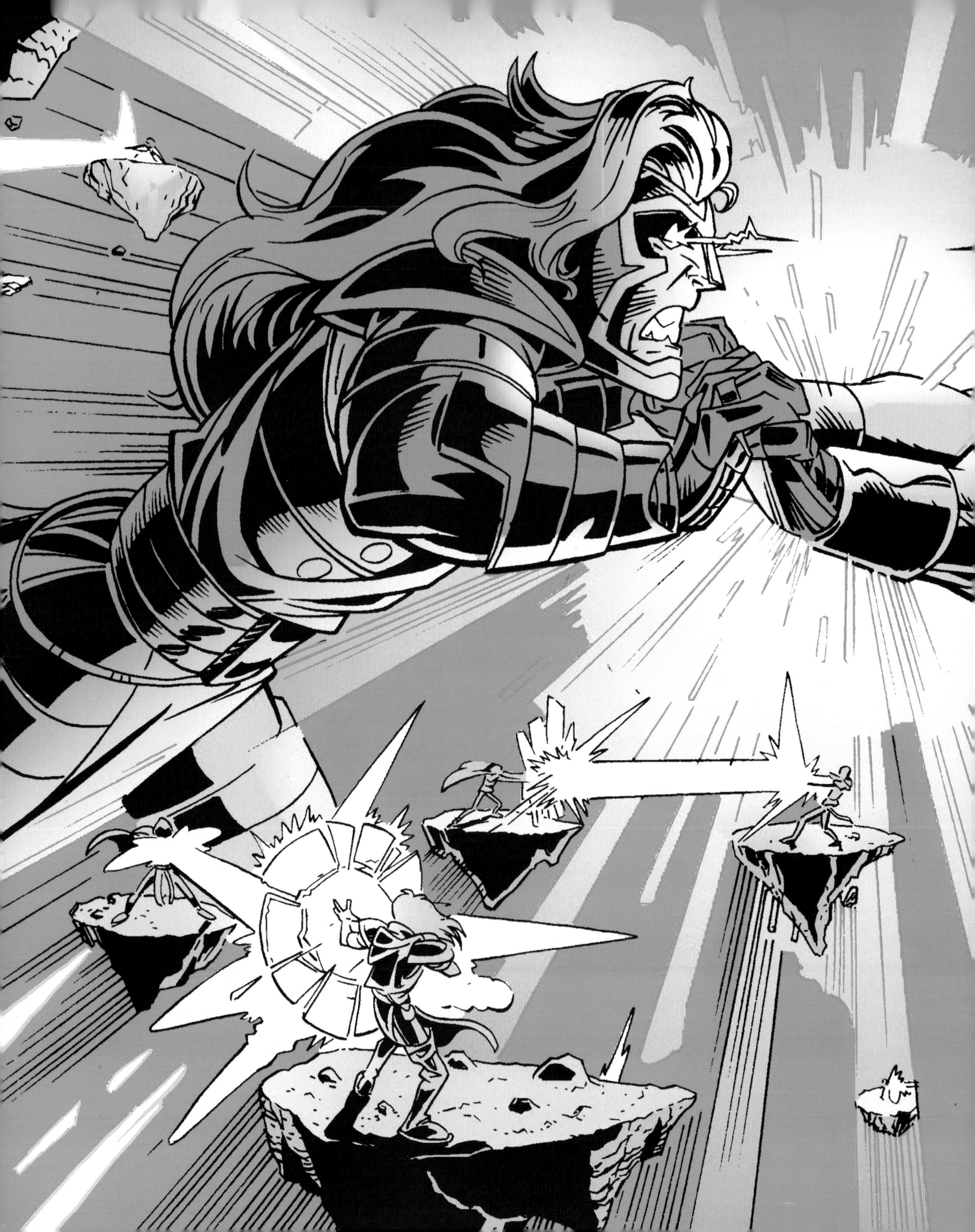

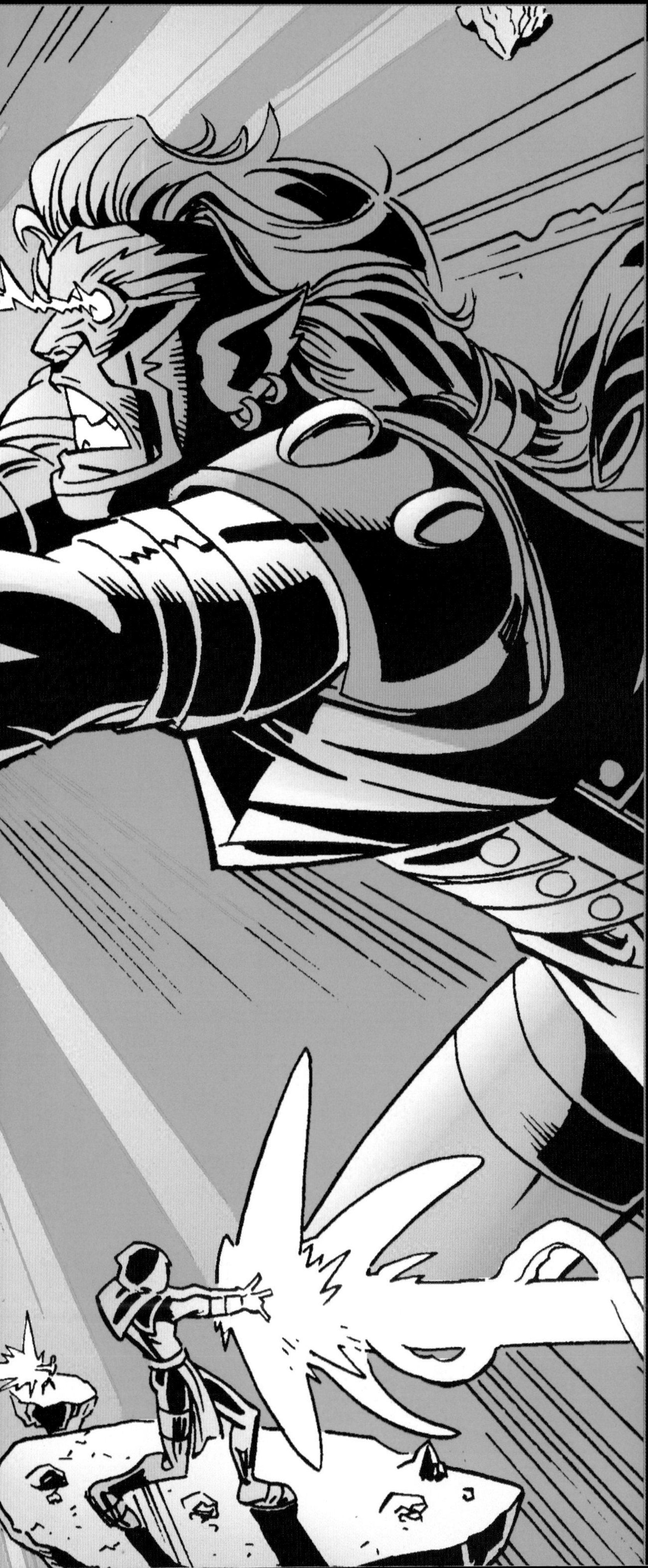

WAR OF THE SEVEN SPHERES

Doctor Strange joined the Vishanti when they requested his aid in a war that raged across the mystical plane. He was reluctant to join them, as the war could—and did—take him away from Earth for thousands of years. At first he declined, but at the cost of losing the title of Sorcerer Supreme. Eventually he relented and fought on the Vishanti's side, helping to defeat their foes, the Trinity of Ashes. Victorious, the Vishanti bent time to return Strange to Earth just before he had originally left.

◀ ***War of magic*** For 5,000 years and across the endless realms, the Vishanti and their evil opposites, the Trinity of Ashes, battled for mystic supremacy.

Sphere of Sara-Kath

After winning the War of the Seven Spheres and enabling Doctor Strange to return safely home, one of the enchanted talismans at the center of the war—the Sphere of Sara-Kath—fell to earth. Here it was accidentally used to release the Gremlin-Lord, Buel. The malevolent creature was eventually subdued by Strange, with a little help from Spider-Man.

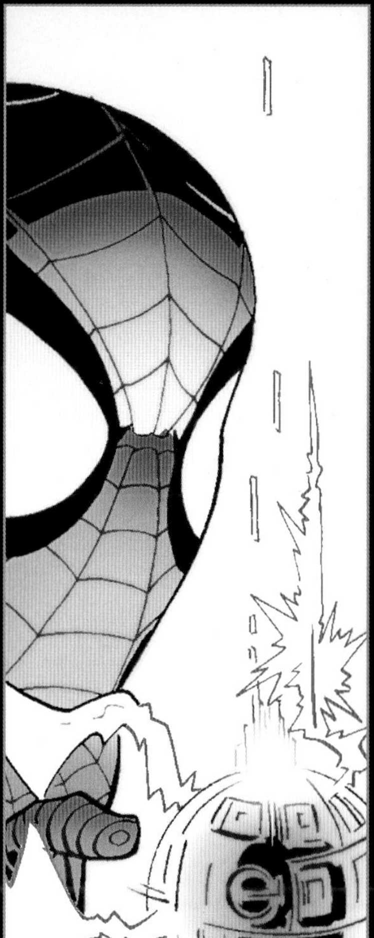

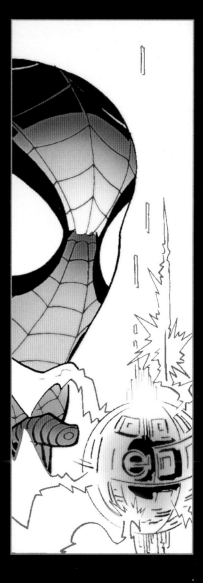

ETERNITY

From the beginning of time until its very end, there is Eternity. This abstract cosmic being is the personification of all life in the universe. Eternity is aware of everything that happens on every plane of existence, but very rarely participates or intervenes—unless events threaten to have serious consequences on a cosmic scale.

▼ *Universe made visible*
When he reveals himself to lesser beings, Eternity adapts a humanoid form that can be easily comprehended.

▲ *A mighty force* With the energy of the entire universe at his disposal, Eternity is able to call upon awesome levels of power.

ALL THAT IS

Eternity was born when the universe came into being. All-knowing, all-seeing, and all-powerful, Eternity is truly one of the most extraordinary entities in existence—although "he" exists without true shape or form. Eternity has complete mastery over time and space, and is able to be in any place at any moment. As the abstract embodiment of the universe, he is immortal. Eternity is able to control and transform all matter, altering and remodeling reality to his will.

While few creatures are even aware of his existence, Eternity has been confronted by contenders for his power. He came under assault when the mad Titan, Thanos,

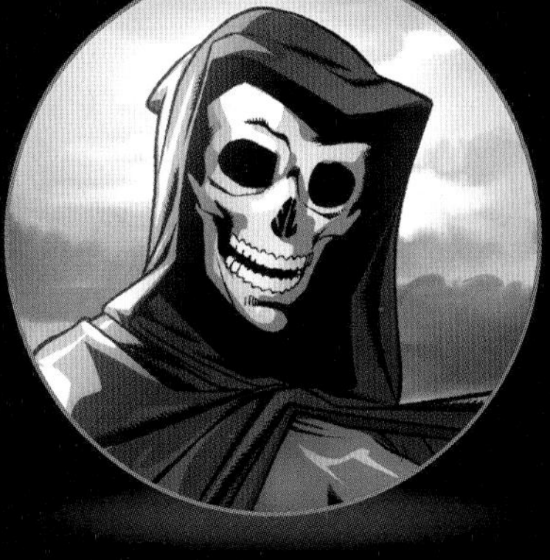

Death
Where Eternity is the presence of life, so his sibling Death is the absence of it. The two exist to keep the universe in harmony.

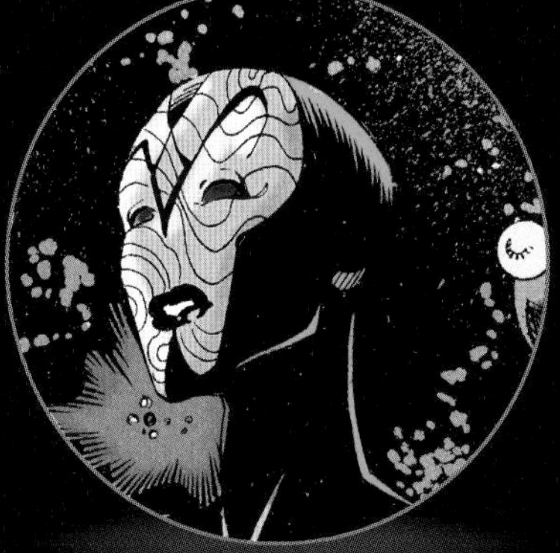

Infinity
Eternity's other sibling, Infinity, encompasses the immenseness of space itself and the universe's need to grow and expand.

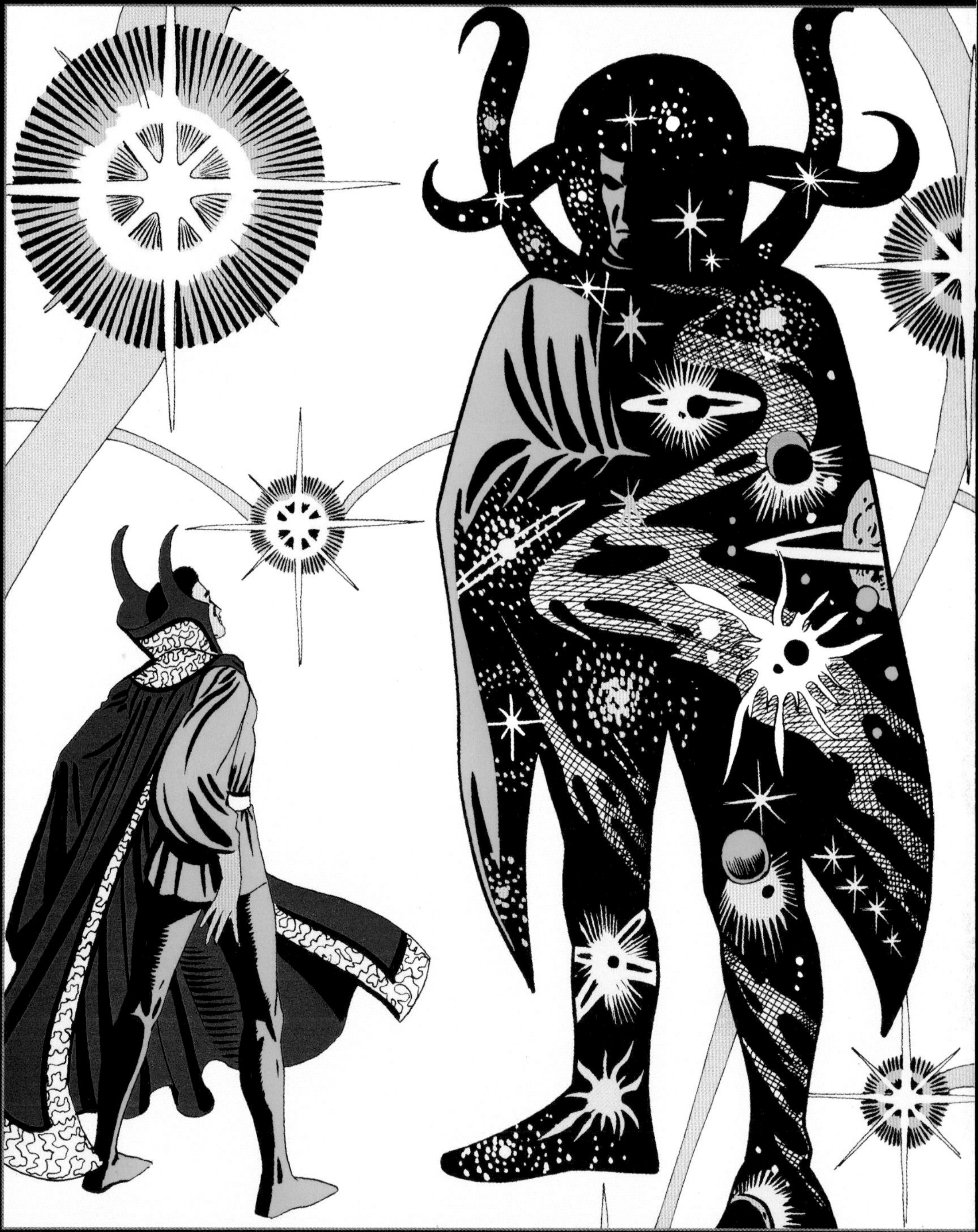

▲ ***Audience with forever*** Seeking additional power to combat Dormammu and Mordo and aid an ailing Ancient One, Doctor Strange came before Eternity.

attempted to kill all life in the universe, and when the Beyonders, a mighty alien race, tried to destroy every powerful cosmic being on every plane of existence.

On rare occasions, Eternity has made his presence known to lesser life forms, taking on a humanoid shape that encompasses the endless expanse of the stars, the planets, and the emptiness of the universe. He has also been seen in this form by those whose awareness of higher powers allows them to perceive him. When deemed necessary, Eternity will sometimes employ mortal agents such as Doctor Strange to do his bidding. For his part, the Sorcerer Supreme has also, on occasion, gone to Eternity's aid.

"NOW YOU WILL FIND THAT I AM NOT ABOVE WRATH."
Eternity

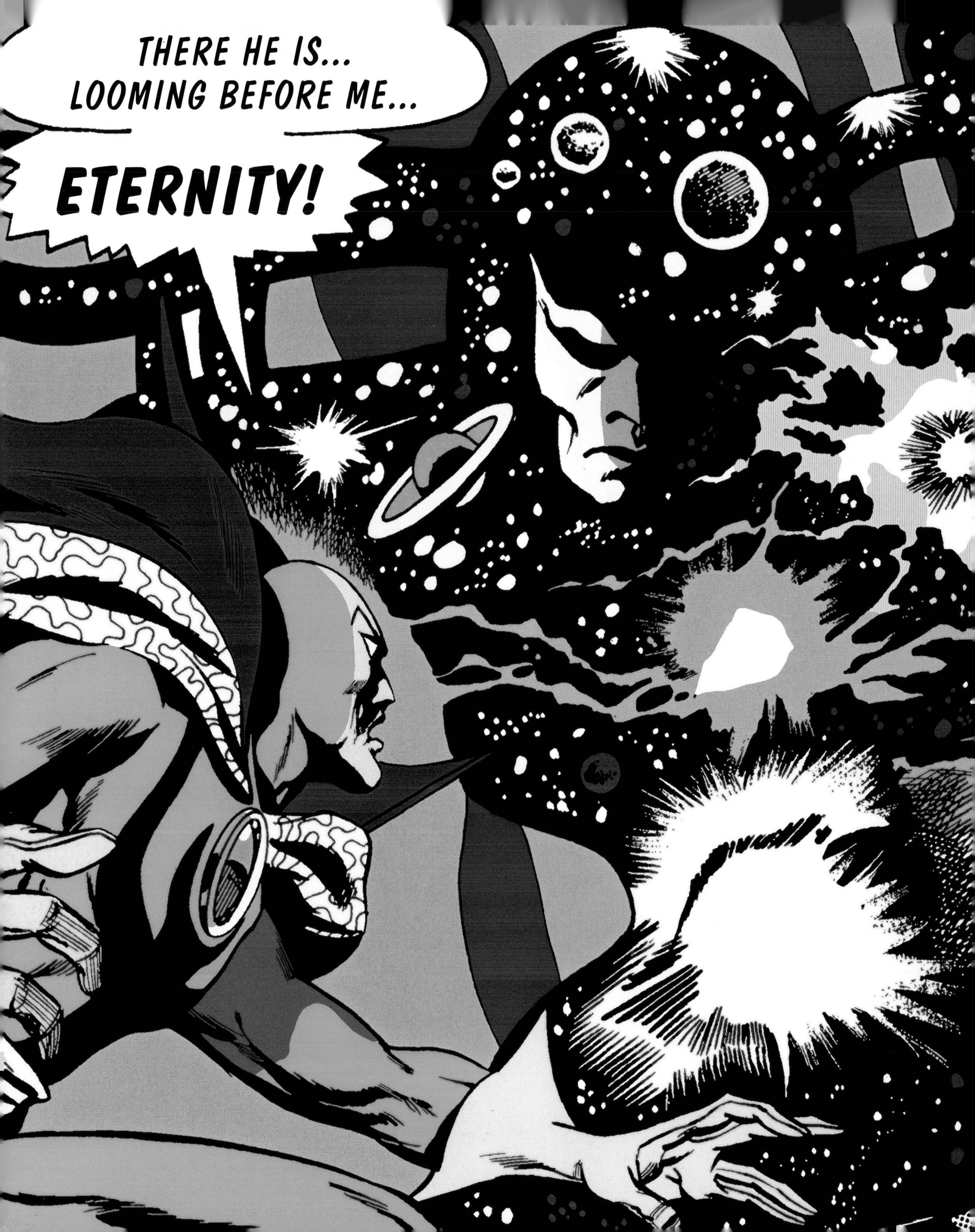
THERE HE IS...
LOOMING BEFORE ME...
ETERNITY!

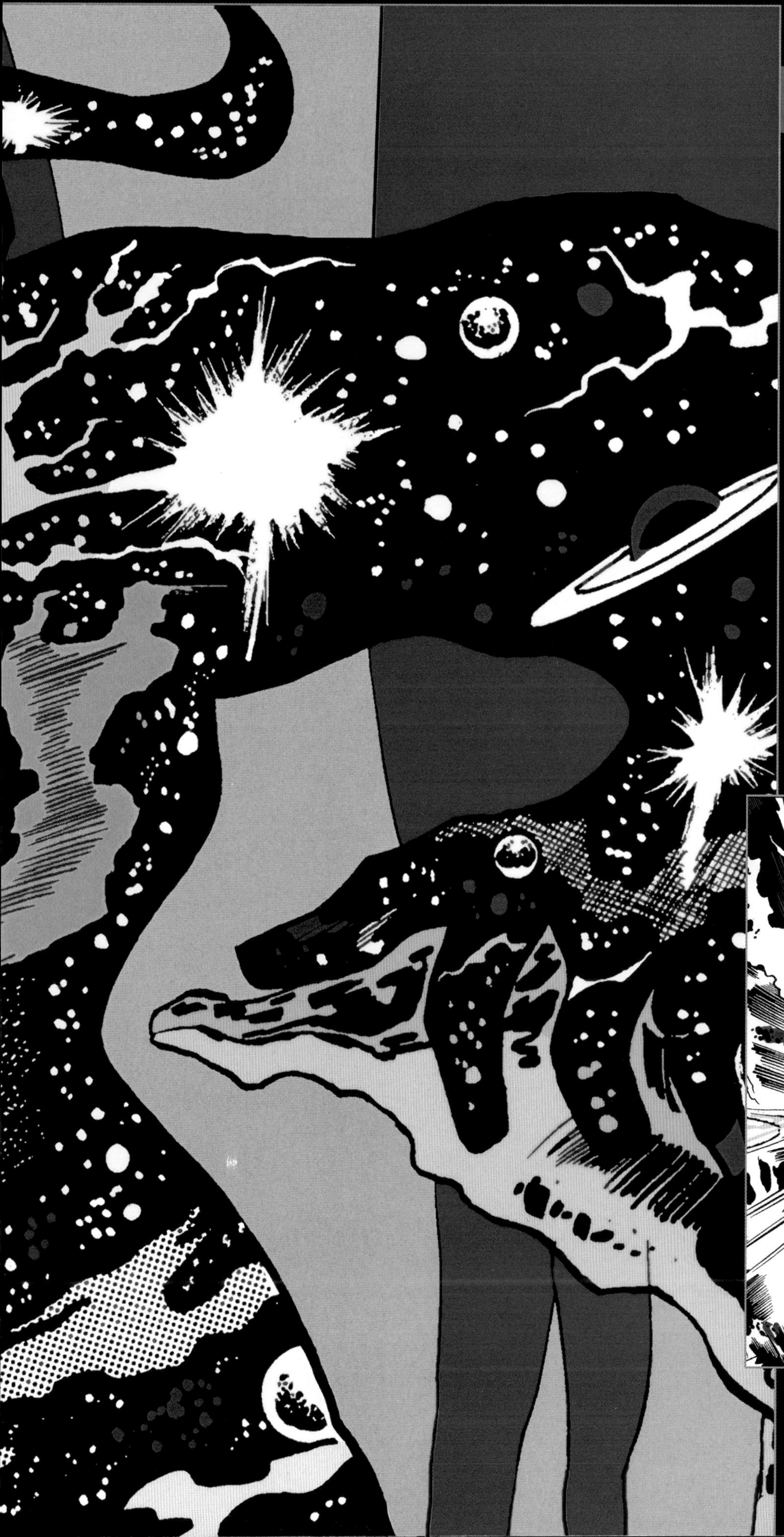

A DREAMING GOD

Doctor Strange once came to the aid of Eternity—and all mankind—against the demon Nightmare. Hatching his most ambitious scheme yet, Nightmare lulled Eternity to sleep by harnessing the combined energies of the universe's slumbering creatures. Now able to influence Eternity's sleeping mind, Nightmare had him dream Earth's destruction. Strange defeated Nightmare, but had a more difficult time convincing Eternity to save humanity, as the human race seemed insignificant to the cosmic being. Eventually, Eternity relented and remade the Earth, leaving only Doctor Strange to know of the utter annihilation that could have been mankind's fate.

◀ ***Searching for Eternity*** In his efforts to counter Nightmare's scheme, Doctor Strange passed through many realities before finally finding Eternity.

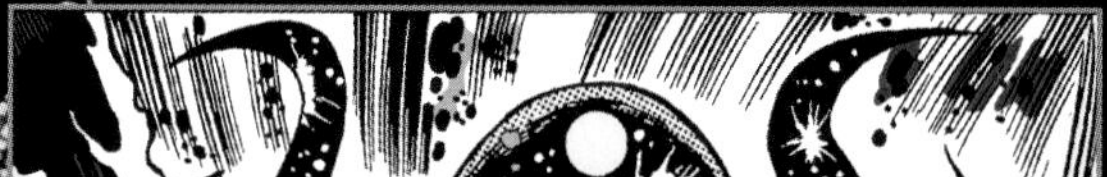

▲ ***Unchained god*** The bonds holding Eternity captive were smashed by Doctor Strange's spells.

THE LIVING TRIBUNAL

At the very limits of what the mind can comprehend, there is the multiverse. Within it are infinite dimensions and alternate realities, all of which coexist in balance. When events in one reality or dimension threaten to upset that balance, the Living Tribunal comes forward to restore order—even if it means the destruction of entire worlds or races. As such, all who stand before the Living Tribunal, including the Sorcerer Supreme, must tread carefully.

▲ *An elevated presence* Though he may appear humanoid, mortal concepts such as good and evil, right and wrong, have no meaning for the Living Tribunal.

REALITY'S JUDGE

The Living Tribunal stands at the very peak of power—both cosmic and mystical—in the known universe and beyond. He has the ability to obliterate entire galaxies and change entire realities on a whim. Yet this extraordinary being does little on whim, for it is his responsiblity to maintain balance across multiple realities. He alone sits in judgment of the multiverse, and his judgments may seem harsh to lesser beings who cannot comprehend his decisions. When Thanos threatened to extinguish life in this reality, the Living Tribunal refused to intervene. He reasoned that the mad Titan's action did not upset the balance of the universe, but in fact followed one of the universe's oldest laws— that only the strongest will survive.

The Living Tribunal presents himself as a giant humanoid with a golden body. He has three covered faces, representing his multiple personalities: equity, necessity, and revenge. Ordinarily, the Living Tribunal speaks through the face of equity. Despite being the most powerful force in the multiverse, the Living Tribunal has stated that even he serves a master—a supreme being known as One-Above-All.

◀ *Above and beyond* Cold, distant, all-powerful: the Living Tribunal is without equal in all reality.

The Stranger

The Living Tribunal has hinted that the enigmatic cosmic entity known as the Stranger was once a fourth part of his personality.

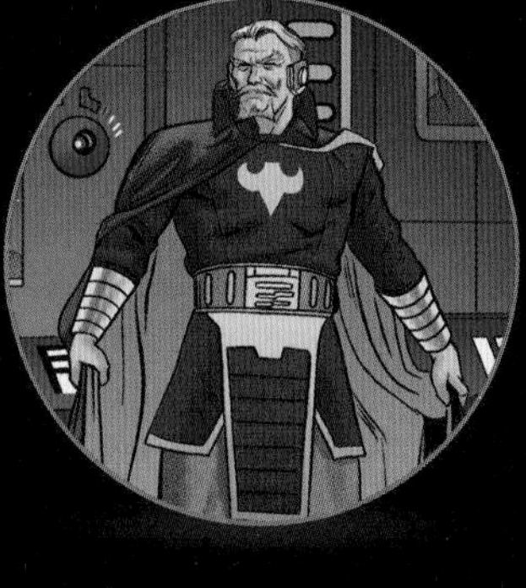

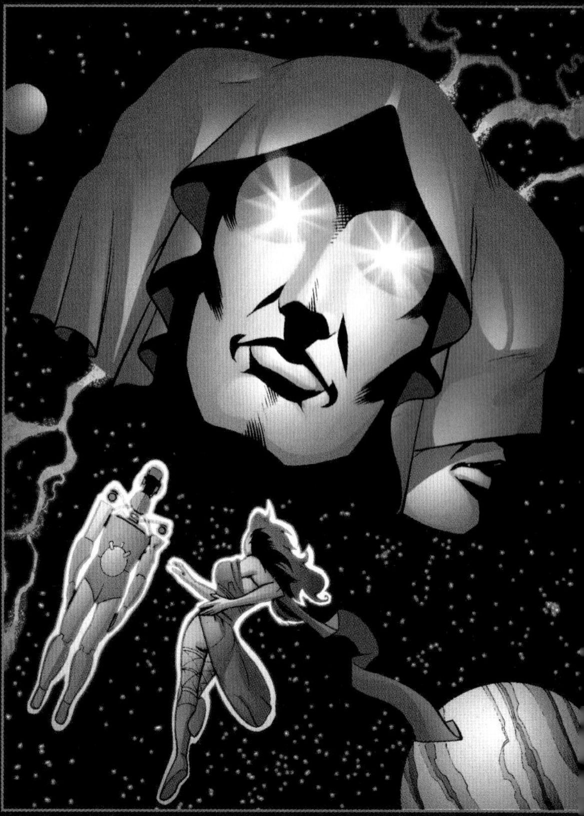

▶ ***Face to face*** The hero She-Hulk was once shown the Living Tribunal's three faces: equity, necessity, and revenge.

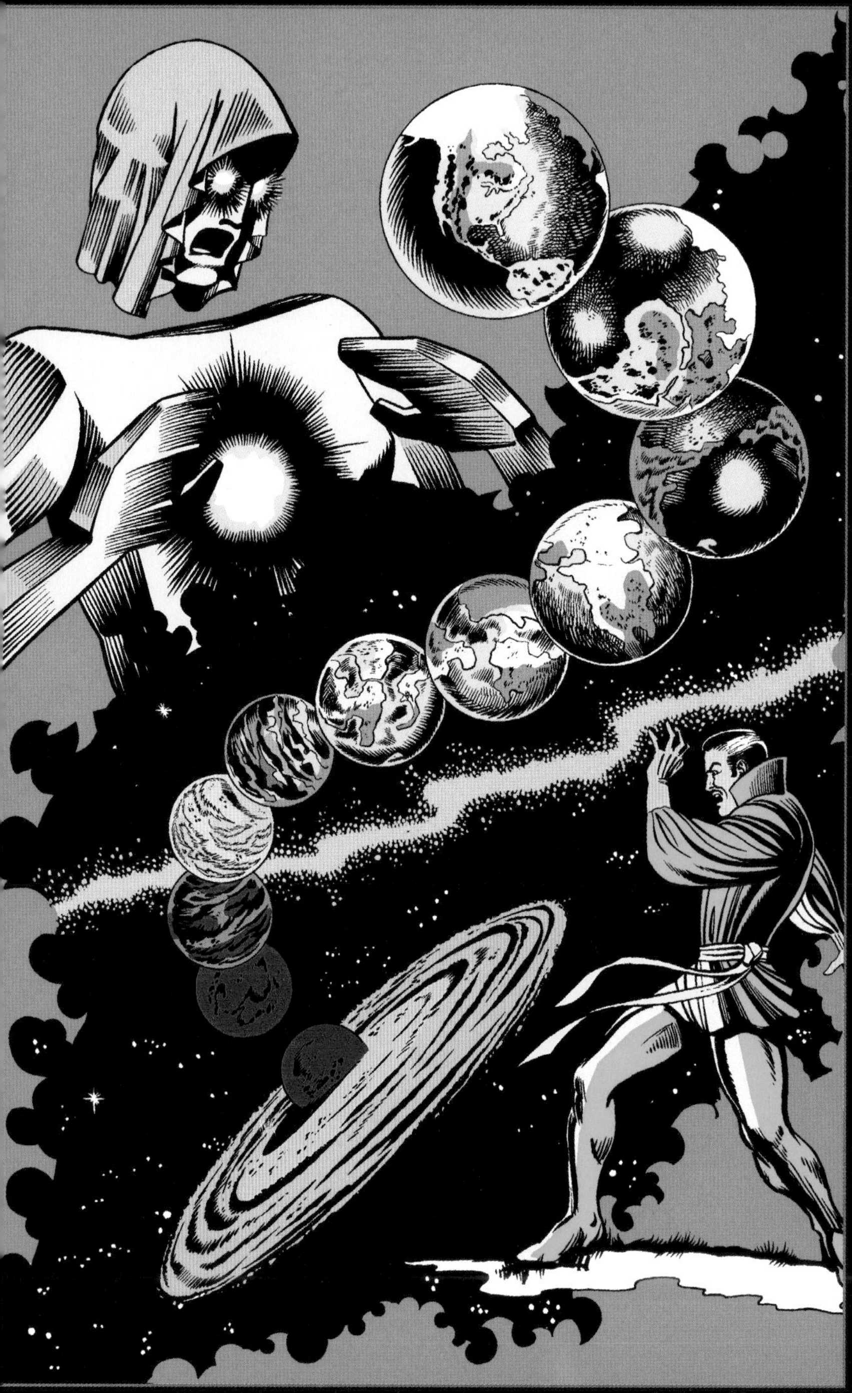

▲ ***Multiversal magistrate*** The Living Tribunal stands in judgment over every aspect of the multiverse—including Doctor Strange.

"MY TASK IS TO JUDGE REALITY'S MOST PRESSING ISSUES."
The Living Tribunal

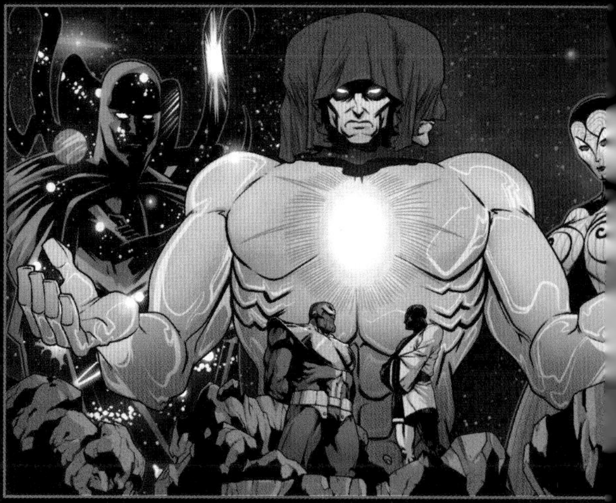

Jury of peers

When Thanos, the mad Titan, was tried for crimes against reality, the Living Tribunal sat in judgment alongside fellow cosmic entities Eternity, the In-Betweener, and Infinity.

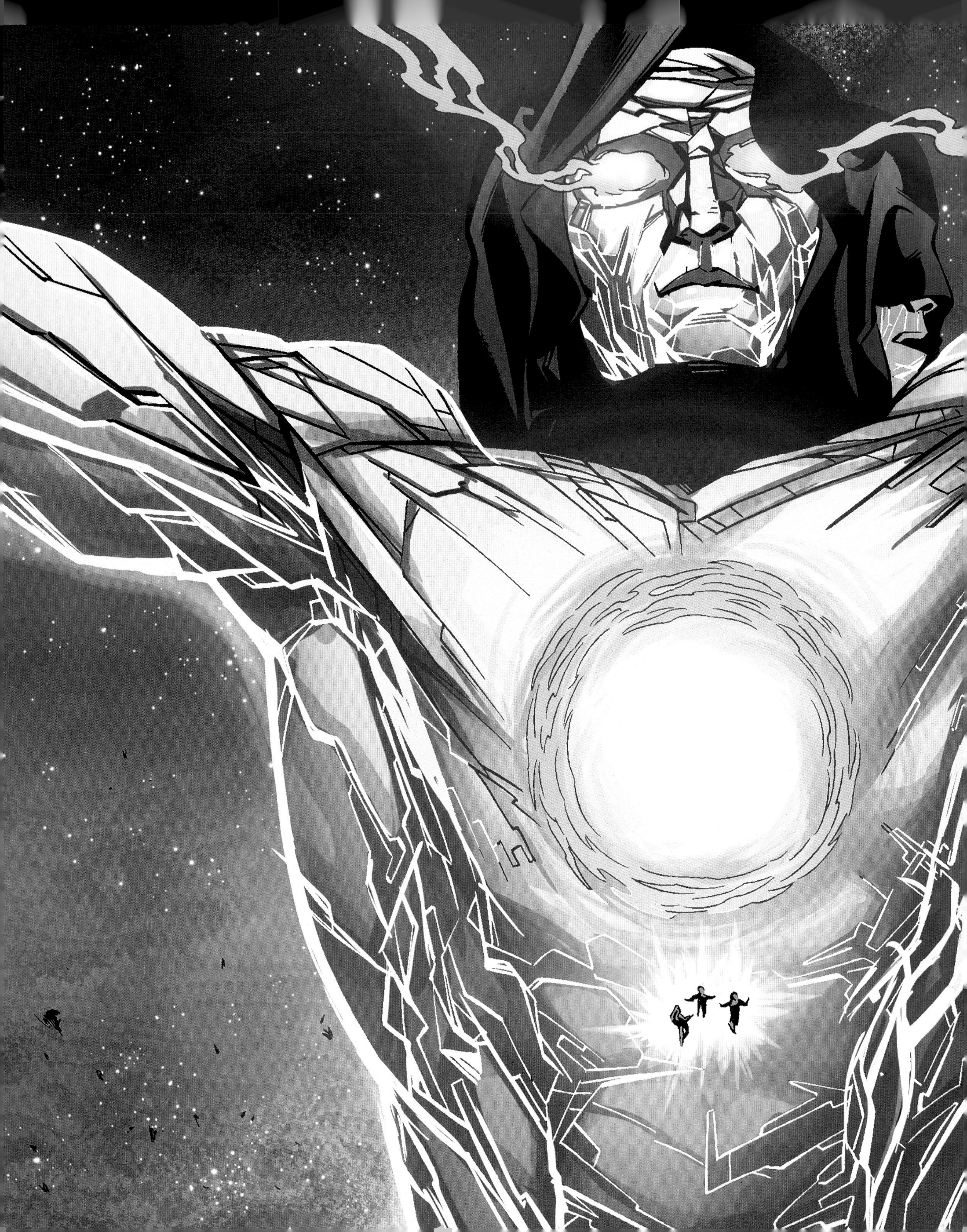

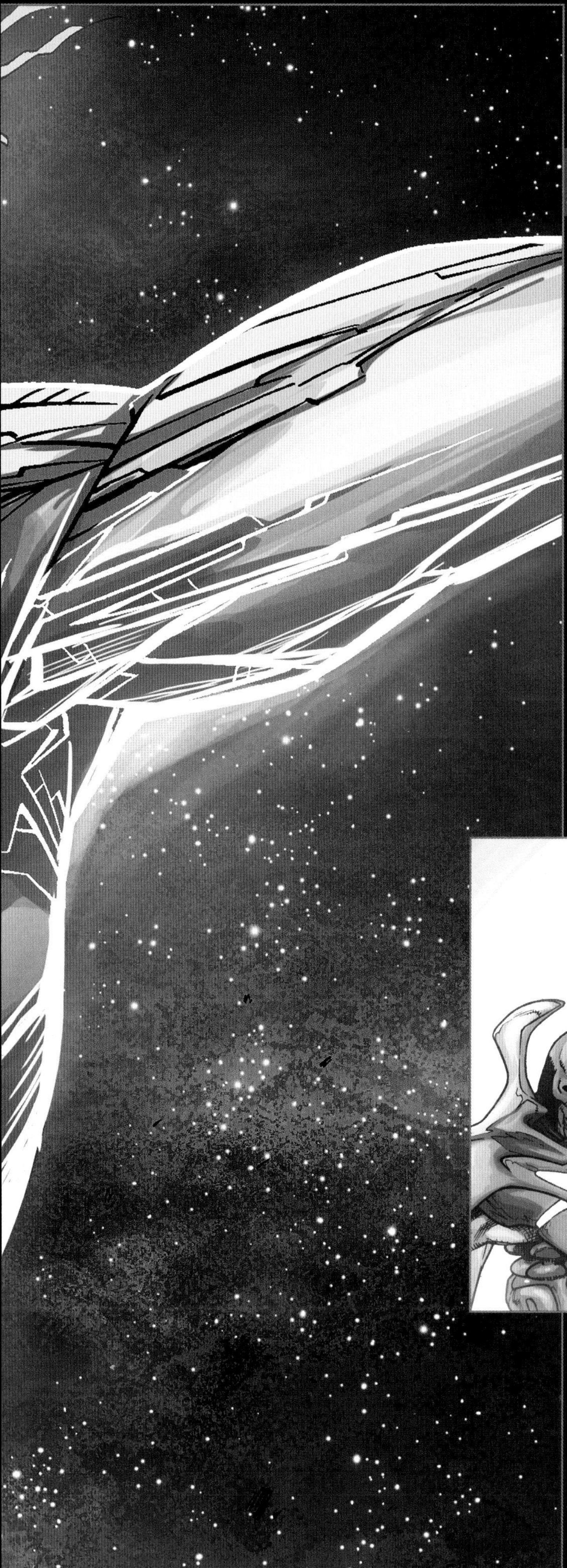

◀ ***Judgment day*** Although the Living Tribunal existed on a scale far greater than the Beyonders, he was still defeated by their combined might.

DEATH OF A TRIBUNAL

As part of an experiment designed to bring about the end of everything, the near-omnipotent extra-dimensional beings the Beyonders set out to destroy every godlike entity in the multiverse. After vanquishing the almighty alien race the Celestials, the In-Betweener, Eternity, and others, the Beyonders finally faced the Living Tribunal. Their battle unfolded across all realities simultaneously, until at last the Living Tribunal fell. He landed on a barren asteroid, his body seemingly as lifeless as his rocky surroundings.

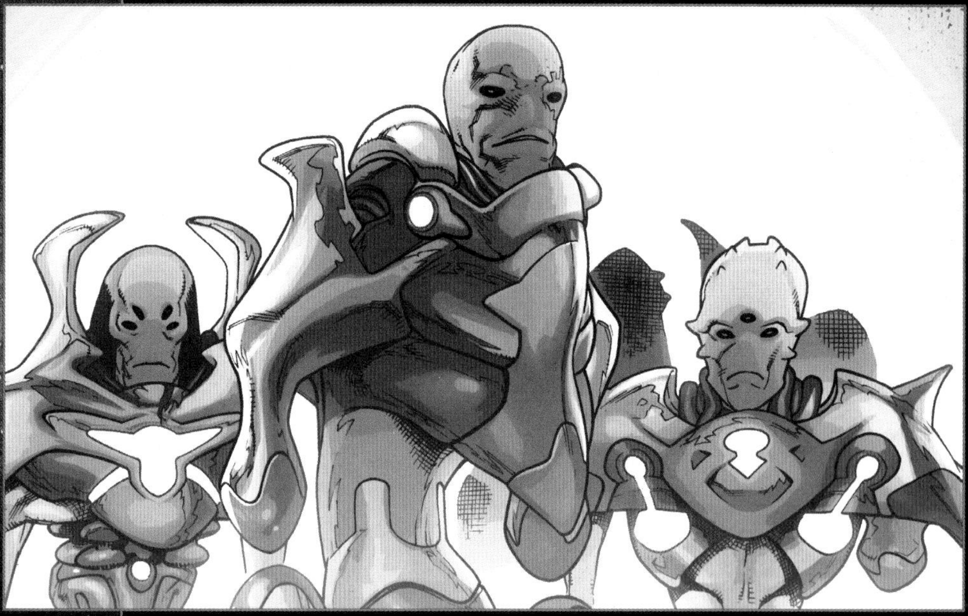

Beyond the Beyonders
The precise link between the Beyonders and the singular cosmic being the Beyonder is unclear. However, when Hank Pym—then under the alias Yellowjacket—encountered the Beyonders, he referred to the Beyonder as a "child unit."

THE IN-BETWEENER

Life and Death. Good and Evil. Love and Hate. Standing in balance between all the divisions of existence is the entity known as the In-Betweener. Fashioned by two of the most powerful forces in the universe, Lord Chaos and Master Order, the In-Betweener was intended to help bring balance to the universe. However, more often than not, his strict interpretation of reality has led to quite the reverse.

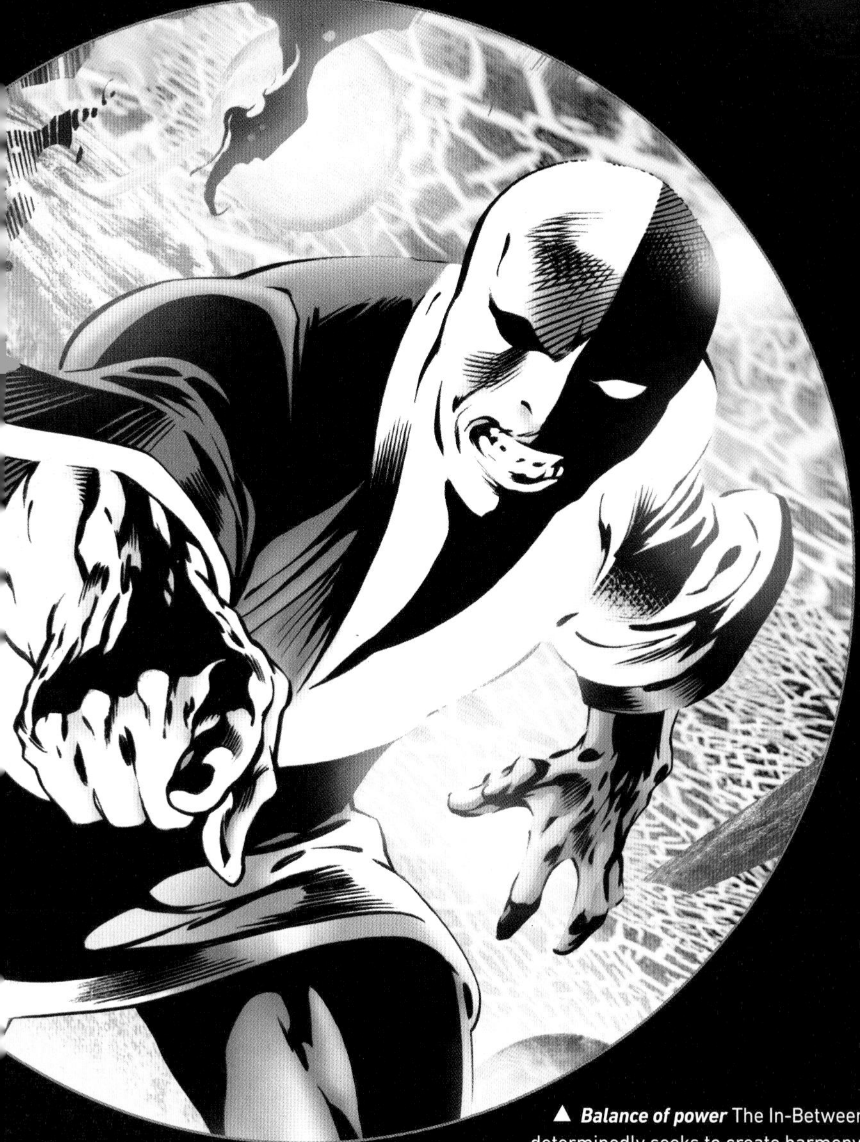

▲ ***Balance of power*** The In-Betweener determinedly seeks to create harmony where there is discord. However, his brashness often led to his undoing.

THE BLACK AND THE WHITE

The In-Betweener's split black-and-white appearance embodies the contradictions of the universe, which he has been empowered to bring into balance. While not as all-powerful as some cosmic entities, he is a formidable force to be reckoned with. He is incalculably strong and can traverse countless galaxies at the speed of thought. He has the power to manipulate matter and to some extent even reality itself. However, even though he is highly attuned to events taking place throughout the universe, he is not all-knowing, and his halfway position between knowledge and ignorance often proves to be one of his greatest vulnerabilities.

As Doctor Strange and other heroes have learned, everything is black and white to the In-Betweener. He has no time for subtleties or shades of gray when choosing a course of action, and his extreme measures have often put the universe in peril. As such, he has come into conflict with beings both mystical and cosmic. Even his own masters, Lord Chaos and Master Order, have been called upon to stop their servant. They even went as far as imprisoning him in a pocket dimension that was in perfect balance, rendering him completely powerless. However, with the universe in constant flux, the In-Betweener will always be ready to restore balance—at all costs.

▼ *Cosmic encounter* In his first confrontation with the In-Betweener, Doctor Strange prevented him from using a group of wizards known as the Creators to remake the universe.

Lord Chaos

Representing the forces of disorder in the universe, Lord Chaos is the physical manifestation of both the reality and the idea of chaos.

Master Order

Inseparable from—yet constantly at odds with his counterpart—Master Order maintains the ideas of equilibrium, discipline, and structure in the universe.

"BY ORDER AND CHAOS I WAS SPAWNED. I AM BEYOND EVEN ETERNITY."
The In-Betweener

◄ *Clash of the titans* While in possession of a powerful Infinity Gem, the In-Betweener had it forcibly taken from him by the death Titan Thanos.

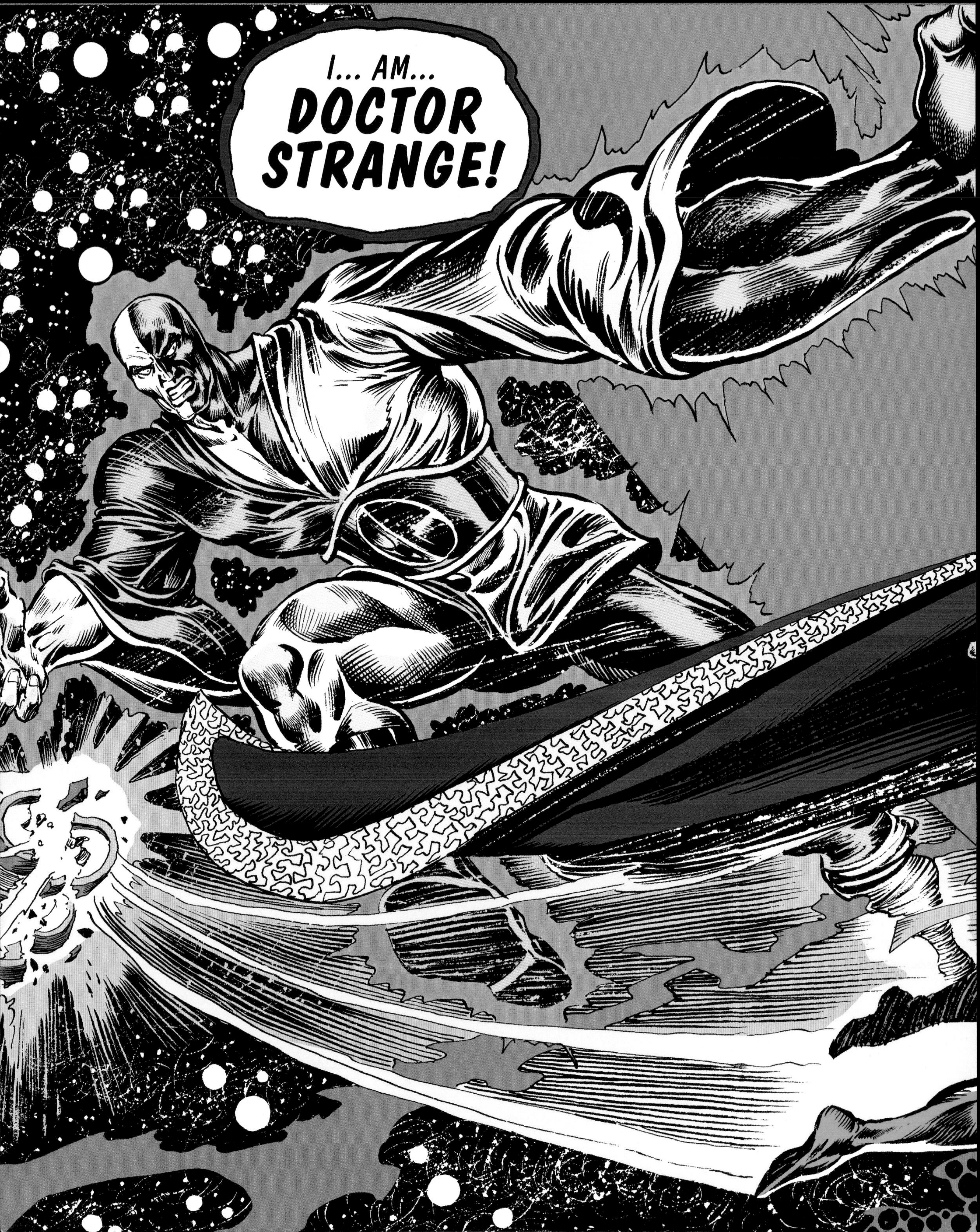
I... AM... DOCTOR STRANGE!

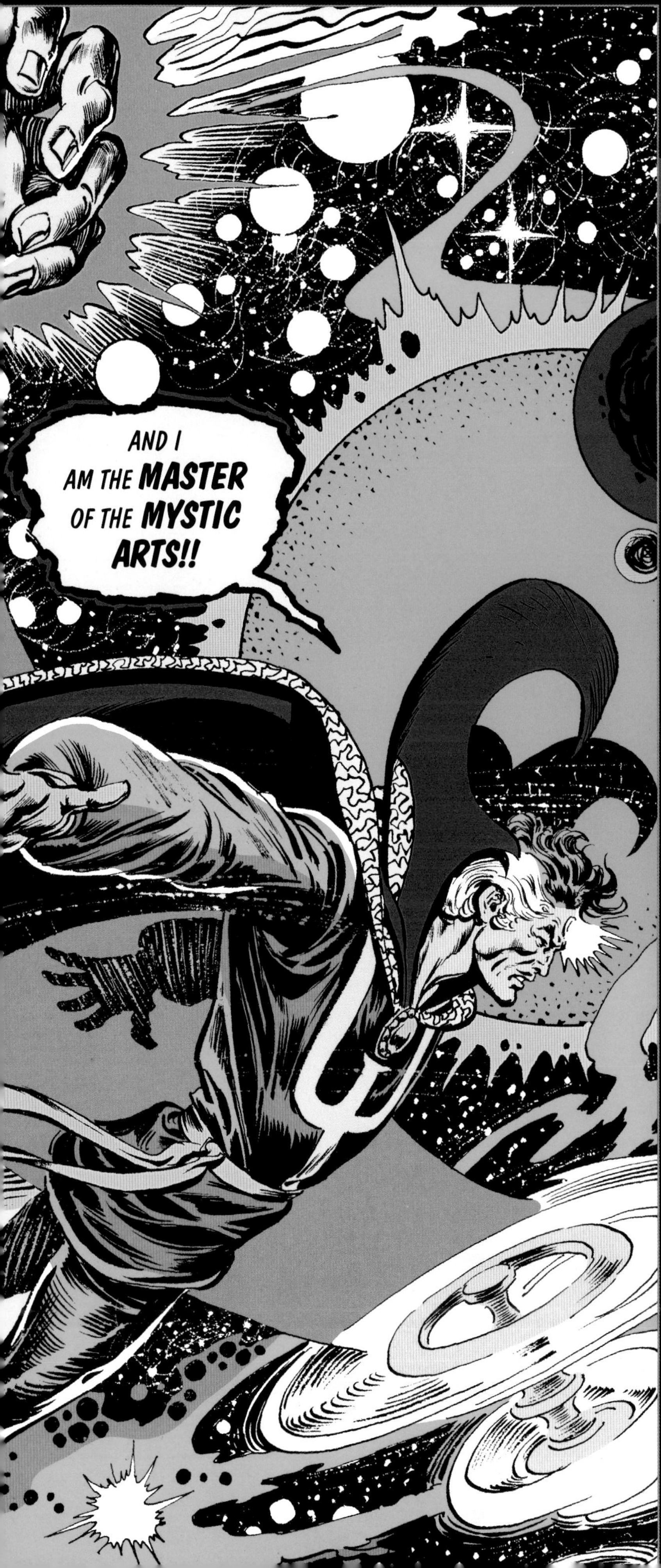
AND I AM THE MASTER OF THE MYSTIC ARTS!!

◀ ***Contest of champions*** When the In-Betweener challenged Doctor Strange, the Master of the Mystic Arts proved more than equal to the contest.

COSMIC COMBAT

In their first encounter, Doctor Strange and the In-Betweener came to blows when the cosmic being sought to prevent the Sorcerer Supreme from returning sanity to a universe gone mad. Their battle raged across dimensions and realities, and almost saw Strange succumb to madness himself. In the end, however, and with the assistance of the Ancient One, Clea, and Wong, the Master of the Mystic Arts was able to best the In-Betweener by turning the power of Lord Chaos and Master Order back on him.

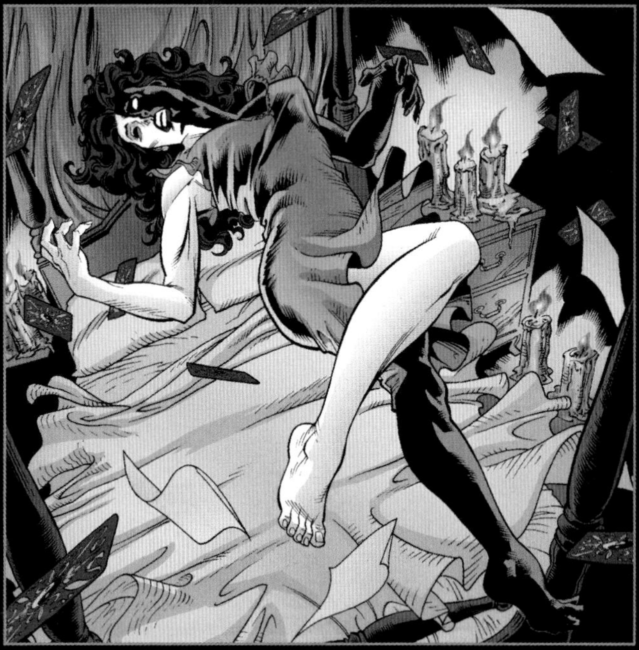

Order out of Chaos
On one occasion, the Chaos half of the In-Betweener possessed the body of the Scarlet Witch in an effort to locate his Order half, which had been taken from him by the villain Scorpio.

As deep and unfathomable as the cosmos itself, the Beyonder's true origins are shrouded in mystery. With reality-altering powers rivaling those of the greatest beings in the universe, he has been said to be many things: the personification of a multiverse in search of purpose; a superhuman whose power became so great that he forgot his Earthly beginnings; and even a portion of escaped energy from the pocket dimensions that power the reality warping Cosmic Cubes. Regardless of his beginnings, the Beyonder is a force to be reckoned with.

▲ *Beyond belief* The Beyonder once transported Manhattan to the asteroid belt, prompting Doctor Strange and the Illuminati to intervene.

◄ *United we stand*
The Beyonder's meddling has often brought him into conflict with Earth's heroes.

Cosmic Cube
Cosmic Cubes are blocks of energy with the ability to reshape reality in any way their possessor wishes.

Beyonder's world
When he was channeled into his own dimension, the Beyonder powered every part of it, including the sun.

FROM BEYOND

At some point in the past, the being known as the Beyonder became intrigued by Earthlings and their capacity for good and evil. Wanting to know more, he kidnapped several heroes and villains, aware that they seemed to possess exceptional extremes of both qualities. He made the heroes and villains fight on a distant planet he created, in the hopes of better understanding them. It proved to be a fascinating experiment that left the Beyonder even more curious about humanity than he was before. Coming to Earth, he continued to interact with heroes, villains, and everyday

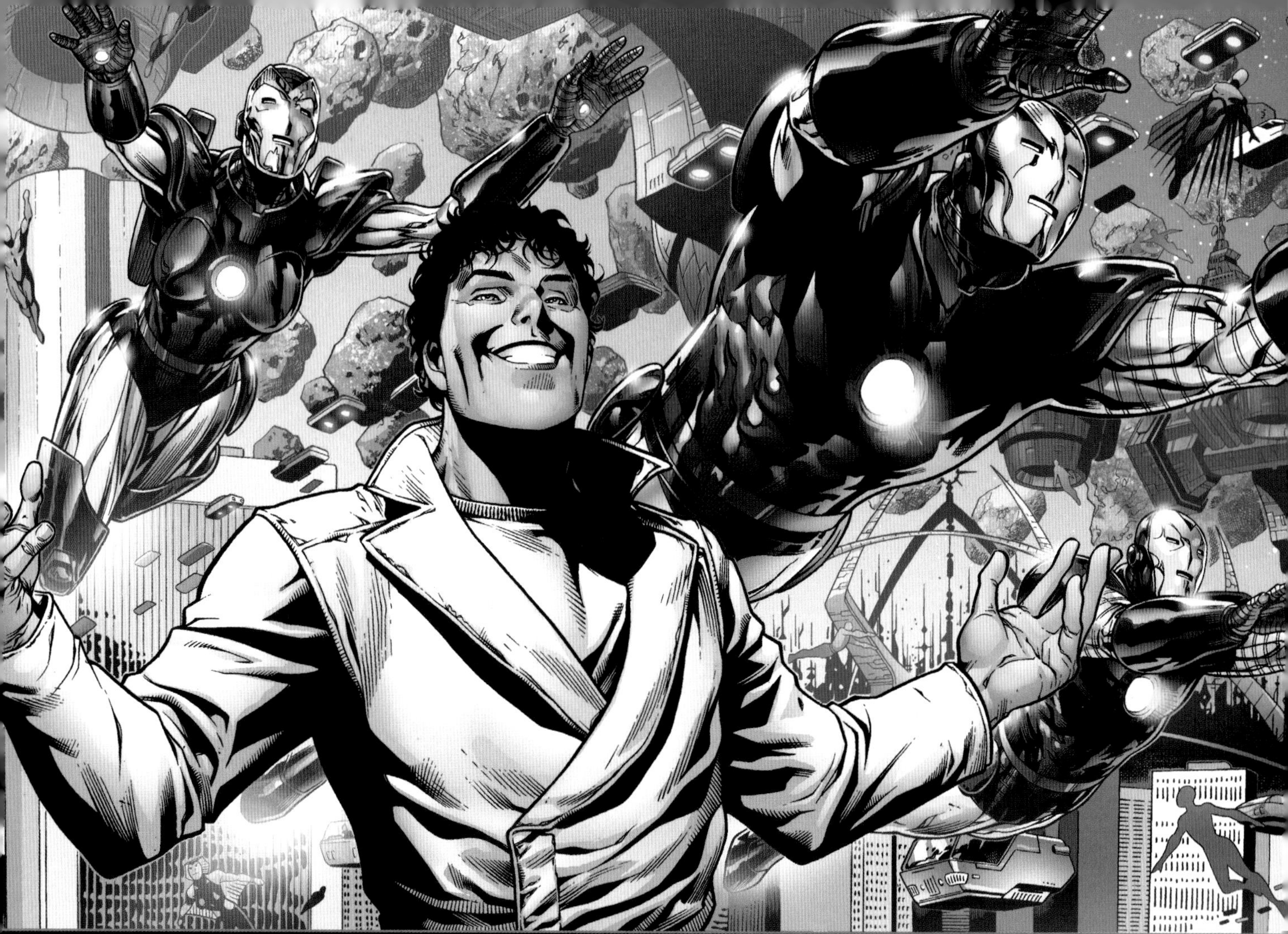

▲ ***Dreams come true*** Such is the Beyonder's power that he can make dreams reality—even Iron Man's desire for armored order.

"I AM SUPREME! IN MY NATIVE REALM I WAS THE UNIVERSE!"

The Beyonder

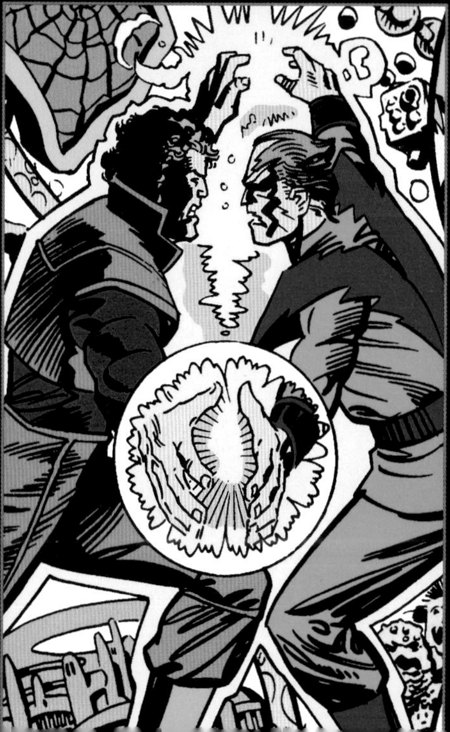

The Molecule Man

A human capable of tapping into the same energies that power the Beyonder, the Molecule Man has clashed with his sometime friend, sometime foe.

people in the hopes of gaining a deeper understanding. Once again, however, the powerful entity often ended up with more questions and confusion than answers.

After having his powers stolen, trying his hand at being a hero, and even attempting to be reborn as a mortal, the Beyonder clashed with Earth's heroes and the equally mighty Molecule Man. The titanic struggle turned the Beyonder to pure energy and transported him into a new dimension, where he found a measure of contentment. Eventually, he himself became a Cosmic Cube—but it is unlikely that the universe has heard the last of the Beyonder.

▶ ***Colliding worlds*** The Beyonders' efforts to end the multiverse caused inter-dimensional Incursions, where realities collided and heroes fought heroes.

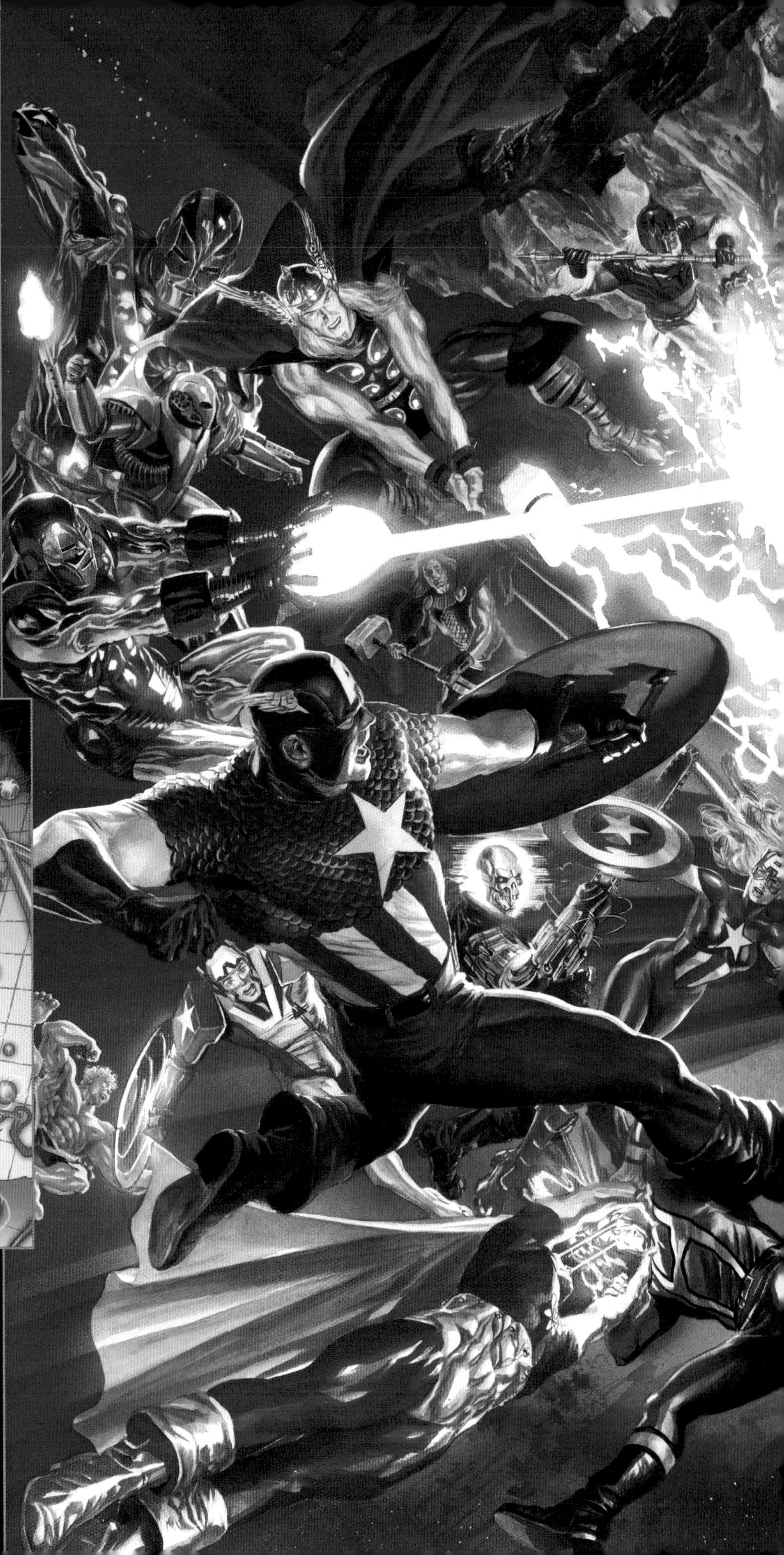

SECRET WARS

A series of cataclysmic events set in motion by the cosmic beings the Beyonders saw heroes from countless realities pitted against one another. Ultimately, all of existence was destroyed, and it was left to Doctor Strange, Doctor Doom, and the Molecule Man to salvage what they could using the stolen power of the Beyonders. Their solution was Battleworld, a patchwork planet composed of fragments of numerous lost worlds. Battleworld was ruled over by Doom—until the Molecule Man and the Fantastic Four's Mr. Fantastic managed to restore reality.

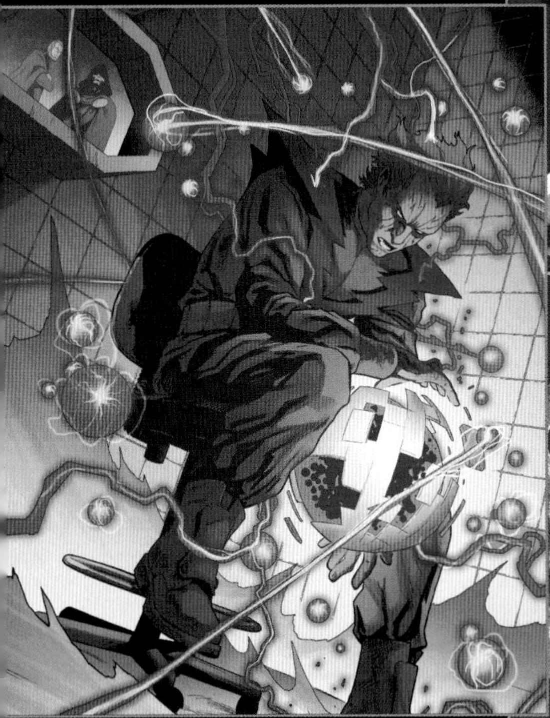

Molecule manipulator
Powered by the same explosive energy as the Beyonder, Owen Reece—alias the Molecule Man—was the key to the otherworldly Beyonders' scheme to destroy reality. However, thanks in part to Doctor Doom, he ended up saving it.

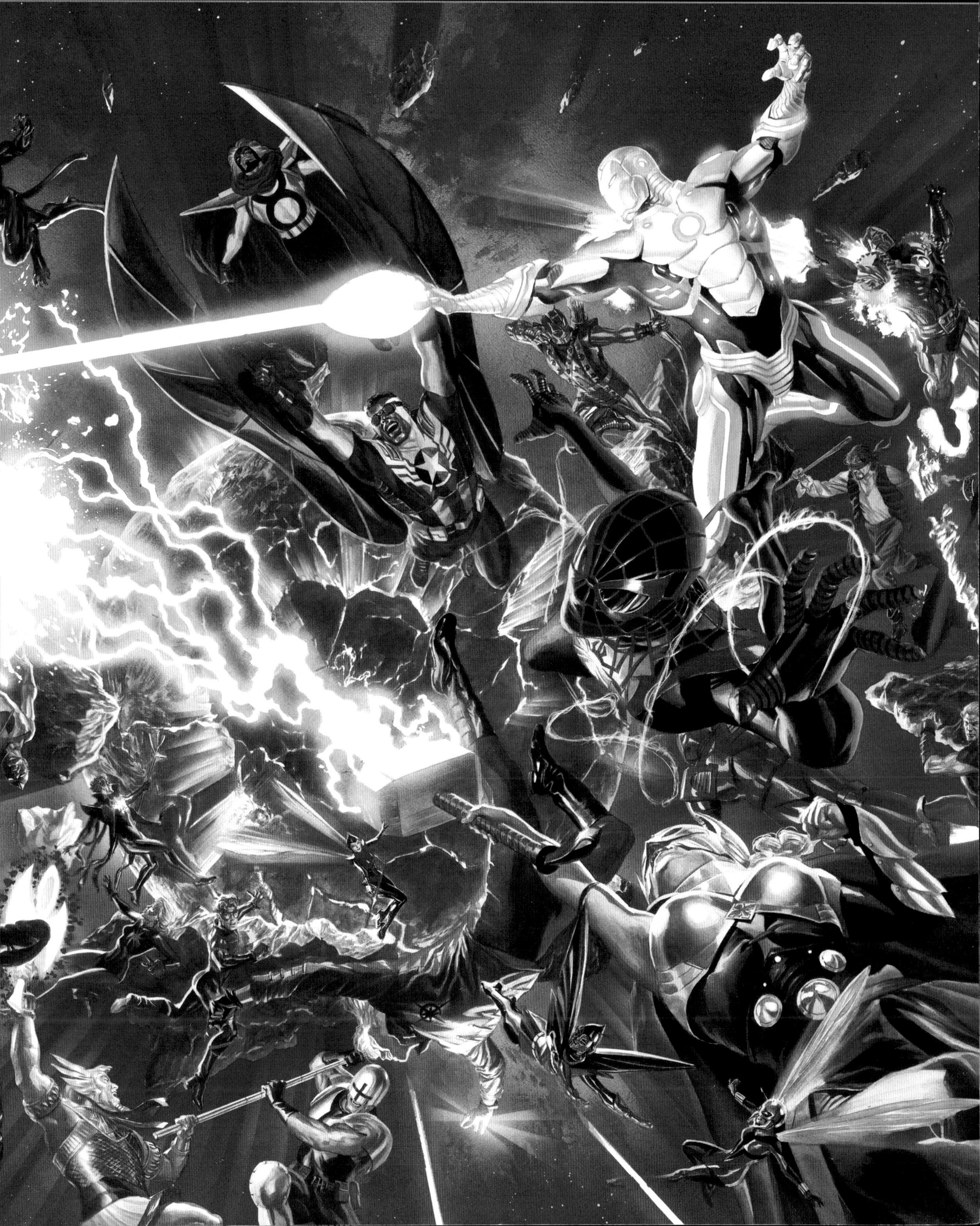

CHAPTER 5
MYSTIC
REALMS

Beyond the Earthly plane of existence, there
lies a myriad of otherwordly domains and
metaphysical dimensions that defy imagination
and description. These weird and wondrous
realms, where time, distance, and the Earthly
laws of physics are meaningless, are largely
hidden from mortal eyes—but not from the
powers of Doctor Strange. From his Sanctum
Sanctorum in New York, he ventures into
these magical regions to seek answers
to mystifying questions or confront
very real threats to his world.

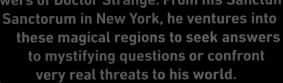

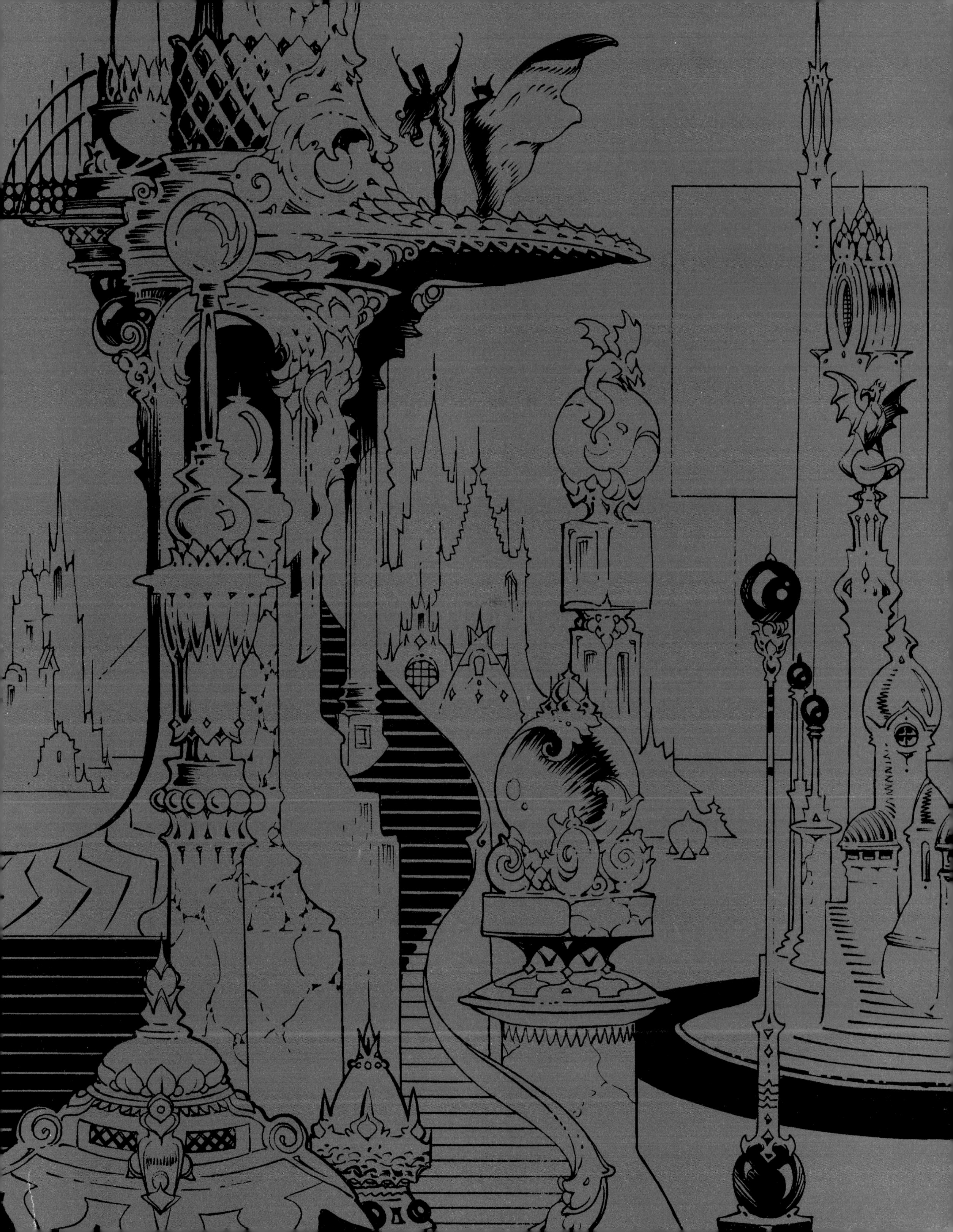

SANCTUM SANCTORUM

Located in the heart of Greenwich Village in New York City, Doctor Strange's townhouse—known as the Sanctum Sanctorum—is not just the home and headquarters of the master mystic. The building also houses his enormous library and collection of magical artifacts, both light and dark, and provides passage to realms far beyond that of this Earth.

Mystic protection

The Sanctum Sanctorum is permanently protected from magical invasion by an intricate web of spells woven by Doctor Strange to augment the house's base energies.

▼ *Strange sanctuary* While locals know the building is the home of an "occult expert," most are unaware of its true purpose.

THE MYSTICAL MANSION

On Bleecker Street, on the corner of Fenno Place, stands a grand, three-story Victorian brownstone, complete with a large, ornate circular window on the sloping roof. Few of the locals are aware that the building is the Sanctum Sanctorum of the Sorcerer Supreme...let alone comprehend the infinite mysteries that lurk within.

Built on the site of pagan sacrifices and Native American rituals from centuries past, and with ley lines running beneath its foundations, the current building is a unique focal point for mystical energies. As a result, it gained a local reputation for being haunted, but it was these energies that drew Doctor Strange to adopt it as his residence and base of operations.

Far from being haunted, the Sanctum Sanctorum—which is run by Strange's loyal manservant, Wong—is indeed "alive" with magic. The exact dimensions of the house are unknown, with the interior seeming to be significantly larger than its external appearances would suggest. While some rooms are fixed in place, they are surrounded by a distortion in time and space, creating labyrinthine corridors and endless chambers that can move around.

The top floor is the most vital area, housing not only Doctor Strange's meditation room but also his mystical library, along with the largest collection of occult objects and artifacts in existence. Strange's prized Orb of Agamotto is also kept here, in its own special anteroom.

Defenders' den

The Sanctum Sanctorum has often been used as a base of operations by Doctor Strange's longtime allies the Defenders.

The Window of Worlds

The distinctive Window of Worlds, which connects to Doctor Strange's meditation chamber, is decorated with a pattern of the Anomaly Rue, the Seal of the Vishanti.

"THERE IS HIS SOMBRE BROWNSTONE… IT STANDS AS PROUD—AS LONELY—AS THE SOLITARY MAN THAT OWNS IT!"

Doctor Strange

▼ *Room of reflection* Doctor Strange's treasured meditation room is located at the top of the Sanctum Sanctorum.

▲ *Under fire* With vast mystical powers contained within its walls, the Sanctum Sanctorum is often threatened. Recently the Empririkul launched a devastating attack on Doctor Strange and his home.

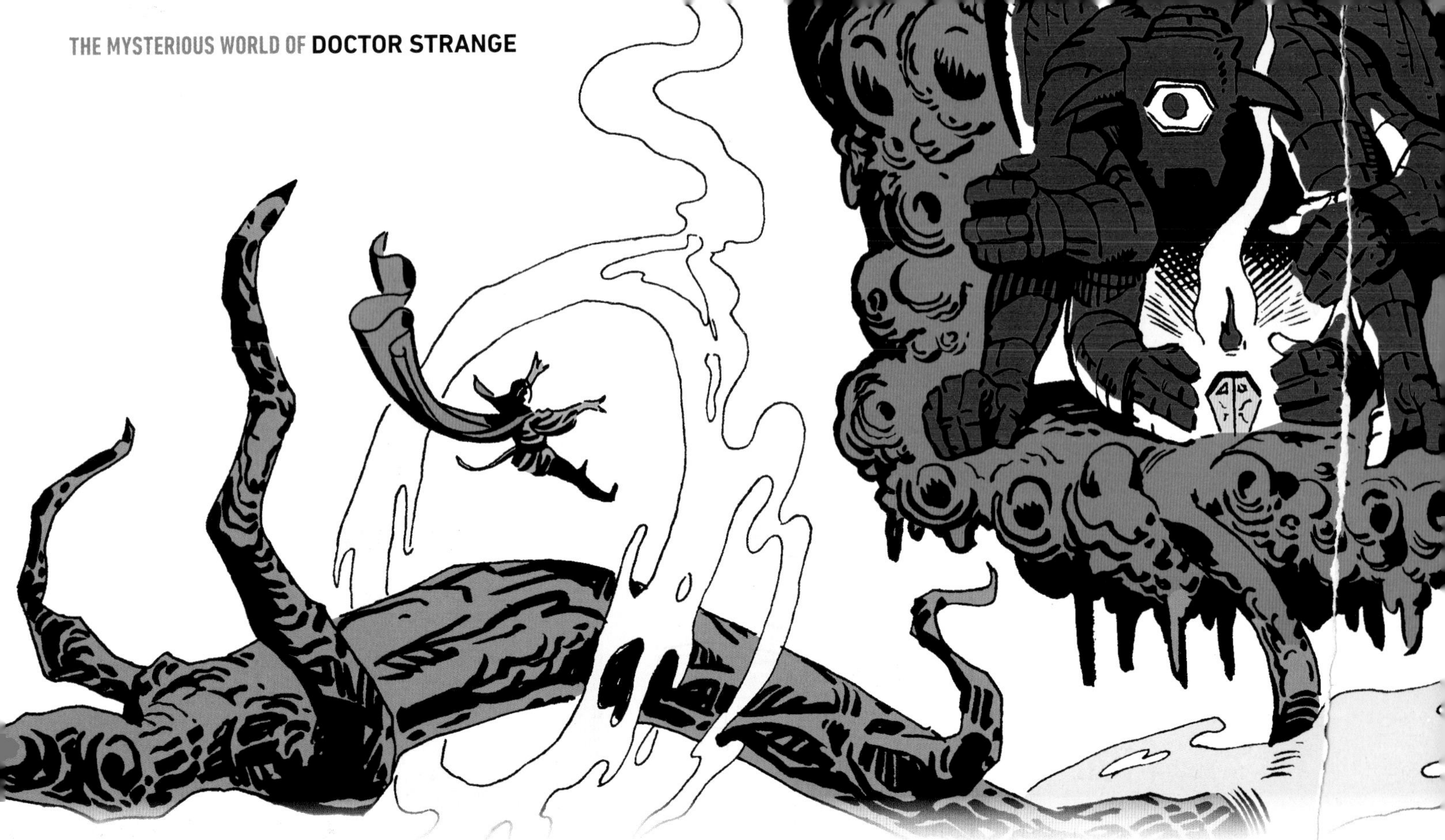

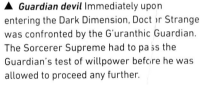

▲ ***Guardian devil*** Immediately upon entering the Dark Dimension, Doctor Strange was confronted by the G'uranthic Guardian. The Sorcerer Supreme had to pass the Guardian's test of willpower before he was allowed to proceed any further.

THE DARK DIMENSION

The Dark Dimension is a vast cosmic realm made up of many realities that fold together to create a universe separate from our own. Ruled over by the tyrannical Dormammu—one of Doctor Strange's most dangerous and determined foes—it was once inhabited by sorcerers named Mhuruuks. Aeons ago, Dormammu and his sister Umar—mother of Strange's beloved, Clea—wrested control of the realm, destroying all opposition. Later, for a time, Clea herself became ruler.

When Doctor Strange first entered the Dark Dimension, he had to pass the challenge of the G'uranthic Guardian, a cyclopean, six-armed, living statue. Having triumphed, Strange found himself in an utterly alien environment, pocked with portals to other realities. One dark dweller after another sprang from these portals to attack Strange and stop him reaching his destination: the domain of the Dread Dormammu.

However, when Doctor Strange finally confronted Dormammu, Clea showed him an even greater peril—the Mindless Ones. Confined to their own region, these marauding monsters were only held at bay by Dormammu's mystical shields, a constant drain on his powers.

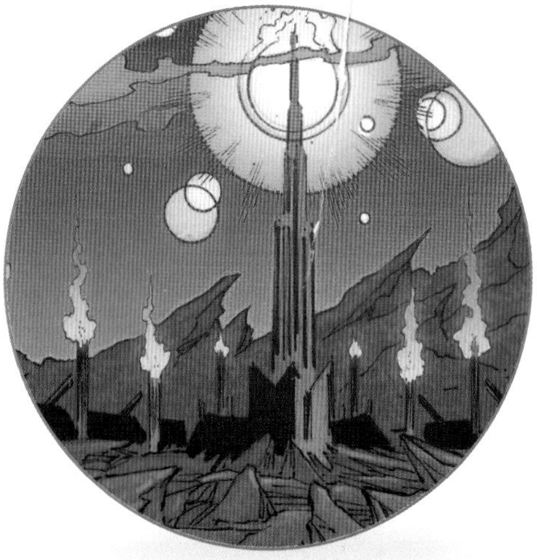

Citadel

The main seat of power in the Dark Dimension is the Citadel. From here, both Dormammu and his sister, Umar, have ruled their realm.

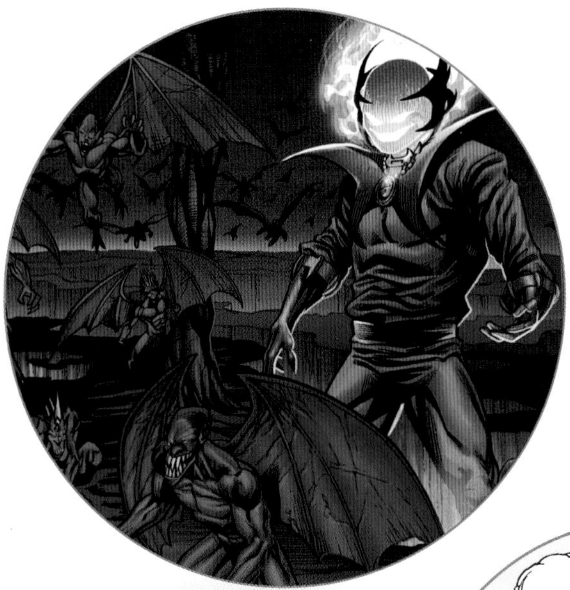

Dark by name...

Ever-changing in appearance, the Dark Dimension has sometimes seemed a hellish place—especially for outsiders who find their way there.

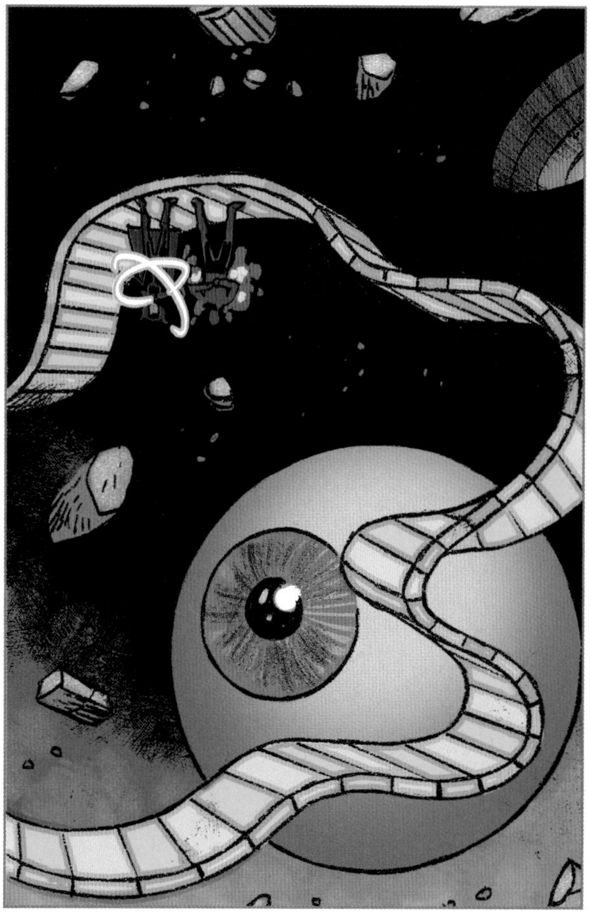

▲ ***Up is down*** The Dark Dimension can be a disorienting domain, as Doctor Strange and the mutant Beast discovered on one visit.

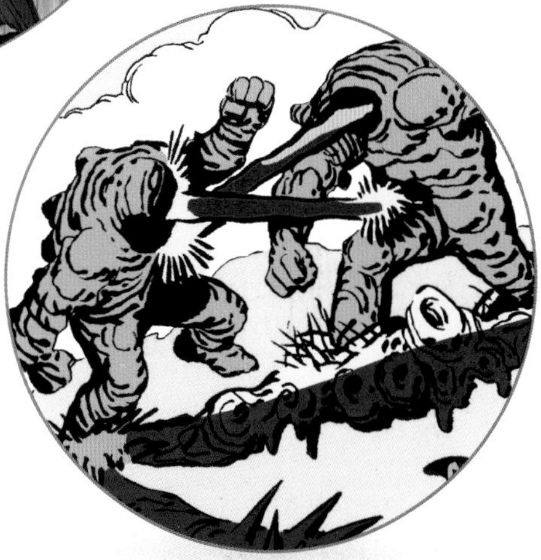

Mindless violence

Clea warned Doctor Strange that if he fought Dormammu, the Mindless Ones might escape their confinement. Sure enough, when Dormammu attacked Strange, the savage, indestructible beasts were released and ran amok.

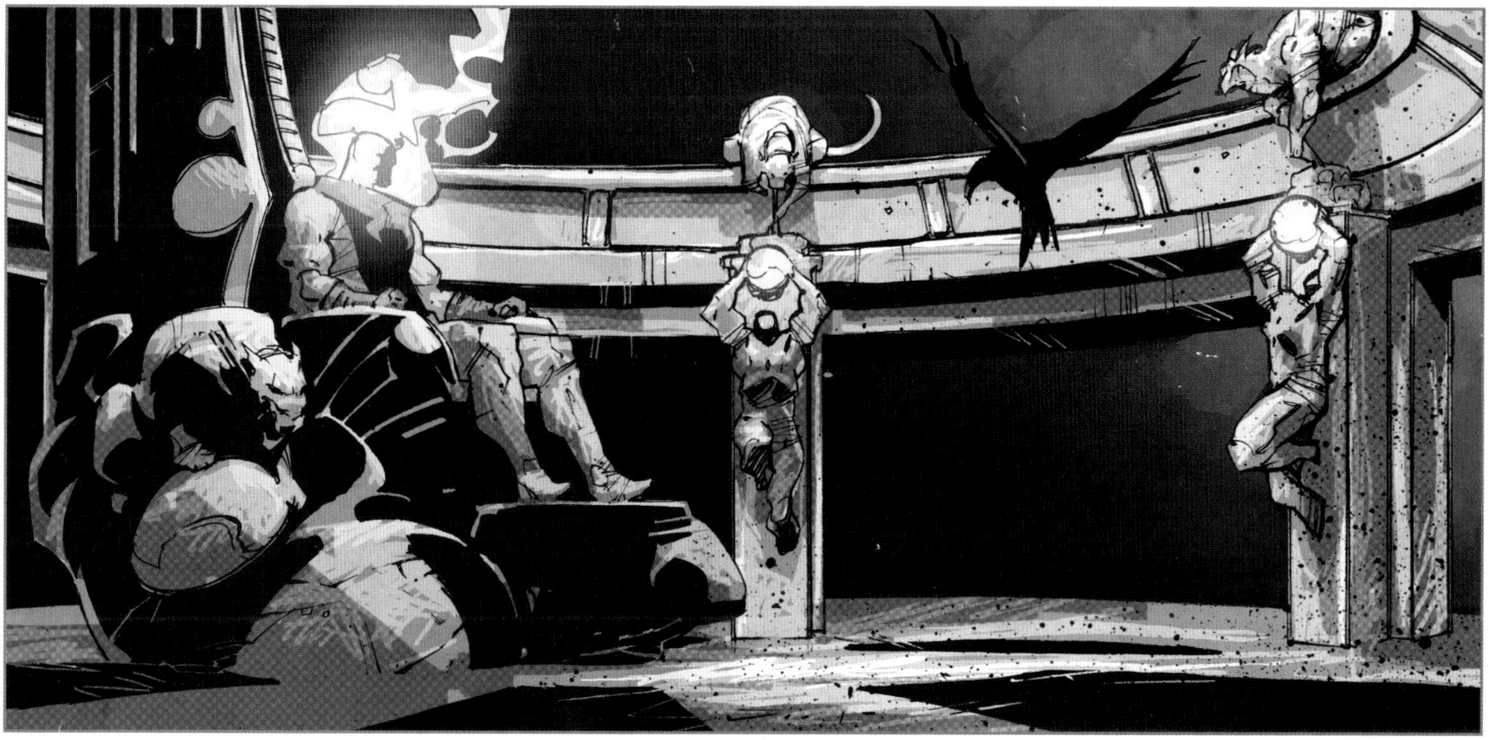

▲ ***Dread despot*** From his stone seat, Dormammu rules the Dark Dimension through sheer force of will. He has sometimes been usurped, but always reclaims his throne.

DIMENSION OF DREAMS

Doctor Strange has faced Nightmare in the demon's Dimension of Dreams many times, but Brother Voodoo also visited the realm when he became the new Sorcerer Supreme, Doctor Voodoo. Through a fiendish plot enacted by Doctor Doom, Voodoo was banished to the Dream Dimension and forced to fight his way back to Earth. Unfortunately, in doing so, he allowed Nightmare to transform Earth into a living unreality—a bad dream made all too real.

▼ ***Dream a little dream*** From the safety of his monstrous Dimension of Dreams, Nightmare manipulated Doctor Voodoo into doing his bidding.

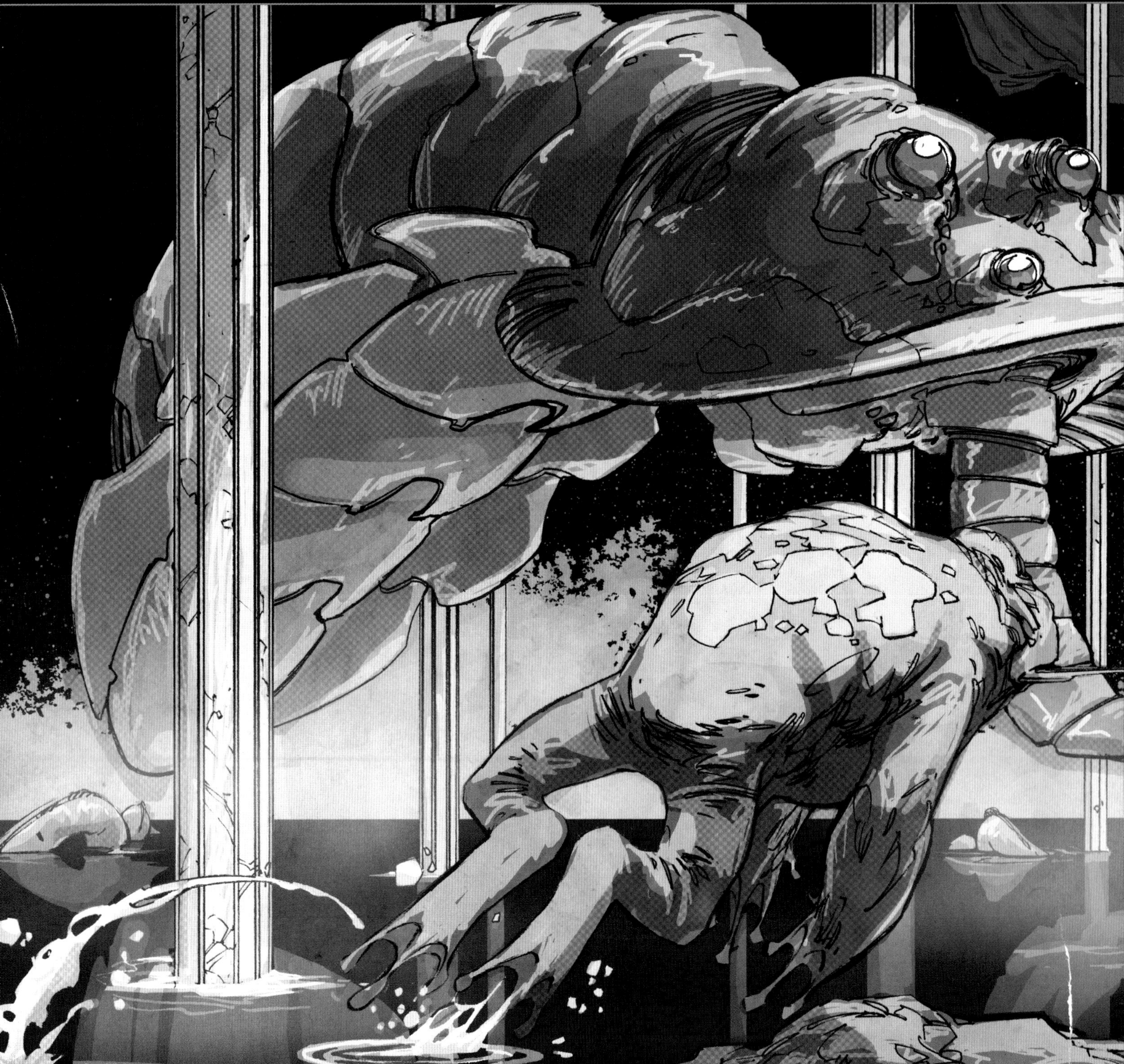

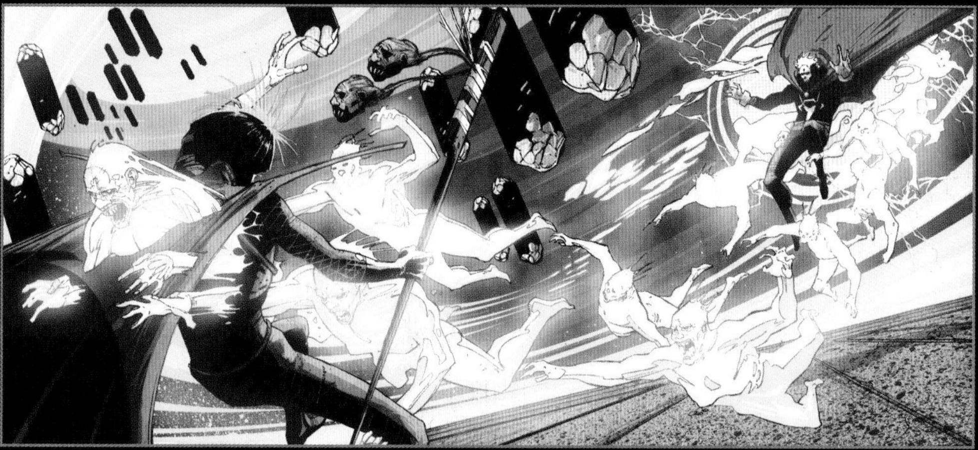

Perchance to scream

When Nightmare gained access to Earth, he reshaped it to resemble his own freakish, hallucinatory realm. Doctor Voodoo opposed Nightmare, and with the reluctant help of Doctor Doom, returned Earth to its rightful state.

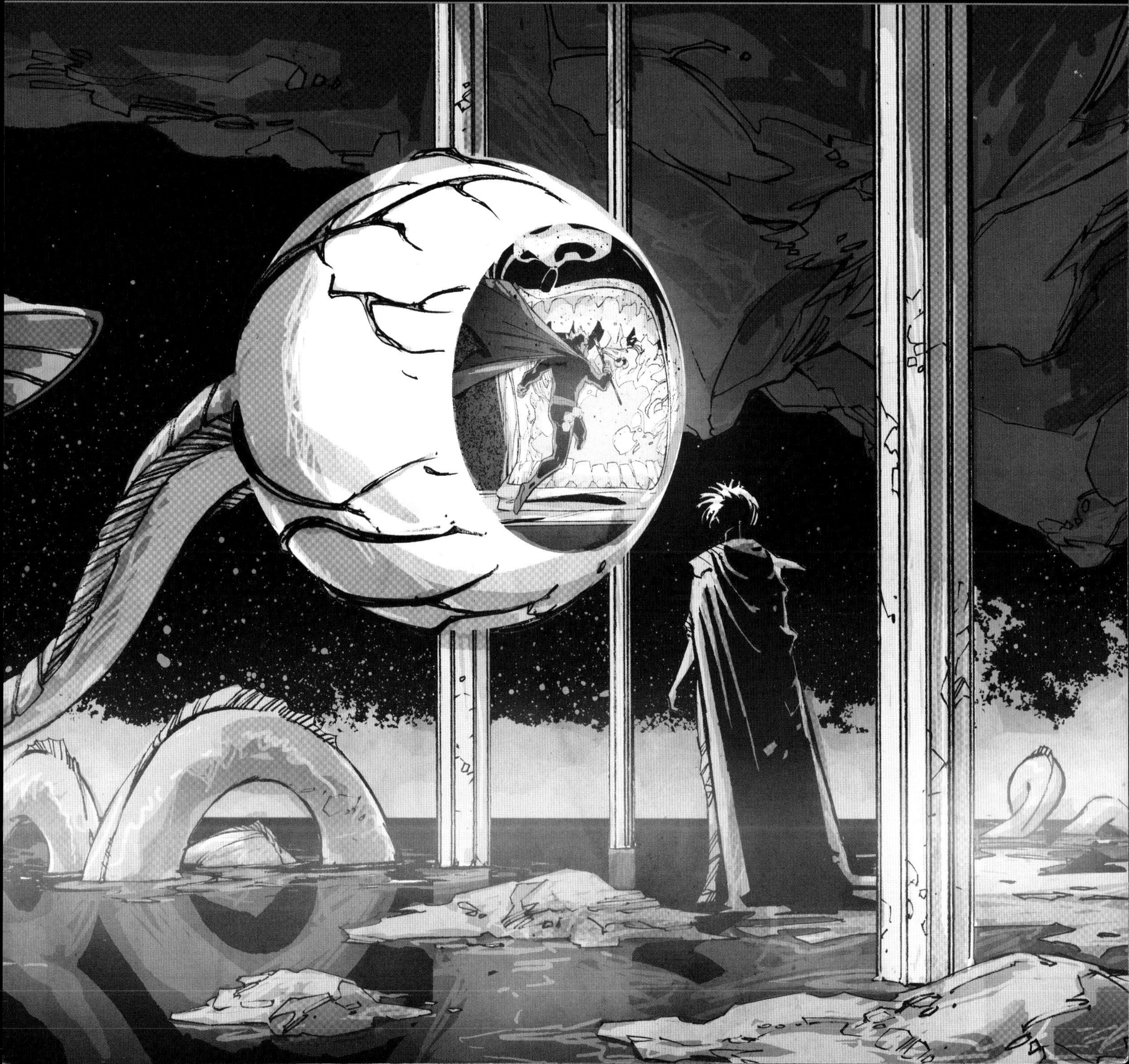

FIRES OF HELL

The unending depths of Hell are the dwelling places of demons and departed souls. Some of Doctor Strange's most formidable foes have laid claim to this underworld domain. The Sorcerer Supreme may have entered the realm of Hell and lived to tell the tale—but most are doomed to be trapped there forever.

▲ *A fiery meeting* In the Devil's Advocacy, the demons gather around the empty throne of Satan to discuss matters of Hell.

INFERNAL REGIONS

Hell—sometimes called Hades—is filled with fire, brimstone, and all manner of evil. It is divided into various territories, which are ruled over by the demonic Hell-Lords. Several of them have been Doctor Strange's greatest enemies over the years, such as Dormammu, Satannish, and Mephisto.

In Mephisto's Realm, time passes extremely slowly, with just a few days on Earth feeling like many years. It was to this abysmal place that Doctor Strange accompanied Doctor Doom on his ceaseless quest to free his mother's soul from Mephisto's clutches.

One of Doctor Strange's fiercest foes in Hell is the demon Pluto. Well-versed in the mystical arts, Pluto has made use of potent items such as the Gem of Tartarus. This magical artifact encased Doctor Strange and his fellow Defenders within an enchanted pillar, though the Gem itself turned out to be fragile and swiftly shattered. Like Mephisto, Pluto has fought many superhumans, and has learned that, for all his power, they cannot be subjugated with ease.

Many demonic beings have claimed the role of Satan—the one true ruler of Hell in its entirety. However, none of these hopeful candidates have ever taken their place on the coveted throne of Satan, which resides in the Devil's Advocacy, a grand hall in a neutral region of Hell. Any demon who has assumed the title of Satan knows that if they try to take the throne, the other demons will turn on them instantly.

◀ *Abyss of agony* Hell teems with demonic beings and the tortured souls of the dead.

Pluto

The immortal Pluto is the Olympian God of the Underworld and would-be monarch of Hell. Pluto possesses unbridled strength and vast magical powers, which he has used in direct mystical combat against Doctor Strange.

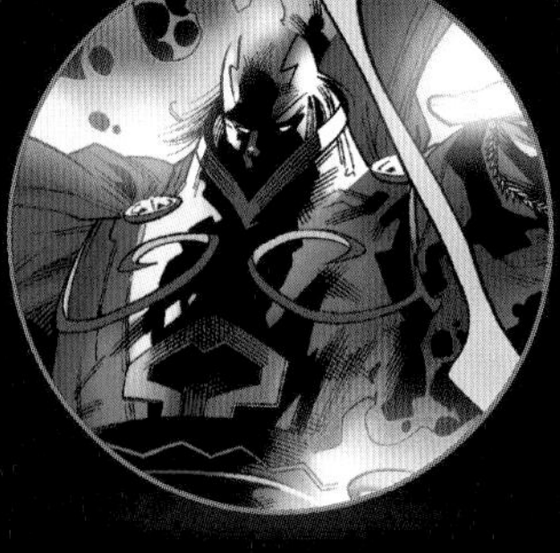

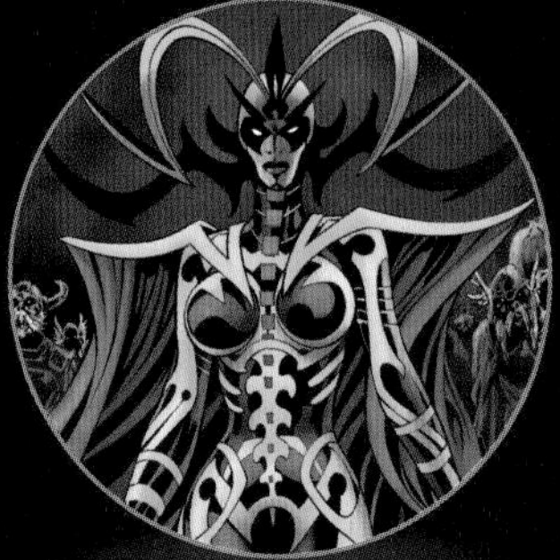

Hela

The Norse Goddess of Death, Hela, was granted rule over the Asgardian realms of Hel and Niffleheim. The Trickster God, Loki, later helped Hela gain control over part of Mephisto's Hell.

Mephisto

The all-powerful Mephisto reigns over much of Hell. The demon often poses as Satan in his efforts to make infernal bargains with humans to take possession of their souls.

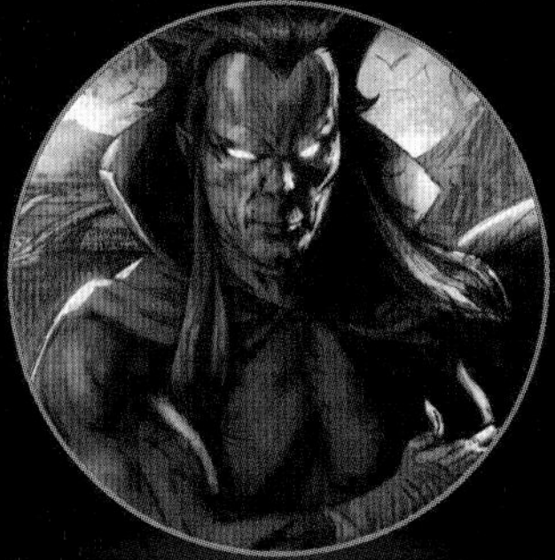

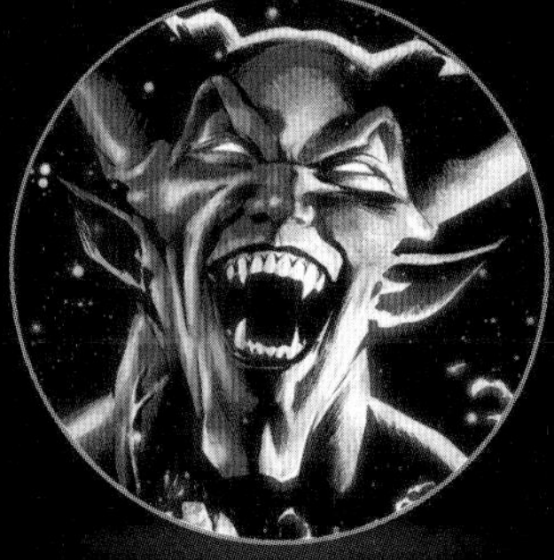

Lucifer

Many years ago, Lucifer was an angel trapped in Hell. During his time there, he became the demon known as the Prince of Lies, and proved himself to be a fearsome ruler.

Marduk Kurios

More than any other demon, Marduk Kurios liked to claim he was the true 'Satan' or the 'Devil'. As such, his child Daimon Hellstrom, a close ally of Doctor Strange, became known as the Son of Satan.

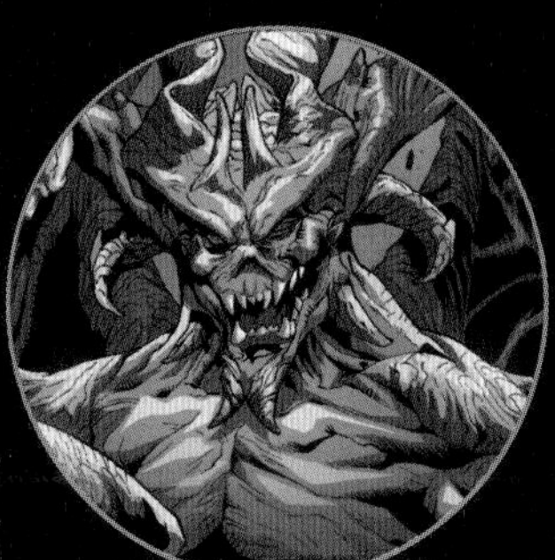

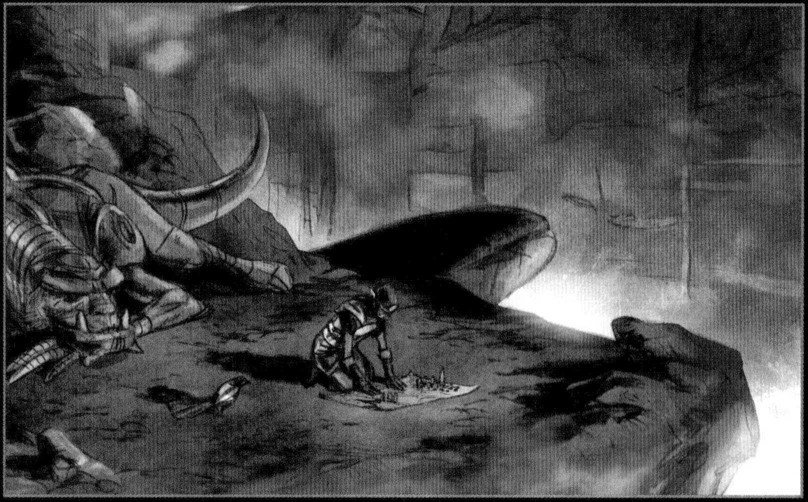

▲ ***Hel and damnation*** The God of Mischief, Loki, journeyed to Hel—the final resting place of Asgardian souls not killed in battle—to stop the evil demon Surtur.

"WELL MAY YOU TREMBLE! FOR YOU GAZE UPON... MEPHISTO!"

Mephisto

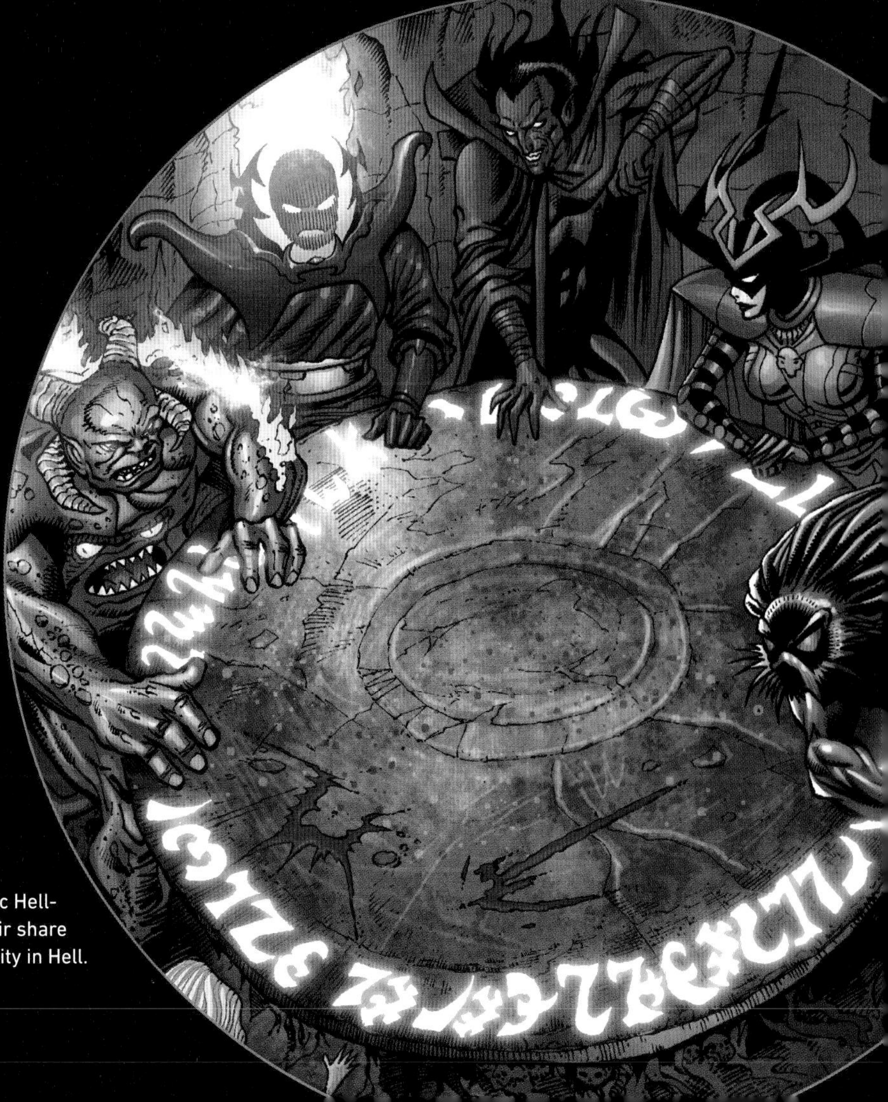

▶ ***Hellish rulers*** The demonic Hell-Lords forever plot to increase their share of souls damned to an eternity in Hell.

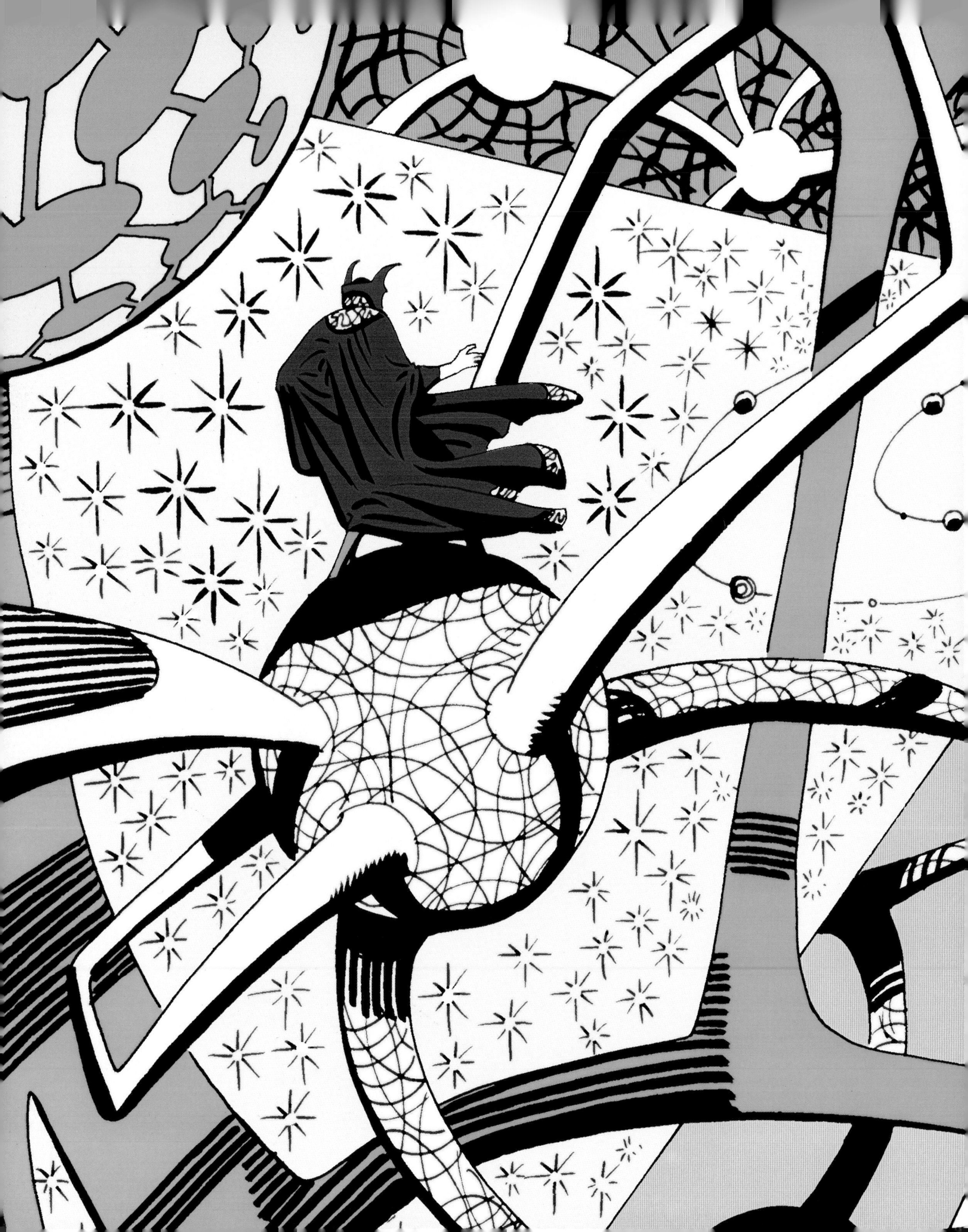

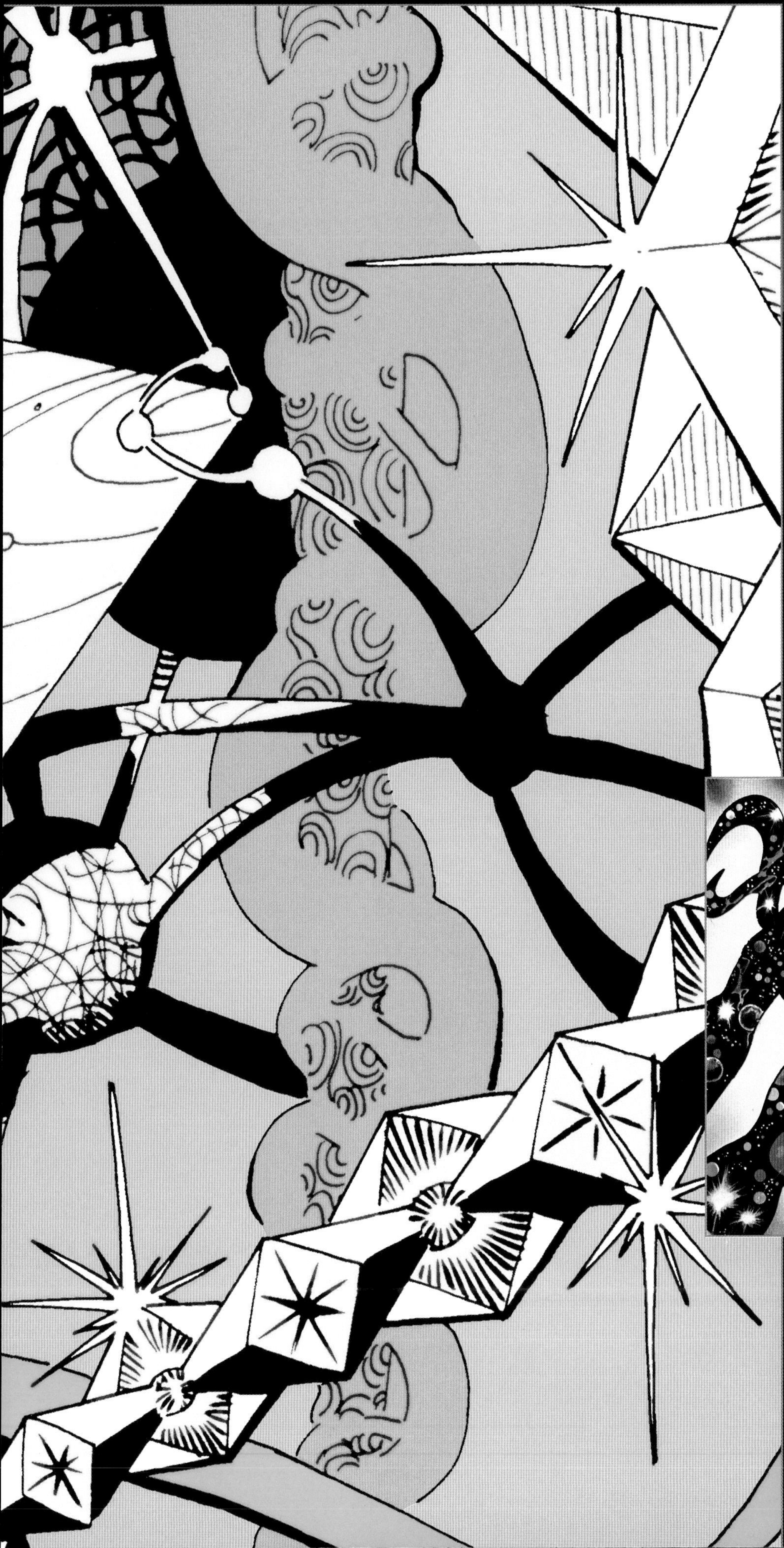

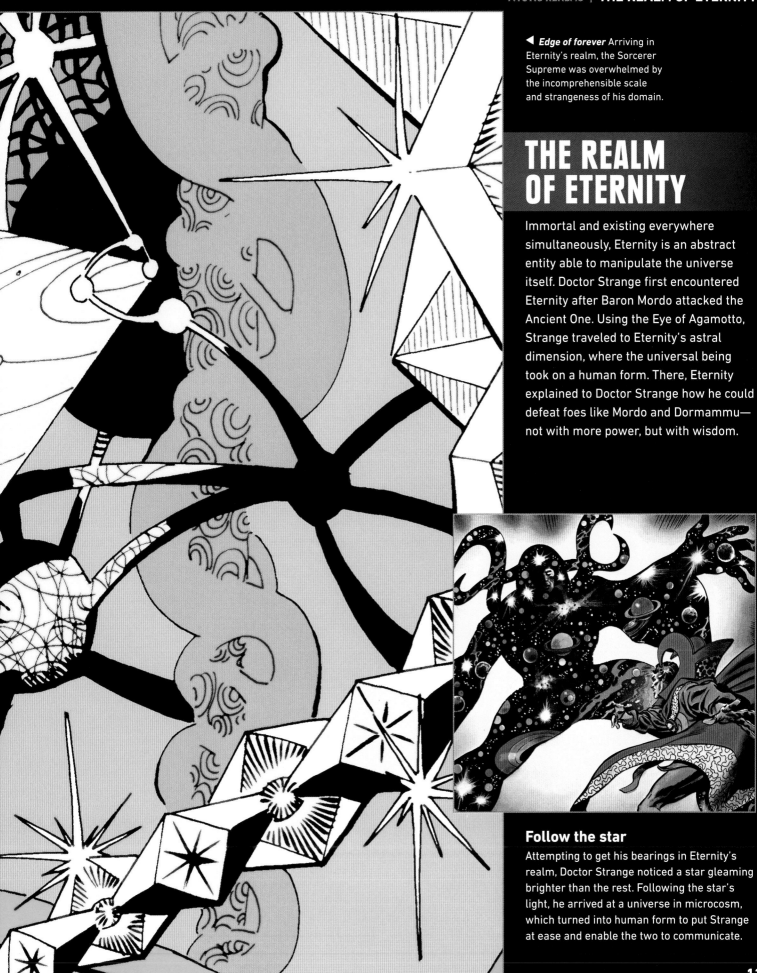

◀ ***Edge of forever*** Arriving in Eternity's realm, the Sorcerer Supreme was overwhelmed by the incomprehensible scale and strangeness of his domain.

THE REALM OF ETERNITY

Immortal and existing everywhere simultaneously, Eternity is an abstract entity able to manipulate the universe itself. Doctor Strange first encountered Eternity after Baron Mordo attacked the Ancient One. Using the Eye of Agamotto, Strange traveled to Eternity's astral dimension, where the universal being took on a human form. There, Eternity explained to Doctor Strange how he could defeat foes like Mordo and Dormammu—not with more power, but with wisdom.

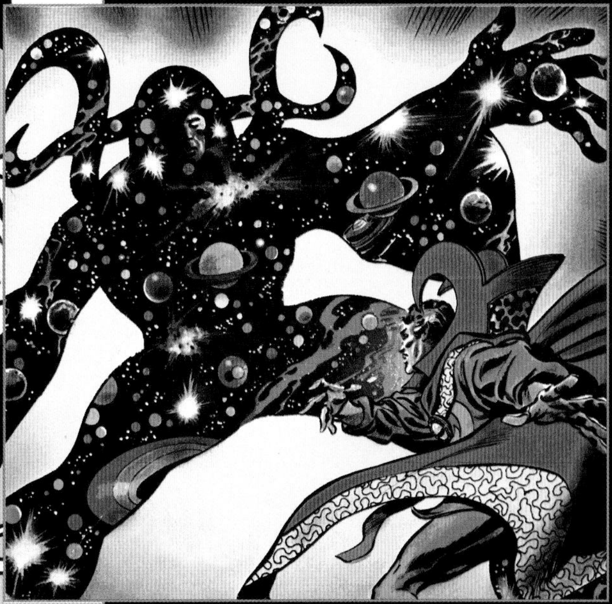

Follow the star

Attempting to get his bearings in Eternity's realm, Doctor Strange noticed a star gleaming brighter than the rest. Following the star's light, he arrived at a universe in microcosm, which turned into human form to put Strange at ease and enable the two to communicate.

REALMS BEYOND IMAGINATION

From his earliest adventures, Doctor Strange has not only traversed the boundaries of Earth, but also the teeming dimensions that exist beyond our own. These are the places where time and space have no meaning, where the rules of physics do not apply, where cosmic vistas collide into an unfathomable whole... and where danger lies.

The Bar With No Doors

Hidden in the back streets of Manhattan is a bar that caters to magic-users of all kinds. Accessed from anywhere in the world, the Bar With No Doors is an ideal gathering place for Doctor Strange to socialize with his fellow sorcerers.

City of Dreams

The empty, eerily quiet City of Dreams stands on the back of a gigantic, slumbering being. When Doctor Strange was attacked by his own dreams in this mystifying dimension, it took quick thinking and illusion spells to escape from the crafty creature's lair.

Strange Matter Dimension

All beings in this plane of existence had been either subjugated or destroyed by Shanzar, the self-declared Sorcerer Supreme of this "Strange World." Doctor Strange fought and defeated Shanzar when the tyrant turned his sights on Earth and took over the Hulk as his host body to invade the planet.

Demonic Limbo

This magical dimension of demons, also known as "Otherplace," is a pocket universe with a corrupting influence. While largely ruled by the demon-sorcerer Belasco, Otherplace was also conquered by Doctor Doom.

Netherworld of Eternal Doom

In his search for the secret of Eternity, Doctor Strange briefly became trapped in a gloomy, bizarre world, where its despotic ruler, the Demon of the Mask, tricked unwary visitors into becoming his slaves.

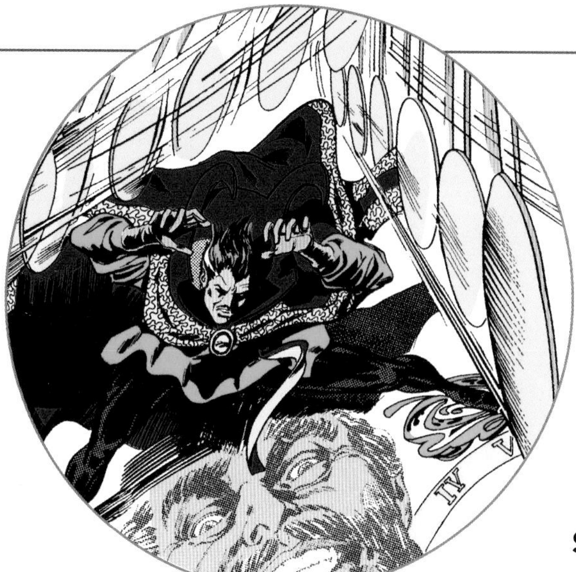

The Clock Dimension

While dueling the wizard Nekron, a disciple of Satannish, Doctor Strange was cast into the menacing Clock Dimension. He found it filled with "Stygian darkness" and razor sharp pendulums, which he struggled to evade.

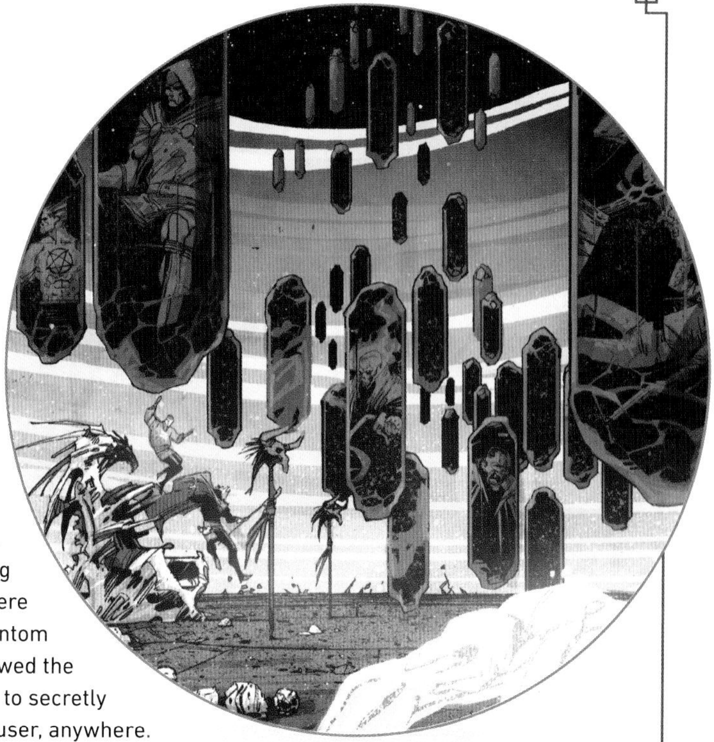

The Scrying Stones of Chthon

In Doctor Voodoo's Haitian sanctum, Hounfour, the Scrying Stones of Chthon were concealed by the Phantom Wall. The stones allowed the Sorcerer Supreme to secretly observe any magic-user, anywhere.

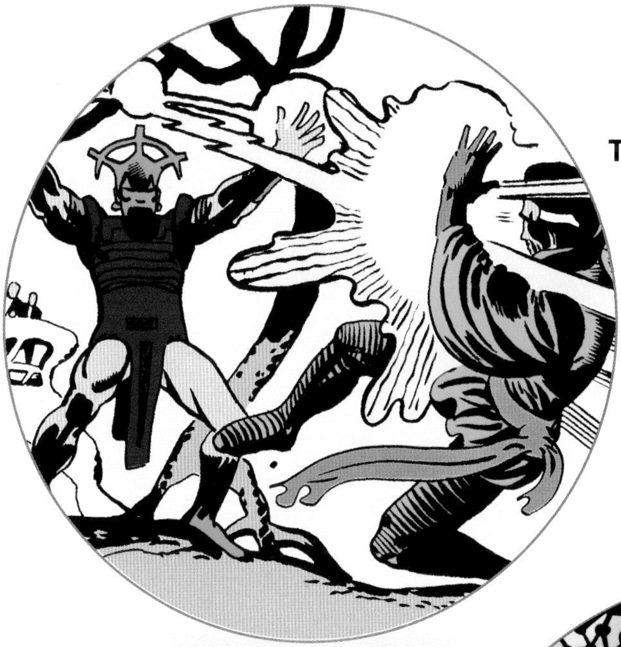

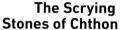

The Sixth Dimension

When the idol of Tiboro appeared on Earth, it was a sign of its owner's impending arrival. The Ancient One advised Strange to venture to the Sixth dimension, Tiboro's home. There, he faced the alien despot in mystical combat.

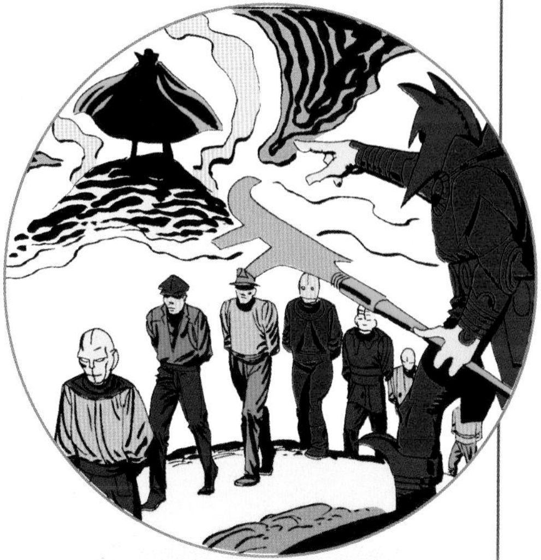

Purple Dimension

This universe is ruled by the ruthless Aggamon, who forced all its inhabitants to mine for jewels. When two hapless crooks stole a gem from Doctor Strange, it transported them to the Purple Dimension. Strange followed them there and challenged Aggamon to a duel to secure the release of the thieves.

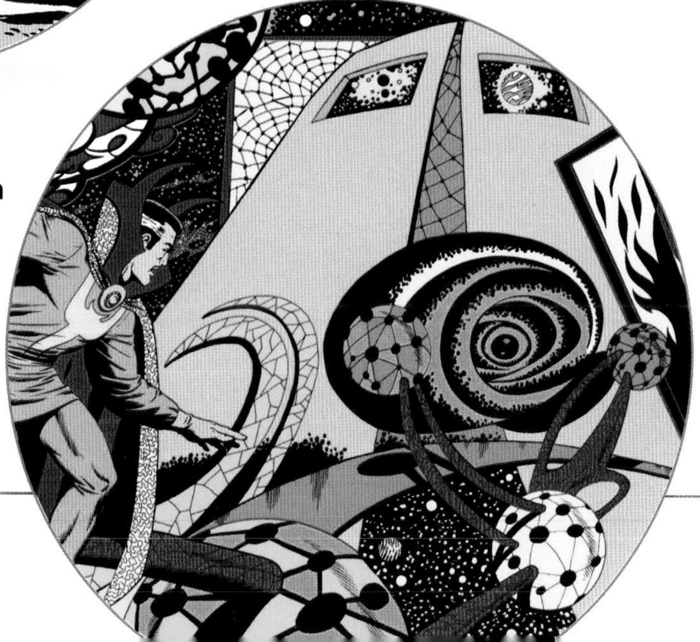

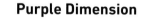

The Realm Unknown

On Doctor Strange's desperate quest to find Clea, who had gone missing, he and Victoria Bentley traveled to the Realm Unknown. There, Strange battled a warrior skeleton, until he realized that everything was a devious illusion created by the Dread Dormammu!

INTO DITKOPOLIS

Of all the dimensions and realms to which Doctor Strange has traveled, one of the most astonishing—and treacherous—was Ditkopolis. The Sorcerer Supreme was lured there by the realm's ruler, a sorceress named Electra, who pleaded with Strange for help to increase her power and save Ditkopolis. In truth, Electra was merely seeking power for its own sake, and would go to any lengths to acquire it.

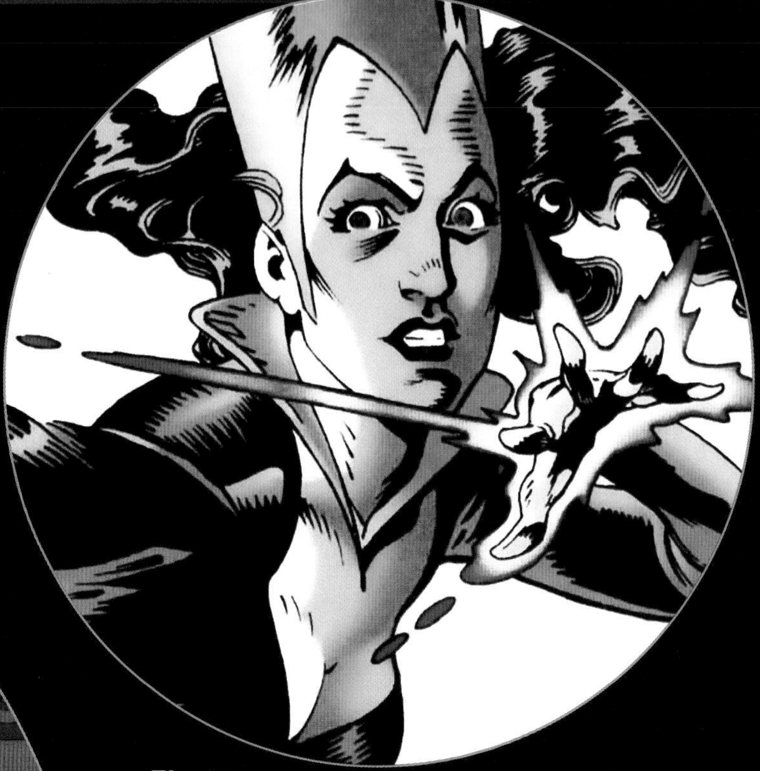

Electra
The sorceress Electra possessed incredible magical abilities, and was able to call upon the energy of the entire realm of Ditkopolis in her spellweaving. Even so, she wanted to add her sister Celeste's power to her own, and brought Doctor Strange to her dimension to aid her in her schemes.

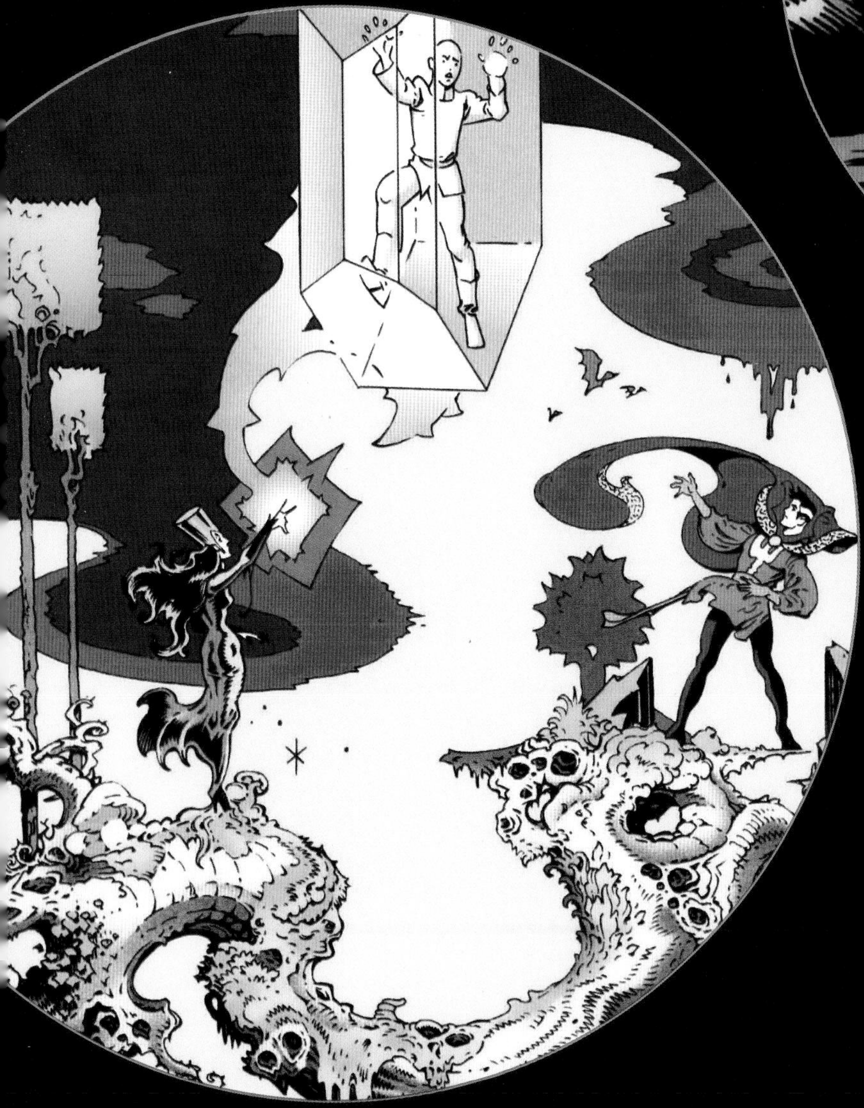

▲ ***Hostage to fortune*** The battle between Doctor Strange and Electra raged across planes of reality and illusion, until at last the sorceress revealed that Wong was held prisoner in a dazzling gem.

REALM OF SPLENDOR AND LIES

Responding to a summons from the Ancient One, Doctor Strange learned that his friend and disciple, Wong, had been kidnapped and transported to a realm unknown to Strange—Ditkopolis. Opening a portal to Ditkopolis, the Sorcerer Supreme discovered a place of great beauty, but was also struck by a sense of foreboding. When the ground suddenly rose up to swallow him, he found himself under attack by the realm's ruler, Electra. Strange engaged Electra in mystical combat, but their battle was curtailed when Electra revealed that she was holding Wong captive, and would kill him unless Strange did her bidding.

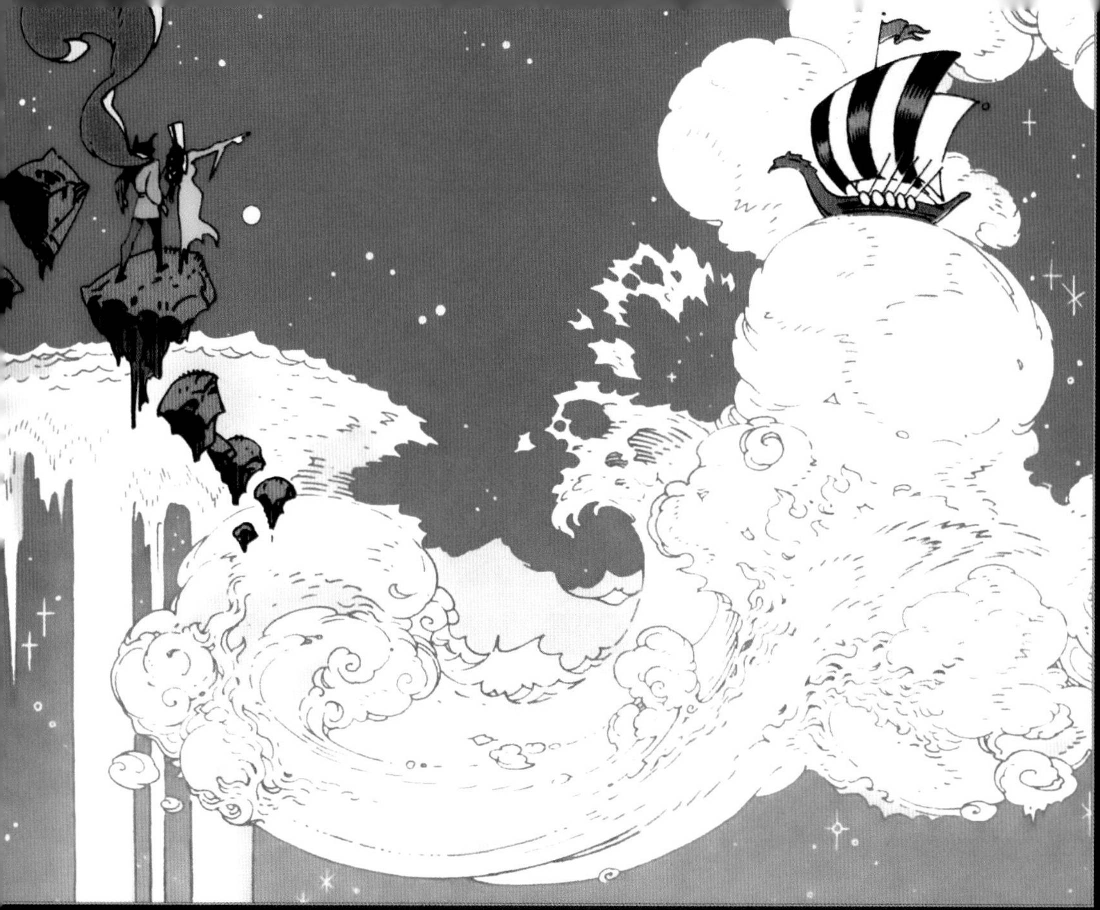

▲ ***Ship ahoy*** To transport herself and Doctor Strange across the ocean to the capital, Electra summoned a ship on the crest of an ethereal wave.

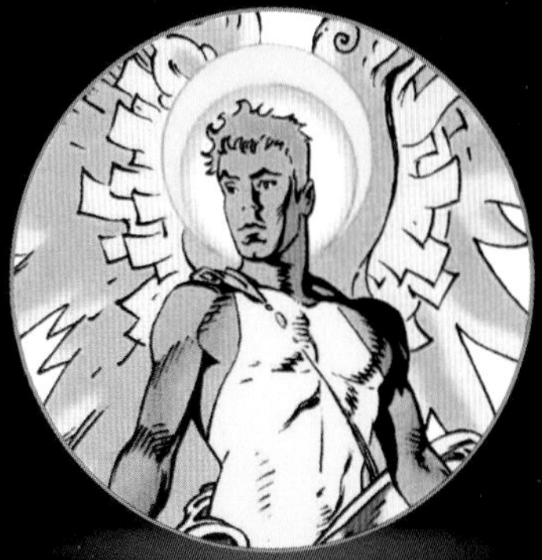

Galtus

The angel-like being Galtus had been found by Electra lying by a river. Electra was entranced by him, but when he set eyes on Celeste, he fell in love with her instead.

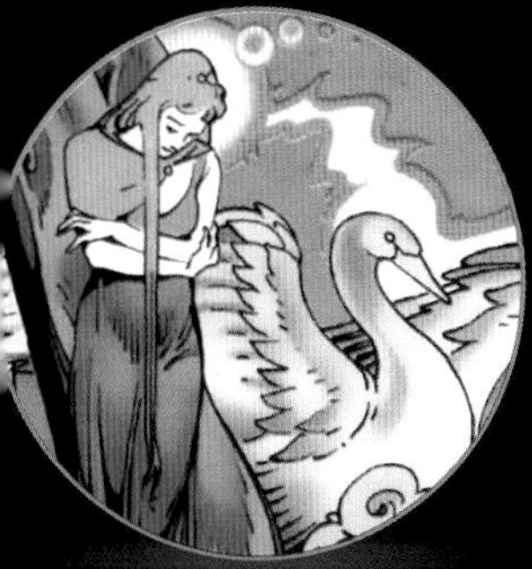

Celeste

When King Roark divided his power between Celeste and Electra, he linked them magically, ensuring one could not harm the other. To counter this, Electra cast a spell that imprisoned her sister's mind and senses, leaving her an empty shell.

Doctor Strange accompanied Electra to her capital city. There she explained that her late father, King Roark, had divided his power between Electra and her sister, Celeste, but that Celeste was now ailing and Ditkopolis was dying. However, Strange soon learned the truth: desiring all the power, Electra had made her sister a mute prisoner of her own mind and turned Celeste's lover, Galtus, into a statue of a swan. Doctor Strange refused to help Electra in her power grab, and instead freed Celeste and Galtus, before returning Wong to Earth. Enraged, Electra attacked Celeste and Galtus, causing all of Ditkopolis to be destroyed.

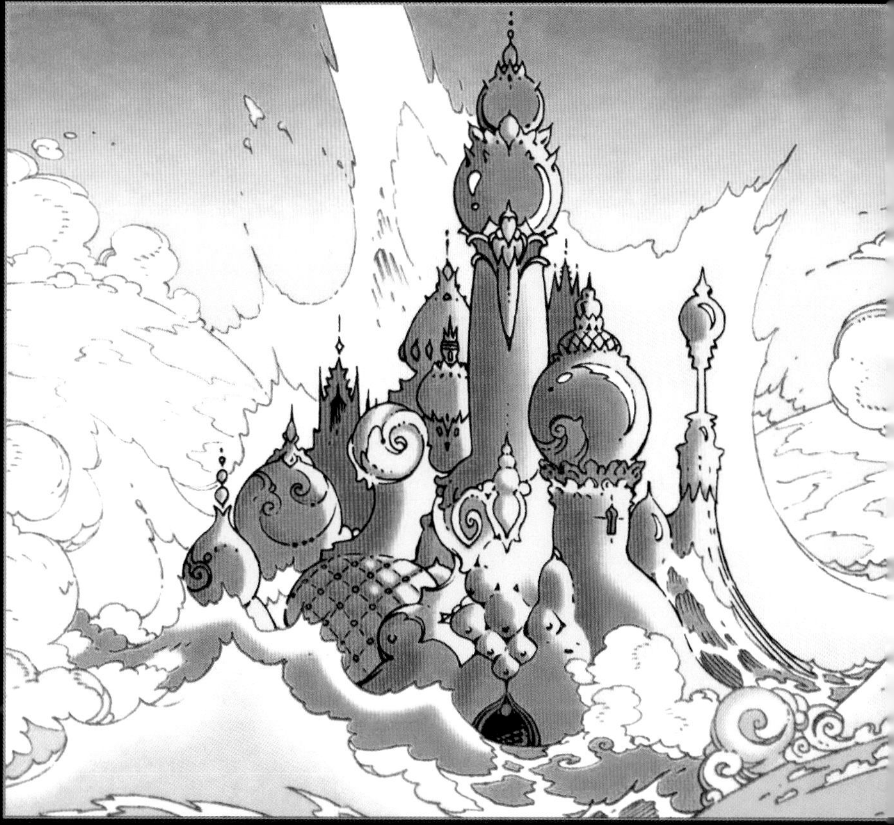

▲ ***City of light and dark*** The capital of Ditkopolis was a city that outwardly appeared glittering, but in reality was decaying, populated by Electra's undead warrior slaves.

FANDAZAR FOO

Described by Doctor Strange as a paradise where magicians could meditate and replenish themselves, Fandazar Foo was a nexus between dimensions rich with magical forces. That tranquility was completely shattered when magic exterminating zealots, the Empirikul, attacked the realm and purged it of any trace of mysticism. When Strange ventured to these mystical crossroads to find the cause of recent magical failures, he was shocked to discover a desolate place littered with the bodies of deceased Sorcerers Supreme.

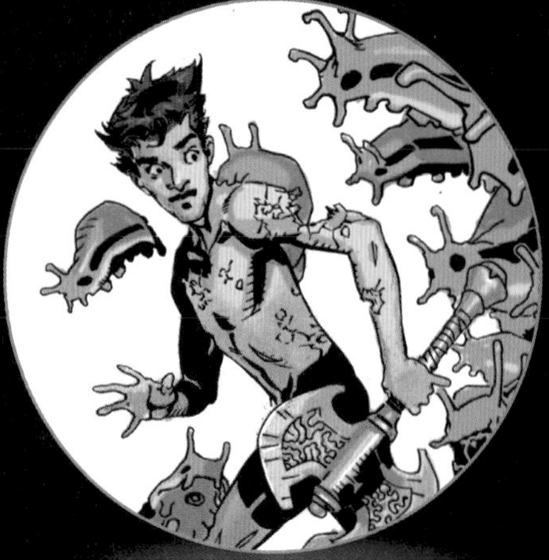

Slug infestation

The Een'Gawori were a race of slugs that fed on mystical energy, and were once abundant on Fandazar Foo. When the Empirikul stripped the realm of its magic, the slugs fled to Earth through a portal in Doctor Strange's Sanctum Sanctorum.

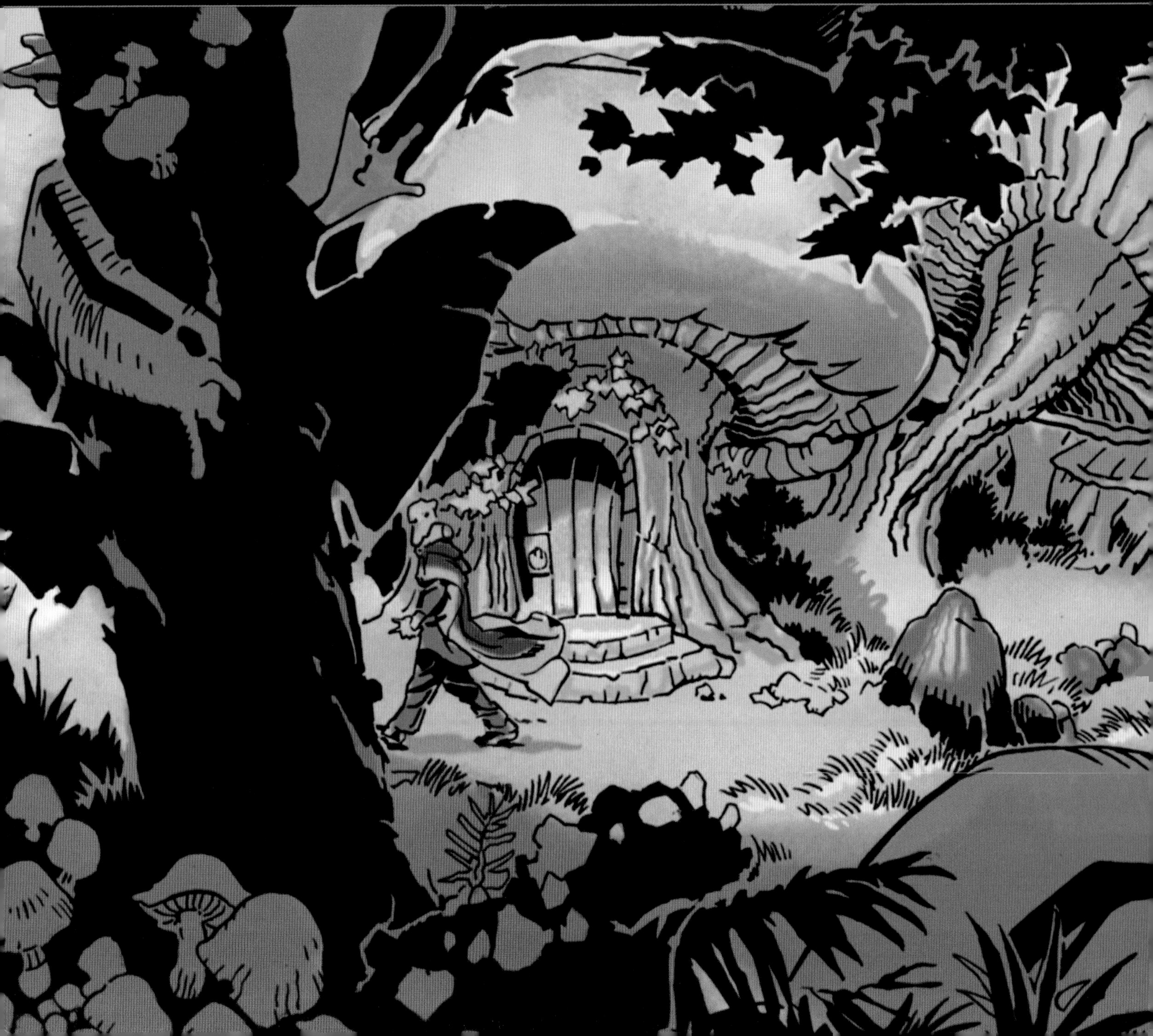

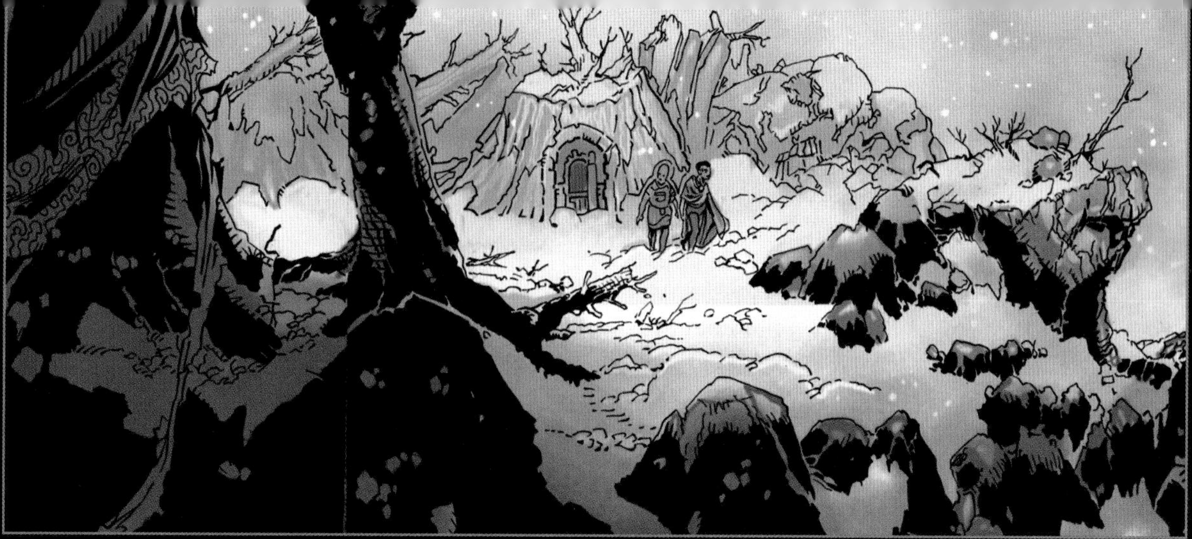

◀ ***Paradise lost***
A magical idyll once defined by serenity, Fandazar Foo was razed to the ground, leaving a barren wasteland.

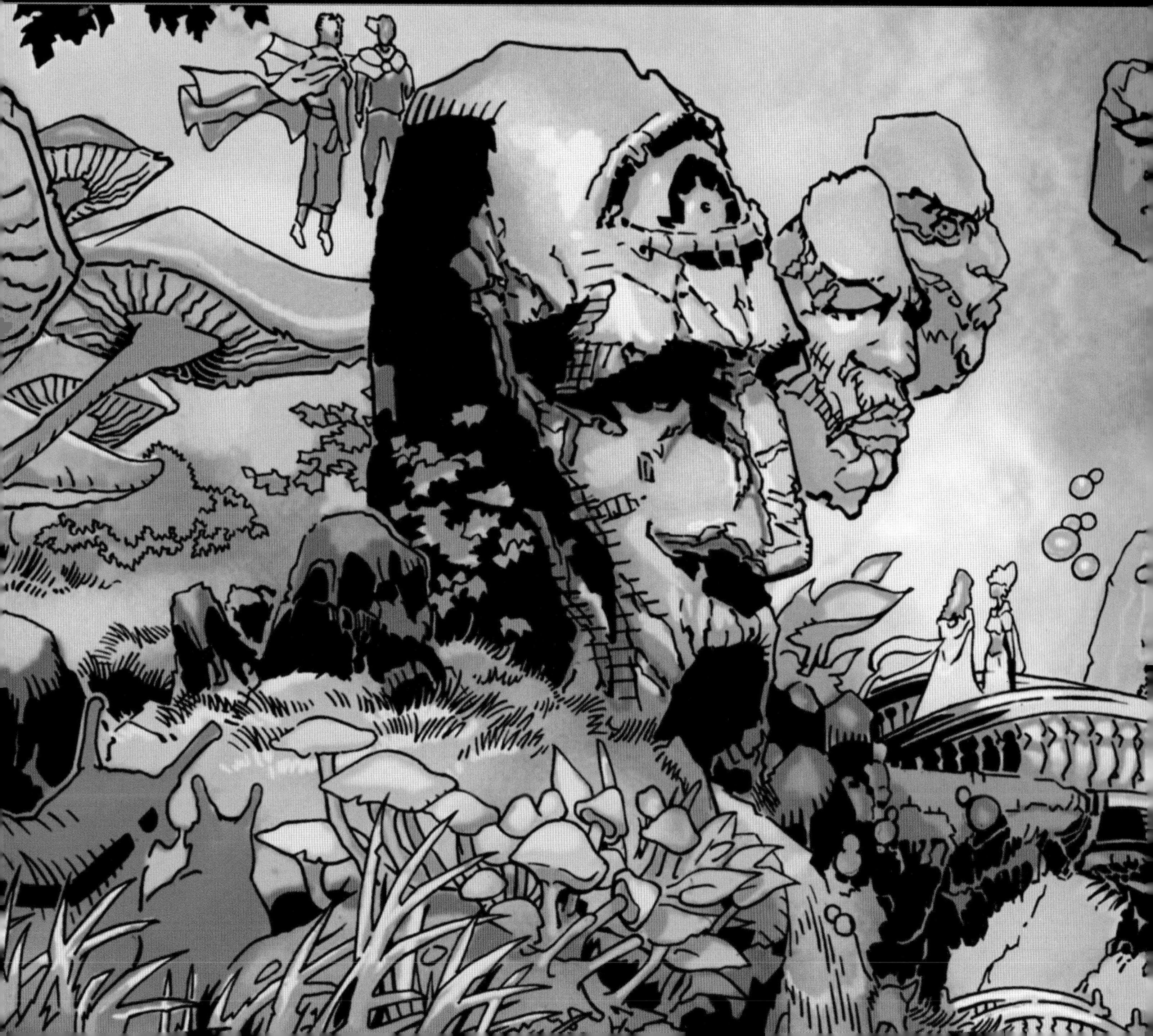

CHAPTER 6

SPELL BOUND

Let demon and man alike beware, for the Earthly realm is protected by the Sorcerer Supreme. Doctor Strange has sworn a sacred oath to watch over mankind and keep humanity free of any and all threats that might enslave it. He commands an astonishing array of mystical abilities that he uses to fight the enemies of Earth. Able to call upon the might of the Vishanti, Raggaddor, Hoggoth, and a pantheon of other supernatural entities, Strange can also deploy the dark energies of his enemies, such as Dormammu and Satannish, to cast spells.

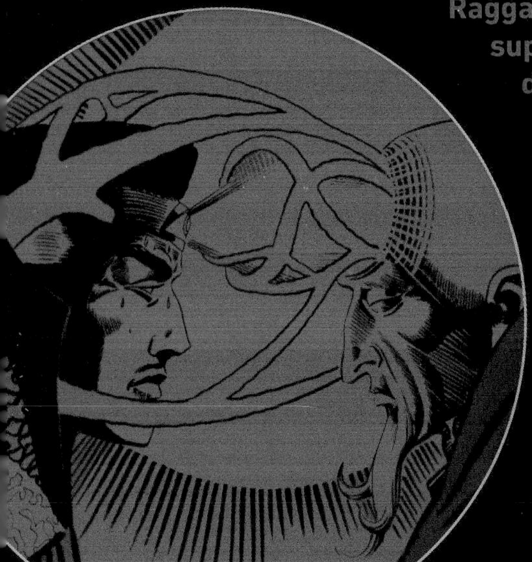

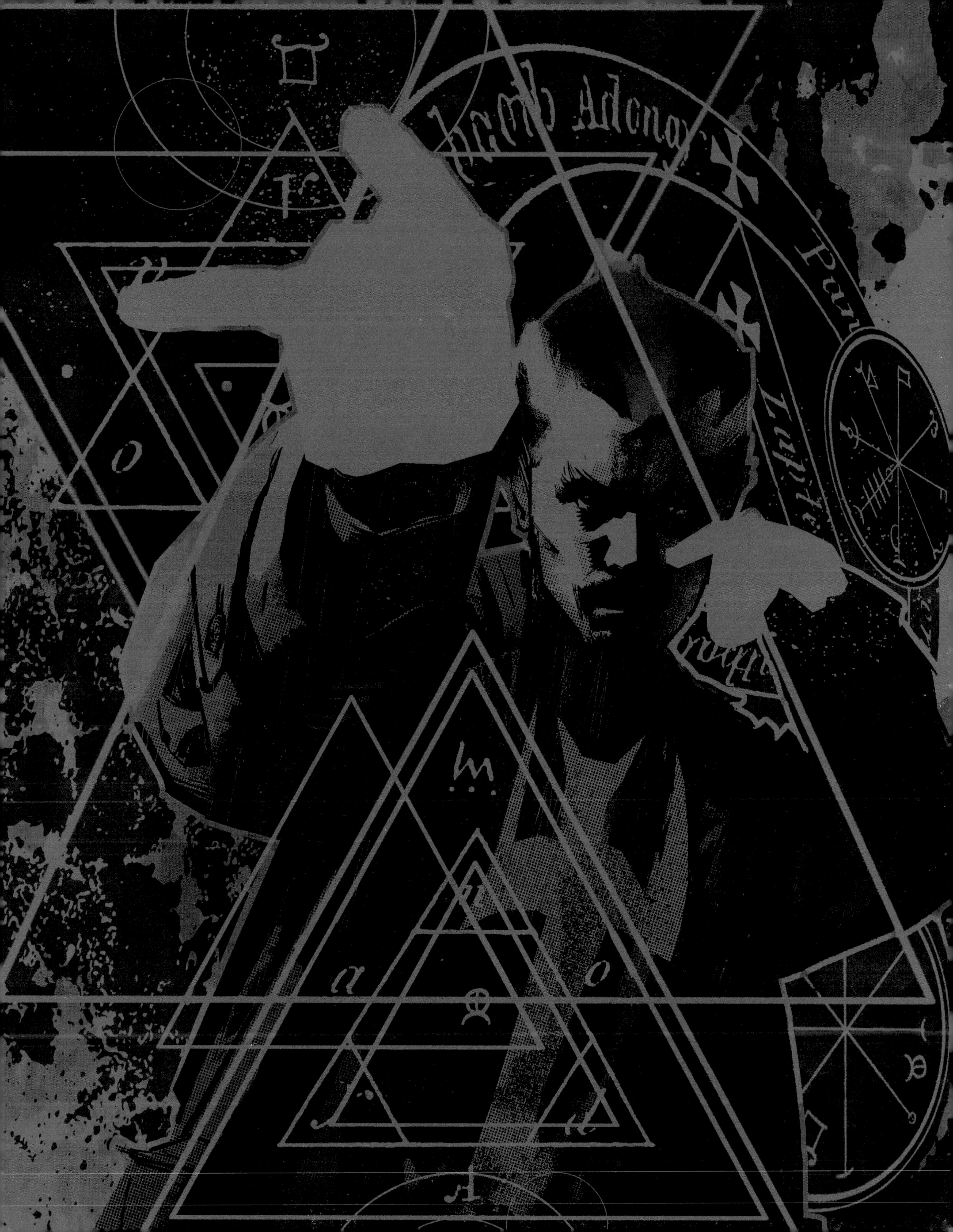

INCANTATIONS AND CONJURATION

Through rigorous training and study of the occult, Doctor Strange has come to possess a wide range of magic-based powers. Accessing his own formidable mental and spiritual resources, he can control and channel ambient mystical energy. He can also cast specific spells and call on powerful entities to lend those spells added potency.

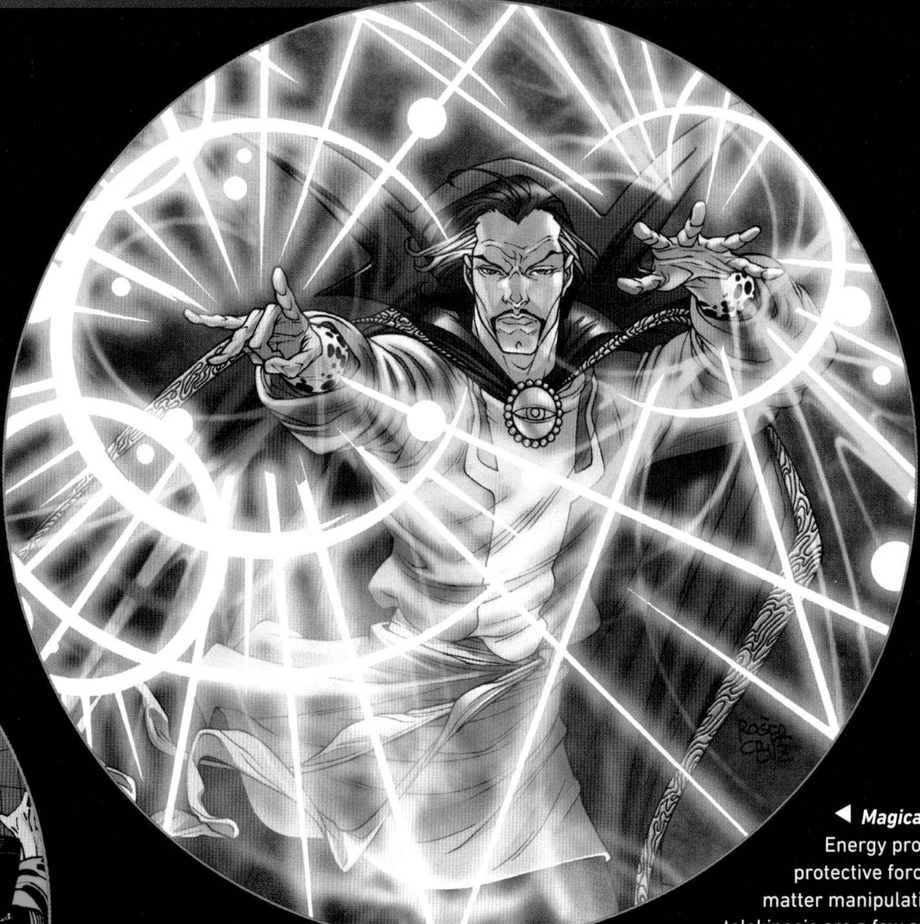

◀ ***Magical arsenal***
Energy projection, protective force fields, matter manipulation, and telekinesis are a few of the many weapons in Doctor Strange's arsenal.

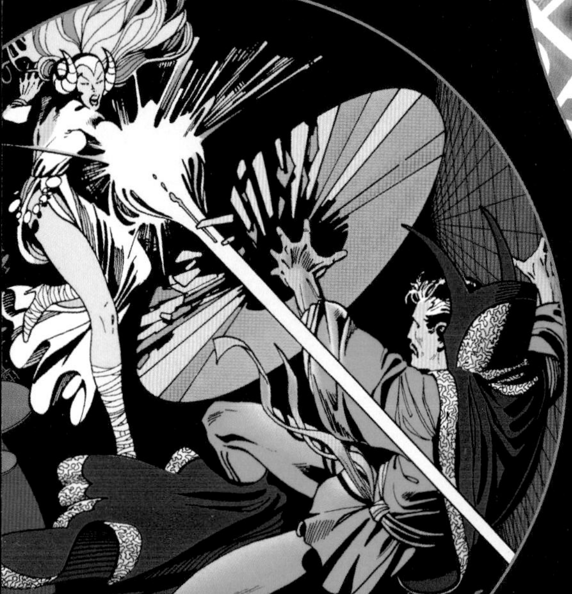

Shield of Seraphim
When Doctor Strange was attacked by the powerful witch, Margali, he used the Shield of Seraphim to protect himself from her mystical bolts.

INVOCATIONS AND ENTITIES

The most powerful weapon at Doctor Strange's disposal is the ability to invoke mystical entities of incredible might. As the Earth's Sorcerer Supreme, he most often calls upon his patrons, the Vishanti. He can call upon them either as a group or, depending on the nature of the spell, their individual personas of Oshtur, Agamotto, and Hoggoth. He may cry out "By the Ageless Vishanti!" to greatly increase the power of a specific protection spell, such as the Shield of Seraphim, or deploy more defined spells if required. For example, the Mists of Hoggoth will open portals to other realms, while their counterpart, the Path of Hoggoth, will create a safe—though narrow—passage for the traveler.

Strange's magical strategies include many tried and tested enchantments. The Moons of Munnopor can conjure

"FIERY BALTHAKK, DREAD KRAKKAN, JOIN THY POWERS NOW IN CHORUS!"

Doctor Strange

Vapors of Valtorr

Doctor Strange uses the Vapors of Valtorr and the Rings of Raggadorr when he wants to increase his speed, such as when he needed to outrace a death spell cast by Umar.

Ancient texts

To master the many facets of magic, Doctor Strange must continually consult ancient and arcane texts, some of which have knowledge of the dark arts predating the dawn of humankind.

illusions and be invoked to help break an opponent's spells. The Rings of Raggador are a potent binding spell used even by the likes of the Living Tribunal. And the Bolts of Balthakk create powerful bursts of mystical energy.

While Doctor Strange mostly uses white magic, he may also summon the dark powers of Satannish and Dormammu. However, he does so warily, for he knows

THE OCTESSENCE

The origins of the entities that comprise the Octessence are shrouded in mystery. Throughout his career, Doctor Strange has invoked their names and cast their spells to create a variety of powerful magical effects.

At some point, long ago, the members of the Octessence began arguing over which of them was greater. They settled on a bet, called the Wager of the Octessence, whereby each entity agreed to create an object that would transfer a small amount of its power to a mortal. These objects were then hidden on Earth. The humans who found the objects were called Exemplars, and they would fight to determine which member of the Octessence would win the bet. The final battle has yet to be won, and the Exemplars continue to trouble Earth.

Farallah
Invoking Farallah can bestow the power to open locked doors and doorways to other dimension. It can also create unbreakable bonds to ensnare an opponent.

Ikonn
Ikonn has the ability to create powerful illusions and control people's minds. His very presence can upset the space-time continuum.

Watoomb
The maker of the Winds of Watoomb, the entity known as Watoomb is also a source for opening portals to other realms. He is invoked as a means of teleportation and of speeding one's journey.

▶ *Exemplars united* The combined might of the Exemplars can be a fearsome force, as the Avengers learned when they battled the group in the skies above New York.

Raggador

Raggador can disrupt an opponent's powers with potent binding spells. He can also impart banishment spells, enhance velocity, and aid in teleportation.

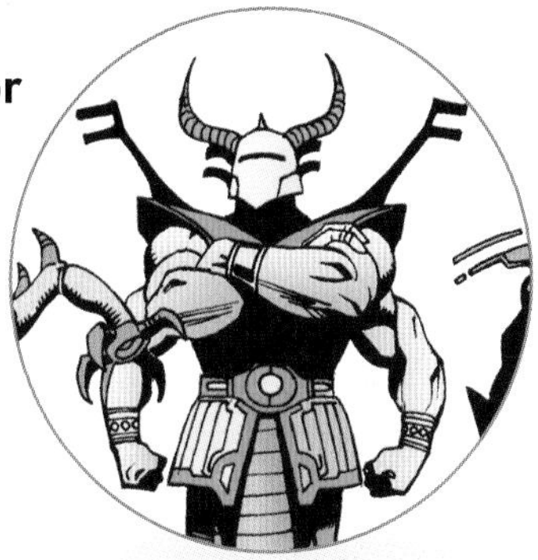

Balthakk

Often appearing in the form of crackling energy, Balthakk can give those who invoke his name the power to fire devastating bolts of pure mystical energy.

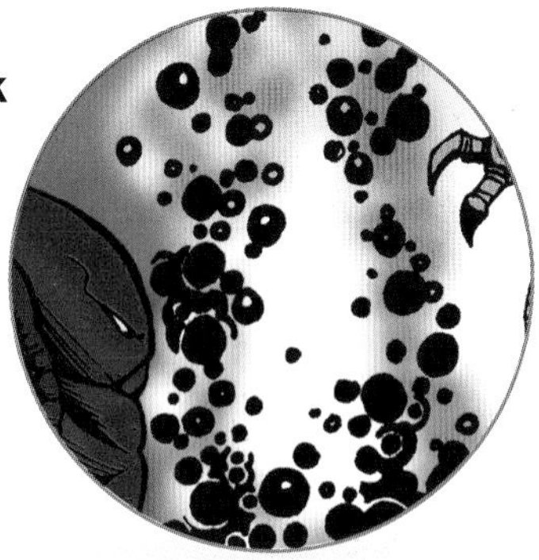

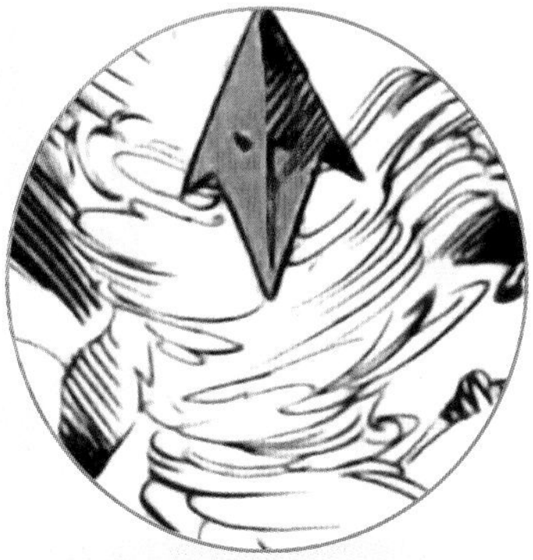

Valtorr

Both dragonlike and ethereal, Valtorr is the source of the Vapors of Valtorr. The powers he grants tend to be highly destructive in nature.

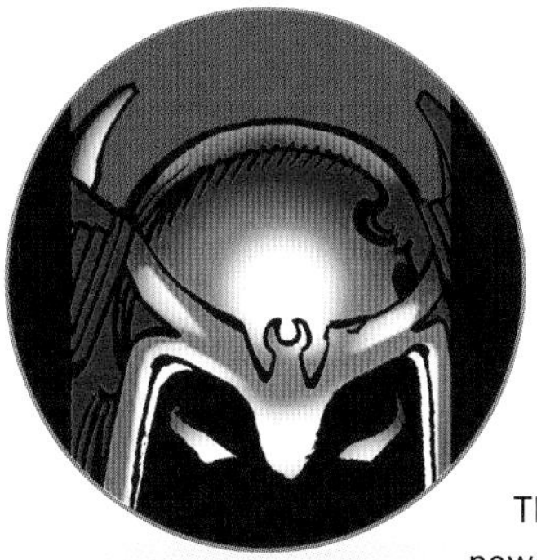

Krakkan

Possibly a demon, Krakkan can bestow the ability to conjure restraining spells. They can weaken an opponent's powers and disrupt their magic.

Cyttorak

Cyttorak can confer great physical power. His Crimson Bands are a spell that can produce nearly unbreakable constraints to secure an opponent.

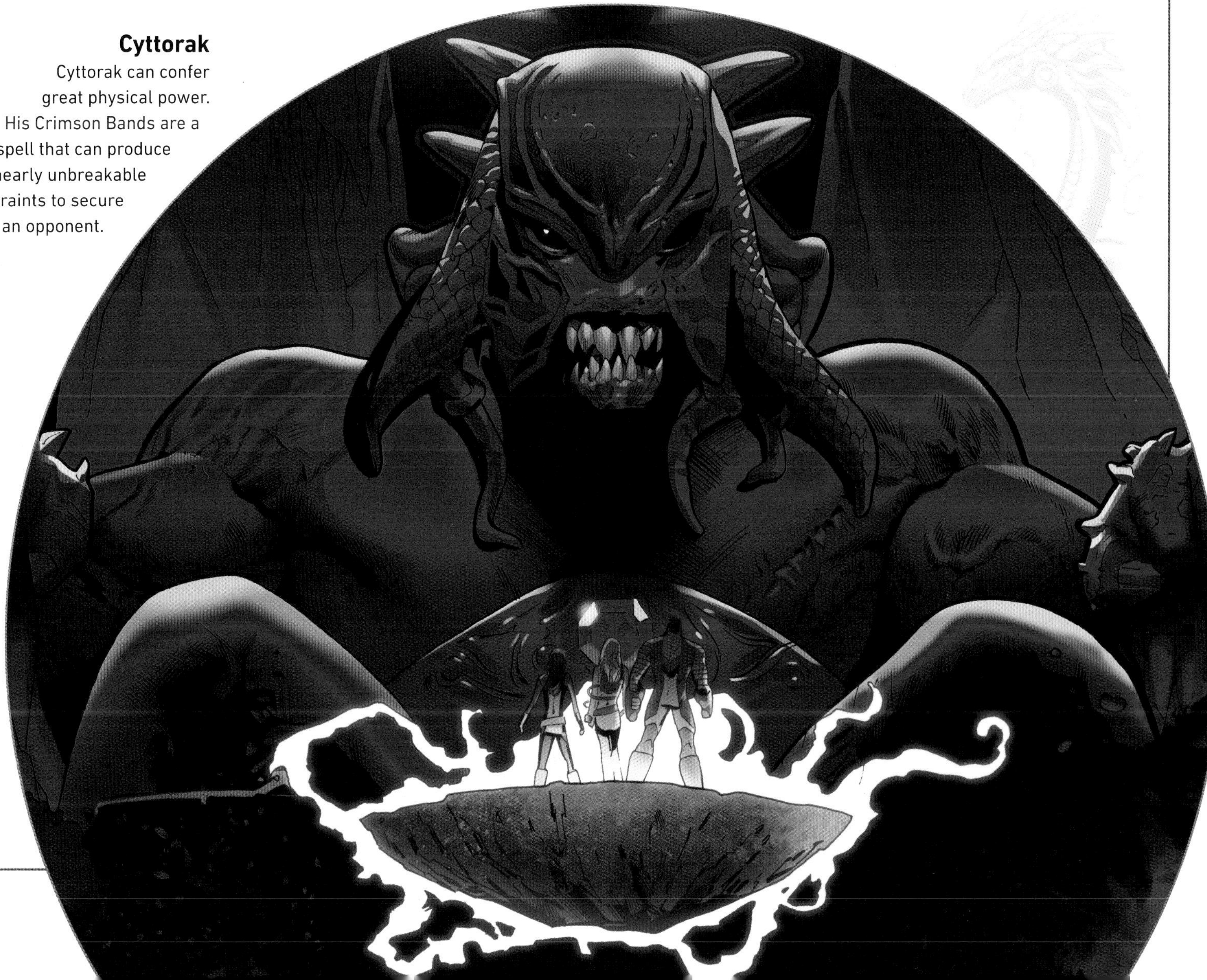

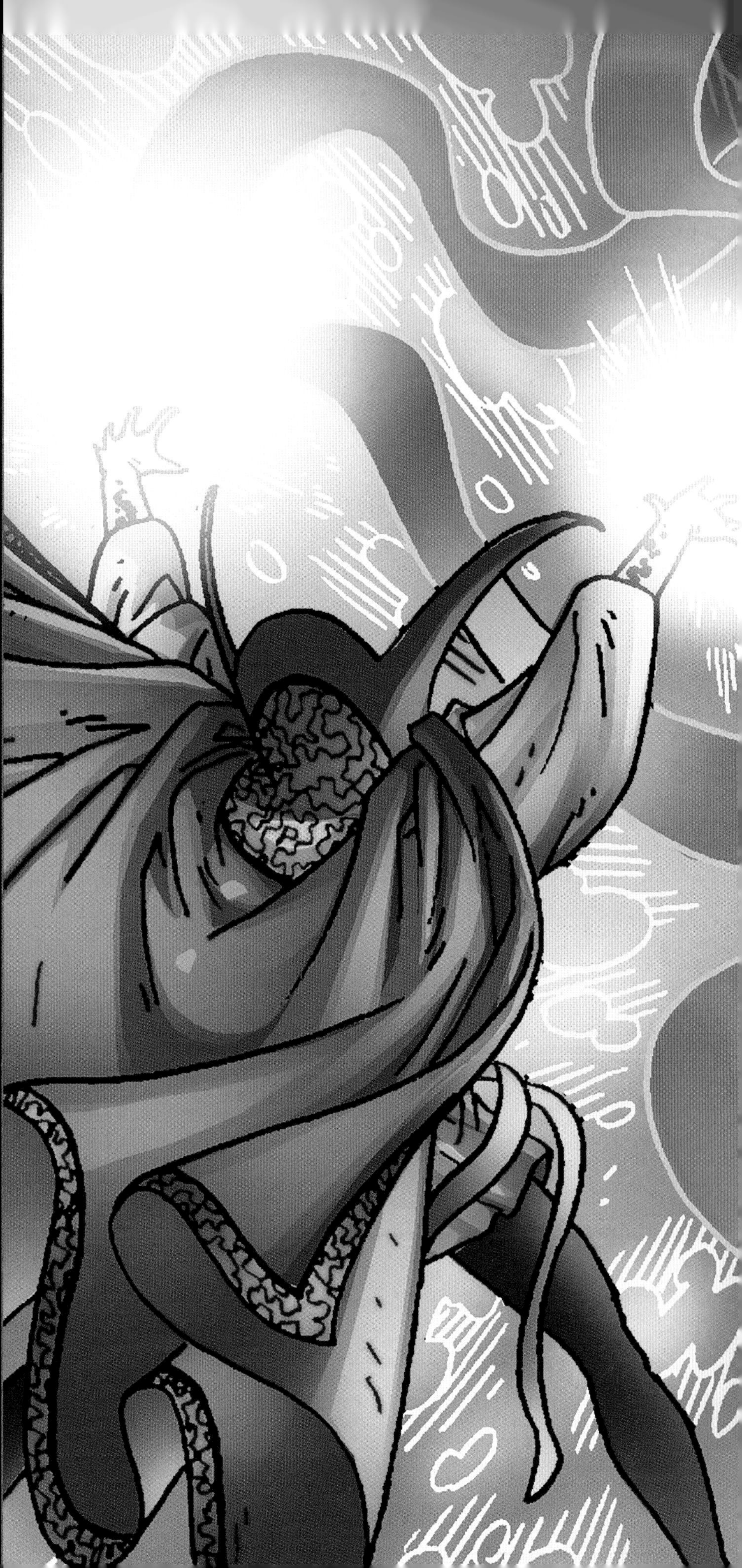

▶ ***Turn the Crimson tide*** Doctor Strange used all his magic against the Iron Maniac, but only the Crimson Bands of Cyttorak had an effect.

CRIMSON BANDS OF CYTTORAK

The Crimson Bands of Cyttorak are an enchantment that can trap an adversary in nearly unbreakable red ribbons of mystical energy, or teleport them away. Doctor Strange has used the Crimson Bands of Cyttorak both offensively and defensively. When a crazed alternate version of Tony Stark—wearing armor more like that of Doctor Doom than Iron Man—arrived from another reality, Strange captured this "Iron Maniac" with the Crimson Bands. Unlike other spells Strange had tried, the binding spell worked for a brief period—until Stark blew up the surrounding area and escaped in the confusion.

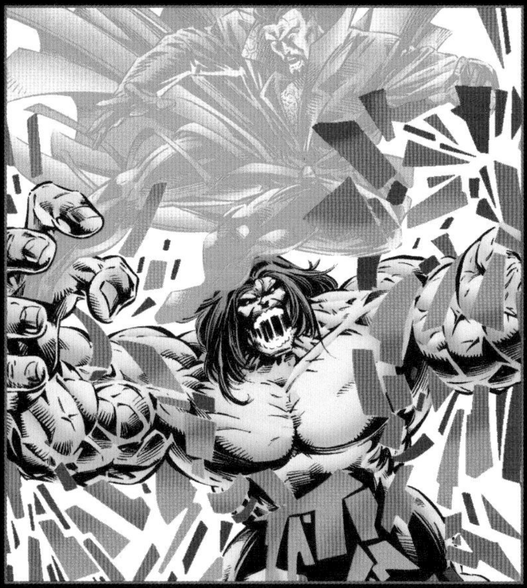

The red and the green

Doctor Strange once used the Crimson Bands of Cyttorak to hold the Hulk. However, despite their magical strength, the green behemoth proved to be one of the few non-magical beings capable of breaking free from them.

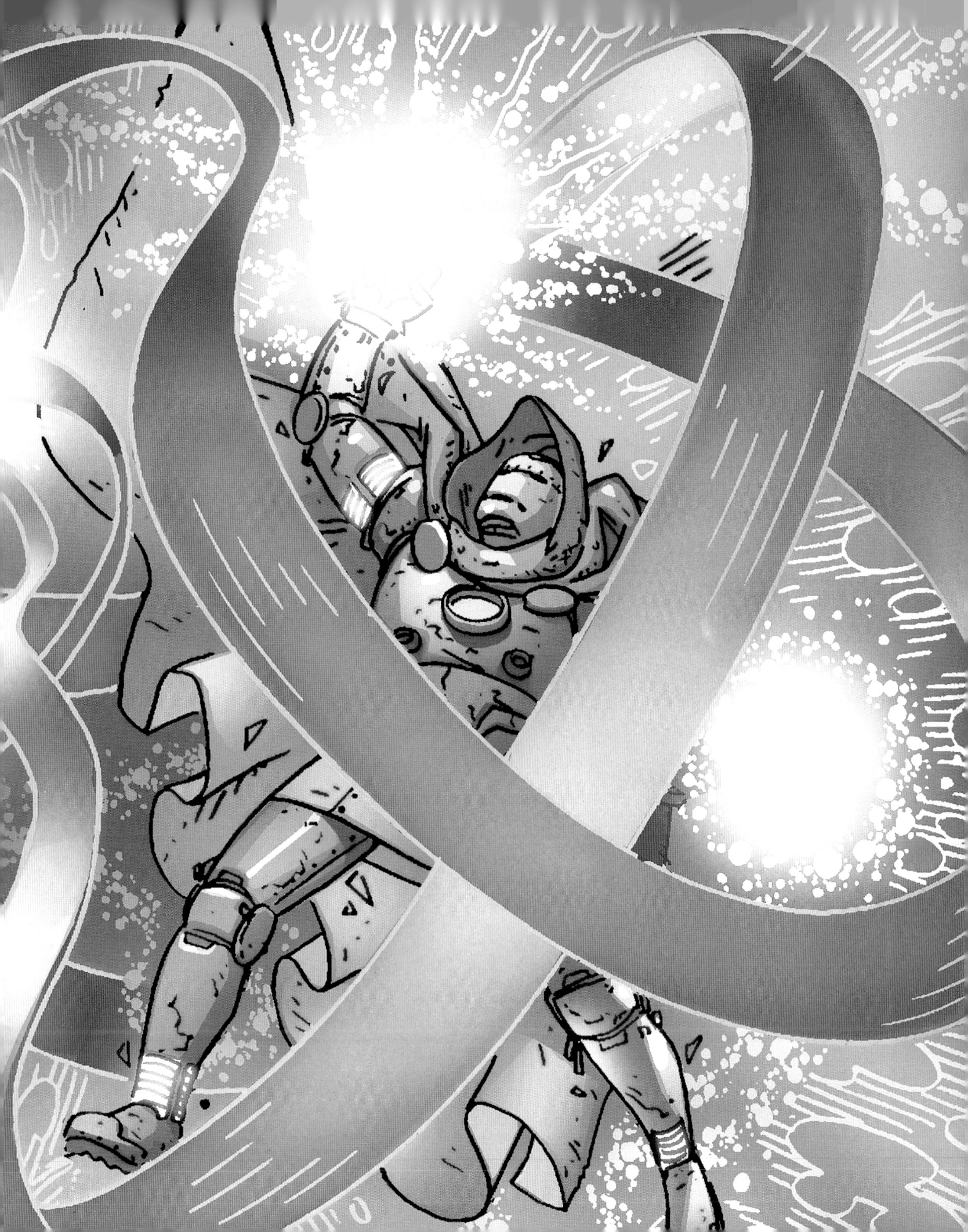

TRAVEL AND TELEPORTATION

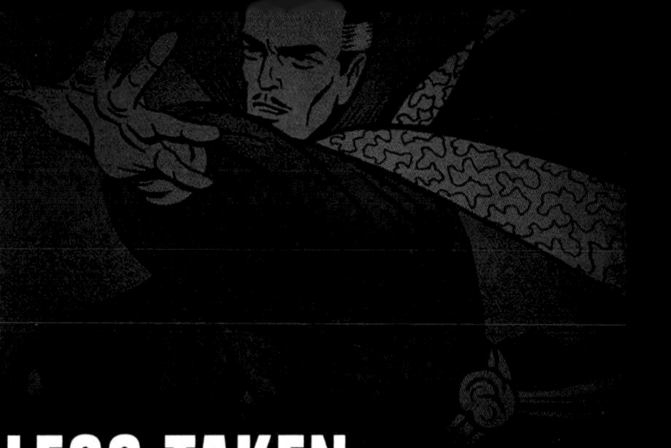

The Sorcerer Supreme's duties span the entire Earth—and often extend to other realms and even beyond the outer reaches of the universe. As such, he calls upon all manner of mystical transportation to reach his destinations and thwart the forces of evil.

▼ ***Doorways to beyond*** Doctor Strange uses a variety of spells to open portals that take him to other places, other times, and other dimensions.

THE PATH LESS TAKEN

The Sorcerer Supreme has many magical means of getting around at his disposal. If it's a matter of moving short distances or quickly flying out of harm's way, he can employ the Cloak of Levitation, which bears him aloft with the slightest mental command. However, when time, distance, and other physical barriers block his path, Doctor Strange can separate his astral form—his spiritual

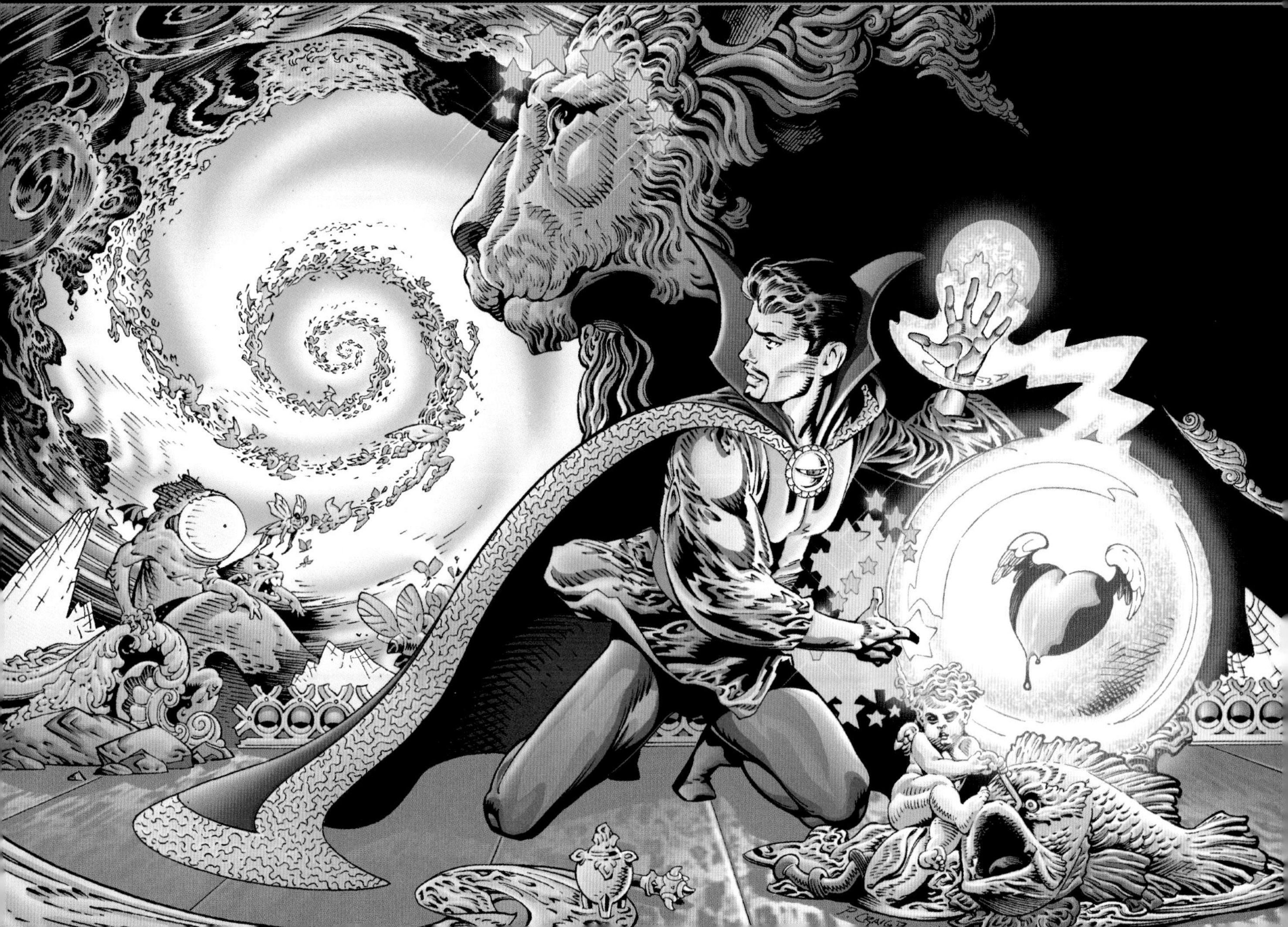

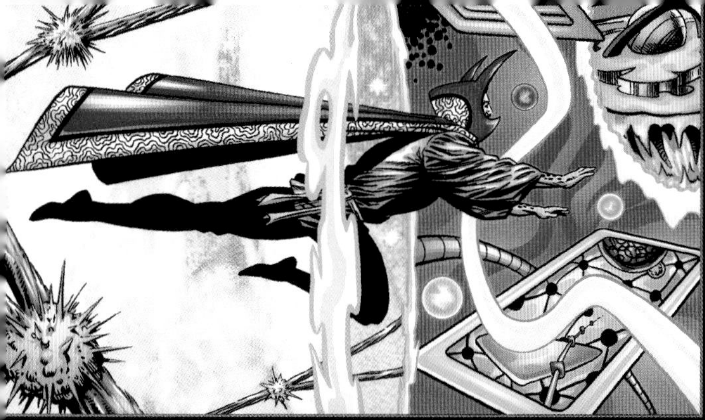

▲ ***To the edge of reason*** Doctor Strange can travel to mind-boggling realities.

essence—from his body. Intangible, his astral form is unshackled from the laws of the physical world, giving him the ability pass through solid objects and traverse great distances instantaneously. In this disembodied state, Strange does not need air, food, or water, and is beyond harm except from the most powerful magic. Doctor Strange has also been known to use astral projection when he needs to communicate quickly and across large expanses with his allies and others on matters of great importance.

To cross great distances or open doorways to other dimensions, the Master of the Mystic Arts can cast spells such as the Winds of Watoomb or Mists of Hoggoth to teleport himself and others. And as Sorcerer Supreme, he commands the magical means to travel in time—although this is never done lightly. Even small changes to the past can greatly affect the future in ways that Strange cannot always foresee.

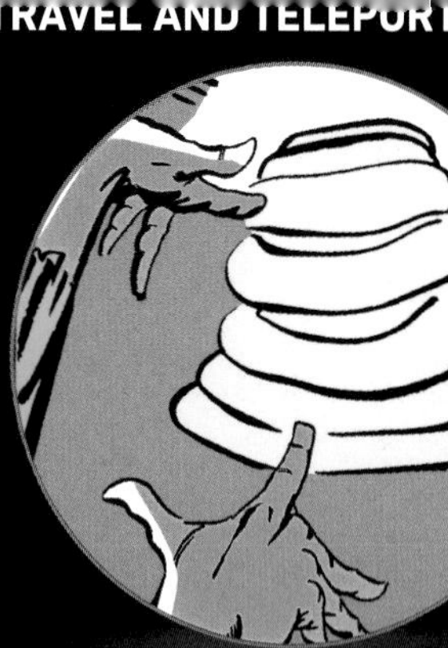

Conjurer's Cone
The Conjurer's Cone is a spell that can be used to teleport an enemy away in a moment of danger. However, it has no effect when used against a foe as powerful as Dormammu.

"A SHIMMERING LUMINESCENCE—LIKE A GATEWAY TO ANOTHER WORLD!"

Doctor Strange

Astral projection
Ghostly and invisible, Doctor Strange's spirit takes flight from his physical form when needed on urgent matters.

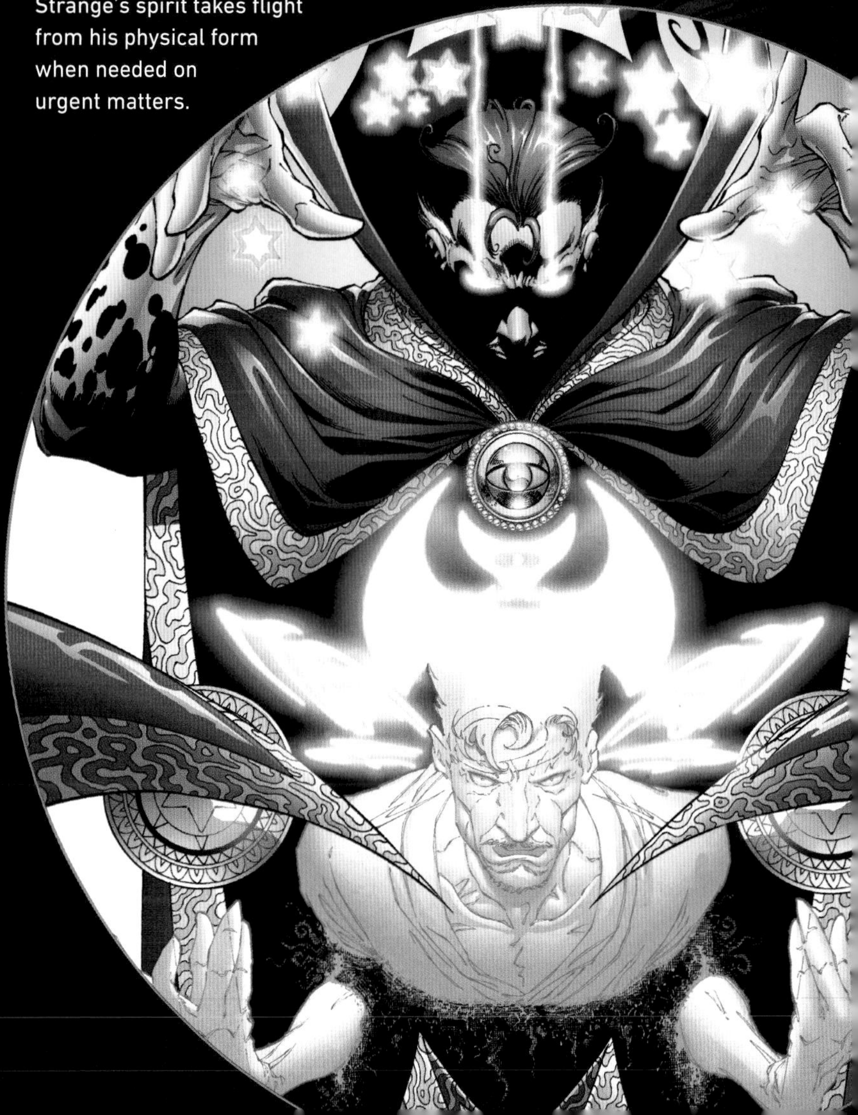

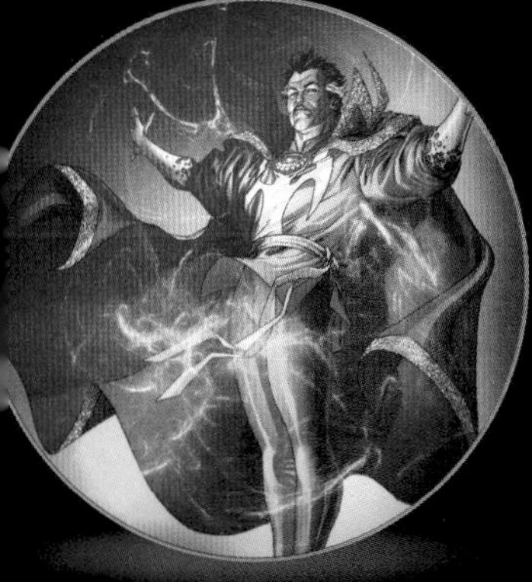

Cloak of Levitation
A vital part of his costume, the Cloak of Levitation allows Doctor Strange to fly from place to place in the Earthly realm and beyond, without the use of other spells.

Eye of Agamotto
Among its many properties, the Eye of Agamotto has the ability to transport Doctor Strange and his allies great distances. It can even teleport across the vast expanse of the universe!

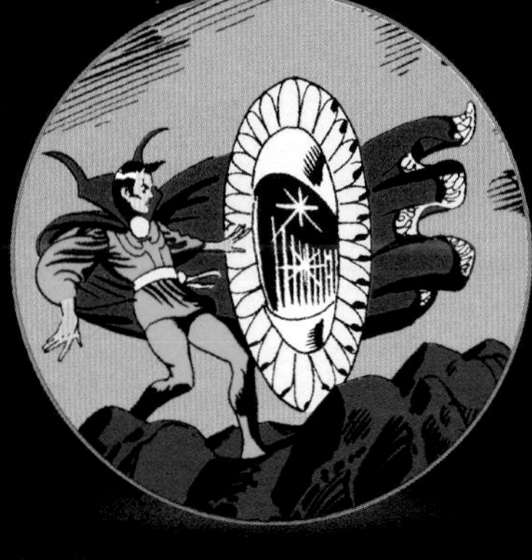

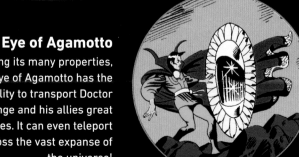

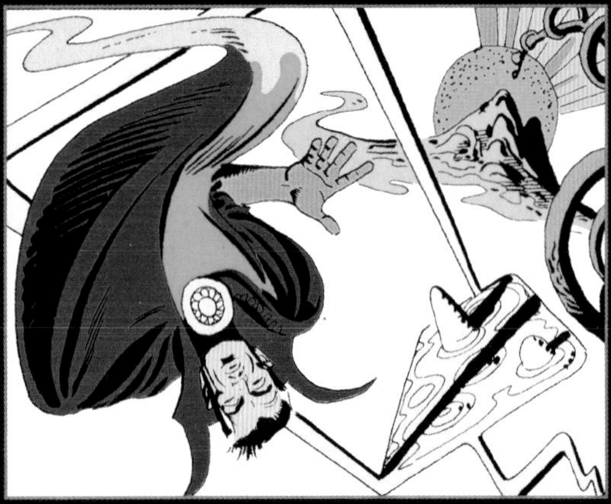

Weird dimensions

Other dimensions do not conform to Earthly laws of physics or matter. Forms and perspective—even time—can differ weirdly and wildly in these dreamlike landscapes.

OTHER REALMS, OTHER WORLDS

Doctor Strange travels to many realms, from the Dark Dimension of the Dread Dormammu, to worlds on the mortal plane and across the cosmos. At times, however, he has traveled closer to home, although with destinations just as perilous and bizarre. On one occasion he journeyed into the soulscape of a young boy who had become inhabited by a nomadic tribe of Soul-Eaters. Besting their monstrous champion, Doctor Strange convinced these denizens of the Nethersphere to move on, leaving the spirit of the boy unharmed.

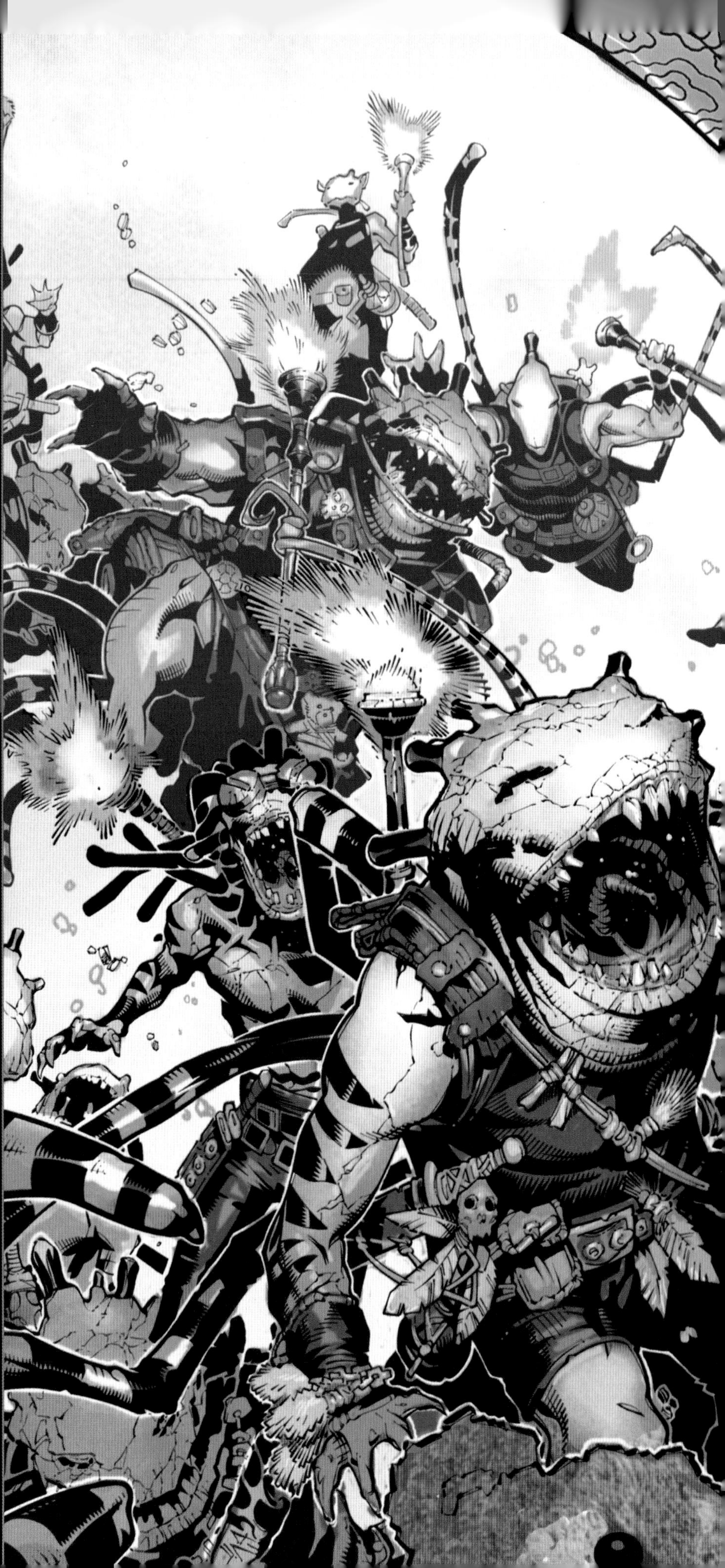

▶ ***Childish things*** The teddy bears and flowers of an innocent child's inner world made for an unusual field of battle when Doctor Strange confronted a sinister band of Soul-Eaters.

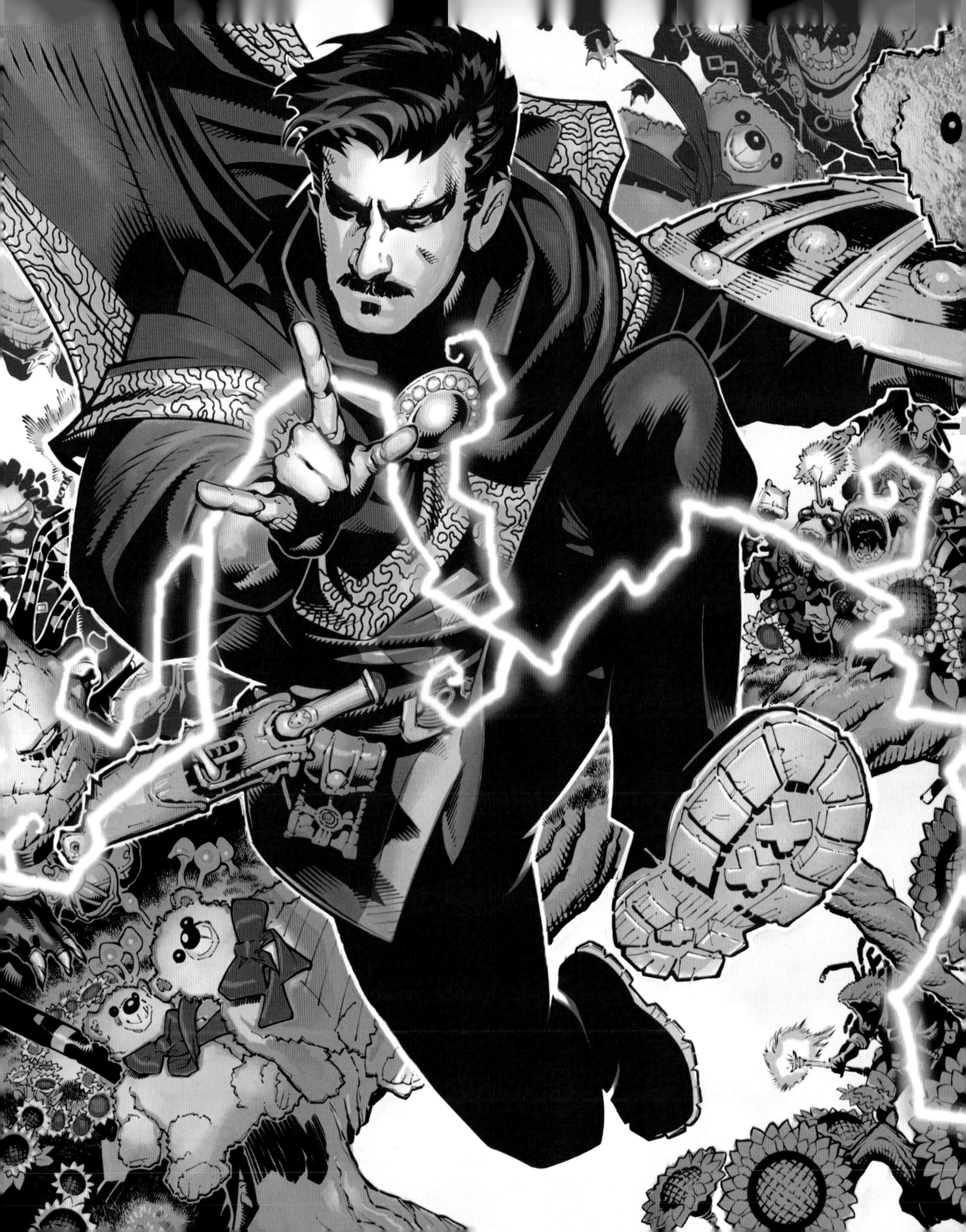

MASTER OF MANY ARTS

As the Sorcerer Supreme, Doctor Strange has mastered many arts and skills involving his body, mind, and soul. His aim has always been to defend the Earth with or without the power of magic.

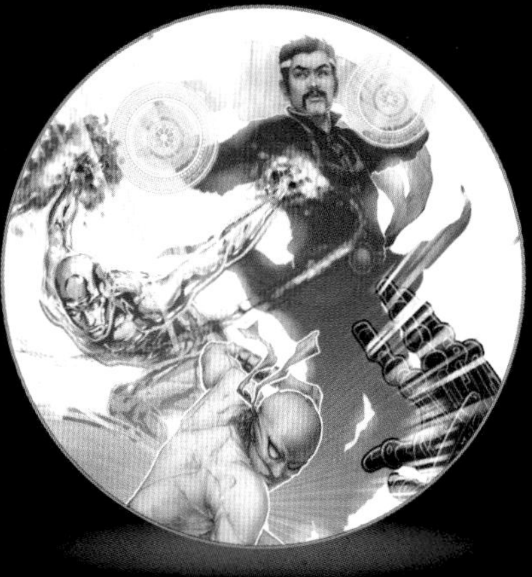

Strategist supreme

In defending the Earth from a multitude of threats from sinister minds, Doctor Strange has proven to be a brilliant strategist. He is also an able leader of his fellow heroes, in groups like the Defenders and the Illuminati.

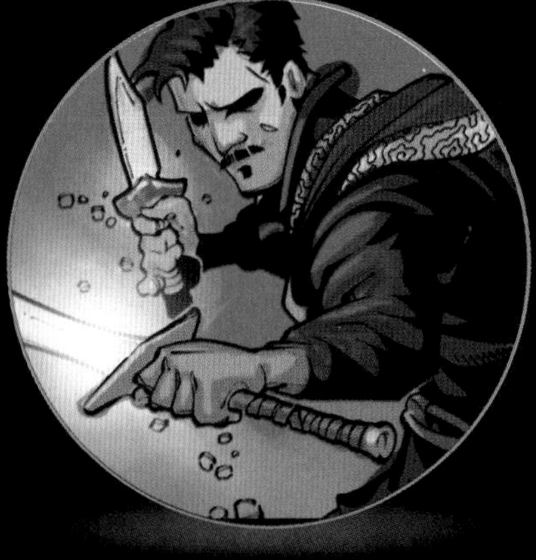

Weapons wizard

Doctor Strange is also skilled with magically infused weapons such as swords and axes, which augment his formidable arsenal of spells.

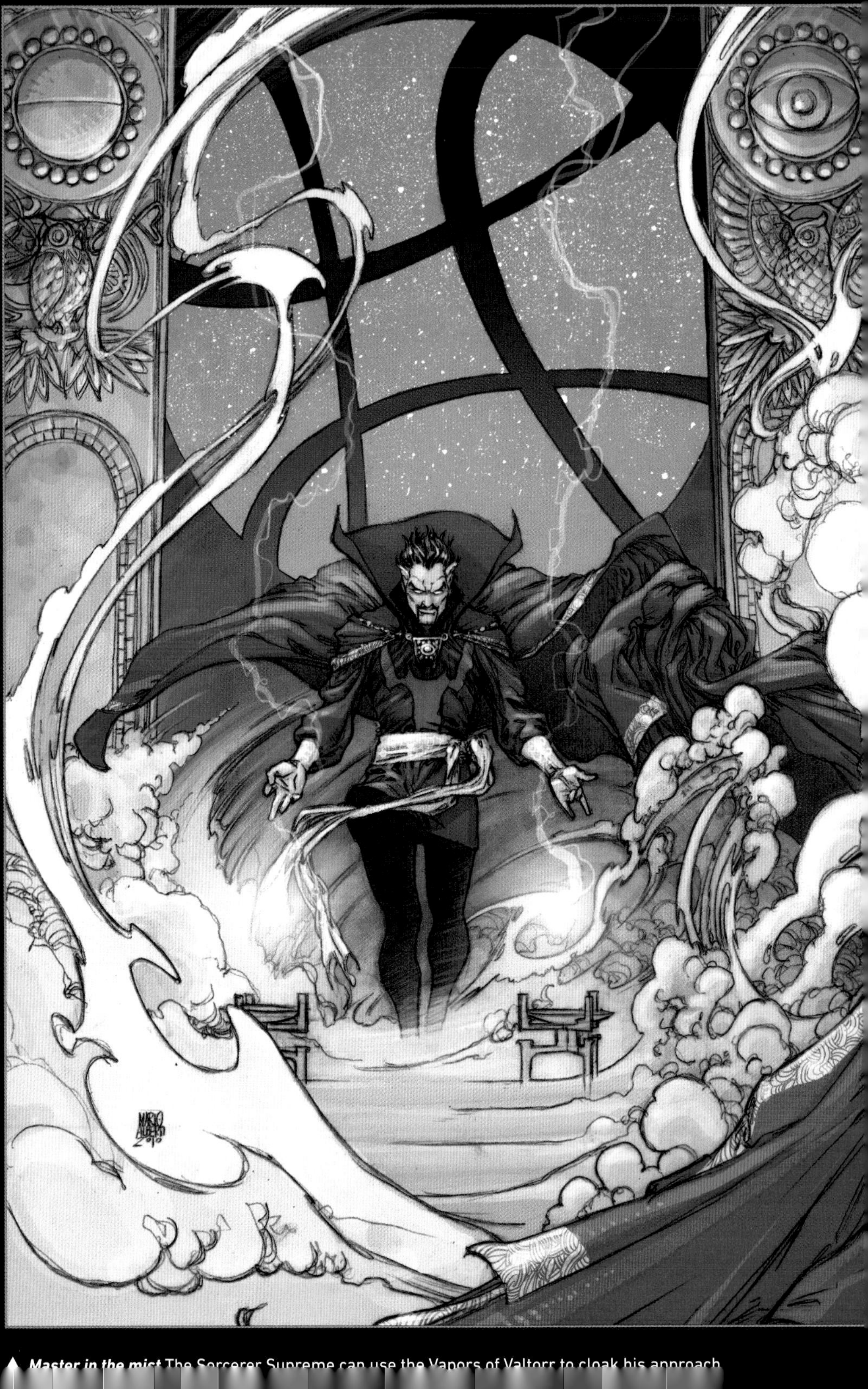

▲ ***Master in the mist*** The Sorcerer Supreme can use the Vapors of Valtorr to cloak his approach.

THE MEASURE OF THE MAN

Since he first became the Ancient One's student, Doctor Strange has been training his body and mind to unlock the latent abilities available to all humans. He enhances those skills with magic. In addition to a talent for hypnotism, Doctor Strange can telepathically read minds and communicate with others. He boosts this ability with the Eye of Agamotto to peer into even more powerful minds. He is attuned to fluctuations in the ambient magical energy coursing through the universe, and through meditation he can focus on specific events, or expand his awareness into other dimensions.

Strange's knowledge of magic allows him to cast spells and call upon the powers of extra-dimensional entities. This enables him to unleash bolts of energy, raise protective shields, cast illusions, and create fire. He can travel to other dimensions either physically or by separating his astral form from his body, and he can also create barriers to keep unwanted entities out of the human world, as well as banish foes to other realms. These are but a few of powers at his disposal.

Doctor Strange has become immortal through the power of magic. He keeps his body in peak physical condition through extensive exercise and martial arts training. Even so, he can still be killed, and his body does require food and rest.

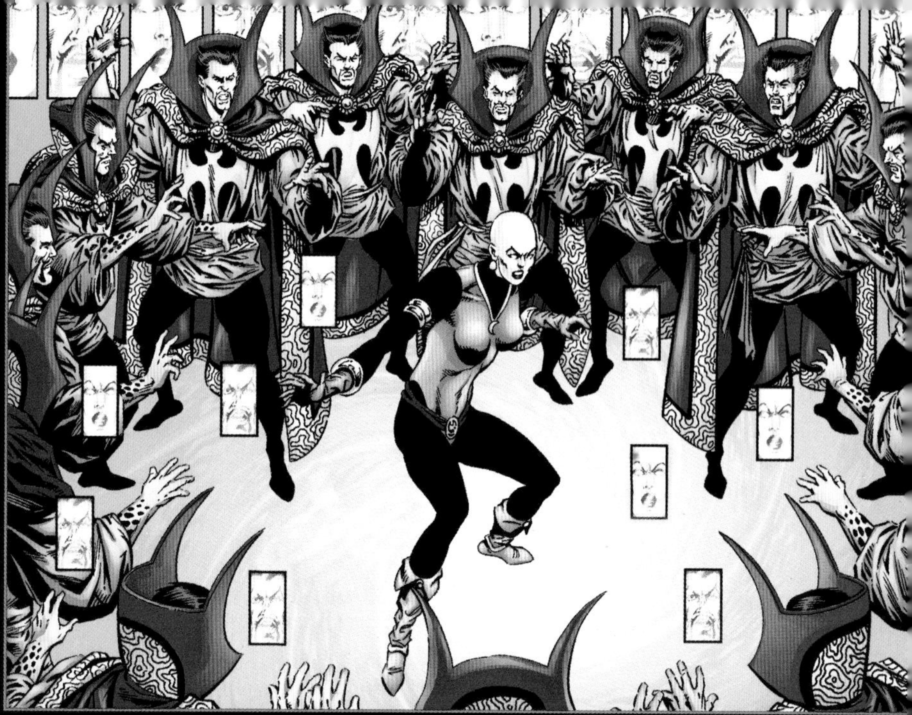

▲ ***Mirror images*** During a magical and mental tussle with Moondragon, Doctor Strange tried to disorient the psychic by conjuring multiple versions of himself.

"THE WORLD MUST NEVER KNOW THE FULL MYSTIC POWER OF DR. STRANGE."
Doctor Strange

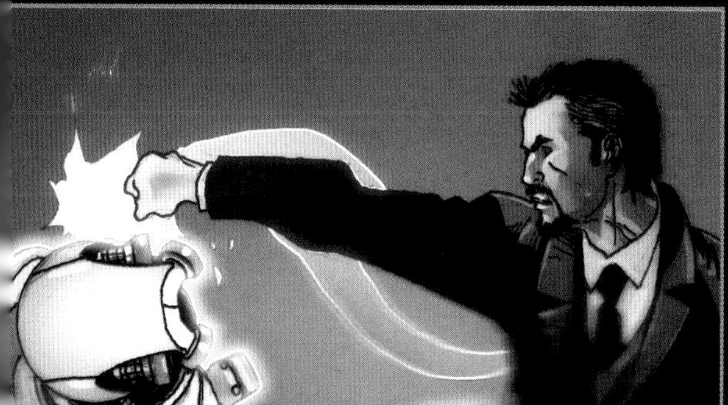

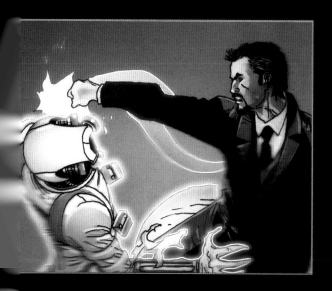

Martial arts master
Doctor Strange has shown villains like the cybernetic saboteur, the Ghost, that he is a master of the martial arts as well as the mystical.

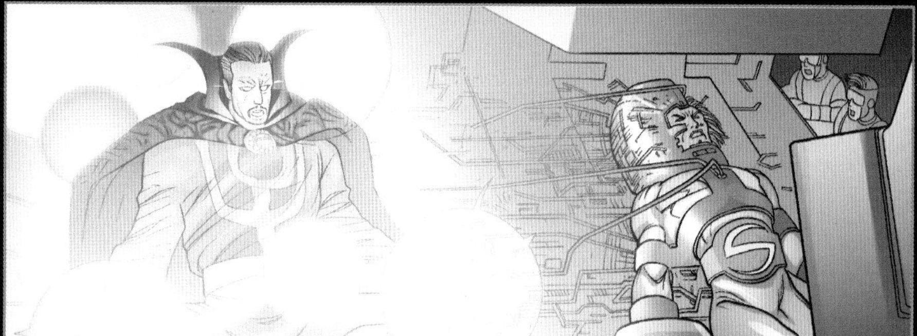

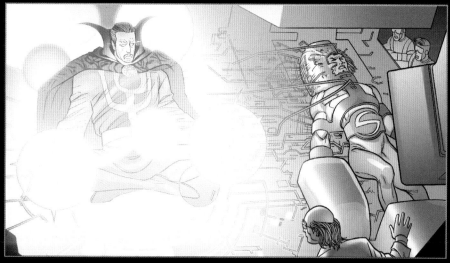

In the mind of the Sentry
Doctor Strange once used his powers in an attempt to heal the shattered mind of the troubled superhero, the Sentry—sadly to no avail.

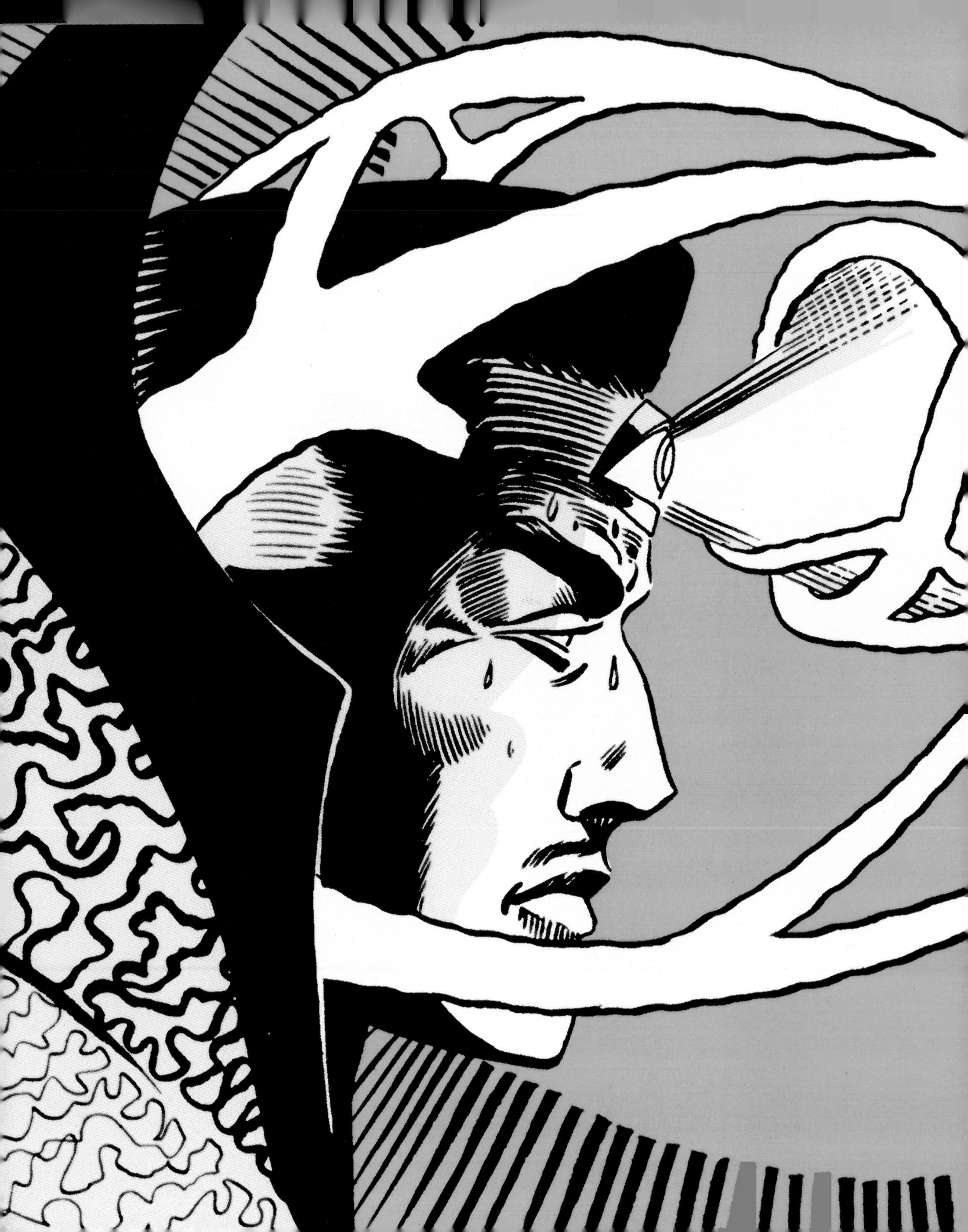

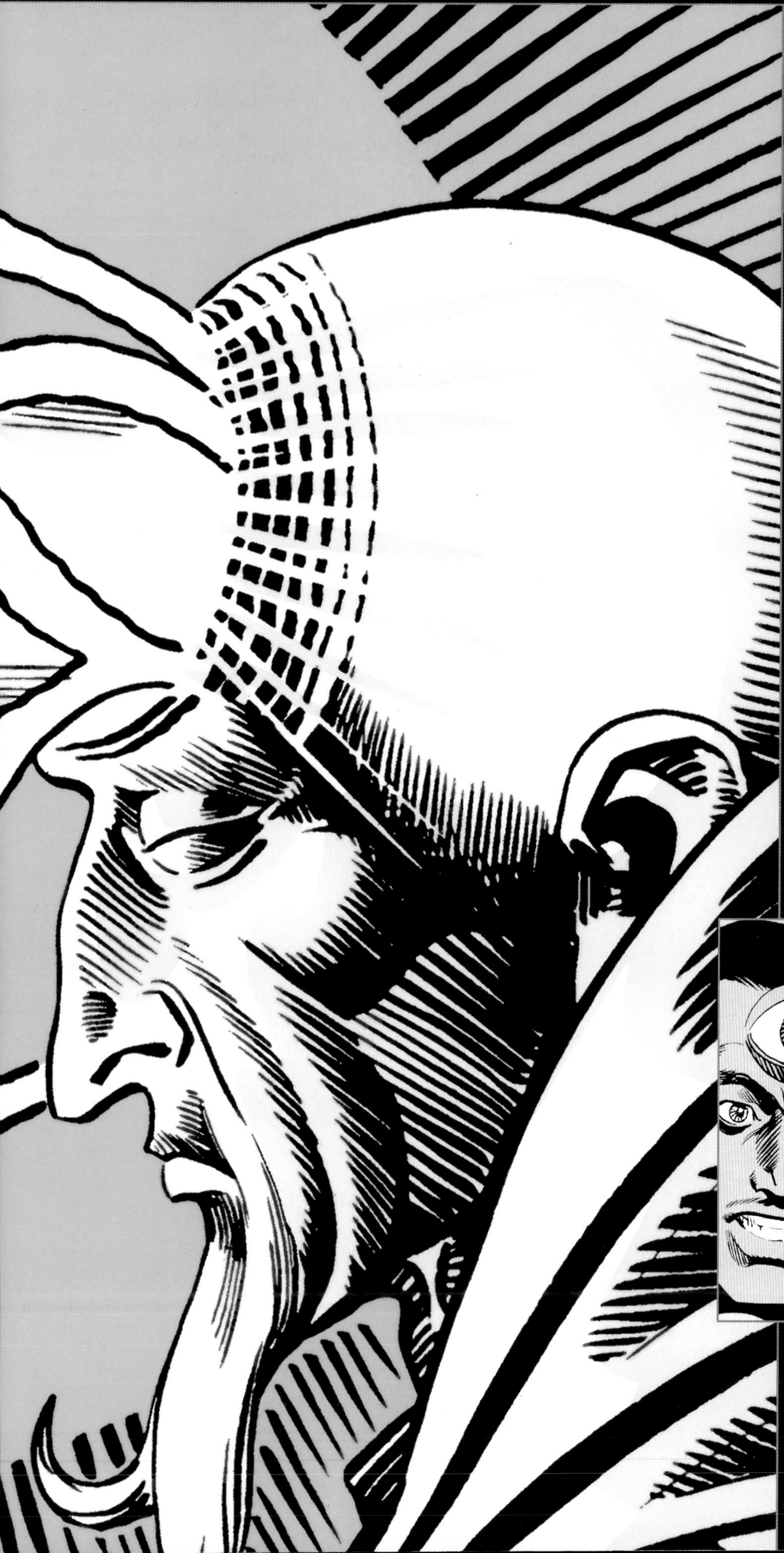

◀ ***Mind over master*** The strain weakened Doctor Strange when he used the Eye of Agamotto to access the Ancient One's mind.

TELEPATHY

While Doctor Strange has the power to read the mind of almost anyone, he has always shared a special link with his former teacher, the Ancient One. Once, when the world was in danger, Strange dared to use the Eye of Agamotto to delve deep into the Ancient One's unconscious mind. But when he did, he found that multiple mystical traps protected the old man's secrets. It was only by dropping his own defenses and allowing his master into his own thoughts that Strange was able to retrieve the information he desperately needed.

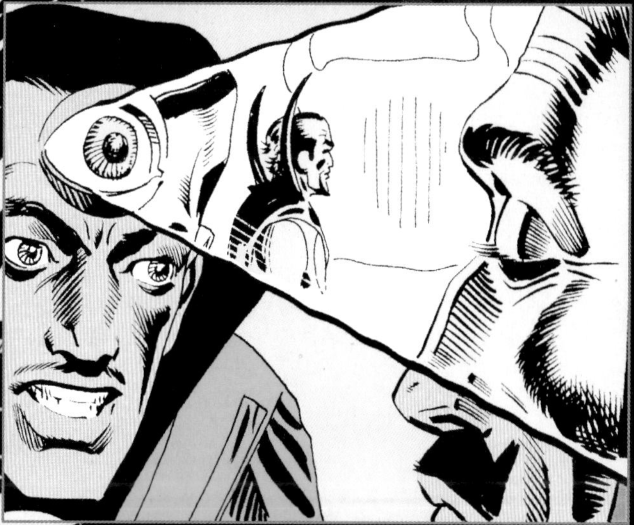

Seeking misdeeds
Doctor Strange once probed the mind of Baron Mordo's servant to find out what evil deeds his old enemy was plotting.

CHAPTER 6
OBJECTS OF ENCHANTMENT

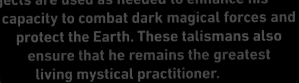

When Doctor Strange became the Sorcerer Supreme—
following extensive training in the mystic arts from
the Ancient One—he took possession of the most
comprehensive collection of magical artifacts and
talismans in existence. While the Eye of Agamotto
and the Cloak of Levitation are essential elements
of Strange's powers—and his costume—other
objects are used as needed to enhance his
capacity to combat dark magical forces and
protect the Earth. These talismans also
ensure that he remains the greatest
living mystical practitioner.

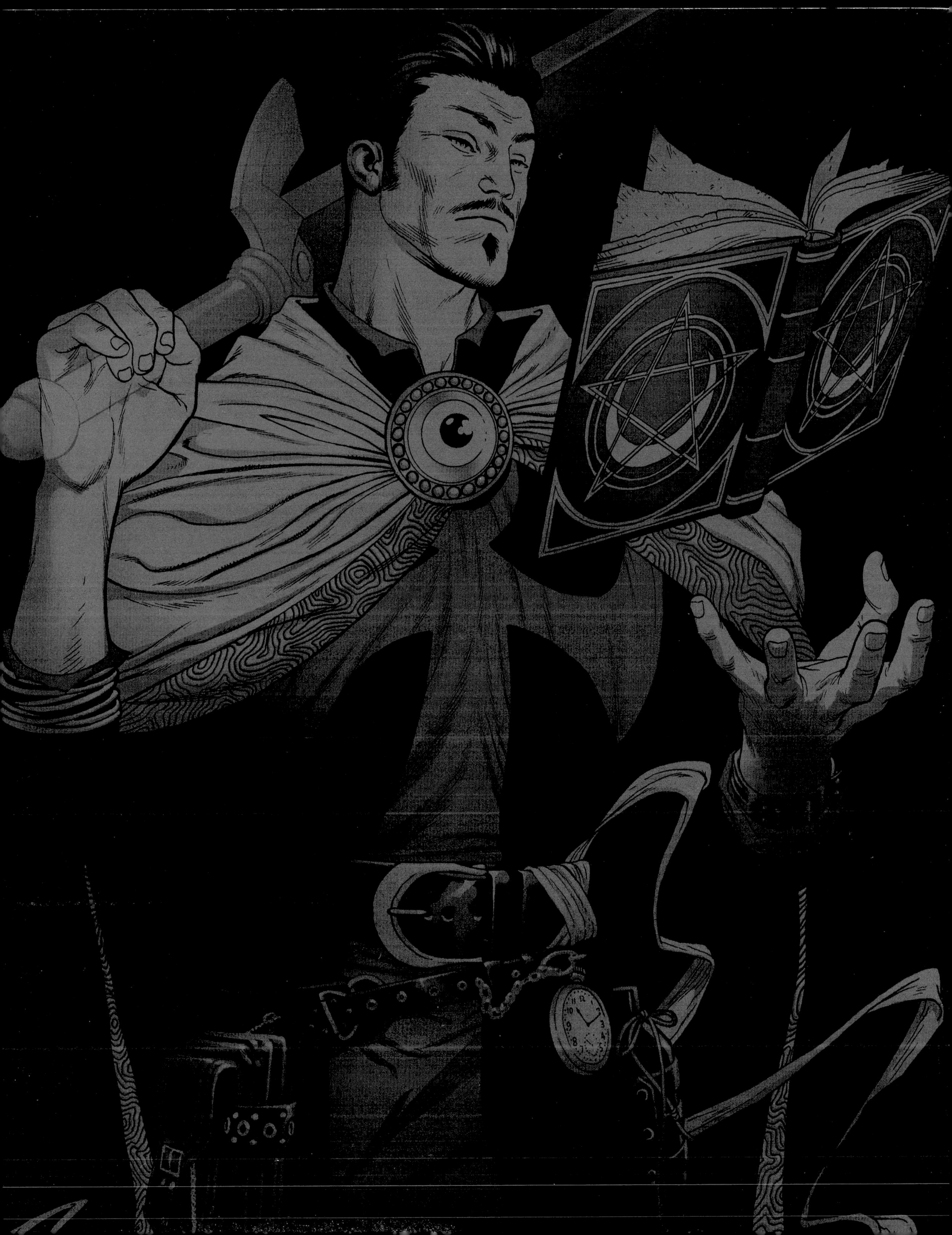

THE EYE OF AGAMOTTO

One of the most powerful mystic conduits on this physical plane, the Eye of Agamotto fastens the Cloak of Levitation—and connects Doctor Strange to the eternal magical realms.

The third of the Vishanti, Agamotto, created three eyes: Truth, Power, and Prescience. The first of these, the Eye of Agamotto, is the mystical amulet worn by Doctor Strange.

It is traditionally bestowed upon the Sorcerer Supreme—a title once held by Agamotto himself. A weapon of wisdom and white magic, the Eye—contained within the amulet—gives Strange the ability to see through all illusions and disguises, thanks to the mystical light that radiates from it depths.

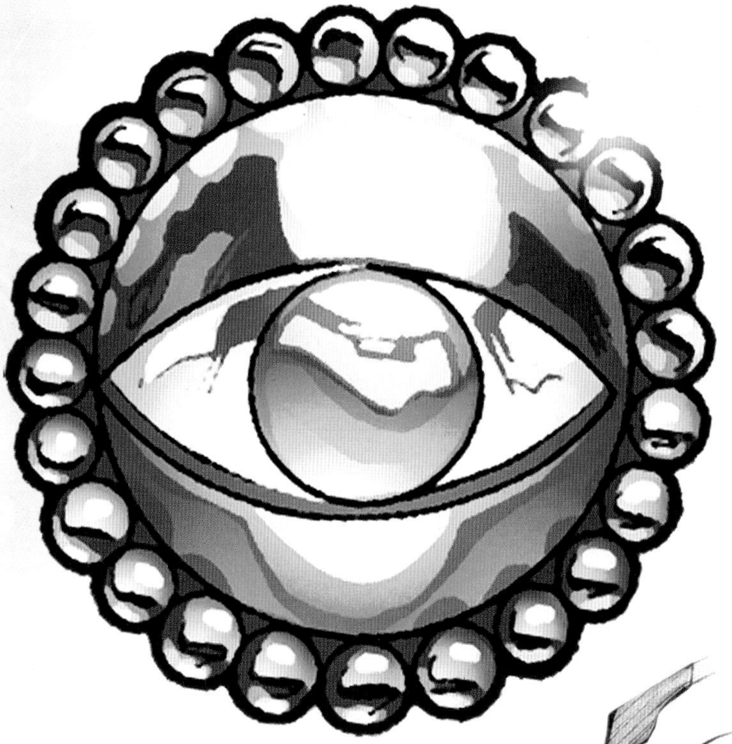

The all-seeing Eye

Enclosed in the amulet, the Eye's incandescent light disperses all shadows and deceptions to reveal the deepest buried truths.

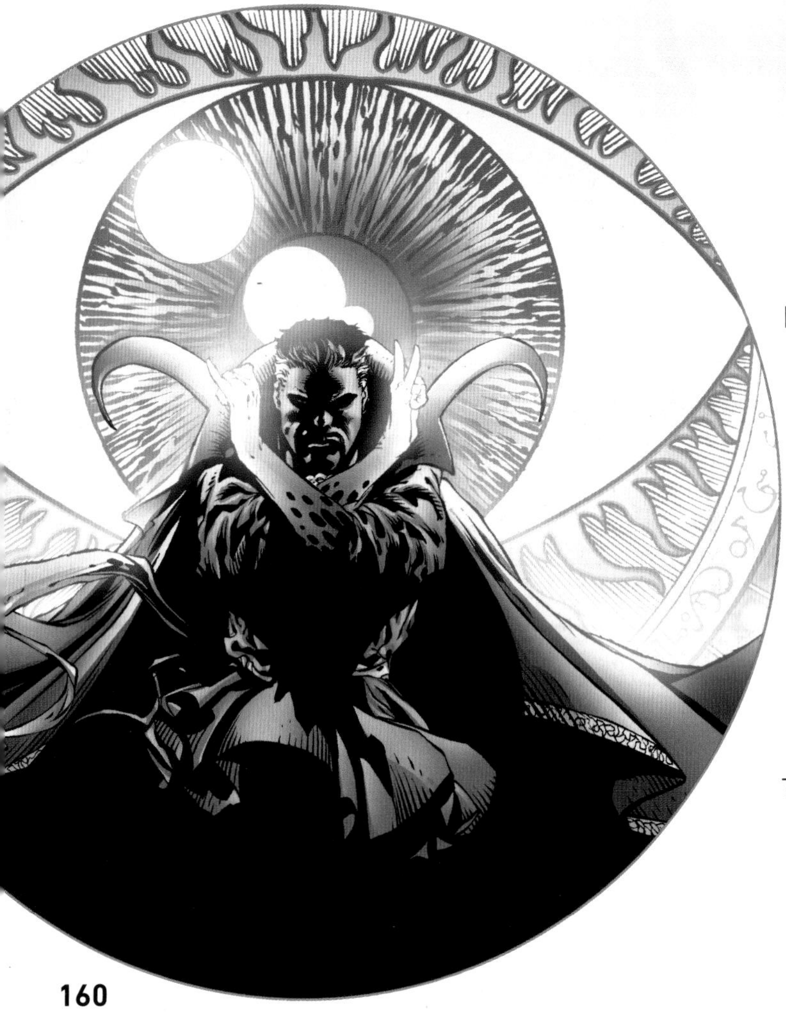

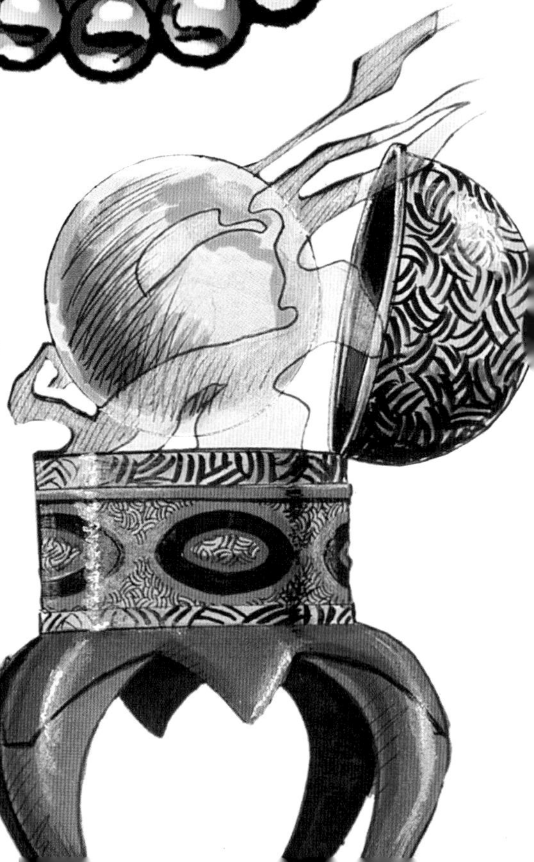

Radiant power

The Eye's enchanted light can weaken various evil beings. These include demons, devils, the undead, extra-dimensional entities, and human practitioners of the dark arts.

Orb of Agamotto

The Eye is mystically linked to the Orb of Amagotto, which can view other dimensions to detect threats to the Earth.

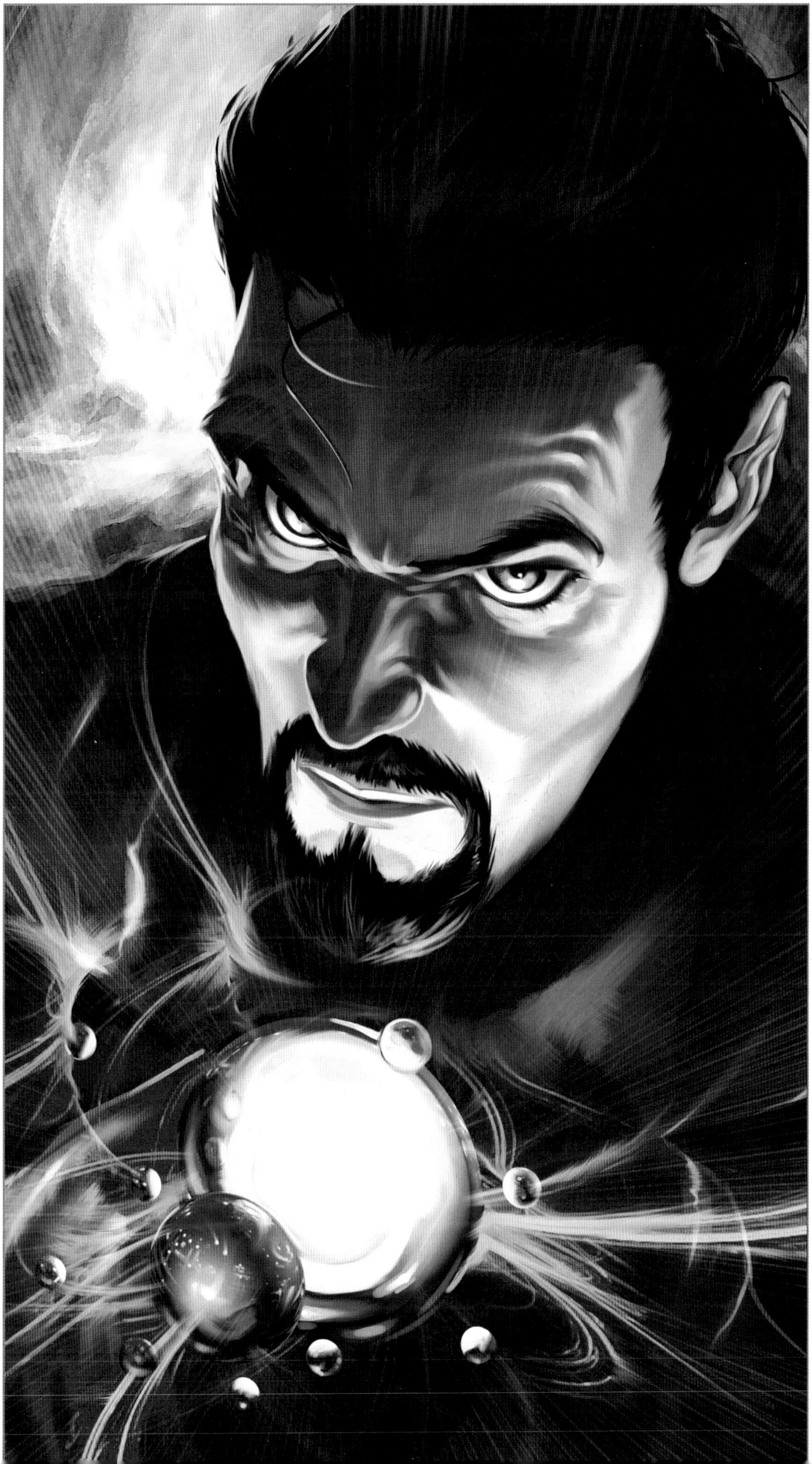

◀ ***Multi-purpose Eye*** Doctor Strange can use the Eye of Agamotto to probe the minds of other beings. He can also use it to create mystical shields, view the past, levitate impossibly heavy objects, and even open portals to other dimensions.

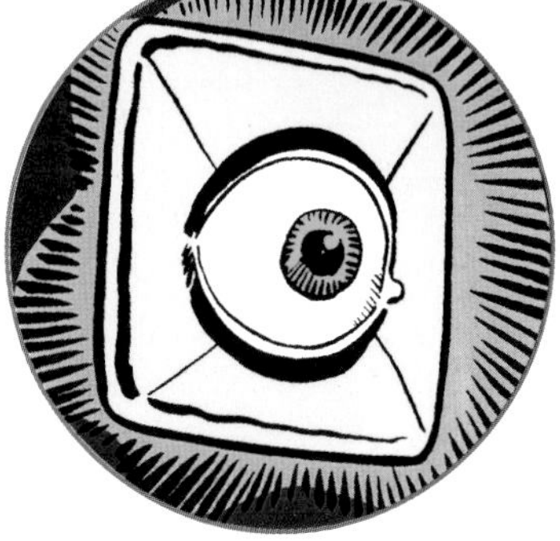

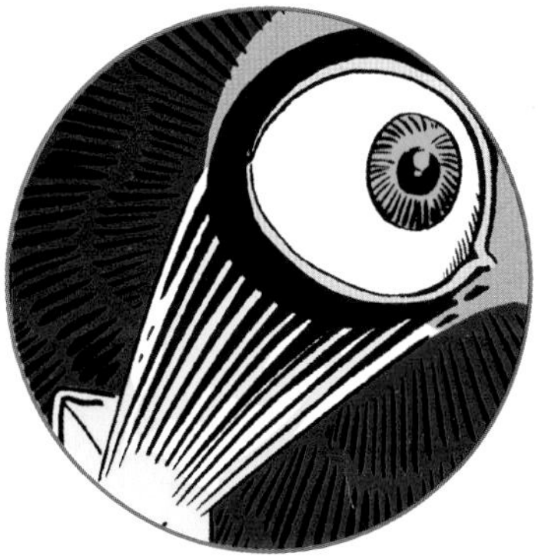

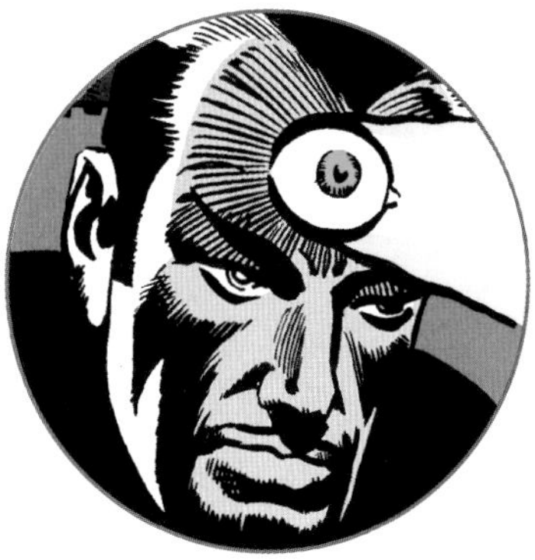

Amulet to Eye

Early on in Doctor Strange's apprenticeship, the Ancient One gave him the Amulet of Agamotto. As he became more adept with his abilities, he was given the more powerful Eye. When the Eye of Agomotto is used, a literal "third eye" appears on the forehead of the mystical practitioner summoning its mighty power.

BOOKS OF MAGIC

Doctor Strange's library in his Sanctum Sanctorum boasts a vast array of arcane books and occult tomes. When evil strikes or the Earth is threatened, it is to these magical texts that the Sorcerer Supreme turns. However, there are other more secret books in Strange's unrivaled collection that contain the ancient knowledge of wizards, demons, gods, and monsters.

▲ **Books abound** Doctor Strange can call upon a huge number of texts in his Sanctum Sanctorum library.

▲ **Enlightenment** Doctor Strange has frequently used The Book of the Vishanti to counter dark magic.

WEIGHTY TOMES

The most prized book in Doctor Strange's possession is The Book of the Vishanti, the greatest source of white magic in the universe. It is believed that the Vishanti themselves were the authors of the initial text, but that it was expanded upon by subsequent generations of wizards. The book originally fell into the hands of the Atlantean sorcerer Varnae, who would become the world's first vampire. It was also owned by Queen Cleopatra, and by the god Marduk, from whom it was liberated by the Ancient One. It finally passed into Doctor Strange's possession when his mentor died.

The Book of the Vishanti's opposite number is the Darkhold, or the Book of Sins, which serves as a record of the Elder God Chthon's knowledge of dark magic. The Darkhold has been used by Morgan Le Fay, Mordred the Mystic, and even by Doctor Strange, who employed the

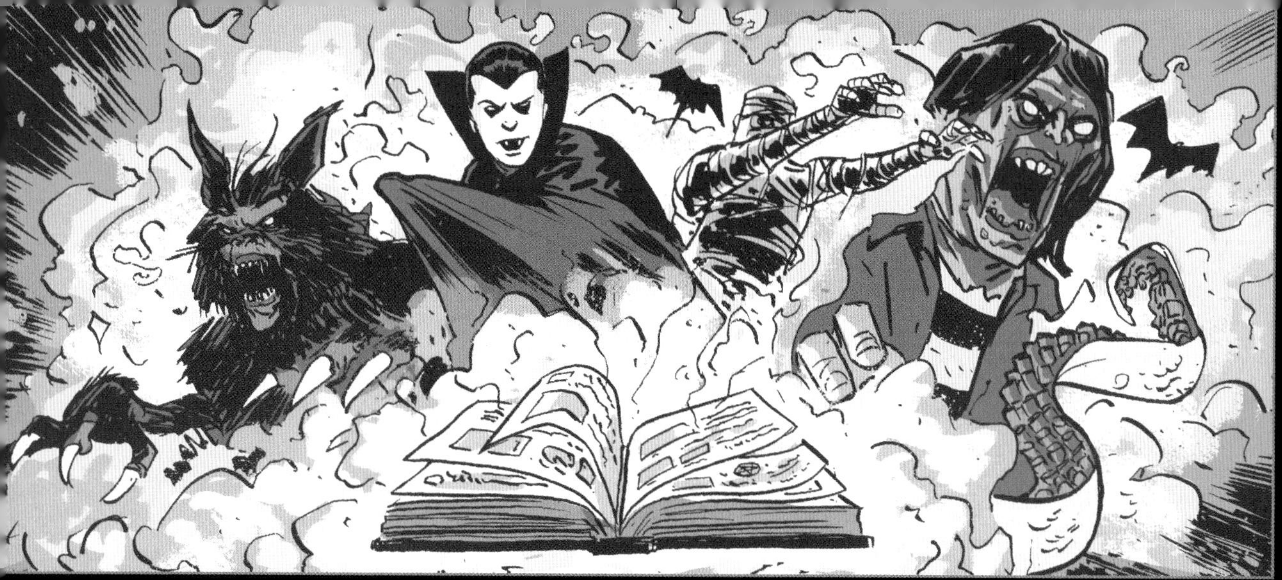

◀ *Dark spells*
The Darkhold contains instructions on how to create vampires, zombies, and werewolves—and how to destroy them.

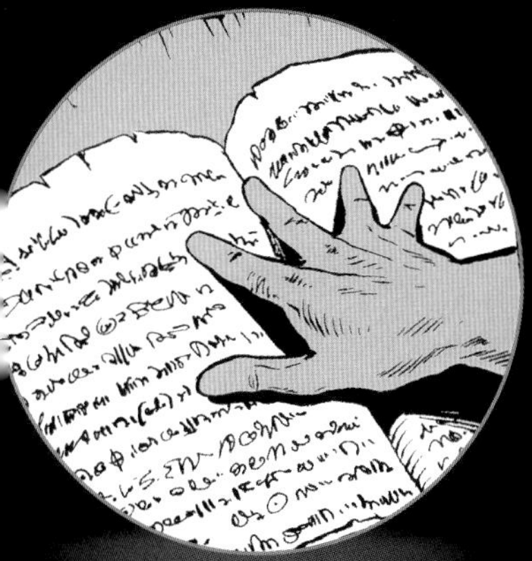

Book of Cagliostro

The Book of Cagliostro was written by an Italian collector of occult wisdom. It contains all his knowledge, additional material from the Darkhold, and some of the obscure teachings of the millennia-old sorcerer Sise-Neg.

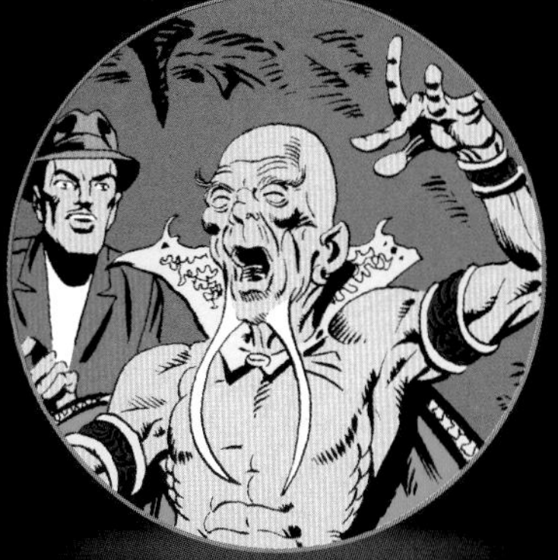

Diary of the Aged Ghenghis

Believed to have been alive since the dawn of man, the Aged Genghis is the oldest living sorcerer on the planet. He wrote down his learning in his Diary, but the book was lost to another dimension.

"EVERY COUNTER-SPELL KNOWN TO THE MYSTIC ARTS IS INSCRIBED WITHIN THESE TIME-WORN PAGES!"

Doctor Strange on The Book of the Vishanti

Montesi Formula described within its pages to eradicate all vampires from Earth. Sections of the book have been spread worldwide by acolytes called Darkholders.

Other revered tomes of wizardry include the Book of Cagliostro, the Diary of the Aged Genghis, the Tome of Zhered-Na, and the Iron-Bound Books of Shuma-Gorath. These last texts were created by Shuma-Gorath and other evil entities, with the purpose of influencing Earth through the use of the books.

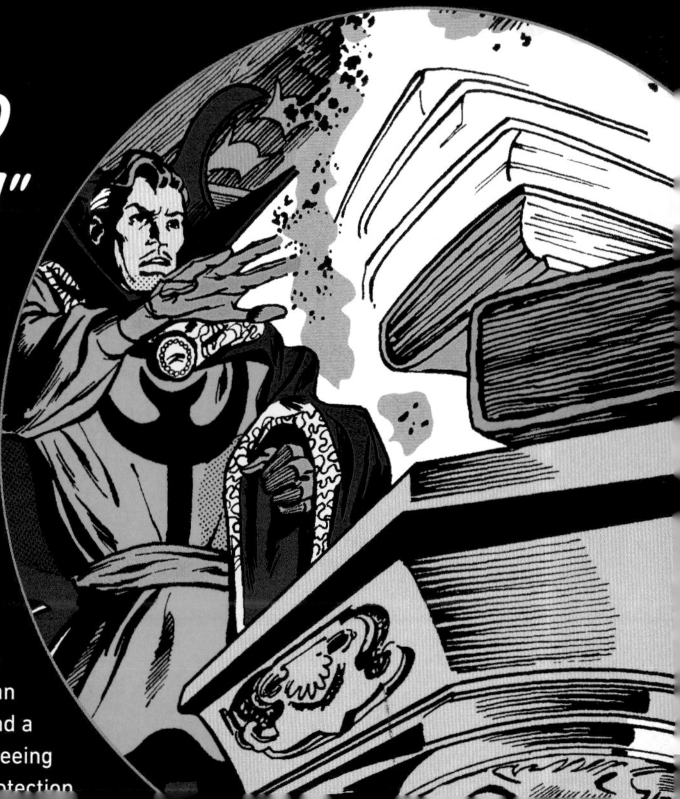

The Book of the Vishanti

So valuable is The Book of the Vishanti that Doctor Strange surrounds it with an enchanted aura and a Shield of Not-Seeing for added protection.

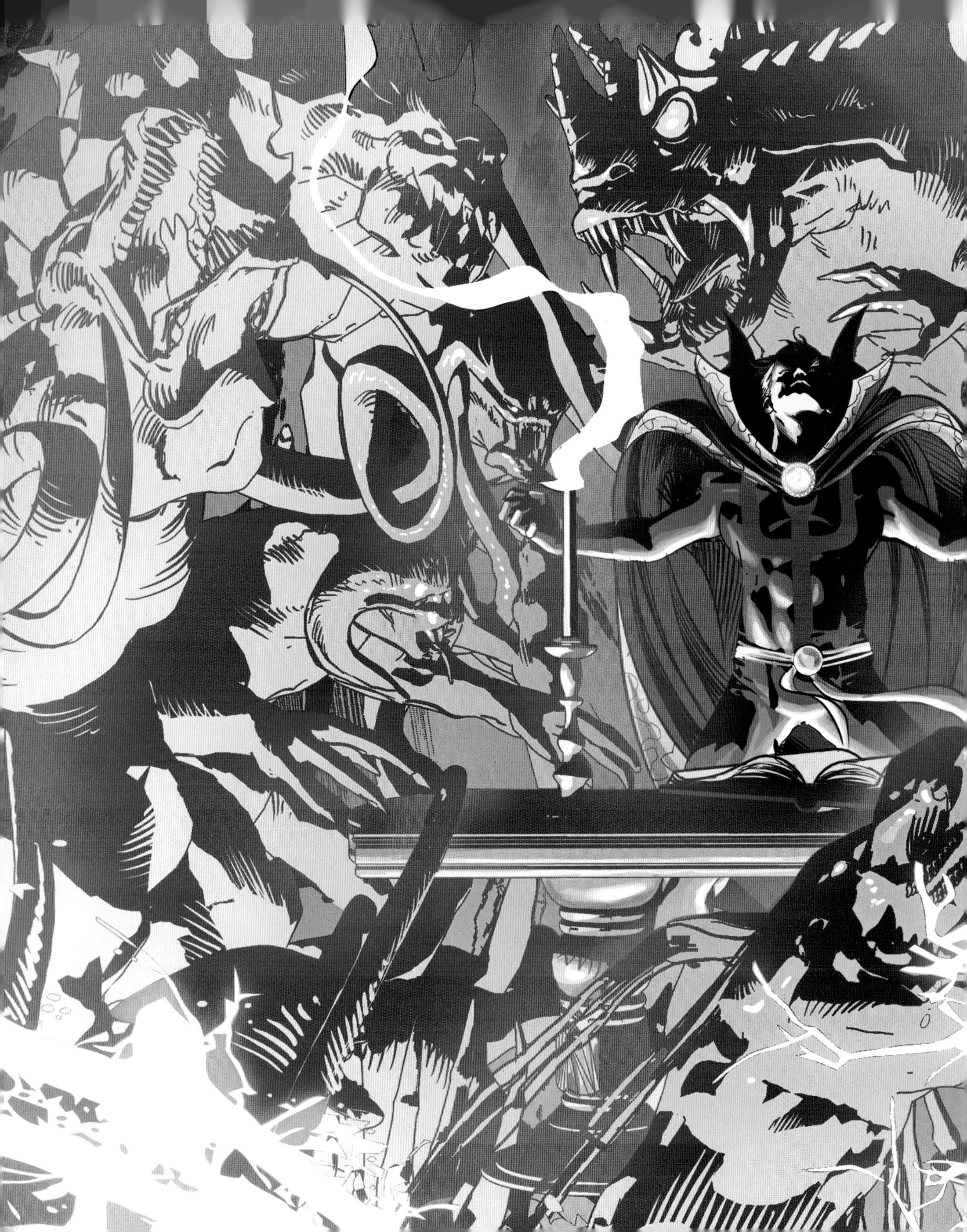

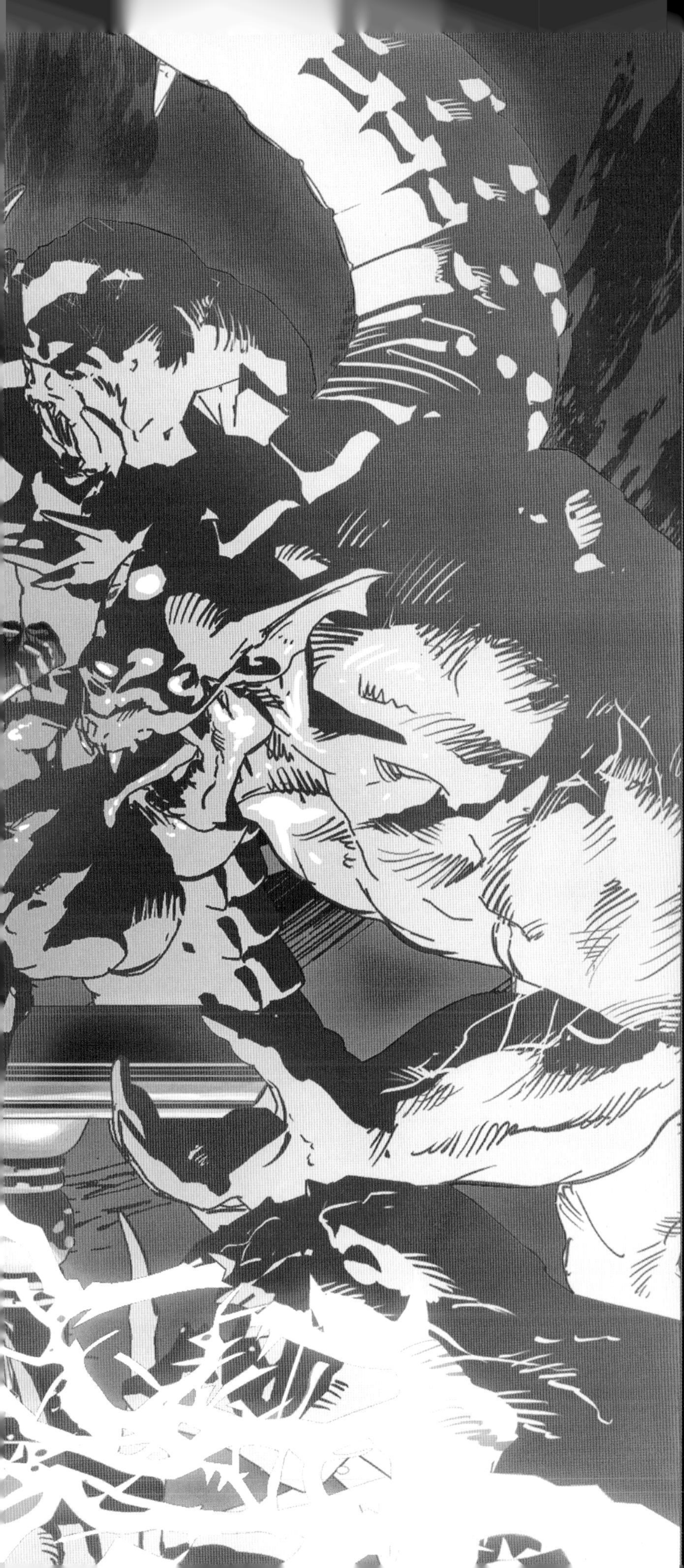

◀ ***Protective magic*** The Book of the Vishanti's hallowed and aged pages enable Doctor Strange to summon vast occult energies—but only ever in defense.

THE BOOK OF THE VISHANTI

The Book of the Vishanti is a vital part of Strange's mystical arsenal, and the undisputed centerpiece of Doctor Strange's library in his New York-based Sanctum Sanctorum. Written in Babylon nearly 20,000 years ago, it possesses a seemingly endless number of pages, and bears a cover marked with the Seal of the Vishanti. The spells within are largely designed to counteract other forms of magic, and as such are never used offensively.

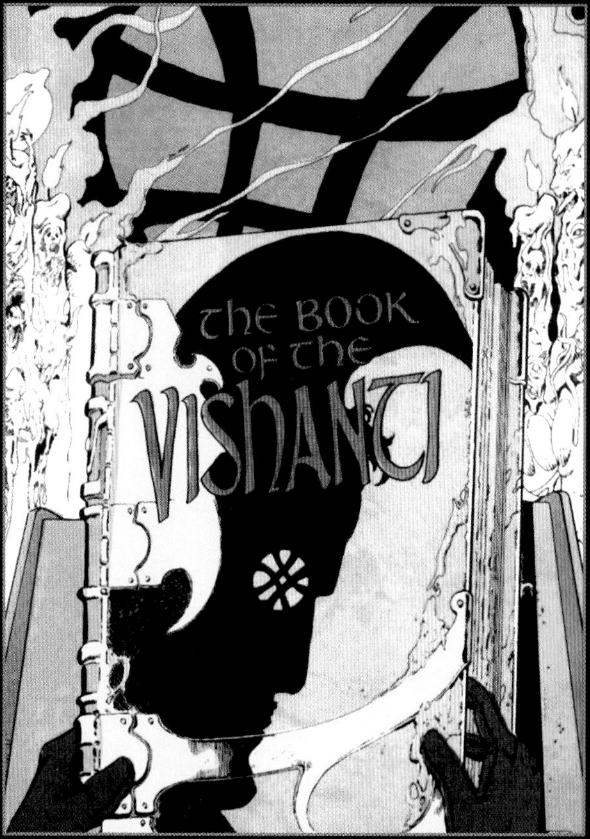
The Book of the
Vishanti

Salvaged secrets

Strange lost the book when the Sanctum Sanctorum was destroyed to prevent his precious artifacts being stolen by the wizard Urthona. However, it was saved by Agamotto, who transported the fabled tome to his own realm and later returned it.

TOOLS OF THE TRADE

Doctor Strange is renowned for having the greatest collection of enchanted objects in existence. Some of these items are vital to his role as Sorcerer Supreme of Earth, forming his striking and flamboyant costume and enhancing his formidable powers. Others enable him to focus his mind on mystical matters. Then there are his mighty magical weapons, including swords and axes, which best reside in his care.

A SORCERER'S ARSENAL

The Cloak of Levitation is an essential element of Doctor Strange's uniform as Sorcerer Supreme. The red-and-yellow cloak once belonged to the Ancient One, until he bestowed it upon Strange as a reward for prevailing in his first battle with Dormammu. The relationship between the Cloak and its wearer is close—the cape responds to commands and depends on the magical might of the wearer.

The Cloak of Levitation is durable, but not indestructible. It has been damaged in many battles, but because of its magical origins and the mystical weaving techniques used to create it, it cannot be repaired by normal means.

One of the most valuable artifacts in the Sanctum Sanctorum is the Cauldron of the Cosmos, which is located in Strange's private meditation chamber. The fumes that rise from the Cauldron provide a view of the universe itself. For the Sorcerer Supreme, it is a crucial aid for meditation.

A particularly coveted item in Doctor Strange's collection is the Wand of Watoomb. One of five Wands in existence, it lay in the possession of various sorcerers until it was seized by Strange. Strange, in turn, has had it stolen from him by sorcerers such as Warren Traveler. The Wand is one of the greatest tools that a Sorcerer Supreme can possess—one that Strange would have to relinquish were he ever to lose his title.

▲ **Battle ready**
Found by Strange in a witch's crypt on the Moon, the Axe of Angarruumus is one of his most ancient and deadly weapons.

Cloak of Levitation
The Cloak of Levitation is able to alter its appearance to other more conventional and handy forms, such as a trench coat, a poncho, or even a magic carpet.

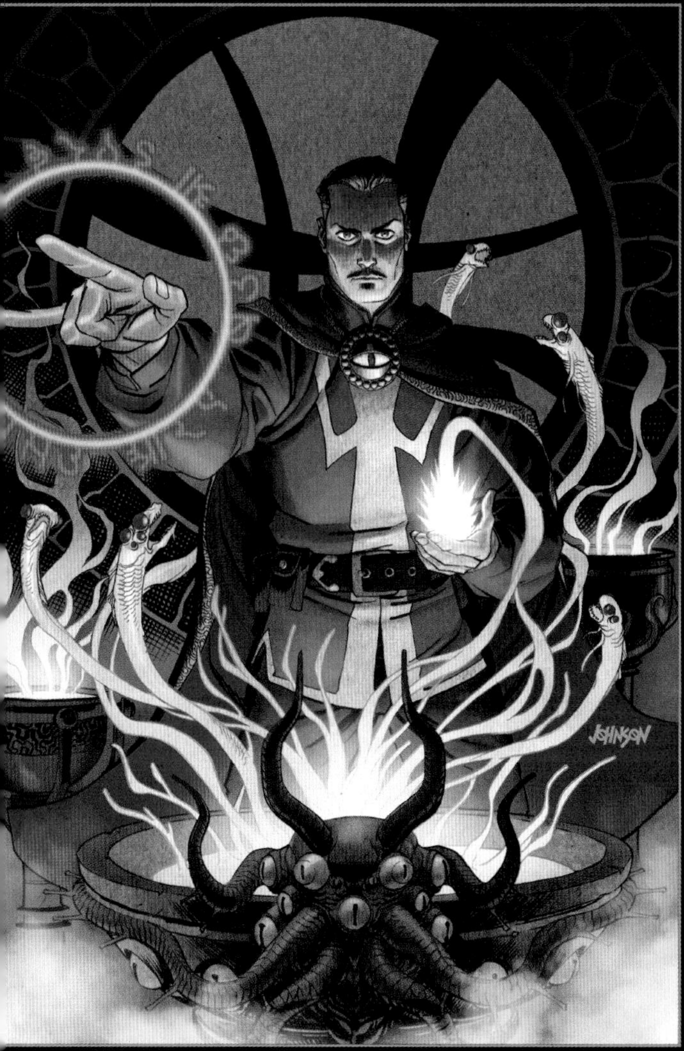
JOHNSON

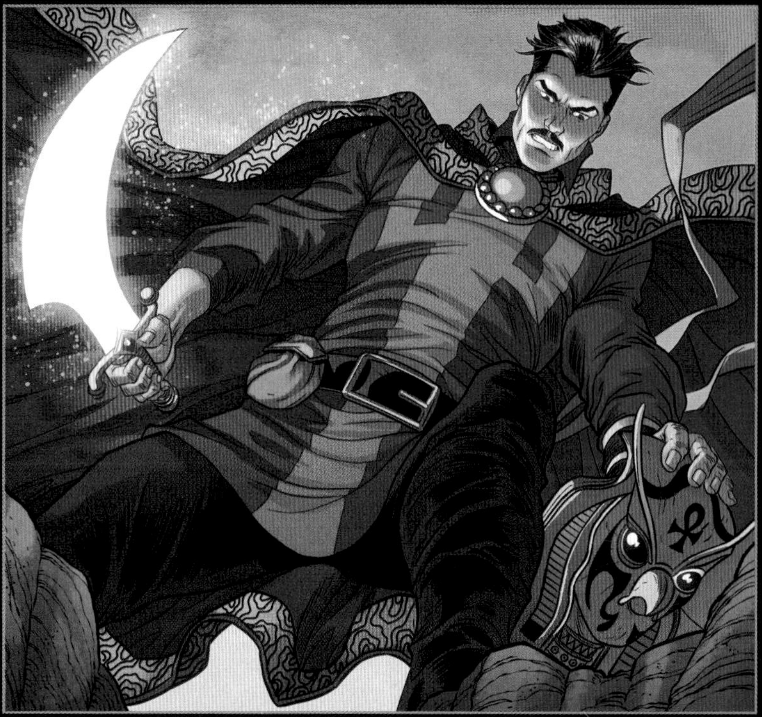

▲ ***Third Eye of Horus*** As well as carrying mystical weapons, Doctor Strange arms himself with useful artifacts like the Third Eye of Horus. This enchanted mask allows the wearer to see things hidden to the human eye, such as magical Shadow Creatures!

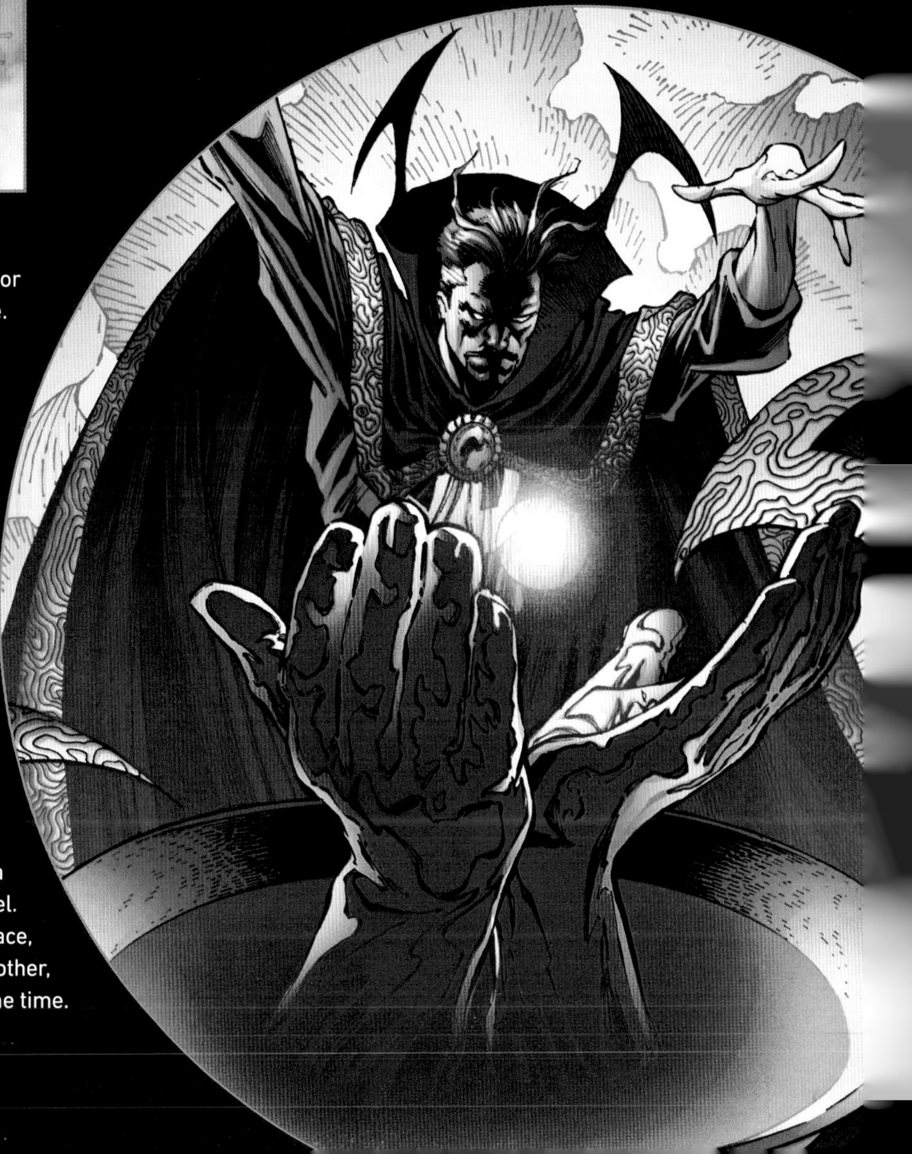

The Cauldron of the Cosmos

The Cauldron of the Cosmos is primarily used by Doctor Strange for meditation, but it can also be used to peer into the past and future.

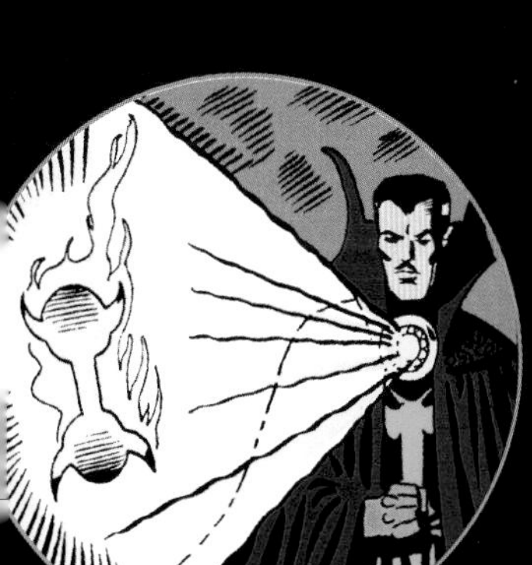

◀ ***Wand of Watoomb*** The Wand is controlled simply by the thoughts of its user. It can be used to manipulate the elements, open portals, intensify mystical energies, and both unleash and block magical attacks.

Hands of the Dead

Created 15,000 years ago, the Hands of the Dead is a set of gauntlets that enable extra-dimensional travel. The wearer can enter the realms of time and space, travel at impossible speeds from one location to another, and even be present in multiple places at the same time.

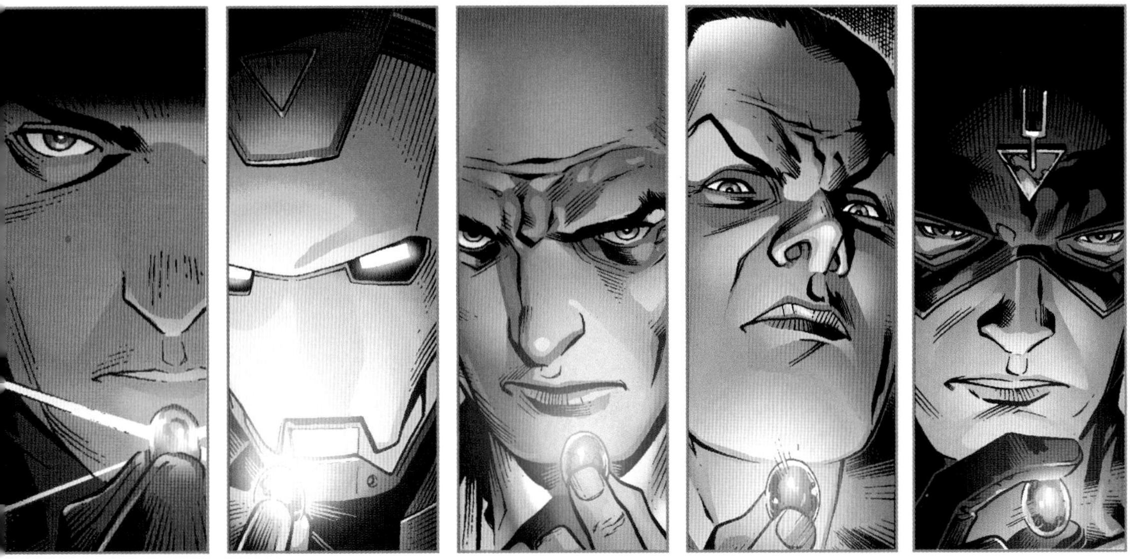

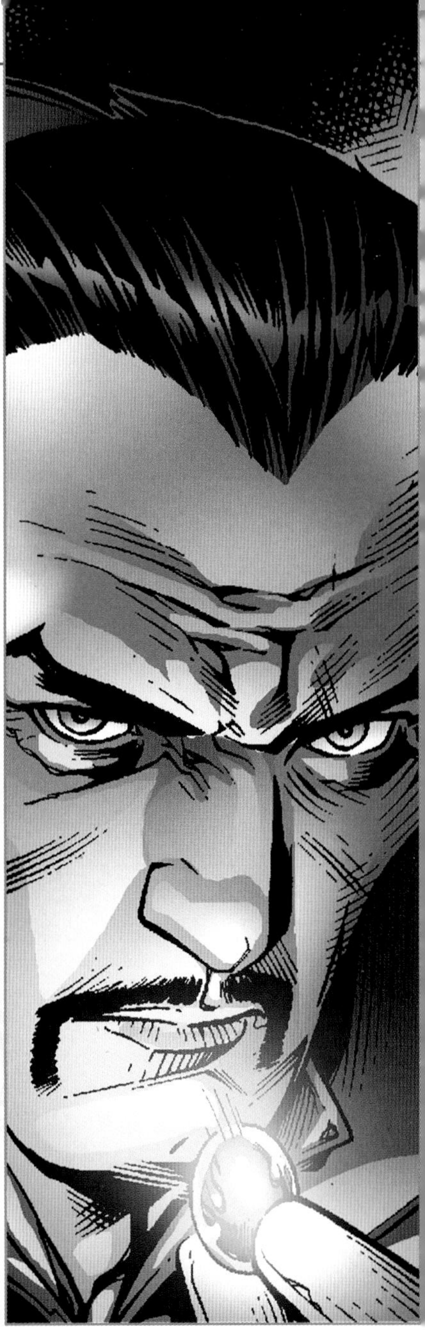

INFINITY GEMS

The Infinity Gems are six unimaginably powerful stones representing soul, power, time, reality, mind, and space. Individually potent, when gathered and used in unison, they provide the bearer with godlike destructive power!
Originally known as Soul Gems, the cosmic stones are the remains of a near-omnipotent being who committed suicide, a fraction of his essence forming the six stones. They were gathered by the Elders of the Universe to combat the Destroyer of Worlds, Galactus. However, the mad Titan Thanos deceitfully took them, setting them in his golden glove and naming it "The Infinity Gauntlet." The gems eventually came into the possession of the clandestine cabal, the Illuminati, who were determined to never let them fall into the wrong hands again.

Soul keeper

The Illuminati gathered the Infinity Gems so that they could not be used to attack Earth. Reed Richards divided the gems among the Illuminati members. He placed the Soul Gem in the care of Doctor Strange, who chose to keep it secure by hiding it in a secret place.

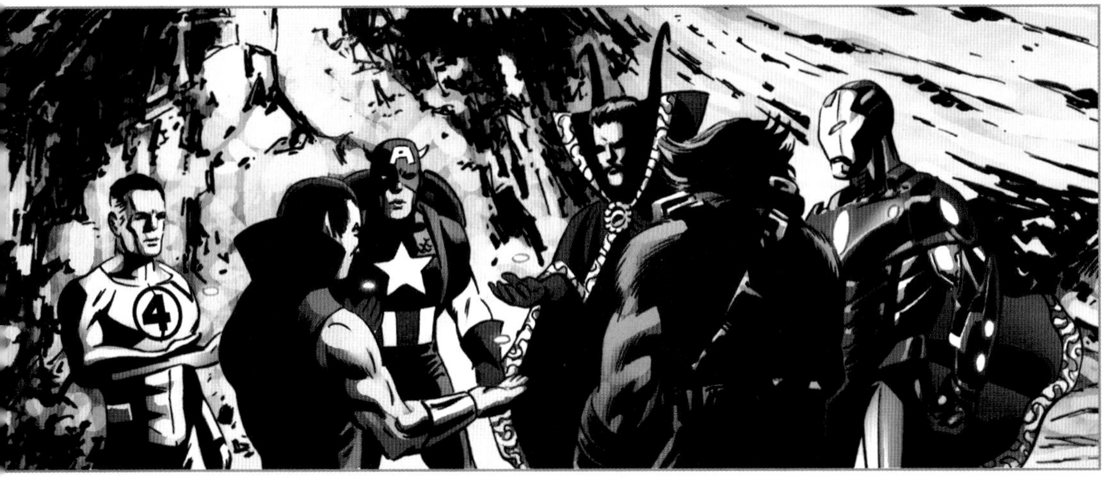

◀ ***Wielding great power*** Strange brought the Soul Gem out of hiding when the Illuminati reluctantly reassembled the Gems to save Earth from the imminent Incursions. The plan failed and the Infinty Gems shattered or vanished.

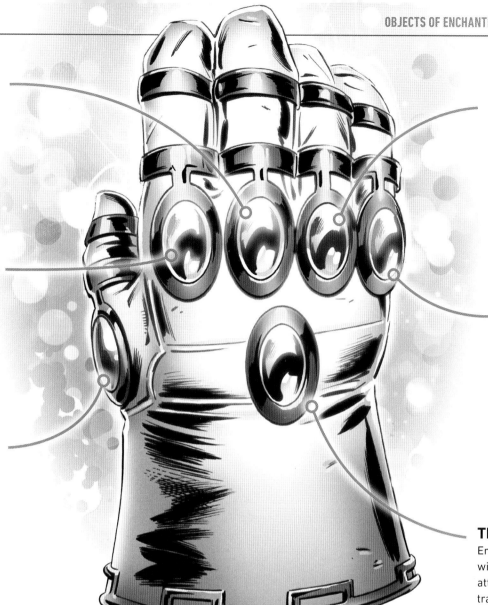

The Mind Gem
Grants the user the power of telekinesis, and psychic abilities including accessing the thoughts and dreams of other beings.

The Reality Gem
Bestows upon the user the ability to control or alter reality, even in direct contradiction to natural laws.

The Power Gem
Gives the wearer access to all power and energy in the universe that ever has been, or will exist, including superpowers.

The Space Gem
Enables the wearer to manipulate space, exist in all dimensions, and move an object anywhere throughout all planes of reality.

The Time Gem
Allows the user to control the past, present, and future, and gives them the ability to slow down or speed up the flow of time.

The Soul Gem
Empowers the wearer with the ability to attack, control, and transform the souls of others, living or dead.

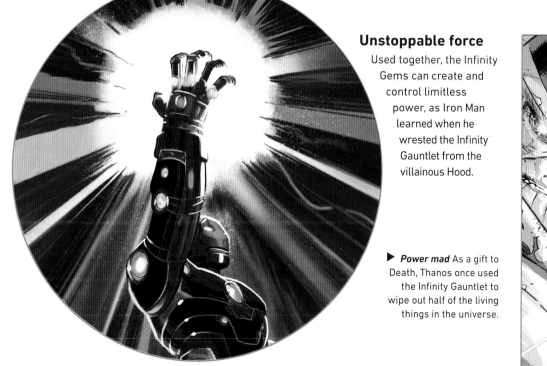

Unstoppable force
Used together, the Infinity Gems can create and control limitless power, as Iron Man learned when he wrested the Infinity Gauntlet from the villainous Hood.

▶ **Power mad** As a gift to Death, Thanos once used the Infinity Gauntlet to wipe out half of the living things in the universe.

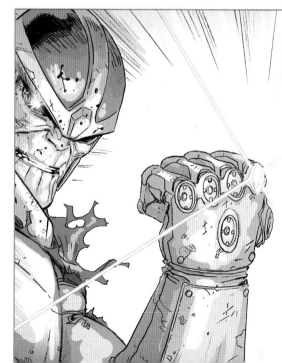

GLOSSARY

Arcane
Something that is mysterious or secret, and understood by very few people.

Astral
A non-physical realm of existence, which can be reached through magical or psychic means.

Cabal
A small group of people—often Super Villains—who work together in secret.

Cosmic being
A being that possess power on a galactic level, far beyond those of humans or even Super Heroes.

Cybernetic
A being that is at least partially composed of mechanical or electrical technology.

Demon
A mystical being that resides in various realms of Hell, and feeds upon the souls of evil people.

Denizens
The inhabitants of a particular place, such as a realm or dimension.

Dimension
A separate universe or realm containing space, matter, and energy.

Doppelganger
A supernatural apparition in the form of the exact double of a living person.

Eldritch
Mysterious and eerie, with connotations of being unearthly.

Extra-dimensional
A being or object that originates from a different dimension or universe.

Incantation
The uttering of words used to conjure a magic spell.

Incursion
A collision between two universes, which results in their total destruction.

Mage
An individual who is highly skilled and knowledgable in magic and sorcery.

Mystic Arts
The skills needed to be a powerful sorcerer, such as spell casting, telepathy, and astral projection.

Multiverse
The collection of various alternate universes, many of which are similar in nature.

Necromancy
The practice of using dark magic in order to communicate with the dead.

Omnipotent
Possessing unlimited, God-like power and control over the universe.

Scrying
The practice of looking into a particular material in order to see images or receive visions.

Succubus
A female demonic creature who feeds upon the life essence of living beings, especially men.

Superhuman
An individual who possesses extraordinary abilities or powers that ordinary humans do not.

Transcendence
The act of going beyond one's normal or physical state.

INDEX

Page numbers in **bold** refer to main entries.

L

M

N

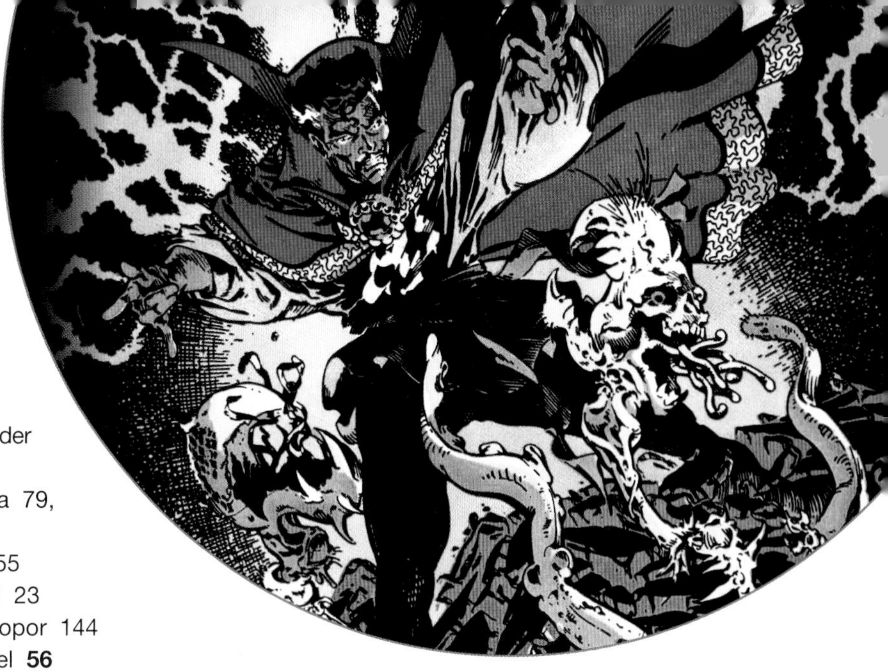

O

P, Q, R

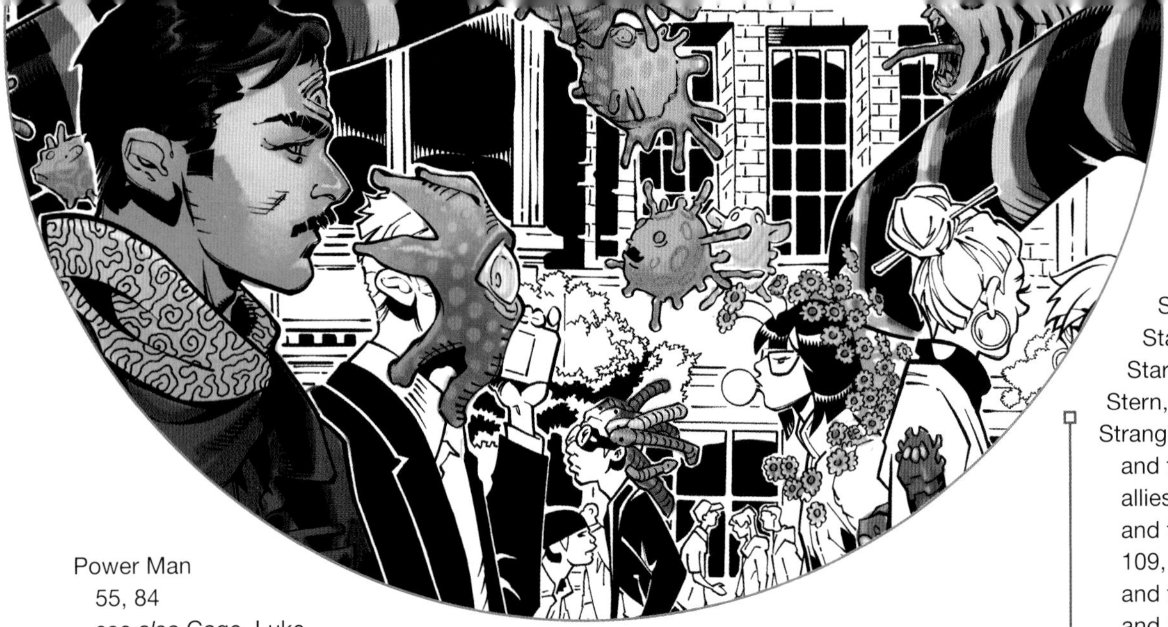

S

T

U

V

W

X, Y, Z

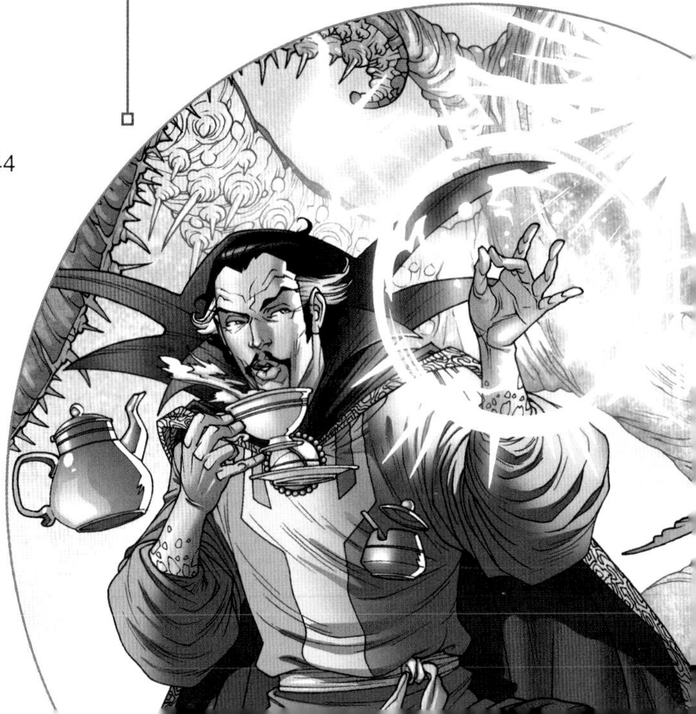

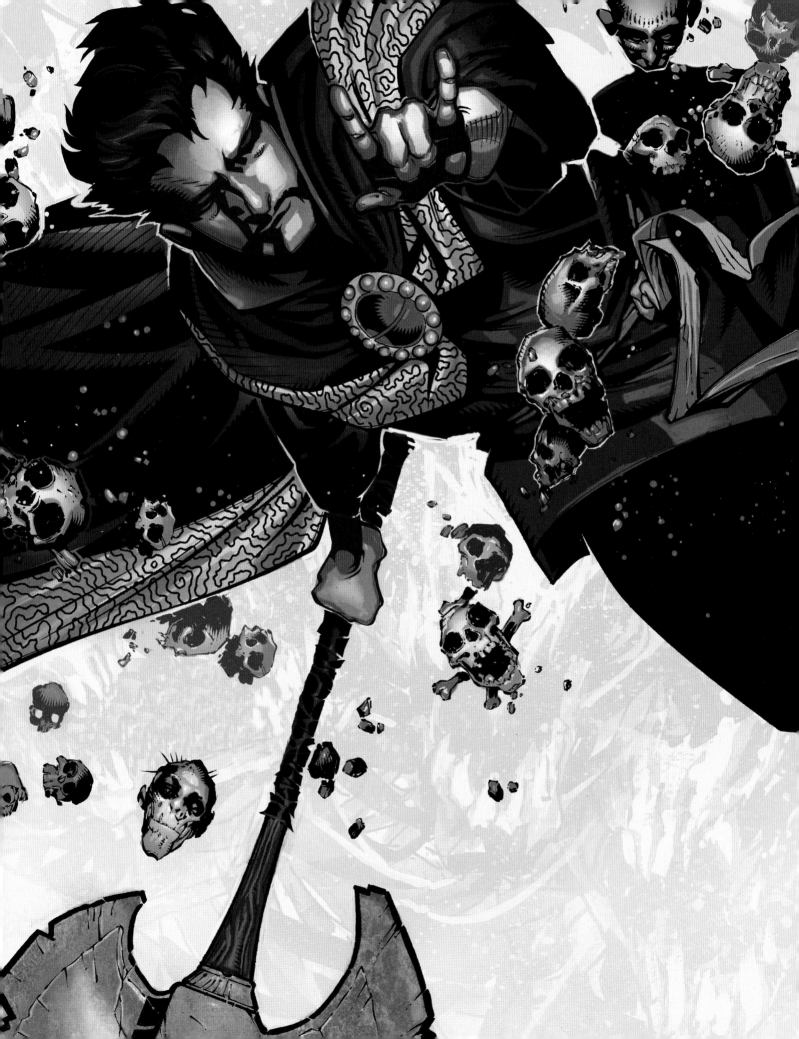